Thinking Spanish Translation

D0023811

The new edition of this comprehensive course in Spanish–English translation offers advanced students of Spanish a challenging yet practical approach to the acquisition of translation skills, with clear explanations of the theoretical issues involved.

A variety of translation issues are addressed, including:

- cultural differences
- register and dialect
- grammatical differences
- genre.

With a sharper focus, clearer definitions and an increased emphasis on up-to-date 'real world' translation tasks, this second edition features a wealth of relevant illustrative material taken from a wide range of sources, both Latin American and Spanish, including:

- technical, scientific and legal texts
- journalistic and informative texts
- literary and dramatic texts.

Each chapter includes suggestions for classroom discussion and a set of practical exercises designed to explore issues and consolidate skills. Model translations, notes and suggestions for teaching and assessment are provided in a Teachers' Handbook that can be found on the Routledge website.

Thinking Spanish Translation is essential reading for advanced under-graduate and postgraduate students of Spanish and translation studies. The book will also appeal to a wide range of language students and tutors through the general discussion of the principles and purposes of translation.

The late **Sándor Hervey** was Reader in Linguistics at the University of St Andrews.
Louise M. Haywood is Senior Lecturer at the University of Cambridge and **Michael Thompson** is Senior Lecturer at the University of Durham.

Titles of related interest

Thinking Arabic Translation
A course in translation method: Arabic to English
James Dickins, Sándor Hervey and Ian Higgins

Thinking German Translation
A course in translation method: German to English
Sándor Hervey, Ian Higgins and Michael Loughridge

Thinking Italian Translation
A course in translation method: Italian to English
Sándor Hervey, Ian Higgins, Stella Cragie and Patrizia Gambarotta

Routledge Encyclopedia of Translation Studies
Second edition
Mona Baker and Gabriela Saldanha

In Other Words
A coursebook on translation
Mona Baker

Becoming a Translator
An accelerated course
Douglas Robinson

The Scandals of Translation
Lawrence Venuti

Translation Studies
Susan Bassnett

Thinking Spanish Translation

A course in translation method:
Spanish to English

Second edition

Louise M. Haywood
Michael Thompson
Sándor Hervey

 Routledge
Taylor & Francis Group

LONDON AND NEW YORK

First published 1995
by Routledge

This edition published in 2009
by Routledge
2 Park Square, Milton Park, Abingdon, Oxon OX14 4RN

Simultaneously published in the USA and Canada
by Routledge
711 Third Avenue, New York, NY 10017

Routledge is an imprint of the Taylor & Francis Group, an informa business

© 1995 Sándor Hervey, Ian Higgins and Louise M. Haywood,
© 2009 Louise M. Haywood, Michael Thompson and Sándor Hervey

Typeset in Times New Roman PS by
Florence Production Ltd, Stoodleigh, Devon

British Library Cataloguing in Publication Data
A catalogue record for this book is available from the British Library

Library of Congress Cataloging in Publication Data
Haywood, Louise M.
    Thinking Spanish translation: a course in translation method,
    Spanish to English/Louise M. Haywood, Michael Thompson,
    Sándor Hervey. – 2nd ed.
        p. cm.
    Includes bibliographical references and index.
    1. Spanish language – Translating into English. I. Thompson, Michael.
    II. Hervey, Sándor.   III. Hervey, Sándor. Thinking Spanish translation.
    IV. Title.
    PC4498.H47 2008
    428′.0261 – dc22   2008025171

ISBN10: 0–415–44005–x (hbk)
ISBN10: 0–415–48130–9 (pbk)
ISBN10: 0–203–88601–1 (ebk)

ISBN13: 978–0–415–44005–9 (hbk)
ISBN13: 978–0–415–48130–4 (pbk)
ISBN13: 978–0–203–88601–4 (ebk)

In memory of Sándor Hervey

To Ian Higgins and our families:
Jon and Jake; Jenn, Lisa and Alex

Contents

Preface to the second edition

This book is a substantially rewritten version of *Thinking Spanish Translation* by Sándor Hervey, Ian Higgins and Louise M. Haywood. It maintains its point of origin as a revised version of a course in translation methodology taught mainly to third- and fourth-year undergraduates of Spanish at the University of St Andrews, which I had the pleasure of co-teaching with Sándor Hervey between my appointment there in 1992 and Sándor's sudden death in 1997 at the age of fifty-five. Sándor originally came up with the idea, and he devised the first translation methodology course to be taught to students of French in collaboration with Ian. Its methodology was then adapted for Spanish, and co-taught by Sándor, first with Catherine Davies, and then with Alan Paterson prior to my appointment at St Andrews. I subsequently learned that in the classroom we drew heavily on source texts contributed by each of them, and I should like to record my personal gratitude to them here. Sándor typed the original version of the book while I sat beside him, commenting on our draft, adding further examples as we went, and passing on typed versions of my classroom notes to him. Many students, graduates of Spanish, friends and colleagues contributed materials. In writing up the course as a book, Sándor and I met frequently with Ian, who gave our manuscript rigorous scrutiny, honing the argument and translations with great humour. It was an honour (and a pleasure) to work with Ian and Sándor, and I mark Sándor's passing and Ian's decision to stop working on the project with regret. It is a pleasure, however, to welcome Mike to the Thinking Translation team.

The current version of the course takes account of subsequent adaptations of versions for French and German, and responds particularly to the challenges that teaching Spanish translation offers in the classroom. As a result of taking adaptations of versions of the course for other languages into account, Ian's thinking and his words echo throughout this course; we are extremely indebted to his rethinking of various aspects of the original course. We hope that the changes are consistent with the thinking behind the course as it has evolved since its first delivery in St Andrews. Although the 'we' of the Preface denotes Louise M. Haywood and Michael Thompson, throughout the rest of the book 'we' includes Sándor. If any credit be deserved, let that go to all three authors; should faults be found that are not in the original version, then they are ours alone.

The most obvious alteration overall is the elimination of the contrastive chapters. In practice, the luxury of a twenty-session course is one that few of us enjoy nowadays, and the presence of optional extra material is merely otiose. In their place, a substantial new chapter, fully integrated into the discussion of the formal properties of texts, deals systematically with translation issues arising from the syntactical differences between English and Spanish (Chapter 7). Conceptually, the most notable refinements bear on the issues of compensation, genre and culture (Chapters 3, 4 and 5). The new chapter on compensation abolishes the elaborate categorization of types of compensation, which proved overly fussy and confusing for practical use, to replace it with a clearer, and better argued and exemplified, discussion. The chapter on genre retains the principles of the broad taxonomy of oral and written categories, but places greater emphasis on generic hybridity in practice and on the importance of relating genres to purposes (of both texts and translations). Revision of the chapter on cultural issues takes account of some significant theoretical developments in translation studies over the past fifteen years or so, a period in which there has been an increased emphasis on the cultural and ideological dimensions of translation. We hope all chapters have benefited from sharper focus, clearer definitions, and fuller and more relevant illustration.

We have also moved the position of the chapter on genre so that it now appears after the one on compensation but before that on cultural issues. Naturally, there are arguments in favour of keeping to a rigorously bottom-to-top structure, with the discussion of genre occurring later in the course toward the end of the discussion of formal properties of texts. Students, for example, often feel happier dealing with genre when they are able to identify and discuss other levels of textual variable. The reason for siting the genre chapter earlier is that the defining element in genre is the relation between textual purpose and textual effect. This relation is often what makes the text 'what it is', and is often what the experienced translator responds to when working on a translation task; and it is in turn the relation between 'what the source text is' and the purpose of the target text that determines the translation strategy. Putting genre in Chapter 4 is a forceful way of conveying these fundamentals. The reason for positioning the chapter on compensation before that on genre is more pragmatic. In the classroom, we have found that students raise the issues it treats for discussion from the earliest classes, and so we have chosen to deal with them as early as is feasible. Moreover, compensation is a key concept that is applicable to all the levels of analysis and types of translation procedure discussed in the following chapters; its previous inclusion in a chapter on cultural issues in translation risked giving the misleading impression that compensation operates only in the cultural domain.

We have, therefore, moved away to a large extent from a structure defined as 'bottom-to-top', now considering strategic questions of genre and culture before moving onto specific textual variables in Chapters 6 and 7. These chapters are based on a systematic linguistic taxonomy starting with phonology and working up through morphology, semantics, syntax and discourse analysis.

In a sense, this represents a retention of the 'bottom-up' principle, but in practice the detailed discussion of the implications for translation emphasizes the need at every level to relate small-scale features (sounds, words, phrases) to large-scale, whole-text factors. We have also maintained the two chapters on language variety to permit greater discussion of regional difference, which is supremely important in the Hispanophone world. This differentiates our course from *Thinking Italian Translation*, and the revised versions of the course for French and German. Where they made use of the space to add further materials, we have excised the contrastive chapters.

We have also reworked the chapter on editing and revision to show the range of considerations and constraints that editors and revisers must keep in mind.

As regards the illustrative and practical material, some has been retained from the first edition, but there is more that is new. Texts are from Latin American and Spanish sources (more of the latter than the former), and belong to a variety of genres. The extensive use of online sources is a new feature, and a number of short examples (oral and written) have been taken from the Real Academia Española's *Corpus de referencia del español actual*. In the first edition, a third of the texts used for Practicals were literary (narrative fiction, poetry and drama); that proportion is now just under a third, but the total number of texts used has increased by about 50 per cent. While we recognize that few aspiring translators are likely to devote a significant part of their working lives to translating novels, poems and plays, we regard the challenges posed by carefully selected samples of imaginative writing as extremely useful for the general development of translation skills and the discussion of translation problems on multiple levels. Students need to begin to get their teeth into more 'real-world' translation tasks, however, and we have therefore increased the number of specialized (technical/scientific/legal), journalistic and factual/informative/persuasive texts used for practicals and illustrative examples. Of course, tutors who find that effective texts from the first edition have disappeared have every right to go on using them in classes.

Finally, we have dropped speed translations from practicals in this edition. This is not meant to imply that translators do not work under pressure of time. Rather, we feel that speed translations belong to a different sort of course focusing more specifically on the practical conditions in which professional translators work. Our aim is to encourage as much planning, discussion and critical reflection on translation processes as possible, which is why the instructions for all practicals emphasize teamwork, collective development of strategies and discussion of outcomes. Completing a translation task within a tight time limit is a sobering experience that helps to keep a translator's feet on the ground, but its usefulness as a learning exercise is limited. It is, of course, open to tutors to impose whatever time limit they deem appropriate on any exercise they choose. If timed translations are used for assessment purposes, we recommend that they be combined with a more extended form of coursework that gives room for planning and reflective commentary.

We hope that Sándor would have agreed to these changes, although no doubt after vigorous discussion. We discussed our proposed changes with Ian, and so we know he supports them. We hope students and tutors enjoy this new edition as much as we enjoyed developing the original.

Louise M. Haywood
Michael Thompson
March 2008

Acknowledgements

We owe a debt of gratitude to a number of friends and colleagues who have helped us in the revision of *Thinking Spanish Translation*: Dr Angeles Carreres, Dr Jennifer Chamarette, Mr Angus Johnston, Prof. David Johnston, Dr Abigail Loxham, Dr Debbie Martin, Mrs Eva Schumacher-Reid, Dr Heiko Ziebell. We are also grateful to the many students at St Andrews, Cambridge and Durham whose response to courses using the first edition has guided us in the preparation of this new version.

We are grateful to all those who have granted us permission to reproduce the extracts listed below. While every effort has been made to trace and acknowledge ownership of copyright material used in this volume, the publishers will be glad to make suitable arrangements with any copyright holders whom it has not been possible to contact:

Practical 2.1 reprinted with kind permission from Julio Cortázar, *Los relatos: 2, Juegos* (Madrid: Alianza, 1976, pp. 57–8), copyright © Julio Cortázar, and Heirs of Julio Cortázar.

Practical 5.2 reprinted with kind permission from Andrés Sopeña Monsalve, *El florido pensil: memoria de la escuela nacionalcatólica*, copyright © 1994 Andrés Sopeña Monsalve.

Text of *Cabellera* by Guillermo de Torre used in Chapter 6. Reprinted with kind permission from Joaquín González Muela and Juan Manuel Rozas, *La generación poética de 1927*, copyright © 1986 Agustina Bravo Ortuña.

Practical 6.3 reprinted with kind permission from Ignacio Carrión, 'Himno', copyright © 1989 Ignacio Carrión.

Practical 6.4 'The wounds of love' reprinted with kind permission from John Kerr, 'The wounds of love', copyright © 1999 John Kerr; 'The wounds of love' reprinted with kind permission from Nicholas Round, 'The wounds of love', copyright © 1999 Nicholas Round; 'You put a bomb in my heart' reprinted with kind permission from Colin Teevan, 'You put a bomb in my heart', copyright © 1999 Colin Teevan.

xvi   *Acknowledgements*

Practical 7.1 ST reprinted with kind permission from Javier Marías, *Corazón tan blanco*, copyright © 1992 Javier Marías, reprinted by permission of the author and Agencia Literaria Mercedes Casanovas.

Practical 7.1 TT reprinted with kind permission from Javier Marías, *A Heart So White*, translated by Margaret Jull Costa, copyright © 1992 Javier Marías, English translation, copyright © 1995 The Harvill Press, reprinted by permission of New Directions Publishing Corp.

Practical 8.4 Spanish ST reprinted from from 'Voto por correo, 2007. Preguntas y respuestas. Elecciones locales 2007', www.elecciones.mir.es/locales2007/faq04.html, copyright © Ministerio del Interior (España).

Practical 8.4 English ST reproduced with kind permission of the Electoral Commission from www.aboutmyvote.co.uk at www.aboutmyvote.co.uk/faq/voting_by_post.aspx, copyright © the Electoral Commission.

Practical 9.2 reprinted from Rubén Darío, 'Sinfonía en gris mayor', *Prosas profanas y otros poemas*, ed. Ignacio M. Zuleta (Madrid: Castalia, 1987, pp. 138–9), copyright © Editorial Castalia.

Practical 13.1 reprinted from 'Contrato de arrendamiento de vivienda', www.idealista.com/informacion/contrato_arrendamiento_vivienda.doc: contract conceded by idealista.com and promein.

Practical 14.2 Text 1 reprinted from Simone Ortega, *Mil ochenta recetas de cocina* (Madrid: Alianza, pp. 359–60), copyright © Simone K. de Ortega, 1972 and Alianza Editorial, 1989.

Practical 14.3 reprinted from Simone Ortega, *Mil ochenta recetas de cocina* (Madrid: Alianza, pp. 359–60), copyright © Simone K. de Ortega, 1972 and Alianza Editorial, 1989.

Introduction

Our experience is that many students who take a course in translation do so with the belief that people either have the aptitude for translation or they do not; sometimes they even report their own lack of aptitude. As teachers of translation know, some people are naturally better than others. However, it is our firm conviction that aptitude for translation is no different from ability in other areas: teaching and practice can help anyone to improve, including the most gifted. Anyone who has taught translation knows that a structured course will help most students to become significantly better at translation – often good enough to earn their living at it. This book offers just such a course. The discussion is systematic and progressive, offering lots of practice in developing rationales for solving different sorts of translation problem. It is not a course in translation theory but in translation method, encouraging thoughtful and logical consideration of possible solutions to practical problems. Theoretical issues do inevitably arise and our approach is informed by developments in translation theory, but our aim is to develop proficiency in the method, not to investigate theoretical implications for their own sake. Interesting and valuable discussions are available elsewhere. We particularly recommend the following useful overviews of translation studies: Bassnett (2002); Gentzler (2001); Hatim and Munday (2004); Munday (2001); Tymoczko (2007).

While the kind of proficiency this book aims to develop is grounded in a realistic appreciation of work carried out by practising translators, most students aiming for a career in translation will need to develop their skills further and acquire more experience of particular fields of specialization by taking a postgraduate training course (and by continuing to update their knowledge thereafter). Nevertheless, this book is intended to provide a solid, all-purpose foundation on which to build the full set of competences required to succeed as a professional translator. Above all, it aims to help students to become thoughtful, alert, self-critical translators of a range of different text types, able to weigh up linguistic and cultural choices and to articulate the reasons for their decisions. They will then be well equipped to undertake further theoretical study and practical training in, for example, commercial or technical translation, interpreting, audiovisual translation, or the use of translation technology. Note that since our aim is to improve the quality of translations produced by students, we do not discuss machine translation, or how to use translation software on the internet.

Let us now briefly outline a few basic assumptions underlying our approach. First, this course is not a disguised version of the traditional 'grammar-and-translation' method of language teaching. Our focus is on how to *translate* from Spanish, not how to communicate in Spanish. We assume that students already have the considerable linguistic resources in Spanish needed to benefit from the course and that they already possess basic dictionary and research skills. Naturally, in using these resources and skills to produce good translations, they inevitably extend and improve their competence in Spanish. This is an important fringe benefit – and for students not intending to work as professional translators, probably the primary benefit of the course, along with a general sharpening of analytical and critical faculties. However, as we have said, our main interest lies in developing useful translation skills and, generally, in improving *quality* in translation work. It should not be forgotten that this quality depends on the translator's command of English as much as of Spanish; indeed, Birgit Rommel, head of the Übersetzer- und Dolmetscherschule Zürich, has lamented the lack of mother-tongue training in universities, concluding that: 'Great stress is laid on improving foreign language proficiency, but excellence in the mother-tongue – the translator's target language – is, quite wrongly, taken for granted' (Rommel 1987: 12). Rommel's comment is a qualified reminder of the common assumption that higher quality can be expected when translating into the mother-tongue than into a foreign language. The predominance in this course of unidirectional translation from Spanish into English reflects our acceptance of this assumption in its qualified form: excellence in the mother-tongue is not taken for granted, but constitutes one of the objectives of the course. It should be pointed out early on that we are both speakers of British English, but we have made an effort to prevent the intrusion of versions that might mystify North American speakers.

Second, the course is not intended as a disguised version of translation theory, or of linguistics. This does not mean that we avoid technical discussion of linguistic or translation-theoretical issues. However, such issues are not treated out of theoretical interest, but out of direct concern with specific types of problem encountered in translating. That is, our approach is *methodological* and practical: where the discussion of theoretical issues facilitates and rationalizes methodological problems of translation, we have freely borrowed theoretical notions from translation theory and linguistics. Throughout the course, we have provided instant and simple exemplification of each theoretical notion invoked, and have tried to link these notions instantly and directly to practical issues in translation. Users are encouraged to familiarize themselves with specialized translation and linguistic terminology, not for its own sake but because it enables precise analysis of texts and problems, and concise articulation of strategies formulated and decisions made.

Third, the course has a progressive overall structure and thematic organization. It begins with the fundamental issues, options and alternatives of which a translator must be aware: translation as process, translation as product, the nature and crucial importance of compensation in translation, and issues relating to genre or text-type. Next, it looks at cultural issues. It then moves on to examine a series of layers of textual variables affecting translation ('upwards' from the nuts and bolts of phonic and graphic details to the organization of complete discourses), and a series of semantic and stylistic topics (literal meaning, connotation and language variety). All these steps are illustrated in the Schema of Textual 'Filters' given at the end of this chapter. We then devote three chapters to specific kinds of specialized translation: scientific and technical, institutional (including legal and financial), and consumer-oriented (including instructions and persuasive/promotional texts). We make no claim to comprehensive coverage of these domains, which tend to present translation difficulties that are far too narrowly specific in subject matter to be suitable for a general coursebook on translation method. None the less, the three chapters identify the most significant kinds of translation problem that arise from these text types, offer general advice on strategies, and provide realistic introductory practice using a selection of texts from a variety of sources. Our aim throughout is to produce an integrated, non-specialized approach to the various aspects that need to be discussed in the context of a general methodology of translation. While we do not claim that this approach is exhaustive, it does have wide scope and a coherent organization, and it is applicable to virtually any type of text likely to be encountered by graduates who go on to translate professionally.

Finally, our claim that the course systematically and progressively builds up a methodical approach to translation practice should not be taken to mean that we are offering a way of 'mechanizing' the process of translation, or attempting to provide rules and recipes to be followed. On the contrary, we believe translation to be a highly creative activity in which the translator's personal responsibility is constantly to the forefront. We have, therefore, tried to emphasize throughout the need to recognize options and weigh up alternatives, the need for rational discussion, and the need for informed decision making. All the material in the course – expository and practical alike – is intended not for silent consumption, but for animated discussion between students and between students and tutor. (In fact, we have found that many of the practicals are best done by students working in small groups and reporting their findings to the class.) Each chapter is, therefore, intended to stimulate and support tutor–student discussion at an early stage in the corresponding practicals; this is because we are not trying to inculcate this or that particular theory or method, but simply to foster the general principle that, whatever approach the translator adopts, it should be self-aware and methodical.

While the course we are presenting is a progressively designed whole, it is divided into a series of successive units intended to fit into an academic timetable. Each unit consists of a chapter outlining a set of related notions and problems, and an accompanying set of exercises in which students are given concrete translation tasks, working on textual material to which the notions and problems outlined in the chapter are particularly relevant. The fifteen units can be managed to fit into different course lengths. Depending on the type of course a particular tutor chooses to give, some chapters can be taken together, such as the first and second, the eight and ninth, and the tenth and eleventh. Likewise, more or less time can be spent on the chapters on specialist, technical, institutional and consumer-oriented translation. Ideally, each unit needs between ninety minutes and two hours of seminar time, and students are also required to prepare in advance for group discussion of the chapter. In practice, however, we have found that if almost no material is given unseen and students prepare thoroughly prior to class, then the course can be delivered in sessions of fifty minutes, with plenty of time for discussion. If teaching the course through seminars, it is important that students should have access to the necessary reference books in class: a monolingual Spanish dictionary, a Spanish–English/English–Spanish dictionary, an English dictionary and an English thesaurus. Some of the practicals will be done at home – sometimes individually, sometimes in groups – and handed in for comment by the tutor. How often this is done will depend on local conditions; in our situation we have found that once a fortnight works well. When an exercise is done at home, this implies that some time should be devoted in the following class to discussion of the issues raised. (More comprehensive suggestions for teaching and assessment can be found in the *Teachers' Handbook*.)

Students doing the course often enquire about the possibility of translation as a career. Useful information can be obtained from the following sources:

- Fédération Internationale des Traducteurs/International Federation of Translators (www.fit-ift.org).
- British Institute of Translation and Interpreting (www.iti.org.uk) – free guides can be downloaded from the 'Getting Started' section.
- Chartered Institute of Linguists (www.iol.org.uk) – have a look at their Discussion Forum for advice on a range of practical topics.
- American Translators Association (www.atanet.org) – a 'Getting Started' booklet can be ordered.
- ProZ Articles Knowlegebase (www.proz.com/translation-articles) – includes a 'Getting Established' section.
- Owens, Rachel (ed.) (1996) *The Translator's Handbook*, 3rd edn, London: Aslib.
- Robinson, Douglas (1997) *Becoming a Translator: An Accelerated Course*, London/New York: Routledge.
- Samuelsson-Brown, Geoffrey (1998) *A Practical Guide for Translators*, 3rd edn, Clevedon: Multilingual Matters.

The abbreviations used in the book are explained in Chapter 1. As for symbols, only one needs any comment: the slash in examples where alternative translations are given. Basically, we use slashes, with no space before or after, to indicate the different possibilities, as in: 'despertar' can be translated as 'wake/awaken/stir up/arouse', etc.

Note that a slash with a space before and after it does not indicate alternatives, but simply a division between, for example, lines of verse, as in 'There was an Old Man of Peru, / Who never knew what he should do'.

Please note, some of the practicals in the course involve work on texts that are not contained in the present volume, but intended for distribution in class. These texts are found in Louise M. Haywood, Michael Thompson and Sándor Hervey, *Thinking Spanish Translation: Teachers' Handbook*, which can be obtained online from www.routledge.co.uk/9780415481304.

Schema of textual 'filters'

The table set out below provides a summary of the specific aspects of translation discussed in the central chapters of this book (4 to 11). Each section of the table – each 'filter' – represents a phase of the analysis of a source text required in order to identify its salient characteristics and determine priorities for translating it. In conjunction with the practical purpose for which a translation is being carried out, systematic analysis of the features of the source text and their relative importance is crucial to the formulation of a translation strategy. The schema provides a checklist of tests that can be carried out on any text to be translated, which can be visualized as a series of filters collecting and sorting relevant textual properties so that their importance for the translation process can be gauged. Different kinds of text will deposit different mixes of significant material: for example, the prosodic level will probably rank as minimally important in scientific texts but as maximally important in some poetic genres, and certain filters or levels will be found to contribute no textually relevant features.

It should also be said that source texts are not the only material that can be passed through the elements of the proposed battery of filters. The process can be applied to translated texts in draft form before they are finalized, comparing their features with those of the source text, or to published translations as a means of evaluating their success.

The analogy of filters is a mechanical one, and in this lies a serious danger of misunderstanding. We do not wish to imply that our schema is intended as a means of mechanizing the process of translation; on the contrary, we believe this process to be an intelligent and 'humanistic' one involving personal, and in the final analysis subjective, choices made by the translator. The schema of filters is not a mechanical device but a mnemonic one: it reminds the translator to consider the full range of textual features as being of potential significance, as well as of the need to rank these features in order of relative textual relevance, as part and parcel of working out a strategy for translating any source text. It also serves to remind translators of options and choices when tinkering with details in editing a provisional target text. But the decisions and choices remain entirely non-mechanical: they are for translators to make in the light of their knowledge and experience.

A further point to be made about the schema of textual filters concerns the time element. Scanning a text in the kind of detail that a full use of the filters would seem to imply is unrealistic when the translator is working against a time limit. In such cases, a more perfunctory use of the schema is still useful in speeding up the process of adopting a translation strategy, and in spotting and handling particular problems of detail. It is worth remembering that the usefulness of the schema is not dependent on making a full and exhaustive use of its scanning potential: it performs a useful function even in speed translation. The translator simply has to make as much, or as little, use of it as time will allow.

Finally, it is worth noting that, through practice, the scanning of texts in the manner suggested by the schema quickly becomes habitual, so that the translator comes to perform the process automatically and rapidly, without having to consult the checklist.

Schema of textual 'filters'

Matrix of features	*Examples of features*
Genre filter (Chapter 4)	
What genre(s) does this text belong to?	
Genre types: empirical	scientific paper, balance sheet
philosophical	essay on good and evil
religious	biblical text
persuasive	constitution, advertisement
literary	short story, poem
hybrid	sermon, parody, job contract
Oral genres: conversation	chat, negotiation
oral narrative	story, joke
oral address	speech, lecture
oral reading	reading out a conference paper
sung performance	song (live or recorded)
dramatization	play, film dialogue, ritual
Oral features in written texts	deictics, address to receiver
Cultural filter (Chapter 5)	
Are there significant issues of cultural difference presenting a choice between:	
Exoticism	wholesale foreignness (sometimes requiring explanation)
Calque	'brave potatoes' (translated literally)

Schema of textual 'filters' . . . *continued*

Matrix of features	Examples of features
Cultural borrowing	'patatas bravas' (assumed to be familiar to target readers)
Communicative translation	'fried potatoes in a spicy sauce'
Cultural transplantation	Barcelona recast as Edinburgh

Formal filter (Chapters 6–7)

Are there significant features on the:	
Phonic/graphic level	alliteration, layout
Prosodic level	vocal pitch, rhythm
Words and morphemes	prefixes and suffixes, semantic fields
Sentential level	syntactical differences (e.g. word order, subjunctive, pronouns)
Discourse level	different ways of achieving cohesion, pragmatics

Semantic filter (Chapters 8–9)

Are there significant instances of:	
Literal meaning	synonymy
Allusive meaning	echo of proverb
Attitudinal meaning	hostile attitude to referent
Associative meaning	gender stereotyping of referent
Collocative meaning	collocative clash
Reflected meaning	homonymic echo
Affective meaning	offensive attitude to addressee

Varietal filter (Chapters 10–11)

Are there significant instances of:	
Social register	shift between chatting with friends and addressing a judge
Tonal register ingratiating tone	
Dialect	Chiapan accent
Sociolect	Buenos Aires working-class *lunfardo*

1 Preliminaries to translation as a process

It is often said that skill in translation cannot be learned and, especially, cannot be taught. Underlying this attitude is the assumption that certain people are born with the gift of being good translators or interpreters, whereas others simply do not have this knack; in other words, skill in translation is an inborn talent: either you've got it or you haven't.

Up to a point, we would accept this view. No doubt it is true, for instance, that some people take to mathematics or physics, whereas others have little aptitude for such subjects, being more inclined towards the humanities. There is no reason why things should be otherwise for translation; some are 'naturally' good at it, others find it difficult; some enjoy translating and others do not.

The twin assumptions behind this book are that it will help its users acquire proficiency in translation, and that we are addressing ourselves to people who do enjoy translating, and would like to improve their translation skills. Indeed, enjoyment is a vital ingredient in acquiring proficiency as a translator. This, again, is quite normal: elements of enjoyment and job satisfaction play an important role in any skilled activity that might be pursued as a career, from music to computer technology. Note, however, that when we talk of proficiency in translation we are no longer thinking merely of the basic natural talent an individual may have, but of a skill and facility that requires learning, technique, practice and experience. Ideally, translators should combine their natural talent with acquired skill. The answer to anyone who is sceptical about the formal teaching of translation is twofold: students with a gift for translation invariably find it useful in building their native talent into a fully developed proficiency; students without a gift for translation invariably acquire some degree of proficiency.

Since this is a course on translation method, it cannot avoid introducing a number of technical terms and methodological notions bordering on the theoretical. (These are set in bold type when they are first explained in the text, and are listed in the Glossary.) Our aims are primarily methodological and practical rather than theoretical, but we believe that methods and practices are at their best when underpinned by thoughtful consideration of a rationale behind them. This book is, therefore, only theoretical to the extent that it encourages a thoughtful consideration of the rationale behind solutions to practical problems encountered in the process of translation or in evaluating translations as texts serving particular purposes.

Throughout the course, our aim is to accustom students to making two interrelated sets of decisions. The first set are what we shall call **strategic decisions**. These are general decisions, which the translator should make before actually attempting a translation, in response to such questions as 'what are the salient linguistic characteristics of this text?'; 'what are its principal effects?'; 'what genre does it belong to, and what audience is it aimed at?'; 'what are the functions and intended audience of my translation?'; 'what are the implications of these factors?'; and 'which, among all such factors, are the ones that most need to be respected in translating this particular text?'. The other set of decisions may be called **decisions of detail**. These are arrived at in the light of the strategic decisions, but they concern the specific problems of grammar, lexis and so on encountered in translating particular expressions in their particular context. We have found that students tend to start by thinking about decisions of detail which they then try to make piecemeal without realizing the crucial prior role of strategic decisions. The result tends to be a translation that is bitty and uneven. This is why, in the practicals, students will usually be asked first to consider the strategic problems confronting the translator of a given text, and subsequently to discuss and explain the decisions of detail they have made in translating it. Naturally, they will sometimes find during translating that problems of detail arise that lead them to refine the original strategy, the refined strategy in turn entailing changes to some of the decisions of detail already taken. This is a fact of life in translation, and should be recognized as such, but it is no reason not to elaborate an initial strategy: on the contrary, without the strategy many potential problems go unseen until the reader of the translated text trips up over the inconsistencies and the obscurities of detail.

Translation as a process

The aim of this preliminary chapter is to look at translation as a process – that is, to examine carefully what it is that a translator actually does. Before we do this, however, we should note a few basic terms that will be used throughout the course. Defining these now will clarify and simplify further discussion:

Text   Any given stretch of speech or writing produced in a given language and assumed to make a coherent, self-contained whole. A minimal text may consist of no more than a single word – for example, '¡Basta!' – preceded and followed by a period of silence. A maximal text may run into volumes – for example, Benito Pérez Galdós's *Episodios nacionales*.
Source language (SL)   The language in which the text requiring translation is couched.

Target language (TL)   The language into which the original text is to be translated.

Source text (ST)   The text requiring translation.

Target text (TT)   The text which is a translation of the ST.

With these terms in mind, the translation process can, in crude terms, be broken down into two types of activity: understanding a ST and formulating a TT. While they are different in kind, these two types of process occur not successively, but simultaneously; in fact, one may not even realize that one has imperfectly understood the ST until one comes up against a problem in formulating or evaluating a TT. In such a case, one may need to go back to square one, so as to reconstrue the ST in the light of one's new understanding of it (just as a translation strategy may need to be modified in the light of specific, unforeseen problems of detail). In this way, ST interpretation and TT formulation go hand in hand. Nevertheless, for the purposes of discussion, it is useful to think of them as different, separable, processes.

The component processes of translation are not qualitatively different from certain ordinary and familiar processes that all speakers perform in the normal course of their daily lives. In this sense, translation is not an extraordinary process. For a start, comprehension and interpretation of texts are common-place processes that we all perform whenever we listen to or read a piece of linguistically imparted information. The act of understanding even the simplest message potentially involves all the beliefs, suppositions, inferences and expectations that are the stuff of personal, social and cultural life. Understanding everyday messages is therefore not all that different from what a translator must do when first confronting a ST –and it is certainly no less complicated. It is, however, true that messages may be understood with varying degrees of precision. For instance, suppose that a mother asked her son to get the blue pen from the top left-hand drawer of the bureau, and he responded by giving her a black one that happened to be handy. She would be justified in thinking that he had not understood her message fully, as he had evidently not paid attention to a number of details in it. Yet he could not be accused of a total lack of comprehension, because he did register and respond to the one salient fact that he had been asked for a pen, according a much lower priority to the other components of the message.

In everyday communication, evidence that a message has been understood may come from appropriate practical response. Another measure of how precisely a message has been understood is appropriate *linguistic* response. Appropriate linguistic response includes such basic things as returning a greeting appropriately, giving a satisfactory answer to a question, or filling in a form correctly. While none of these are translation-like processes, they do show that the element of comprehension and interpretation within the translation process involves what can be a perfectly ordinary, everyday activity requiring no special skill or power of intellect, only an average native command of the language used. Consider a US court case:

| *Defense counsel*: | The truth of the matter is that you are not an unbiased witness, isn't it? You too were shot in the fracas? |
| *Witness*: | No, sir. I was shot midway between the fracas and the navel. |

(Jones, Sevilla and Uelman 1988: 99)

This example shows the importance of understanding or decoding the message content in communication. The witness is intimidated by the formality of the court setting, and assumes that the unfamiliar word, 'fracas', is a polite euphemism. The first step in effective translation is precisely this: ensuring an accurate grasp of the content of the ST, and acting upon it effectively.

One everyday activity that does resemble translation proper is what Roman Jakobson calls '**intersemiotic translation**' (1971: 261), that is, translation between two semiotic systems (systems for communication). 'The green light means go' is an act of intersemiotic translation, as is 'The big hand's pointing to twelve and the little hand's pointing to four, so it's four o'clock'. In each case, there is translation from a non-linguistic communication system to a linguistic one. To this extent, everyone is a translator of a sort.

Still more common are various sorts of linguistic response to linguistic stimuli which are also very like translation proper, even though they actually take place within a single language. These sorts of process are what Jakobson (1971: 261) calls '**intralingual translation**'. A brief look at the two extremes of intralingual translation will show what its major implications are. Take the following scenario: Jill is driving Jack through the narrow streets of a small town. A policeman stops them. As he leans in to speak, Jill can see over his shoulder that, further on, a trailer had tipped over and blocked the road. At one extreme of intralingual translation lies the kind of response typified in this exchange:

Policeman:	There's been an accident ahead, Madam – I'm afraid you'll have to turn left down St Mary's Lane here, the road's blocked.
Jill:	Oh, OK. Thanks.
Jack:	What did he say?
Jill:	We've got to turn left.

The policeman's essential message is 'Turn left'. But he does not want to sound brusque. So he mollifies the driver with a partial explanation, 'There's been an accident', and then cushions his instruction with 'I'm afraid you'll have to ...'. 'Down St Mary's Lane' gives a hint of local colour and fellow-citizenship; but he does add 'here' just in case the driver is from out of town. Finally, he completes his explanation with the information about the road being blocked.

When Jack asks what he said, however, Jill separates the gist of the police-man's message from the circumstantial details and tonal subtleties, and reports it in her own words. This type of intralingual translation is called **gist translation**. The example also shows two other features which intralingual translation shares with translation proper. First, Jill's is not the only gist translation possible. For instance, she might have said 'We've got to go down here'. Among other things, this implies that at least one of them may not know the town: the street name has no significance. A third possibility is 'We've got to go down St Mary's Lane': if Jack and Jill do know the town, the policeman's gist is accurately conveyed.

The other feature shared by intralingual translation and translation proper is that the situation in which a message is expressed and received affects how it is expressed and received. By 'situation' here we mean a combination of three elements: the circumstances in which a speaker and addressee find themselves (such as being stopped in a car and having to take a diversion or being a witness in a law court), the accumulated experience they carry with them all the time (knowing or not knowing the town, familiarity or unfamiliarity with conventions for giving and receiving instructions; liking or disliking the police, etc.), and the linguistic context. 'Context' is often used metaphorically in the sense of 'situation' (and sometimes even in the sense of 'meaning'). In this book we shall use it specifically to denote the rest of a text in which a given expression or stretch of text occurs. For example, the context of Jack's question is the exchange between Jill and the policeman and her reply to Jack; the context of the policeman's words is everything that follows them; the context of Jill's reply to Jack is everything that precedes 'We've got to turn left'. As will become clear, the whole context is an important consideration in translation; but the more immediate the context, the more crucial a factor it becomes in making decisions of detail.

There are always so many variables in the message situation that it is impossible to predict what the gist translation will be or how the addressee will take it. For example, Jill might simply have said, 'Turn left', a highly economical way of reporting gist – no bad thing when she has to concentrate on driving. However, depending on how she says it and how Jack receives it, it could give the impression that the policeman was brusque.

Another reason why 'Turn left' could sound brusque is that, grammatically, it looks like direct speech (an imperative), whereas all the other gist translations we have given are clearly indirect speech (or 'reported speech'). Now all translation may be said to be indirect speech, inasmuch as it does not repeat the ST, but reformulates it in the translator's words. Yet most TTs, like 'Turn left', mask this fact by omitting the typical markers of indirect speech, for example 'The author says that . . .', and changes in point of view (as in changing '*I'm* afraid *you'll* have to turn left' into '*he's* afraid *we'll* have to turn left'). As a result, it is easy for reformulation consciously or unconsciously to become distortion, either because the translation misrepresents the ST or because the reader misreads the TT, or both.

In other words, gist translation, like any translation, is a process of *interpretation*. This is seen still more clearly if we take an example at the other extreme of intralingual translation. Jill might just as easily have interpreted the policeman's words by expanding them. For example, she could build on an initial gist translation as follows:

> We've got to go down St Mary's Lane – some fool's tipped a trailer over and blocked the High Street.

This puts two sorts of gloss on the policeman's message: she adds details that he did not give (the tipping over, the name of the street ahead) and her own judgement of the driver. We shall use the term **exegetic translation** to denote a translation that explains and elaborates on the ST in this way. The inevitable part played by the translator's accumulated experiences becomes obvious in exegetic translation, for any exegesis by definition involves explicitly bringing considerations from outside of the text into one's own reading of it – here, the overturned trailer, Jill's knowledge of the town, and her attitude towards other road-users.

An exegetic translation can be shorter than the ST, as in this example, but exegesis is usually longer, and can easily shade into general observations triggered by the ST but not really explaining it. Knowing the town as she does, Jill might easily have gone on like this: 'The street's just too *narrow* for a thing that size.' This explanation is admissible as exegesis, but it probably goes beyond the limit of exegetic translation.

Finally, gist translation and exegetic translation often occur in close association with one another. Sometimes, they seem to be inseparable, especially in the rewording of metaphor (see the examples from *El sombrero de tres picos* below). But this is not confined to intralingual translation or to literary texts. Here is an example from a company annual report concerning the regulations which affect the conduct of its General Assembly:

ST	TT	
Sin embargo, el Consejo de	However, the Company's	
Administración de la sociedad en su	Board of Directors in its	
reunión de 30 de marzo de 2006	meeting on the 30th March	
aprobó proponer a la Junta General la	2006 resolved to propose to	
modificación de dicho Reglamento con	the General Assembly the	5
el fin de adaptarlo a la nueva redacción	modification of such Rules,	
de la Ley de Sociedades Anónimas	in order to adopt the new	
según modificación introducida por	text of the Spanish Law on	
la Ley 19/2005 de 14 de noviembre	Public Limited Companies.	
sobre la Sociedad Anónima Europea	Through this modification the	10
domiciliada en España ampliando a un	minimum notification period of	
mes (en lugar de quince días) el plazo	fifteen days for the call for a	
mínimo de anterioridad para la	General Assembly was extended	
publicación del anuncio de convocatoria.	and is now of thirty days.	
(Europac 2005b: 41)	(Europac 2005a: 41)	

As these examples show, it is not only sometimes hard to keep gist translation and exegetic translation apart, it can be hard to see where translation shades into comment pure and simple. It certainly seems very difficult to achieve an ideal **rephrasing**, a halfway point between gist and exegesis that would use terms radically different from those of the ST, but add nothing to, and omit nothing from, its message content. And yet, with its constant movement between gist and exegesis, intralingual translation happens all the time in speech. It is also common in written texts. Students regularly encounter it in annotated editions. Many good examples appear in the well annotated Biblioteca Clásica series published in Barcelona by Crítica, in which footnotes gloss the text. The following example is from Eva F. Florensa's edition of Pedro Antonio de Alarcón's *El sombrero de tres picos*:

> Dormitaban en la meseta de la escalera y en el recibimiento[1] otros alguaciles y ministros,[2] esperando descansadamente a su amo, mas cuando sintieron llegar a Garduña desperezáronse dos o tres de ellos, y le preguntaron al que era su decano y jefe inmediato:[3]
> – ¿Viene ya el señor?
>
> [1] *meseta*: 'descansillo, rellano'; *recibimiento*: 'recibidor, vestíbulo'. [Both virtually synonymous rephrasings, for readers unfamiliar with nineteenth-century domestic lexis; a good example of how any rewording involves presuppositions regarding the target audience's accumulated experience]
> [2] «*Alguacil* es ministro de la Justicia para echar mano de los malhechores» (Covarrubias) [Quotation of an exegetical rephrasing from an established authority; lends weight to the editor's own notes; presumption of target audience's recognition of that authority but lack of knowledge of the term]; *ministros*: 'funcionarios que ejercen un cargo cualquiera en la administración de justicia'. [Exegetic rephrasing.]
> [3] *decano*: 'miembro más antiguo o viejo de una corporación'. [Exegetic rephrasing.]

(Alarcón 1993: 141, 111)

This type of expository interpretation can, as here, easily develop into a full-scale textual exegesis that tries to analyse and explain the implications of a text (perhaps with the addition of cross-references, allusions, critical apparatus, complementary notes and so on). Indeed a few chapters further on, the editor uses a footnote to observe that the description of a fight at a windmill may be inspired by Cervantes (144), which she cross-references to an endnote in which she supplies bibliographical references, and notes an alternative reading of the passage (203). This process may not tally with everyone's view of translation, but it does share some common features with translation proper, especially with certain kinds of academic translation: both cases involve an ST, which is subjected to interpretation, and a TT, which is the result of a creative (extended and expository) reformulation of the ST.

The attainability of ideally precise rephrasing is a controversial question that will continue to occupy us in what follows. From the examples just cited, it is clear that precision is a relative matter. 'Stop!' is perhaps a successful intersemiotic rephrasing of 'red traffic light' (but it omits the associations of danger and the law), while 'yours truly consumed a small quantity of alcohol' is a distinctly less exact (intralingual) rephrasing of 'I had a little drink'. These examples illustrate what is surely a fundamental maxim of translation, namely that rephrasing never allows a precise reproduction of the total message content of the ST, because of the very fact that the two forms of expression are different, and difference of form always entails a difference in communicative impact. We shall return to this in Chapter 2, in discussing the concept of translation loss.

So far, then, we have suggested that there are three basic types of translation-like process, defined according to the degree in which the TT abstracts from, adds to, or tries to reproduce faithfully, the details contained in the ST message.

It should be added that there are two important respects in which these three types of process are on an equal footing with one another, as well as with translation proper. First, they all require intelligence, mental effort and linguistic skill; there can be no substitute for a close knowledge of the subject matter and context of the ST, and a careful examination and analysis of its contents. Second, in all three cases, mastery of the TL is a prerequisite. It is salutary to remember that the majority of English mother-tongue applicants for translation posts in the European Commission fail *because of the poor quality of their English* (McCluskey 1987: 17). In a translation course, TL competence needs as close attention as SL competence. There is, after all, not much point in people who do not have the skill to rephrase texts in their native language trying their hand at translation proper into their mother-tongue. Consequently, synopsis-writing, reported speech, intralingual rephrasing and exegesis are excellent exercises for a translator, because they develop technique in finding, and choosing between, alternative means of expressing a given message content. That is why the first practical exercise in this course is a piece of intralingual translation in English.

Practical 1

1.1 Intralingual translation

Assignment

(i)   Identify the salient features of the content and expression in the following ST, and say what its purpose is.

(ii) Recast the story in different words, adapting it for a specific purpose and a specific public (i.e. a specific readership or audience). Say precisely what the purpose and the public are. In this case, you may treat the ST EITHER as if you were recasting the whole book of Genesis, of which it is a part, OR as a text in its entirety. (As a rule, unless we explicitly state otherwise, *whenever* you do a translation as part of this course, you should proceed as if you were translating the whole text from which the ST is taken. Many STs will repay some preliminary research.)

(iii)   Explain the main decisions of detail you took in making the textual changes, and the reasons for these alterations. (Insert into your TT a superscript note-number after each expression you intend to discuss, and then, starting on a fresh sheet of paper, discuss the points in numerical order. This is the system you should use whenever you annotate your own TTs.)

Contextual information

This ST is from the Authorized Version of the Bible, first published in 1611. The best way of making sense of it is to read Genesis 10 and 11 (of which it is the start). God punished humankind with a flood but saved Noah, his sons, and the animals from destruction. Noah's sons repopulate the earth.

Source text

AND the whole earth was of one language, and of one speech.
    And it came to pass, as they journeyed from the east, that they found a plain in the land of Shinar; and they dwelt there.
    And they said one to another, Go to, let us make brick, and burn them throughly. And they had brick for stone, and slime had they for morter.   5
    And they said, Go to, let us build us a city and a tower, whose top may reach unto heaven; and let us make us a name, lest we be scattered abroad upon the face of the whole earth.
    And the LORD came down to see the city and the tower, which the children of men builded.   10
    And the LORD said, Behold, the people is one, and they have all one language; and this they begin to do: and now nothing will be restrained from them, which they have imagined to do.
    Go to, let us go down, and there confound their language, that they may not understand one another's speech.   15
    So the LORD scattered them abroad from thence upon the face of all the earth: and they left off to build the city.
    Therefore is the name of it called Babel; because the LORD did there confound the language of all the earth: and from thence did the LORD scatter them abroad upon the face of all the earth.   20

                                                                      (Genesis 11, v. 1–9)

1.2 Gist translation

Assignment

You will be asked to produce a gist translation of a passage given to you in class by your tutor. The tutor will give you any necessary contextual information, and tell you how long you should take over the translation.

2 Preliminaries to translation as a product

As we saw in Chapter 1, translation can be viewed as a process. It can, however, also be viewed as a product: and that is how we shall look at it in this chapter. Here, too, it is useful to start by examining two diametric opposites, in this case two opposed types of translation, one showing extreme SL bias, the other extreme TL bias.

At the extreme of SL bias is **interlineal translation**, where the TT attempts to respect the details of SL grammar by having grammatical units corresponding point for point to every grammatical unit of the ST. Here is an example:

> ST1   Le gustaba todo lo que le gustara a su mujer, pero no que su mujer les gustara tanto a los hombres.
>
> (Butt and Benjamin 2004: 339)

> TT1   To him was pleasing all that which to her was pleasing to his wife, but not that his wife to them was pleasing so much to the men.

Interlineal translation is rare and exists only to fulfil specialized purposes in, say, language teaching, descriptive linguistics or in certain kinds of ethnographic transcript. Since it is of little practical use to us, we shall not, in fact, give it much consideration, other than to note its position as the furthest degree of SL bias. Interlineal translation is actually an extreme form of the much more common **literal translation**, where the literal meaning of words is taken as if from the dictionary (that is, out of context), but TL grammar is respected. The **literal** – or 'cognitive' or 'denotative' – **meaning** of an expression is the appropriate conventional referential meaning given for it in the dictionary, regardless of any connotations or nuances it has in a particular context. (Lexis will be discussed in relation to compensation in Chapter 3, and literal meaning will be discussed as a topic in Chapter 8.) For our purposes, we shall take literal translation as the practical extreme of SL bias. A possible literal version of ST1 is:

> TT2   He liked everything that his wife happened to like, but not that men liked his wife so much.

At the extreme of TL bias is **free translation**, where there is only a global correspondence between the textual units of the ST and those of the TT. The following example contrasts a literal and a free translation of a stock conversation in Chinese between two people who have just been introduced:

Literal TT		*Free TT*	
A	Sir, are you well?	A	How do you do?
B	Are you well?	B	Pleased to meet you.
A	Sir comes from where?	A	Do you come here often?
B	I come from England.	B	No, this is my first visit.
A	How many persons in your family?	A	Nice weather for the time of year.
B	Wife and five children. And you?	B	Yes, it's been quite warm lately.

The type of extreme freedom seen in the second version from the Chinese example is known as **communicative translation**, which is characterized, in this example, as follows: where, in a given situation (like introducing oneself to a stranger), the ST uses a SL expression standard for that situation, the TT uses a TL expression standard for an analogous target culture situation. We discuss below, in Chapter 5, questions of target- and source-language bias, as well as the translation of culturally specific terms without analogous target culture situations. This degree of freedom is no more to be recommended as general practice than interlineal translation. (Translators have to use their own judgment about when communicative translation is appropriate.) Communicative translation is, however, often mandatory for many culturally conventional formulas that do not allow literal translation. Public notices, proverbs and conversational clichés illustrate this particularly clearly, as in:

Prohibido el paso.	No entry.
Antes que te cases, mira lo que haces.	Marry in haste, repent at leisure.
¿Qué hay?	How's it going?

Between the two extremes of literal and free translation, one may imagine an infinite number of degrees, including a balanced translation representing some sort of a compromise or ideal half-way point between the two. Whether this ideal is actually attainable is the question that lies behind our discussion of 'equivalence' and 'translation loss' below. For the moment, we simply suggest that translations can be usefully judged on a scale between the two polarities of extreme SL bias and extreme TL bias. We have schematized five possible points on this scale – excluding interlineal translation – in the following diagram, which is heavily adapted from Newmark (1981: 39):

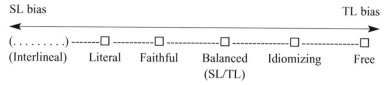

SL bias   TL bias

(. . . . .) -------☐ ----------☐ ------------☐ --------------☐ --------------☐

(Interlineal)   Literal   Faithful   Balanced   Idiomizing   Free

(SL/TL)

Before going any further we should say what we mean by an **idiomizing translation**. This is a translation that respects the ST message content, but typically uses TL idioms or familiar phonic and rhythmic patterns to give an easy read, even if (as in our example at TT5, below) this means sacrificing nuances of meaning or tone. By **idiom** we mean a fixed figurative expression whose meaning cannot be deduced from the literal meaning of the words that make it up, as in 'football's not *my cup of tea*', 'you've *hit the nail on the head*', 'tiene salud *de piedra*', 'perdió *los estribos*', etc. Note that 'idiomizing' is not synonymous with 'idiomatic': throughout this course, we use the term **idiomatic** to denote what sounds 'natural' and 'normal' to native speakers – a **linguistic expression** that is unexceptional and acceptable in a given context. In certain situations, such as informal discussion between two friends, TT5, below, might be regarded as an idiomizing translation of ST1, above. The other TTs below are listed in order of the number of **grammatical transpositions** – the replacement or reinforcement of given parts of speech or grammatical categories in the ST by others in the TT – employed. Were grammatical transposition regarded as the sole measure of degrees of freedom on our adapted Newmark scale, TT2 might be considered to be the most SL-biased or literal of the TTs and TT6, the most TL-biased or free of the TTs. Of these five examples, more than one might be considered idiomatic but only TT5 is idiomizing (note the use of contracted forms, 'to be keen on' and 'fancy'):

> TT2 He liked everything that his wife happened to like, but not that men liked his wife so much.
>
> TT3 He liked whatever his wife liked, but not the fact that men liked her so much.
>
> TT4 He liked all the same things as his wife except for the fact men were attracted to her.
>
> TT5 He and his wife liked all the same things but he wasn't so keen on the fact that other men fancied her so much.
>
> TT6 He shared all his wife's likes and dislikes, but didn't like the idea of sharing her.

The five examples call for further comment. In TT2 (the most literal of our examples), there are three grammatical transpositions of the intransitive verb, 'gustar', 'to be pleasing', rendered as the more idiomatic transitive verb 'to like'. (For more detailed discussion of 'gustar', see Chapter 7). Further, the subjunctive mood of 'gustara' following the subordinating conjunction 'que' has been conveyed (i) in the first subclause through the addition of 'to happen to' to mollify the indicative mood, and (ii) in the second clause by indicative 'liked'. In TT3, there are the three grammatical transpositions of 'gustar', and two of the subjunctive mood to the indicative. The first ST subjunctive clause is introduced in the TT by the compound relative 'whatever' to give the generalized and indefinite sense achieved by 'todo lo que' + subjunctive, which is missing from the more all-encompassing 'everything' in TT2. In addition, there is one further grammatical transposition: the negated conjunction 'pero no' is rendered as the nominal clause by 'the fact that'. TT3 might be regarded as faithful since it maintains the ironic use of a single verb in all three clauses, and is marginally more idiomatic than ST2 in that it suppresses the repetition of 'his wife' by replacing the noun in the second clause with a third-person object pronoun. TT4 is the most balanced translation of those offered with regard to grammatical transposition: four more take place: (1) the nominal phrase 'todo lo' becomes a nominal object phrase 'all the same things', with the knock-on effect that (2) the conjunction 'que' becomes the conjunction 'as', expressing comparison without a verbal clause; (3) the negated conjunction 'pero no' is rendered by the prepositional phrase 'except for'; (4) the intransitive imperfect subjunctive verb 'gustara', whose subject is 'su mujer', is replaced by a past perfect continuous 'were attracted to her', with 'men' as the verbal subject, and the choice of verb makes explicit the sexual connotations implicit in 'gustar'. In addition, it shares the grammatical transposition of 'gustaba' and the suppression of the subjunctive mood in the final clause with the more SL-bias translations, and the suppression of 'que' in the final that-clause with TT3. Seven grammatical transpositions, then, but they are unexceptional and acceptable: like the ST, this balanced translation is in a neutral register, and it is rendered more idiomatic than the other TTs through the elimination of repetition of the verb 'to like', however, the ironic tone is somewhat sacrificed.

Another important point about degrees of freedom is that the dividing lines between them are fluid. Each of the TTs is open to query, and others could be suggested. For instance, is 'He liked everything that' really an accurate rendering of 'Le gustaba todo lo que'? Do 'He liked everything that his wife liked', 'He liked whatever his wife liked' and 'He and his wife liked all the same things' mean the same thing? Depending on the answers to these questions, it might even be argued that, in this case, the suggested balanced translation is the only accurate literal translation. As for the free translation, it only gives partial overlap with the ST – the message is the same 'The couple like the same things apart from other men's interest in the wife'; but it suggests that they dislike the same things, and implies that she enjoys other men's interest in her. If all these issues are discussed in class, it will become clear that the five categories are fluid, and that, depending on context, any of these TTs – or others – could be the preferred choice.

However, some contexts offer less choice than others. This brings us to our final point: in certain circumstances, a freer TT may in fact hardly be a choice at all! This is often the case if the ST contains an SL idiom, proverb, or other expression standard for a given situation. In such cases, using a TL communicative solution is often inescapable. So, in many contexts, the following TTs will generally seem mandatory, although you may wish to discuss in class their validity and alternatives in a variety of possible contexts:

ST	TT
Les tiene en ascuas.	He's keeping them on tenterhooks.
Ni hablar.	Nothing doing.
Haz tu santa voluntad.	Do whatever you like.
De tal palo, tal astillo.	A chip off the old block.
Quien espera desespera.	A watched pot never boils.
Objetos perdidos.	Lost property.
Bien inmueble.	Property (UK). Real Estate (US).

To recap, communicative translation is produced when, in a given situation, the ST uses an SL expression standard for that situation, and the TT uses a TL expression standard for an equivalent target-culture situation. We will discuss communicative translation more in Chapter 5. For the moment we will point out a seeming paradox: inasmuch as they diverge greatly from ST literal meanings, the ready-made communicative translations are examples of free translation.

Note that although 'He hated other men fancying his wife' would be a very free and colloquially plausible rendering, it is not a communicative translation, because it is not the standard expression in the given situation. (There is no standard expression for this situation.) So its freedom is gratuitous, and might well be considered excessive: it might be out of character for the speaker to use 'fancying' in this sense, and the TT is in any case, and possible more significantly, avoidably different in message content and tone from the ST. It should also be noted that a free translation does not have to be a colloquial one. It could just as easily be highly formal, as in: 'The gentleman and his wife held their opinions in common; however, he objected to the interest other men showed in her.'

Equivalence

In characterizing communicative translation, we used the term 'analogous target culture situation' and discussed 'equivalent' idioms and proverbs. Before going any further, we should make it clear what we mean – or rather, what we do not mean – by the terms 'equivalent' and 'equivalence'. We shall not go in detail into the philosophical implications of the term 'equivalence': this is not a course on translation theory.

The literature on translation studies has generated a great deal of discussion of what is generally known as *the principle of equivalent effect*. In so far as 'equivalence' is taken as a synonym of 'sameness' (which is often the case), the concept runs into serious philosophical objections, which we will not go into here (for good discussions see Bassnett 2002: 30–36, Hatim and Munday 2004: 40–56, Hermans 1999, Holmes 1988, Koller 1995, Nida 1964, Snell-Hornby 1988, and Toury 1980 and 1995). The claim that ST and TT effects and features are 'equivalent' in the sense of 'the same' is in any case unhelpful and misleading for the purposes of translation methodology, for two main reasons.

First, the requirement that the TT should affect its recipients in the same way as the ST does (or did) its original audience raises the difficult problem of how any one particular recipient responds to a text, and of the extent to which texts have constant interpretations even for the same person on two different occasions. Before one could objectively assess textual effects, one would need to have recourse to a fairly detailed and exact theory of psychological effect, a theory capable, among other things, of giving an account of the aesthetic sensations that are often paramount in response to texts. Second, the principle of equivalent effect presumes that the theory can cope not only with ST and SL audience but also with the impact of a TT on its intended TL audience. Since on both counts one is faced with unrealistic expectations, the temptation for translators is covertly to substitute their own subjective interpretation for the effects of the ST on recipients in general, and also for the anticipated impact of the TT on its intended audience.

It seems obvious, then, that if good translation is defined in terms of 'equivalence', this is not an objective equivalence, because the translator remains ultimately the only arbiter of the imagined effects of both the ST and the TT. Under these circumstances, even a relatively objective assessment of 'equivalent effect' is hard to envisage.

More fundamentally still, unlike intralingual translation, translation proper has the task of bridging the cultural gap between monolingual speakers of different languages. The backgrounds, shared knowledge, cultural assumptions and learnt responses of monolingual TL speakers are inevitably culture-bound. Given this fact, SL speakers' responses to the ST are never likely to be replicated exactly by effects on members of a different culture. The notion of cross-cultural 'sameness' of psychological effect is a hopeless ideal. Even a small cultural distance between the ST audience and the TT audience is bound to produce fundamental dissimilarity between the effects of the ST and those of the TT – such effects can at best be vaguely similar in a global and limited sense; they can never be 'the same'.

To take a simple example: a translator who decides that the effect of a given ST is to make its audience laugh can replicate that effect by producing a TT that makes its audience laugh. However, claiming 'sameness' of effect in this instance would only be at the expense of a gross reduction of the effects of a text to a single effect. In fact, of course, few texts can be attributed such a monolithic singleness of purpose, and as soon as a ST is acknowledged to have multiple effects, it is unlikely that the TT will be able to replicate them all. (In any case, humour itself is a highly culture-bound phenomenon, which means that even the genuine cross-cultural equivalence of laughter is questionable.)

Another point one must query about the principle of objective equivalent effect concerns the requirement that the TT should replicate the effects of the ST on its original audience. This might conceivably be possible for a contemporary ST, but for a work of any appreciable age it may not be feasible or even desirable. It may not be possible for the translator to determine how audiences responded to the ST when it was first produced. But even if one assumes that such effects can be determined through historical research, one is still faced with a dilemma: should the effects of the TT be matched to those of the ST on its original audience, or on a present-day audience? The extract from Teresa de Jesús's *Su vida* used in Practical 8.1 is a good example of these problems. Even if it were translated into early modern English, could one ever know if the TT would produce the same effects on an English-speaking readership in the 1990s as the ST did on its contemporary Spanish readers? The choice between modernizing a TT or making it archaic is fraught with difficulties whatever one decides: on the one hand, the TT may be rendered trivial without the effects it produced on its original audience; on the other, the original cultural impact of the ST may even be incomprehensible, or unpalatable, to a modern TL audience. For example, in the case of Fernando de Rojas's *Tragicomedia de Calisto y Melibea,* many people in his contemporary audience would have appreciated the rhetoric in Pleberio's lament for its own sake, as well as the ideas and feelings expressed; but today, few readers in Spain – or in Britain – have enough knowledge of rhetoric to be able to appreciate it as some of Rojas's original readers must have done.

In short, we find the principle of equivalent effect, in so far as it implies 'sameness', too vague to be useful in a methodology of translation. At best, a good TT produces a carefully fabricated approximation to some of the manifest properties of the ST. This means that a sound attitude to translation methodology should avoid an absolutist attempt at maximizing sameness in things that are crucially different (ST and TT), in favour of a relativist attempt at minimizing relevant dissimilarities between things that are clearly understood to be different. Once the latter approach is accepted, there is no objection to using the term 'equivalence' as a shorthand for 'not dissimilar in certain relevant respects'. It is in this everyday sense of the word that we use it in this book.

Translation loss

Our position is best explained in terms of an analogy with engineering. All engineering is based on the premise that the transfer of energy in any mechanical device is necessarily subject to a certain degree of 'energy loss'. A machine that permits energy loss is not a theoretical anomaly in engineering: engineers are not puzzled as to why they have not achieved perpetual motion, and their attention is directed, instead, at trying to design machines with increased efficiency by reducing energy loss. By analogy, believing in translation equivalence in the sense of 'sameness' encourages translators to believe in the elusive concept of a perfect translation, representing an ideal mean between SL bias and TL bias. But it is far more realistic to start by admitting that the transfer of meaning from ST to TT is necessarily subject to a certain degree of **translation loss**; that is, a TT will always lack certain culturally relevant features that are present in the ST. The analogy with energy loss is, of course, imperfect. While energy loss is a loss *of* energy, translation loss is not a loss *of* translation, but of exact ST–TT correspondence *in* (the process of) translation. Similarly, the very factors that make it impossible to achieve 'sameness' in translation also make it impossible to measure translation loss absolutely and objectively. Nevertheless, once one accepts the concept of inevitable translation loss, a TT that is not a replica of its ST is no longer seen as a theoretical anomaly, and the translator can concentrate on the realistic aim of reducing translation loss, rather than on the unrealistic one of seeking the definitive translation of the ST.

Using the term 'loss' rather than, for example, 'difference' may seem unduly negative. It is indeed meant to be negative, but constructively so. The danger in talking of 'translation difference' is that 'difference' may be understood in a trivial sense. 'Of course the ST and the TT are different – just look at them, one's in Spanish and the other's in English.' 'Loss' is more likely to direct attention to the relation between ST and TT as terms in a system of relationships, rather than to the texts in themselves (cf. 'just look at them') as static, substantial, autonomous entities. Crucially, 'loss' is a reminder that, if you read a translation of *Cien años de soledad*, you are not reading *Cien años de soledad*, you are reading a reading of it.

It is important to note that translation loss embraces any failure to replicate a ST exactly, whether this involves losing features in the TT or adding them. Our concept of translation loss is, therefore, not opposed to a concept of translation gain; where the TT gains features not present in the ST, this is a form of translation loss. For example, in rendering 'brasero' as 'electric element heater', an obvious translation loss is that the TT lacks the concision of the ST, as well as its cultural specificity (even though there is a gain in explicitness) as a circular heater, traditionally using hot coals but now more usually with an electric element, typically placed under a table; but rendering 'electric element heater' by 'brasero' entails an equally obvious translation loss, in that the TT does not have the explicitness of the ST (even though there is a gain in concision and vividness, as well as cultural appropriateness). Similarly, translating the adjective 'tuerto' as 'blind in one eye' is an instance of translation loss, even though the TT is not only literally exact, but has 'gained' several words and makes explicit reference to blindness and to eyes. In addition 'tuerto' can also be translated as one-eyed, and used as a noun 'a person blind in one eye', 'a one-eyed person'. A third example exhibits still more sorts of translation loss: the translation of 'capital transfer tax' by 'impuesto sobre plusvalía de cesión'. The English is more concise, but its grammar is a potential source of ambiguity for the unwary; for instance, is this a transfer tax that is capital, or a tax that is a capital transfer, or a tax on transfers that are capital, or a tax on the transfer of capital? The grammar of the Spanish expression eliminates all such ambiguity, but it is more cumbersome than the English. As these three examples show, translation loss, in the way we have defined it, is inevitable, even where the TT gains in, say, economy, vividness, cultural specificity or avoidance of ambiguity. The challenge to the translator is, therefore, not to eliminate translation loss altogether, but to reduce it by deciding which of the relevant features in the ST it is most important to respect, and which can most legitimately be sacrificed in doing so.

For all translators, but particularly for students, there are two great advantages in the notion that translation loss is inevitable, and that a so-called gain is actually a loss. First, they are relieved of the inhibiting, demoralizing supposition that, if only they were clever enough or lucky enough to find it, the perfect TT is just round the corner; and, second, they are less tempted to try crudely to outweigh losses in their TT with a greater volume of gains.

Our approach assumes, then, that the translator's ambition is not an absolutist one to maximize sameness, but a relativist one to minimize difference: to look, not for what one is to put into the TT, but for what one might save from the ST, and therefore to forget the mirage of gain and to concentrate instead on the real benefits of compensation. (We shall discuss compensation in the next chapter.) Once this approach is adopted, the culturally relevant features in the ST will tend to present themselves to the translator in a certain hierarchical order. The most immediately obvious features which may prove impossible to preserve in a TT are 'cultural' in a very general sense, arising from the simple fact of transferring messages from one culture to another – references or allusions to the source culture's history, geography, literature, folklore and so on. We shall, therefore, discuss such issues in Chapter 5 (after consideration of general issues of compensation and genre in Chapters 3 and 4). The next step will be to analyse the objectively ostensible formal properties of the ST; we shall suggest a systematic framework for discussing these properties in Chapters 6–7. Subsequent ST features that will inevitably be lacking, or changed, in any TT will have to do with nuances of literal or **connotative meaning**; yet others will stem from such aspects of language variety as dialect, sociolect and register. We shall be discussing literal and connotative meaning in Chapters 8 and 9 respectively, and questions of language variety in Chapters 10 and 11.

Practical 2

2.1 Strategic decisions and decisions of detail: translation loss

Assignment

(i)   You are translating the extract from a short story by Julio Cortázar to appear in the magazine, *Astounding Stories*, read by teenaged fans of science fantasy and tales of the supernatural. Discuss the strategic

decisions that you have to take before starting detailed translation of this
ST, and outline and justify the strategy you adopt.

(ii)   Translate the text into English.

(iii)   Paying special attention to the places where you managed to avoid
unacceptable translation loss, discuss the main decisions of detail you
took, explaining what the threatened loss was and how you avoided it.

Contextual information

The passage is from Julio Cortázar's short story 'Estación de la mano' (1967),
in which the narrator tells of a mysterious disembodied hand which visits him
for a period and which incites attraction and fear. (Students are advised to
investigate the context of the full text before translating the passage.)

Source text 1

Le puse nombres: me gustaba llamarla Dg, porque era un nombre que sólo
se dejaba pensar. Incité su probable vanidad olvidando anillos y brazaletes
sobre las repisas, espiando su actitud con secreta constancia. Alguna vez
creí que se adornaría con las joyas, pero ella las estudiaba dando vueltas
en torno y sin tocarlas, a semejanza de una araña desconfiada; y aunque   5
un día llegó a ponerse un anillo de amatista fue sólo por un instante, y lo
abandonó como si le quemara. Me apresuré entonces a esconder las joyas
en su ausencia y desde entonces me pareció que estaba más contenta.

Así declinaron las estaciones, unas esbeltas y otras con semanas teñidas
de luces violentas, sin que sus llamadas premiosas llegaran hasta nuestro   10
ámbito. Todas las tardes volvía la mano, mojada con frecuencia por las
lluvias otoñales, y la veía tenderse de espaldas sobre la alfombra, secarse
prolijamente un dedo con otro, a veces con menudos saltos de cosa
satisfecha. En los atardeceres de frío su sombra se teñía de violeta.
Yo encendía entonces un brasero a mis pies y ella se acurrucaba y   15
apenas bullía, salvo para recibir, displicente, un álbum con grabados o un
ovillo de lana que le gustaba anudar y retorcer. Era incapaz, lo advertí
pronto, de estarse largo rato quieta. Un día encontró una artesa con arcilla
y se precipitó sobre ella, horas y horas modeló la arcilla mientras yo, de
espaldas, fingía no preocuparme por su tarea. Naturalmente, modeló una   20
mano. La dejé secar y la puse sobre el escritorio para probarle que su obra
me agradaba. Era un error: a Dg terminó por molestarle la contemplación
de ese autorretrato rígido y algo convulso. Cuando lo escondí, fingió por
pudor no haberlo advertido.

Mi interés se tornó bien pronto analítico. Cansado de maravillarme, quise   25
saber, invariable y funesto fin de toda aventura. Surgían las preguntas
acerca de mi huésped: ¿Vegetaba, sentía, comprendía, amaba? Tendí
lazos, apronté experimentos. Había advertido que la mano, aunque capaz
de leer, jamás escribía. Una tarde abrí la ventana y puse sobre la mesa un

lapicero, cuartillas en blanco y cuando entró Dg me marché para no pesar   30
sobre su timidez. Por el ojo de la cerradura la vi cumplir sus paseos
habituales; luego, vacilante, fue hasta el escritorio y tomó el lapicero. Oí
el arañar de la pluma, y después de un tiempo ansioso entré en el estudio.
En diagonal y con letra perfilada, Dg había escrito: *Esta resolución anula
todas las anteriores hasta nueva orden.* Jamás pude lograr que volviese a   35
escribir.

(Cortázar 1976: 57–8)

2.2 Translation loss

Assignment

(i)   Taking the first half of the text in Spanish below (*Source text 1*), identify
       the salient features of its content and expression.
(ii)   Taking the TT printed next to it as a whole, place it on a scale of degrees
       of freedom given on p. 19, and explain your decision.
(iii) Taking the detail of the TT discuss the main differences between it and
       the ST, paying special attention to cases where it incurs, or manages
       to avoid, unacceptable translation loss.
(iv)   Where you think the TT can be improved, give your own revised
       version and explain the revision.
(v)   In the light of this work on the first part of the ST, outline and justify
       your strategy for translating the rest of it.
(vi)   Translate the rest of the text (the section entitled 'Datos e Internet' –
       Source text 2) into English.
(vii) Paying special attention to cases where you managed to avoid
       unacceptable translation loss, discuss the main decisions of detail you
       took, explaining what the threatened loss was and how you avoided it.
(viii) Compare your TT with the published one, which will be given to you
       by your tutor.

Contextual information

The ST is from the annual report for 2006 of Telefónica, S.A., one of the
world's largest telecommunications groups. The TT was published as the
English version of the report. The first part of the ST comes from the section
of the report that deals with Telefónica's corporate identity, and the second from
the section dealing with Telefónica's achievements. Although there are graphs,
charts, and full-colour illustrations throughout the report, including in these
sections, the summary of Telefónica's performance appears later with detailed
financial statements, and balance sheets. The annual report thus combines
publicity with information on the company's main activities, aimed at retaining
present shareholders, and attracting new ones.

Source text 1	Target text
Gestión medioambiental	*Environmental Management*

Para garantizar el cumplimiento de este compromiso contamos con una norma interna de "Requisitos Mínimos Ambientales", cuyo objetivo final es la certificación ambiental de todas nuestras operaciones. Con una metodología común aseguramos que todas las empresas del grupo tienen un comportamiento responsable en esta materia. Para facilitar el cumplimiento de la norma establecimos cinco pasos de actuación: el compromiso, requisitos de aplicación, mejora del comportamiento, implantación de sistemas y certificación.

El seguimiento del cumplimiento de la norma se hace a través de los comités de medio ambiente país, presentes en Argentina, Brasil, Colombia, España, México y Perú. El seguimiento de las actividades ambientales de todos los comités se presentan periódicamente a la Comisión de Reputación y Recursos Humanos.

(Telefónica 2007b: 84)

To ensure compliance with this commitment, we have an internal standard of "Minimum Environment Requirements" with the ultimate goal of   5
environmental certification for all our operations. Through a common methodology we can ensure that all of the group's companies behave responsibly in this field. To facilitate compliance with   10
the standard, we have established five stages in the process: commitment, requirements for application, improvement in behaviour, implementation of systems and certification.   15

Compliance with the standard is monitored through the Environmental Committees Argentina, Brazil, Chile, Colombia, Spain, Mexico and Peru. All of these committees regularly submit the   20
results of their monitoring to the Reputation and Human Resources Committee.

(Telefónica 2007a: 84)

Source text 2

Datos e Internet

Telefónica parte de una sólida posición para aprovechar las oportunidades que ofrece el nuevo entorno digital.

Los accesos de banda ancha fija alcanzaron los 8 millones, con un crecimiento interanual del 41,1% y una ganancia neta de 2,3 millones de   5
accesos.

En 2006, Telefónica se ha posicionado como el primer operador de ADSL de América Latina, con más de 3,7 millones de accesos de banda ancha en la región.

En España, Telefónica gestiona más de 3,7 millones de accesos   10
minoristas a Internet de banda ancha, con una ganancia neta de 1,5 millones en el ejercicio. A este crecimiento han contribuido decisivamente las ofertas combinadas (dúo, trío . . .) que ya superan los 2,7 millones de suscripciones.

Telefónica O_2 Europa presentó un crecimiento en el número de accesos 15
de banda ancha del 93,4%, como consecuencia de la ganancia de 179.000
líneas en República Checa y el lanzamiento de la oferta de ADSL en
Alemania.

(Telefónica 2007b: 16)

3 Lexis and compensation

Everyone is familiar with dictionaries. They present what purports to be a list of the practical totality of the words, often with commonly used phrases, in a given language at a particular time (and some include archaic words and senses). This totality is known as the **lexis** of a language (adj. **lexical**). For reasons of educational bias (for instance, the paramount use that students make of dictionaries and lexically arranged encyclopedias), people are far more directly aware of individual words than of other units and structures of language. In particular, mentioning 'meaning' or the semantic properties of languages (and therefore also of texts) tends to evoke first and foremost the level of individual words. Yet meanings are certainly not exclusively concentrated in words individually. Any text shows that the combination of words (and their use in contexts) creates meanings that the individual words do not possess in isolation, and even meanings that are not wholly predictable from the literal senses of the words combined.

As our multi-level approach to textual variables – discussed in Chapters 6 and 7 – indicates, lexical translation losses (such as want of an exact translation for a particular word) are just one kind of translation loss among many. There is no a priori reason, as long as the overall sense of the ST is successfully conveyed by the TT, why they should be given a heavier weighting than other kinds of translation loss. In fact, communicative translation is often more important than word-for-word correspondences. For instance, 'no se puede saber' can be plausibly translated in most modern contexts as 'you never can tell', rather than as 'one can never know'; even then, the choice of 'you' instead of 'one', 'a body' or even 'a girl' would be entirely a matter of context.

Lexical translation losses, then, are no more avoidable than other kinds of translation loss. Exact synonymy between SL and TL words is the exception rather than the rule, and problems arising from this should be neither maximized nor minimized, but treated on a par with other translation losses that affect the overall meaning of the TT. None the less, in specific situations compensation may be necessary to mollify the effects of loss.

Comparing the lexical meanings of words across languages underlines the fact that lexical translation losses are as likely to result from **particularization** (where the TT word has a narrower meaning than the ST word) as from

generalization (where the TT has a wider meaning than the ST word). So, for example, translating, in a given context, Spanish 'alma' as 'soul', rather than as 'mind' or 'spirit', is an inevitable particularization, because one has to choose one of these three TL words, each of which has a narrower range of reference than Spanish 'alma'. Conversely, translating '¡tiene un revólver!' as 'he's got a gun!' is a case of generalization, because 'gun' can also mean 'escopeta', 'pistola', 'fusil' and 'cañón' – that is, it has a wider range of reference than 'revólver'. The translation problems arising from particularization and generalization are very common, and we shall return to them in Chapter 8.

Another reason why, in ordinary language, no TL word is ever likely to replicate precisely the 'meaning' of a given SL word is that, in each language, words form idiosyncratic associations with sets of other words. Such associations may hold by virtue of the forms of words, as in the homonymic association between 'crane' (bird) and 'crane' (machine); or by virtue of the literal meanings of the words, as with the associations of relative value in the series 'gold', 'silver' and 'bronze'; or by virtue of culture-bound prejudices and assumptions, as in the association of 'law and order' (or 'brutality') with 'police'. The exact associative overtones of words in the overall context of a ST are often difficult enough to pinpoint, but it is even more difficult, if not impossible, to find TL words that will, over and above conveying an appropriate literal meaning, also produce exactly the right associative overtones in the context of the TT. This is another source of lexical translation loss, and another potential dilemma between choosing literal meaning at the expense of associative overtones, or vice versa. We shall return to these questions in Chapter 9.

The issue of undesirable, yet inevitable, translation losses raises a special problem for the translator. The problem consists in knowing that the loss of certain features sacrificed in translation does have detrimental effects on the quality of the TT, but seeing no way of avoiding these unacceptable compromises. So, for instance, 'sword' is admittedly far from being an exact translation of the literal meaning of 'estoque'; it lacks the association with the weapon's ceremonial use in bullfighting which is so much part of the meaning of the word. Nevertheless, translating 'estoque' as 'sword' may be an acceptable compromise if the ST merely makes casual mention of it. However, this is less acceptable in, say, an anthropological text examining the aesthetic and ideological aspects of the bullfight; and such a compromise is quite unacceptable if 'estoque' is the sole means by which the cultural context of bullfighting is evoked in the ST.

As can be seen from this discussion, it may be necessary to find ways of compensating for certain unavoidable TT effects. This can be illustrated well when considering the translation of cultural clichés and proverbs, such as when translating the following Hungarian ST into English. (We choose Hungarian because it is unfamiliar to most readers, and therefore capable of giving a genuinely exotic impression.) Waking on the first morning of the holiday, the children are disappointed to find that it is raining heavily. Their mother comforts them with a proverb, suggesting that it will soon clear up: 'Nem baj! Reggeli vendég nem maradandó' (literally, 'No problem! The morning guest never stays long'). The only advantage of a literal translation is its exoticism, but this advantage is cancelled by two things: the obscurity of the TT, and its lack of contextual plausibility. If there were good reasons for preserving the exoticism, one could mitigate these disadvantages by obliquely signalling in the TT that the mother is using what is, for TL readers, an exotic proverb: 'Never mind! You know the saying: the morning guest never stays long'. The translation of the proverb itself is a **calque**, an expression that consists of TL words and respects TL syntax, but is unidiomatic in the TL because it is modelled on the structure of a SL expression. The phrase 'You know the saying' is added to show that the aphorism is an established proverb and not a flight of poetic creativeness on the part of the mother. Without the addition, the unfamiliarity of the calque would have an exotic quality that is completely absent from the ST, and it would also imply something about the mother's character. As it is, the exotic quality is maintained but the expression's lack of idiomaticity is palliated for the reader. Depending on the purpose of the TT, these effects could be instances of translation loss, a significant betrayal of ST effects. Adding 'You know the saying' does not make 'the morning guest never stays long' any more familiar in itself, but it does make it less likely to have these misleading effects. And giving it a quasi-proverbial style preserves the sentitious tone, which would be lost in a literal translation.

These procedures together are a good examples of **compensation**: that is, where any translation (whether literal or otherwise) would entail an unacceptable translation loss, this loss is reduced by the freely chosen introduction of a less unacceptable one, such that important ST effects are rendered approximately in the TT by means other than those used in the ST. In other words, one type of translation loss is mitigated by the deliberate introduction of another. In this example, adding 'You know the saying' incurs great translation loss in terms of economy and cultural presupposition, but this is accepted because it significantly reduces the greater loss in terms of message content that would be incurred by a literal translation or a misleading communicative translation. And the pseudo-proverb is grammatically, rhythmically and phonically very far from the ST proverb: but this loss, too, is welcomed because it preserves the sentitious tone, which a literal translation would lose.

Note that these departures have not been forced on the translator by the dictates of TL grammar. The changes have been deliberately and freely chosen to compensate for the lack of a TL proverb that does what the ST one does. The question of choice versus constraint is vital to the understanding of compensation as we shall see. Compromise in translation means reconciling oneself to the fact that, while one would like to do full justice to the 'richness' of the ST, one's final TT inevitably suffers from various translation losses.

Often one allows these losses unhesitatingly. For instance, a translator of prose (particularly in the commercial sector) may without any qualms sacrifice the phonic and prosodic properties of a ST in order to make its literal meaning perfectly clear, while a translator of verse (for instance, song lyrics) may equally happily sacrifice much of the ST's literal meaning in order to achieve certain desired metric and phonic effects. These are just two examples of the many kinds of compromise translators make every day, guided by the strategic priorities decided upon for each translation task.

Compromises should be the result of deliberate decisions taken in the light not only of what latitudes are allowed by the SL and TL respectively, but also of all the factors that can play a determining role in translation: the nature of the ST, its relationship to SL audiences, the purpose of the TT, its putative audience, and so forth. Only then can the translator have a firm grasp of which aspects of the ST can be sacrificed with the least detriment to the effectiveness of the TT, both as a rendering of the ST and as a TL text in its own right. Much of the material in this book will in fact draw attention, in both principle and practice, to the different kinds of compromise suggested – perhaps even dictated – by different types of text. It virtually always entails a difference in kind between the ST textual effect and the TT textual effect. For instance, it may involve making explicit what is implicit in the ST. One area where what is explicit in the ST also quite often needs to be explicit in the TT is in the differences between the marking of gender as a grammatical category in Spanish and English. The contrast in Spanish between masculine and feminine forms of nouns, adjectives and the definite article is one that frequently causes problems. In English many nouns, adjectives and the definite articles do not permit the expressive power that a Spanish ST may derive from the contrast between feminine and masculine gender. Consider the opening sentences of Dora Alonso's short story 'Los gatos'. It comes from an anthology of stories particularly selected by the author because they all have female protagonists (human or animal):

> La gata dilataba las pupilas en la oscuridad. Maullaba con insistencia y parecía intranquila. Lola despertó y, adivinándola entre la sombra, la llamó en voz baja:
> – Galana, ven.
> La gata se arrimó a la mano seca que la buscaba y esta palpó el redondo vientre que saltaba y se removía.
>
> (Alonso 1980: 133–4)

If encountered in a gender-neutral text, the first sentence might harmlessly be grammatically transposed as 'The cat's pupils dilated in the darkness'; however, it would almost certainly not be adequately translated without some reference to female gender in the context of this feminist ST. As 'The cat's pupils dilated in the darkness' cannot create the gender-based link between feline motherhood and human motherhood, which is such a crucial motif of the ST, this option represents an unacceptable translation loss. One way of overcoming this loss might be to compensate in kind to make the cat's gender explicit in the TT, by translating 'La gata dilataba las pupilas en la oscuridad' as 'The pupils of the *she-cat* dilated in the darkness' (but 'she-cat' might be perceived as translationese), or even as 'The *mother* cat's pupils dilated in the darkness', or as 'The cat dilated *her* eyes'. Alternatively, mention of feminine gender may have to be delayed to a subsequent sentence in the TT where it can be signalled by anaphoric 'she', which, in this context, would be a mandatory choice over the frequent allusion in English to animals, even domestic pets, as 'it'.

A further example of compensation for the loss of an explicit meaning in the ST by the introduction of implicit meanings in the TT comes from poem LXXVII of Machado's *Soledades, galerías y otros poemas* (1903). The Predmore version (Machado 1987) represents a literal rendering, whereas in the Trueblood translation (Machado 1982b) the literal meaning of Spanish 'usual' as 'usual/normal' is compensated for by the connotations of tedium carried by 'same old':

> Y es esta vieja angustia
> que habita mi usual hipocondría.
>
> (Machado 1982a: 125)

> and it's this old anguish
> that inhabits my usual hypochondria.
>
> (Machado 1987 [trans. Predmore]: 207)

> The old distress is back,
> Stirring inside the same old fancied ills.
>
> (Machado 1982b [trans. Trueblood]: 97)

Further, connotative meanings in the ST may be compensated for by literal meanings in the TT. This type of compensation can be illustrated by comparing two translations of another extract from Machado (poem LX). Once again, the Predmore translation (Machado 1987) represents a literal rendering of 'noria' through his use of an obscure but established loan-word with strong culturally specific connotations. The obscurity of TL 'noria' may render the oxymoron ineffective for many readers, who fail to see the explicit link between the noria's use as a water wheel, and its description as 'seca', thus occasioning a loss in the TT of the connotative oxymoron implicit in the ST's juxtaposition of 'seca' and 'noria', and of the latent SL connotations of 'ferris wheel'. While also sacrificing the latent connotations of ferris wheel, the Trueblood translation (Machado 1982b) restores the oxymoron by explicitly referring to 'water wheel', thus juxtaposing 'water' and 'dry':

Colmenares de mis sueños
¿ya no labráis? ¿Está seca
la noria del pensamiento . . .

(Machado 1982a: 117)

Beehives of my dreams,
do you work no more? Has
the noria of my thought run dry . . .

(Machado 1987: 179)

Have the beehives of my dreams
stopped working, the water wheel
of the mind run dry . . .

(Machado 1982b: 93)

(We shall discuss literal and connotative meaning in Chapters 8 and 9.)

Third, where, for example, the humour of the ST hinges on the comic use of calque, the TT may have to derive its humour from other sources, such as a play on words. Successful examples of this sort of compensation in kind abound in the Astérix books; compare, for instance, *Astérix chez les Bretons* with *Asterix en Bretaña*:

Obelix:	Pourquoi parlez-vous à l'envers?
Jolitorax:	Je demande votre pardon?

(Goscinny and Uderzo 1966: 9)

Obelix:	¿Por qué habla al revés?
Buentorax:	Le ruego me perdone.

(Goscinny and Uderzo 1967: 9)

In the ST, the comic effect of Jolitorax's anglicism is achieved by the substitution of a calque on English 'I beg your pardon' for 'Plaît-il?' or 'Comment?' (the ST expression in fact means 'I ask your forgiveness'). In the Spanish TT, where '¿Qué?' or '¿Cómo?' would be expected (cf. 'Comment?'), the comic effect hinges on the generic incongruity of a phrase only found in business correspondence, never in speech; that is, the translator has compensated for the element of humour by means other than those used in the ST.

In literary, political or journalistic STs, a significant part of the effect is often produced through the sounds of words. If the strategy is to produce similar effects in similar ways in the TT, this will almost certainly only be possible using different sounds in different places, as in the following examples from Fidel Castro's address to the UN in New York on 12 October, 1979 (repetition is underlined, and other sound effects in bold):

Hablo **en n**ombre de los **n**iños que **en** el mundo **no tienen** un **p**edazo de
pan; hablo **en n**ombre de los **en**fermos que **no tienen** medi**c**inas.
(Castro 1979a)

Here, the rhetoric is obviously reinforced by the alliteration and assonance,
and by the repetition of 'hablo en nombre de' and 'no tienen'. By **alliteration**
we mean the recurrence of the same sound or letter sequence at the beginning
of a word, and by **assonance**, the recurrence of a sound or letter sequence in
the middle of closely occuring words. The power of the statement derives from
the acoustic association of the two categories of individual introduced through
alliteration and assonance on n, and the word 'no' which refers to their lack
of access to basic resources. The phonic association cannot be replicated in
an English TT: the key words do not alliterate, and 'children' and 'sick' or
'ill' have no sound in common with one another or with 'no', as the following
rather literal TT shows:

I speak in the name of the children in the world who do not have a piece
of bread. I speak in the name of the sick who do not have medicine.
(Castro 1979b)

A possible TT might try to convey the rhetorical effect by compensation for
the loss of alliteration with an increase in syntactical parallelism, and by
substituting the SL idiom 'un pedazo de pan' for a suitable TL idiom:

I speak in the name of the children who do not have a bite to eat. I speak
in the name of the sick who do not have medicine.

Sound effects might also involve using phonic reinforcement in different places
in the TT than in the ST. Consider the following extract from *Cola de lagartija*
by the Argentinian novelist Luisa Valenzuela:

Centelleante con escamas de plata montado en flete de luna voy
cantándole al sol poniente la grandeza de mi destino voy. A escasas leguas
de Capivarí sé de la felicidad que siento y de la que sentiré cuando se me
reciba como a una aparición. De mis músculos se ha borrado el cansancio
y mis brazos han olvidado el remar y sólo mis muslos están tensos y alertas   5
para mantenerme sobre el lomo de este brioso corcel que ahora ¿por qué?
se detiene de golpe y recula. Pega unos pasos de costado – corcovea, casi,
por nada del mundo acepta seguir su camino. Y de golpe oigo el siseo
aterrador y veo (y se me paran los pelos en punta, creo que se me caen
todas las escamas, los dientes me castañetean de terror, es una corriente 10
indefinible que pasa del caballo a mi entrepierna y me recorre el cuerpo).
    Bajo esa luz sin sombras del ocaso las veo y por primera vez sé del
espanto verdadero. Es el nudo de víboras, la rueda del mundo girando,
apareándose, las víboras de cascabel sacudiendo sus crótalos, la de coral

con sus venenos, la yarará, todas, no alcanzo a distinguirlas, son colores 15
que se mezclan, colas y cabezas tan iguales y todas copulando. La gran
rueda de cópula girando, volteándose a los lados. La víbora, animal de
dos falos. La envidiable, la envidiosa, aglutinadas en masa única,
bisbiseante, y mi caballo se yergue en sus patas traseras y ya no puedo
retenerme, me dejo deslizar hasta el suelo.   20

(Valenzuela 1983: 298–9)

As a class exercise, identify phonic patterns of alliteration and repetition in the
text above and discuss their implications for translation. Look for recurrences
not only of individual sounds and groups of sounds but also of words and
phrases, and discuss the relationship between phonic effects and meaning.
When translating a text that makes use of such effects as extensively as this
one does, phonic reinforcement of the same lexical items in ST and TT will
not always be possible and some compensation is likely to prove necessary.
(For a fuller discussion of the phonic level, see Chapter 6.) Here is Gregory
Rabassa's published TT of the Valenzuela extract for class discussion:

Glittering with silver scales, mounted on a moon-bearer, I go; singing
to the setting sun the grandeur of my destiny, I go. A few miles from
Capivari I acknowledge the happiness I feel and will feel when I am
received as an apparition. Fatigue has been banished from my muscles
and my arms have forgotten all the rowing and only my thighs are tense 5
and alert, holding me up on the haunches of this fiery steed that now, why?
suddenly stops and draws back. I give it some kicks on the side – it almost
bucks, for nothing in the world will it follow its path. And suddenly I hear
the terrifying hissing and I see them – and my hair stands on end, I feel
all my scales falling off, my teeth chattering from terror, it's an ineffable 10
current that passes from my horse to my crotch and runs up my body.
   Under the shadowless light of dusk I see them and for the first time I
know true fright. It's the vipers' knot, the wheel of the world, spinning,
pairing off, the rattlesnakes shaking their rattles, the coral snakes and their
poison, the pit viper, the *curiyú* viper, all of them, I can't make them out, 15
they're colors that mingle, tails and heads so much alike, and all copu-
lating. The great wheel of copulation, spinning, fluttering to the sides. The
viper, an animal with two phalluses. The envied one, the envious one,
joined in a single mass, hissing, and my horse rears on his hind legs and
I can no longer hold back, I let myself slip to the ground.   20

(Valenzuela 1992: 277–8)

All these sorts of substitution may be confined to single words, but they more
usually extend to whole phrases, sentences, or even paragraphs. For example,
series of words can be distributed in contrastive and recurrent patterns that
signal or reinforce the thematic development of the text: see Chapter 7 for fuller
discussion, especially of the patterned use of lexical sets over an entire text in

the rhyme 'One for sorrow' (p. 115). In Aphek and Tobin (1988), the term **word system** is used to denote this phenomenon. A word system is a pattern (within a text) of words having an associative common denominator, a pattern which 'nurtures the theme and message of the text with greater intensity' (Aphek and Tobin 1988: 3). In the following extract from Juan Goytisolo's novel *Reivindicación del conde don Julián*, the author builds up a word system of nouns that derive directly from Arabic (many of which begin *al-*), and which refer to something introduced into Spain by its Muslim inhabitants in the Middle Ages:

> y galopando con ellos en desenfrenada razzia saquearás los campos de algodón, algarrobo, alfalfa
> vaciarás aljibes y albercas, demolerás almacenes y dársenas, arruinarás alquerías y fondas, pillarás alcobas, alacenas, zaguanes
> cargarás con sofás, alfombras, jarros, almohadas
> devastarás las aldeas y sacrificarás los rebaños, despojarás a la ilusionada novia de su ajuar, a la dama aristócrata de sus alhajas, al rico estraperlista de su fulana, al hidalgo provecto de su alcurnia
> retirarás el ajedrez de los casinos, el alquitrán de las carreteras
> (Goytisolo 1988b: 196)

The novel was first published in 1970, and reflects Goytisolo's antipathy towards Francisco Franco's regime. The list occurs towards the end of the third part of the novel, in which Goytisolo offers a biting satire of the notion of the unity and purity of Castilian in the face of Arabic influence, and undermines the institutions that insist on the existence of linguistic purity. The power of Goytisolo's attack depends on a prevalent, officially sanctioned negative attitude towards Islam, Africa, and Arabic as impure and corrupting. In other words, Arabic would generally be regarded as of lower prestige than Castilian, but Goytisolo collapses the privileging of Castilian culture over Arabic. Unless they were particularly vigilant, many native speakers would not be immediately aware of the Arabic origins of these words on seeing or hearing them out of this particular context even if they were aware of the link between the opening syllable *al-* and Arabic. And even those familiar with the link between an opening *al-* and Arabic, only a very limited number of readers would also be familiar with the Arabic origin of 'razzia', 'dársena', 'fonda' and so on. The translator of this passage would need to consider whether it was possible to use a word system of words with Arabic origins. In such a case, the negative connotations of Arabic would be lost on the target audience since Anglophone culture does not relegate the Arabic language to a position of low esteem, and very few readers indeed would be aware of the origins of such words. French and Latin are the most obvious languages with which English has a similar relationship of linguistic borrowing but both of these languages are held in high esteem. On account of the areas of Arabic influence semantic word systems also emerge: military, agriculture, domestic, social organization, and so on. The translator would also need to consider the extent to which he or she wished to convey the extensive range of areas of activity to which the second-level word systems point. The published translation would repay discussion in class:

> And galloping with them as they mount their furious attack, you will lay waste to their fields of cotton and alfalfa and carob beans
> you will demolish arsenals and magazines, sink feluccas, pillage alcoves
> you will carry off sofas and divans, mattresses, muslins, and jars
> you will kill albatrosses
> you will deprive the astrologer of his azimuth, the alchemist of his elixirs, the assassin of his scimitar
> you will remove chess from the casinos, and the asphalt from highways
> (Goytisolo 1989: 166)

This example and that drawn from Valenzuela's *Cola de lagartija* show that it is worth scanning certain types of text for theme-reinforcing word systems (such as a series of thematic key-words, or phonetic patterns, or an extended metaphor), because such things may be important textual devices. Where a word system is found in the ST, the construction of some analogous word system in the TT may be desirable; if so, this will be a strong factor influencing the translator's lexical choices. In the case of our example, the word system in question hinges on a phonic/graphic common denominator which is highly specific, but not unique, to Spanish; constructing a similar **phonic/graphic** word system seems virtually impossible in an English TT. Two of the translator's first strategic decisions will, therefore, be how much priority to give to this type of pattern, and how to construct an appropriate word system in the TT.

Quite apart from these examples, sometimes an entire text is affected by the need for compensation. For instance, beyond lexical and grammatical considerations, if a poem is heavily marked by rhyme and the translator decides that rhyme would lead to unacceptable translation loss, compensation might consist of heavily marking the TT with something different, such as rhythm, assonance or expressive breaks between lines. Ted Hughes' 1998 translation of *Phèdre*, which deliberately introduces translation loss on every level, is a resoundingly successful example of wholesale compensation on this scale. However, if a translator judges that an adequate TT could not afford to lose all trace of the salient and insistent sound-symbolic effects, then full-scale compensation might be indicated. Consider the following extract from Nicolás Guillén's 'Mulata' (*Motivos de son*, 1930):

> **Tanto tren con tu cueppo,**
> **tanto tren;**
> **tanto tren con tu boca,**

tanto t**ren**;
tanto t**ren con** t**u** sojo,
tanto t**ren**.
(Guillén 1976: 104)

Here the element of sound symbolism that is so central to the poem as a whole is reinforced by alliterations and assonances which concentrate particularly, on the one hand, on the consonants [t] and [n], and, on the other, on the vowel [o]. This phonetic reinforcement cannot be precisely, and equally intensively, replicated in an English TT because the key words do not alliterate in the required ways. The following TT attempts at least partly to compensate for this by using phonetic reinforcement distributed in different places from where it occurs in the ST:

So much **fuss 'bou**t you' **b**ody
so much **fuss;**
so much **fuss 'bou**t you' **mou**t',
so much **fuss;**
so much **fuss 'bou**t you' eyes,
so much **fuss**.
(Unpublished translation by
Gustavo San Román)

Humour is notoriously difficult to translate without using compensation. Successful examples abound in the Astérix books. In this example from *Asterix en Bretaña*, as in the one discussed above, the humour derives from Jolitorax speaking a different dialect. Without cultural transplantation, this is impossible to convey, so the TT obtains its humour by compensation:

Jolitorax: Je serai ravi, j'en suis sûr, *d'aller dans la votre maison*!
(Goscinny and Uderzo 1966: 9; our italics)

Buentorax: *Me gustará*, estoy seguro, ir a vuestra casa.
(Goscinny and Uderzo 1967: 9; our italics)

One of the comic effects of the ST is achieved by the grammatical incongruity of 'aller dans la votre maison'. In the Spanish TT the corresponding 'ir a vuestra casa' is grammatically correct, but contextually inappropriate, and the comic effect is transferred to the incongruous 'me gustará'. Compensation in place (achieving the desired TT effect in a different place) is also needed in translating the phrase 'un galán maduro, algo calvo', probably best rendered as 'a mature gentleman, handsome but slightly balding'. This example illustrates the fact that **grammatical transposition** – the reorganization of a ST grammatical structure into a different, more idiomatic, structure in the TT – often amounts to a type of compensation in place.

Compensation also very often involves a change in 'economy'. For example, ST features carried over a relatively long stretch of text (say, a complex phrase or a compound word) might be condensed into a relatively short stretch of the TT (say, a simple phrase or a single word). In some cases, such condensation is the only way to strike a fair balance between doing justice to the literal meaning of a piece of ST and constructing an idiomatic TT, as in the example 'estuvo bastante tiempo sin resolverse'. An accurate literal translation of this phrase might be produced by translating word for word; but the resulting TT phrase would be far too long-winded and ponderous to be suitable in most contexts, and certainly out of place in a colloquial one. The semantic contents of the ST expression are rendered accurately, and in a more streamlined fashion, through compensation by merging, as 'he shilly-shallied'.

The following item provides two examples where compensation by merging offers the most plausible solution ('es necesario que' merged into 'should' and 'de aspecto deportivo' merged into 'sporty-looking', with appropriate reordering of the sentence):

> Es necesario que al paso de un joven de aspecto deportivo cualquier señorita musite: '¡Adiós, Pirri! ¿Quieres que sea la Sonia Bruno de tu existencia?'

Where the context allows, and there is no single TL word that covers the same range of meaning as a given ST word, it may be possible to state explicitly the most important notions conveyed. A simple example is furnished by the Spanish verb 'escasear', which, for literal exactitude, has to be translated as 'to be in short supply'.

The following example is more complex, but no less typical. In most contexts 'el toreo' can be effectively rendered as 'bullfighting' (a solution which, in itself, represents a degree of culturally necessary circumlocution). In certain contexts, however – for instance where a Spanish ST deals with the exposition of the ethics and aesthetics of the 'toreo' – the English reader needs, for obvious cultural reasons, to be reminded that 'bullfighting' should be seen as more than a mere sport or a mere popular spectacle. In such contexts, a translator might render 'el toreo' as '*the art of* bullfighting'. The ST's implicitly (culturally) connoted notion of bullfighting as an art form is rendered in the TT by literal means through the explicit addition of 'the art of'. We will not pursue this any further, because what is involved is the question of literal versus connotative meaning, and these questions are not addressed until Chapters 8 and 9. Suffice it to say that the TT exhibits the substitution of literal meaning for connotative meaning.

It has been necessary in this chapter to anticipate certain elements of topics that are treated at length in later chapters. What we wish to emphasize by placing the discussion of compensation here is that it is a key concept that applies to all aspects of the process of translation: it plays a crucial role in dealing with translation problems arising from genre, cultural difference, phonic and graphic effects, syntactical and discourse features, literal and connotative meaning, and language variety.

We conclude with a word of caution: while compensation exercises the translator's ingenuity, the effort it requires should not be wasted on textually unimportant features. The aim is to reduce some of the more serious and undesirable translation losses that necessarily result from the fundamental structural and cultural differences between SL and TL.

Practical 3

3.1 Compensation

Assignment

(i)   Discuss the strategic problems confronting the translator of the following text and outline your own strategy for translating it, focusing particularly on compensation options.
(ii) Translate the text into English, assuming that the target readership of the TT comprises employers and employees in the Canary Islands whose knowledge of Spanish is limited.
(iii) Explain the main decisions of detail you made in producing your TT.

Contextual information

The ST is from an article issued by the Oficina Técnica de Prevención de Riesgos Laborales, a service run by the Spanish trade union, UGT (Unión General de Trabajadores) in the Canary Islands. It was published on 2 October 2007 on the website Salud Laboral. The extract comprises the first two paragraphs and the last paragraph of the article. The text in between, omitted here, is the 'decálogo' referred to in the second sentence, which is a list of ten advantages to be gained by increasing the involvement of employees in the management of health and safety risks.

Source text

> La integración de trabajadores y trabajadoras en la gestión preventiva de la empresa
>
> Aunque la Ley de Prevención de Riesgos Laborales contempla que la gestión preventiva debe integrarse en la empresa, no son raros los casos de resistencia a hacer partícipes a los trabajadores de la toma de 5
> decisiones en esta materia. Mediante la exposición del siguiente decálogo pretendemos hacer ver de manera sintética algunas de las ventajas de este hecho y así valorar positivamente la implicación en la gestión de la prevención de todos los miembros de la organización.

El artículo 16° de la Ley de Prevención de Riesgos Laborales – en   10
adelante LPRL – ('Plan de prevención de riesgos laborales, evaluación de
los riesgos y planificación de la actividad') establece que 'la prevención
de riesgos laborales deberá integrarse en el sistema general de gestión de
la empresa (. . .)', cuestión ésta que, en la actualidad, y a la vista de lo que
trasmiten los representantes sindicales en general y los delegados y   15
delegadas de prevención en especial, no se está llevando a cabo tal y como
preceptúa la ley, ni en su texto ni en su espíritu. Como organización
sindical, UGT-CANARIAS, tiene el deber de reivindicar el cumplimiento
de lo establecido en la normativa vigente en materia de prevención
de riesgos laborales, puesto que la salud y la seguridad laboral de los   20
trabajadores y trabajadoras son cuestiones de vital importancia sobre
las que no se puede negociar ni transigir. Es prioritario que todos los
protagonistas de la prevención descubran, vean y participen, con absoluta
convicción, de lo que se entiende como 'integración de la prevención'.
Y en el seno de la misma, los trabajadores y trabajadoras, y sus repre-   25
sentantes tienen un papel clave que, si las empresas dejaran desarrollar en
toda su plenitud de derechos, se alcanzarían más objetivos reales de cara
a reducir los índices de siniestralidad en nuestra Comunidad Autónoma,
y a contribuir en la mejora de las condiciones de trabajo.
   [. . .]   30
Todas estas razones van más allá de una mera justificación amparada
en un artículo de la ley y, desde la Unión General de Trabajadores de
Canarias, estamos convencidas y convencidos de que serían reales si la
integración del trabajador en la gestión preventiva de la empresa fuera
cierta y efectiva, y no sólo formal o inexistente.   35

(Unión General de Trabajadores 2007)

3.2 *Literal meaning and compensation*

Assignment

Working in groups, analyse instances of compensation in the TT below. Give
your own version where you can improve on the published TT.

Contextual information

The ST is an extract from Juan Goytisolo's *Señas de identidad,* first published
in 1966. It is the first volume in a trilogy of works which experiment with
narrative technique. In this volume the protagonist reflects on his own identity
and experience. Goytisolo was a bitter opponent of Franco's regime and his
early novels were banned in Spain. He has lived the life of a political and
cultural exile. The TT is from *Marks of Identity*, Gregory Rabassa's translation
of *Señas de identidad*, published in 1988 by Serpent's Tail (Goytisolo 1988a).

Source text

en el centro
en medio de un cuadrado de césped señalado por cuatro mojones
un zócalo sobrio realzaba la estatua ecuestre de un guerrero en bronce regalo de la Ciudad
eso decía la lápida
a su Caudillo Libertador   5
buscaste refugio a la sombra de los pórticos
los turistas discurrían en grupos compactos hacia el museo del Ejército fotografiaban
    la estatua ecuestre se aglomeraban a la entrada de las tiendas de souvenirs hacían
    girar los torniquetes de tarjetas postales visitaban el almacén de Antigüedades
    Heráldica Soldados de Plomo   10

                       ENTRADA LIBRE
                       ENTRÉE LIBRE
                       FREE ENTRANCE
                       EINTRITT FREI

el cartel anunciador de una corrida de toros atrajo bruscamente tu atención   15

        SOUVENIR   SOUVENIR
        DE ESPAÑA   DE ESPAÑA
        Plaza de Toros Monumental
        Grandiosa corrida de toros
        6 Hermosos y Bravos Toros 6   20
        con la divisa rosa y verde de
        la renombrada ganadería de
        Don Baltasar Iban de Madrid
        para los grandes espadas
        LUIS MIGUEL DOMINGUÍN   25
ICI VOTRE NOM – HERE, YOUR NAME – HIER, IHRE NAMEN
        ANTONIO ORDÓÑEZ
        con sus correspondientes cuadrillas
        Amenizará el espectáculo la Banda
        'La popular Sansense'   30

pasaste de largo
una multitud de curiosos examinaba dos composiciones fotográficas en las que un torero
    (sin cabeza) clavaba (con estampa de maestro) un par de banderillas y una gitana (sin
    cabeza igualmente) se abanicaba (muy chula ella) frente a una maqueta de la Giralda
en endiablado esperanto un caracterizado ejemplar de hombrecillo español de la estepa 35
    explicaba que se trataba de una imagen trucada con la que los señores y caballeros
    messieurs et dames ladies and gentlemen aquí presentes podrían sorprender a sus
    amistades y conocidos vestidos de toreros y gitanas toreadors et gitanes matadors
    and gypsies de regreso a sus respectivos países vos pays d'origine your native
    countries y afirmar así su personalidad affirmer votre personnalité your personality 40
    con el relato de sus aventuras españolas aventures espagnoles Spanish adventures
                               (Goytisolo 1976: 407–9)

Target text

in the center
in the middle of a square of grass marked off by four stones
a somber base held up the equestrian statue of a bronze warrior the gift of the City
the plaque said so
to its Liberator and Caudillo   5
you took refuge in the shade of the porticos
the tourists were going through in compact groups toward the Army museum they were
    photographing the equestrian statue they were clustered around souvenir stands they
    were turning the card racks they were going into the shop with Antiques Heraldic
    Material Lead Soldiers   10

              ENTRADA LIBRE
              ENTRÉE LIBRE
              ENTRANCE FREE
              EINTRITT FREI

the bullfight poster suddenly drew your attention   15

              SOUVENIR   SOUVENIR
              OF SPAIN   OF SPAIN
              Monumental Bullring
              Great Bullfight
              6 Beautiful and Brave Bulls 6   20
              with the pink and green colors
              of the famous ranch of
              Don Baltasar Iban of Madrid
              for the great bullfighters
              LUIS MIGUEL DOMINGUÍN   25
   ICI VOTRE NOM – YOUR NAME HERE – HIER, IHRE NAMEN
              ANTONIO ORDÓÑEZ
              with their respective teams
              Music furnished by the Band of
              'La Popular Sansense'   30

you passed by quickly
a crowd of curious people was examining the photographic compositions in which a
    bullfighter (headless) was placing (with the stamp of a master) a pair of *banderillas*
    and a Gypsy woman (also headless) was fanning herself (very flashy she was)
    opposite a mock-up of the Giralda   35
in a devilish Esperanto a characteristic example of a little Spaniard from the steppe
    was explaining that it was a matter of a cut-off image with which the señoras y
    caballeros messieurs et dames ladies and gentlemen here present could surprise their
    friends and acquaintances dressed as bullfighters and Gypsies when they returned
    to sus respectivos países leur pays d'origine your native countries and afirmar así 40
    su personalidad affirmer leur personalité show your personality with the story of
    your aventuras españolas aventures espagnoles Spanish adventures
                                       (Goytisolo 1988a: 340–1)

3.3 Compensation: phonic effects

Assignment

Working in groups:

(i)   Discuss the strategic problems confronting the translator of the following ST, and say what your own strategy would be.
(ii) In the light of your findings in (i), translate the text into English, paying particular attention to cultural transposition and compensation.
(iii) Explain the main decisions of detail you made in producing your TT.

Contextual information

The text is an extract from Julio Cortázar's *Rayuela* (1984; first published 1963). It appears as a self-contained unit (item 7) in the section 'Del lado de allá'. The Argentinian's novel contrasts life in Paris and Buenos Aires. 'Del lado de allá' deals with the narrator's relationship with la Maga while he is in Paris. The novel is noted for its ludic qualities.

Source text

Toco tu boca, con un dedo toco el borde de tu boca, voy dibujándola como si saliera de mi mano, como si por primera vez tu boca se entreabriera, y me basta cerrar los ojos para deshacerlo todo y recomenzar, hago nacer cada vez la boca que deseo, la boca que mi mano elige y te dibuja en la cara, una boca elegida entre todas, con soberana libertad elegida por mí   5
para dibujarla con mi mano en tu cara, y que por un azar que no busco comprender coincide exactamente con tu boca que sonríe por debajo de la que mi mano te dibuja. Me miras, de cerca me miras, cada vez más de cerca y entonces jugamos al cíclope, nos miramos cada vez más de cerca y los ojos se agrandan, se acercan entre sí, se superponen y los cíclopes   10
se miran, respirando confundidos, las bocas se encuentran y luchan tibiamente, mordiéndose con los labios, apoyando apenas la lengua en los dientes, jugando en sus recintos donde un aire pesado va y viene con un perfume viejo y un silencio. Entonces mis manos buscan hundirse en tu pelo, acariciar lentamente la profundidad de tu pelo mientras nos besamos   15
como si tuviéramos la boca llena de flores o de peces, de movimientos vivos, de fragancia oscura. Y si nos mordemos el dolor es dulce, y si nos ahogamos en un breve y terrible absorber simultáneo del aliento, esa instántanea muerte es bella. Y hay una sola saliva y un solo sabor a fruta madura, y yo te siento temblar contra mí como una luna en el agua.   20

(Cortázar 1984: 160)

4 Genre

Text type and purpose

The table of textual filters on pp. 6–7 places the **genre** of the ST at the top of the list of textual features to be taken into account in the development of a translation strategy. Analysis of the type of text to be translated is the indispensable starting-point, involving not only recognition of characteristic textual conventions but also identification of the purpose of the ST within the culture in which it was produced and is used. Most of the texts being produced around the world, and especially those likely to get translated, fulfil concrete functions – providing information, persuading, making a record of agreements or transactions, building or consolidating human relationships – and the verbal (or visual) forms they take are generally determined by those functions. Everyday conversations may seem largely aimless, but they tend to be motivated and structured by underlying purposes and social dynamics, such as establishing one's status within a group or reinforcing an emotional bond with someone who may provide support. Literary texts can in a sense be defined in terms of not having a specific practical or informative function, yet they are certainly published, purchased and read for particular reasons: to be marketed and consumed as a leisure activity, often alongside other media products; to be studied as part of educational curricula; to provide emotional experiences and influence opinions; to enhance the prestige of cultural institutions.

The other essential foundation for the planning of a translation is its own purpose, which does not necessarily coincide exactly with that of the ST, either because of cultural differences (as discussed in Chapter 5) or because of the specific operational requirements of the person or organization commissioning the translation (the initiator). Some translation theorists use the term **skopos** (meaning 'aim', 'purpose' or 'goal' in Greek, traditionally used in the analysis of rhetoric) to refer to the defining purpose of translation when it is seen as a task carried out in order to meet the needs of a specific commissioning agent. Hans Vermeer sums up this functionalist view of translation in the following 'Skopos rule': 'Translate/interpret/speak/write in a way that enables your text/translation to function in the situation in which it is used and with the people who want to use it and precisely in the way they want it to function' (quoted in Nord 1997: 29).

A very specific example of a translation skopos is to provide consumers who speak one language with instructions for the use of a product made by speakers of another language, by means of translating an existing leaflet into the target language in such a way that the readers will be able to use the product successfully. In its fullest sense, the skopos embraces both the manufacturer's basic requirement that their customers can use the product and the translator's overall definition of what kinds of features the TT will need to have in order to achieve this. The basic definition of textual genre is simple: instructions for the use of a consumer product. However, the translator needs to take account of other genre-related considerations: there may be different conventions governing the composition of instruction leaflets in the two countries (for example, the degree of formality with which the user is addressed), or the product itself may be unfamiliar in the target market, requiring more detailed instructions that take nothing for granted (that is, the genre of the TT becomes 'instructions for the use of a product by *uninitiated* consumers'). A different, less concrete purpose would be: to make a prestigious or successful literary text available to people unable to read it in the original language, either for purely commercial reasons (to sell more books) or as part of a non-profit-making project to promote intercultural understanding.

A further consideration with regard to skopos is that the purposes of a ST and the TT produced from it are not necessarily exactly the same. Some TTs are designed to be received as if they were TL originals; others acknowledge their status as translations. A translation of a legal document may not need to have legal force in its own right; a translation of a poem may not always be required to work as verse in the TL; a translation of a play may be intended as an authoritative version for publication (with notes and introduction) rather than as a performance script. A translation into English of a campaign speech by a South American politician is more likely to have the function of informing foreign policy analysts than of actually persuading TL readers to vote for the speaker; in this case (assuming that more than a gist translation is required), the TT needs to convey the effect of the rhetoric and the implications of what was said but does not need to be designed to convince its readers. Consequently, even when the genre of the ST can apparently be replicated by an equivalent genre in the TL, the ways in which SL and TL readers perceive and experience them are never exactly the same.

Any given ST will share some of its properties with other texts of the same genre, and will be perceived by a SL audience as being what it is on account of such genre-typical properties. Therefore, the translator must, in order to appreciate the nature of the ST, be familiar with the broad characteristics of the appropriate source-culture genre. Furthermore, since any source culture presents a whole array of different textual genres, the translator must have some sort of overview of genre types in that culture. This does not imply an exhaustive theory of genres – even if such a theory were available, it would be too elaborate for a methodology of translation. All that is needed is a rough framework of genre types to help a translator to concentrate on character-istics that make the ST a representative specimen of a particular source-culture genre.

The most elementary division we propose is between **oral discourse** and **written discourse**. We then divide these into broad genre categories, each of which implicitly contains a range of specific text types. Although the main emphasis of this book is on the translation of written texts, we start here with oral genres because their key features are more specifically identifiable, and because those features are in turn imitated by many examples of written language.

Oral genres

In the case of oral genres, we suggest the following broad categories, based primarily on the ways in which utterances are delivered to listeners and the circumstances in which communication takes place:

1 conversation
2 oral narrative
3 oral address
4 oral reading
5 dramatization
6 sung performance.

1 Conversation

As a genre, conversation is characterized by its genuinely unscripted nature: it is unplanned discourse, often chaotic in its organization and not always following rules of syntactical cohesion (see the discussion of cohesion and coherence in Chapter 6). It tends to be dominated by **deictic** (referring to the circumstances of the communication) and **phatic** (serving to cement a personal relationship) elements, which often make explicit textual cohesion unnecessary. Its guiding structural principle is 'turn-taking', that is, the rule-governed alternation between participant speakers, who signal their understanding of each other's utterances and fill in any gaps in the explicit verbal content. Some of the most distinctive markers of dialect and social register (discussed in Chapters 10 and 11) emerge in conversation, and may be imitated by written texts.

2 Oral narrative

The genre of oral narrative includes the continuous (though not necessarily uninterrupted) telling, by one speaker, of tales, stories, anecdotes, jokes and the like, and the recounting of events (whether true or apocryphal). Character-istic of such texts is the fact that they are organized by a narrative structure, which may be a familiar template specific to a particular subgenre (for example, the Shaggy Dog Story or 'There was an Englishman, an Irishman and a Scotsman . . .'). Written narrative genres, both fictional and non-fictional, often incorporate features of oral narrative – 'Let me tell you a story'.

3 Oral address

In this category are placed all forms of public speaking (lectures, talks, seminars, political speeches, verbal pleadings in a court of law, and so on). The defining feature of this genre type is that, nominally at least, a single speaker holds the floor, and elaborates on an essentially non-narrative theme. The discourse in this case is planned, at least to some extent, and may effectively amount to the oral delivery of a written text. A formal debate or meeting in which several speakers defend more or less prepared positions combines the expository and rhetorical nature of the address with the turn-taking of conversation. There is a clearly felt intuitive distinction between oral narratives and oral addresses: while stories are 'told', addresses are said to be 'delivered'. (Though an address may be interspersed with items of oral narrative, for instance anecdotes or jokes, its structural guiding principle is clearly not narrative, being geared to information, instruction or persuasion rather than to entertainment.)

4 Oral reading

Oral reading is introduced as a separate genre type in order to distinguish, not only 'reading aloud' from 'silent reading', but also the 'flat' reading-out of written texts from 'dramatized reading'. In other words, what is typical of oral reading is that readers do not attempt to act out the script by assuming the characters of imaginary unscripted speakers. (This, incidentally, is distinct from the habitual manner of poetry recitation, where the reader normally assumes and interprets the part of the poet.) Where dramatized reading tries to give the impression of unscripted oral performance, oral reading is simply the vocalized delivery of a written text. Oral reading is also distinct from oral address: witness the clear intuitive difference between a lively lecturing style (oral address) and the technique of 'reading a paper' at a seminar or conference.

5 Dramatization

By this category we mean the entire gamut of plays, sketches, dramatized readings, films and the like, manifested in actual spoken performance, whether on stage, screen, radio or television. Such texts are characterized by the necessary role of an actor or actors in their performance – that is, people explicitly *playing roles*, speaking words motivated by a planned scenario (whether fully scripted or not) and directed implicitly at an audience who are not usually part of the imaginary situation in which the words are uttered but are physically present (in the theatre or at a screening of a recording of the performance). Their effectiveness depends on a dramatic illusion entered into by both actors and audience, and on the relationship between verbal language and other semiotic systems. All four of the types of oral language listed above appear in texts designed for dramatized performance, together with a parallel apparatus of specialized non-oral discourse in written scripts or transcripts (stage directions, camera directions, names of characters).

6 *Sung performance*

The category of sung performance includes all oral texts set to music, whether figuring as songs performed in isolation or as part of a longer work (for instance, an oratorio, or an opera), and operatic recitative. While improvized song is possible, this genre consists predominantly of the oral performance to music of a written text, often denoted by the cover-term 'lyrics'. What we are concerned with here, however, is not written lyrics as such but the verbal content of actual oral renderings of songs, musicals, operas, operettas and the like. Consequently, it is important for translators in this genre not to deal with the lyrics in the abstract, but to consider verbal texts as forming part of a live musical performance.

This list, while it does not claim to be exhaustive, gives a good general coverage of oral genre types in western cultures. Each category can, of course, be further subdivided (for example, oral narrative into folk tales, ghost stories, anecdotes, autobiographical accounts, jokes and so forth). However, even as it stands, the list enables us to pick out the basic features that concern translators of oral texts.

The defining property all these genres have in common is the fact that they are realized in a vocal medium. Though a truism, this fact has important implications. First, an oral text is received by listeners in real time: it is in essence a fleeting and unrecoverable event. A speaker can be asked to repeat or clarify, and a recording can be paused and replayed, but an oral utterance is essentially designed to be received and understood instantaneously. Second, vocal utterance tends to be accompanied by visual cues (such as gestures or facial expressions) which may be secondary to it, and equally transitory, but form a part of the overall text and play a role in colouring its meaning. And third, deictic and phatic language play prominent roles in oral discourse. We have already mentioned this as being especially important in conversation (participants referring to 'me' and 'you', 'here' and 'now', and 'this' and 'that', as well as sending emotional signals by saying 'How's it going?' or 'Sorry' or 'Never!'), but more formalized oral genres also contain such markers, often of a more elaborate kind: 'Ladies and gentlemen', 'We are gathered here today . . .', 'With all due respect . . .', 'Have you heard the one about . . .?'. This all means that, on every level of textual variable, oral texts must obey the 'rules' of a spoken language first and foremost. It also means that an effective oral text avoids problems of comprehension arising from information overloading, elaborate cross-reference, excessive speed and so forth. In all these respects, what is true for oral STs is also true for oral TTs – an obvious fact, but one that is all too often overlooked.

Another important implication is the appearance of spontaneity that charac-terizes the majority of oral genres (with the exception of oral reading). This goes not only for impromptu conversation or unrehearsed narrative, but for prepared texts as well: stories told and retold in a carefully formulated version; memorized lines in a play or film; even such texts as speeches or lectures, where the speaker may stick closely to a script but the delivery is imitative of unscripted oral texts. To a lesser degree, dramatized reading, recited verse, song lyrics and libretti, if well performed, all give the audience a chance to enter into the illusion of spontaneous vocal utterance.

As these remarks suggest, an oral text is always quite different in nature and impact from even its most closely representative written version. For instance, a recited poem is quite distinct from its printed counterpart, and so is a performed song from the bare text set down on paper. Even the most unspontaneous oral reading has certain nuances of oral delivery, such as intonation and stress, that make its reception quite different from the experience of silent reading. An awareness of these properties of oral texts and genres is a necessary starting-point for discussing the particular types of problem that confront anyone wanting to engage in any of the following modes of translation with an oral dimension:

1   Oral ST > oral TT or written TT.
2   Written ST intended for (or a transcript of) oral delivery/performance > written TT suitable for oral delivery/performance.
3   Written ST containing features characteristic of oral discourse > written TT.
4   Written ST > oral TT.

The most specialized branch of oral-to-oral translating is on-the-spot interpreting. (In fact, terminologically, interpreting is usually distinguished from other kinds of translating.) There are three major types of **interpreting**.

The first is consecutive interpreting. The interpreter listens to an oral text (usually a section at a time), makes highly condensed notes and, from these, produces an oral TT that relays the general message, key pieces of detail and some of the nuances of the ST. The training for consecutive interpreting is intensive, and takes several months at least.

The second type is simultaneous interpreting. Here, the interpreter relays an oral TT at the same time as listening to the oral ST, either remotely – using microphones and earphones – or by whispering. This is the most specialized form of interpreting, and requires the longest training. Grasping the content and nuances of a continuous oral ST, while at the same time producing a fluent oral TT that does justice to the content and nuances of the ST, can be very taxing. Trainees do not usually start learning simultaneous interpreting until they have acquired considerable skill in consecutive interpreting.

The third type is bilateral (or liaison) interpreting of conversation, where the interpreter acts as a two-way intermediary in unrehearsed dialogue. Bilateral interpreting can be the most relaxed of the three types; as part of the multilingual social situation, the interpreter can even clarify obscure points with the speakers. The method is usually consecutive (waiting until each speaker has completed an utterance before translating it), but may have a simultaneous (whispered) element. What this kind of interpreting requires mainly is a broad facility in understanding and speaking the languages involved, familiarity with the relevant cultures, and sensitivity to the conversational nuances of both languages (including awareness of tonal registers and of visual cues of gesture and facial expression).

Since it is a specialized skill, interpreting is not part of this course and we shall not dwell on it. (For a detailed theoretical and practical introduction to interpreting, see Pöchhacker 2004.) It is very useful, however, to try a simplified session of consecutive interpreting, partly as an exercise in gist translation but mostly because it sharpens awareness of specifically oral textual variables, which may require special attention in translating any kind of text, spoken or written. (Practical 4.2 therefore comprises a suggestion for a basic consecutive interpreting exercise to be done in class.)

An exercise in interpreting will also confirm that spoken communication has stylistic quirks and constraints that are very much language-specific. The eternal problem of translating jokes is a good example of this. It is not merely that some jokes are hard to translate because they depend on word-play, but that both humour itself and techniques of joke- and story-telling are to a great extent culture-specific. Translating oral jokes is an especially clear illustration of the fact that oral translation is not simply a matter of verbal transposition from one spoken language to another: the genre-related norms and expectations of the target culture must be respected as well, including gestures, facial expressions, mimicry and so on. Texts in most oral genres are not only utterances, but also dramatic performances. Translating them often involves the production of a written TT, but this will only be an interim approximation to the combination of phonic and prosodic features essential to a successful, performed, oral TT.

Audiovisual translation (for film or television) and translation for the theatre raise particularly interesting issues in relation to crossing over between oral and written language. The text to be translated in both cases consists primarily of dialogue. Theatre translation usually involves the translator starting with a written script, transferring to considerations of how the ST might be performed orally and then composing a TT that is a script suitable for eventual oral performance. Audiovisual translation usually involves the translator starting with an oral ST and its transcript, and producing either a TT suitable for silent reading alongside the images (subtitles) or an oral TT designed to be performed in a way that matches the timing and rhythms of the ST as far as possible (dubbing).

Dramatic traditions in different cultures, despite various degrees of cross-fertilization, can be markedly different not only in broad terms of genre patterns but also with regard to practical details such as acting styles and conventions for stage directions (such as the confusing fact that play texts in English designate 'stage left' and 'stage right' from the point of view of the actor on stage facing the audience, while those in Spanish usually refer to 'izquierda' and 'derecha' as seen by the audience). This implies that the translation of stage plays will often involve an element of genre transposition, in deference to the different expectations and tastes of TL audiences. On the other hand, complete transposition of the TT into some traditional TL genre may mean that the point is lost, and with it the merits of the ST. Thus, a translation of Calderón de la Barca's *La vida es sueño* as an imitation of the genre of Jacobean comedy would fail on at least two counts: the TT would convey none of the technical merits of the genre of Calderón's play, and retain little or nothing of the merits of the genre of Jacobean comedy. The translations of stage drama that are most successful from the performing point of view are usually based on compromises between reflecting some of the features that confer merit on the ST and adopting or adapting features of an existing TL dramatic genre.

The defining characteristic of a theatre script is that it is a blueprint for a continuous live performance in a space shared by performers and audience. Whether it contains explicit stage directions or not, it has been written with the intention that it will prompt the creation of 'texts' using semiotic systems other than words to complement the oral TT – gestures, facial expressions, bodily movements, space and ways of occupying it, costumes, physical objects, non-verbal sounds. Ultimately, what needs to be translated is not just the words of the ST but the implicit relationship between the various signifying systems.

Both kinds of audiovisual translation are tightly constrained by the technicalities of making the TT fit the images on the screen. Dubbing allows oral features of accent, intonation and rhythm to be reproduced, but the need to synchronize the oral TT with the gestures, facial expressions and lip movements of the screen actors may have the effect of pushing the translator towards retaining ST structures and therefore limiting communicative translation. Subtitling allows the audience to hear the original SL intonation and rhythms, but the need to present the written TT in such a way that it can be read by the audience as the film is running means that it is usually not feasible to convey all the qualities (or translate all the words) of the spoken ST. Consequently, subtitling is essentially a form of gist translation, which nevertheless aims to convey some of the characteristics of the oral style of the ST so that the TT is recognizable as dialogue. These may include features of social register, tonal register, dialect, sociolect, and so on. For a recent guide to subtitling, see Díaz Cintas and Remael (2006).

Written genres

There are, in Western cultures, so many different varieties of written text that any typology of practical use for translation is bound to be even more approximate than the one suggested for oral genres. The broad taxonomy we outline below lays no claim to originality or precision. It is traditional but flexible, assuming that all innovations in types of writing can be fitted into this scheme. Its categories are not exclusive: specific genres at a more detailed level of classification may belong to more than one category, and most actual texts will also turn out to have characteristics of more than one of them:

1   literary/fictional/imaginative
2   religious/devotional/ritual
3   theoretical/philosophical/speculative
4   empirical/descriptive/analytical
5   persuasive/prescriptive/normative.

Unlike the oral classification offered earlier, this one is primarily based on a global view of textual subject matter, or, more precisely, on the author's implicit attitude to the treatment of subject matter – which essentially consti-tutes *skopos* as defined at the beginning of this chapter. Of course, these five categories can also be applied to oral discourse, but from the point of view of developing translation strategies we regard it as more useful to give priority to the performance-based classification set out in the previous section. At this general level, the physical medium in which the text is presented to readers (manuscript, printed book, leaflet, computer screen and so on) is not the determining factor, acquiring greater importance in relation to more specific genres within these top-level categories.

1   Literary/fictional/imaginative genres

The essence of texts in this category is that they are about a fictive, imaginary world of events and characters created autonomously in and through the texts themselves, and not controlled by the physical world outside. However close a text of this type may be to autobiography or history, it still approaches its subject matter by recreating experience in terms of a subjective, internal world, which is fundamentally perceived as fictive, for all its similarities to real life. In texts in this category, the author is understood to be ultimately in control of events and characters.

Literary genres can, of course, be subdivided almost infinitely. Even poetry, which is just one genre in this category, has split up over the last two centuries into innumerable subgenres, each with different characteristic styles. As for prose fiction, there are not just the genres of novel and short story, but a wide variety of minor genres such as detective stories, thrillers, historical romances and science fiction. The translator attempting to classify a literary ST needs to be as specific as possible but take nothing for granted – recognizing conventional generic features but also being aware that there is no such thing as 'literary style', nor even such a thing as a single 'detective story style'. Originality of style has not always been a requirement of literary writing, but it has acquired significant prestige value in the past two centuries. Literary genres evolve over time, and during the twentieth century were repeatedly challenged and destabilized, resulting in ever more blurring of the boundaries between 'high' literary culture and popular or mass culture. They have also always echoed and played with oral forms of language.

2 Religious/devotional/ritual genres

The subject matter of devotional and religious works implies belief in the existence of a 'spiritual world'. Seen from the outside, there may seem to be little difference between this and the imaginary subject matter of literary/ fictional genres. However, seen in terms of the author's attitude to the treatment of the subject matter, there is nothing fictive about the spiritual world dealt with in religious texts: it has its own extratextual realities and unshakable truths. That is, this category has more in common with 'empirical/descriptive/ analytical' and 'theoretical/philosophical/speculative' than with 'literary/ fictional' genres. The author is understood not to be free to create the world that animates the subject matter, but to be merely instrumental in exploring or revealing it. Another way of viewing this category is as a variant of the 'persuasive/prescriptive/normative' – religion is merely ideology. Again, however, from the perspective of the author and the primary target readership, the point is shared revelation, not simply authorities imposing laws.

Of all five categories of genre, this one seems to have changed and diversified least of all. Even the Good News Bible represents only a minor departure from the Authorized Version, and Thomas Aquinas or Julian of Norwich have only to be brought modestly up to date to feel remarkably modern. While it shares some characteristic textual forms with the literary/ fictional class (for example, narrative and verse), its stylistic possibilities tend to cover a narrower range. One of the key features of religious texts is a ceremonial quality: shared, reiterative language (often marked by distinctive oral features) used as part of a communal emotional experience.

3 Theoretical/philosophical/speculative genres

These genres have as their subject matter a network of ideas, which are understood to exist independently of the individual minds that think them. Pure mathematics is the best example of the kind of subject matter and approach to subject matter that define theoretical/philosophical/speculative genres. The vehicle used by authors is not fictional imagination or spiritual faith, but reasoning. (In Western cultures, the primary form of abstract, rational thinking is deductive logic.) The author of a text of this kind, however original it may be, is understood not to be free to develop theoretical structures at will, but to be constrained by standards of rationality.

The proliferation of genres in this category has been less spectacular than that of literary genres, but it is strikingly diverse nonetheless – compare, for instance, Spinoza's *Tractatus theologico-politicus*, Kierkegaard's *Lidelsernes evangelium* and Kant's *Kritik der reinen Vernunft*. While some texts may display stylistic distinctiveness, there is in general likely to be less experimentation and playfulness than in literary genres, and greater attention to discursive **cogency**.

4 *Empirical/descriptive/analytical genres*

Genres in this category purport to treat of the real objective world as it is experienced by specialist or first-hand observers. An empirical/descriptive/ analytical text is one with a necessarily factual reference (though, again, sceptics may refuse to accept that factuality); it is a text that sets out to give an objective account of phenomena, even if those phenomena consist of personal experiences and perceptions.

This category has diversified in direct proportion to the creation and diversification of specialized scientific and technical disciplines. Each discipline and each school of thought tends to develop its own technical vocabulary and its own style. In this way, a virtually endless list of minor genres – some with tightly circumscribed stylistic conventions – is being constantly generated.

5 *Persuasive/prescriptive/normative genres*

The essence of these genres is that they aim at influencing readers to act and think in textually prescribed ways. This aim can be pursued through various means: practical instructions; authoritative statements; oblique suggestions. Thus, we are uniting in a single category the entire gamut of texts from instruction manuals, through documents stating laws, rules and regulations, to propaganda, advertisements and so forth. Like the other four genre categories, this one can be broken down into an indefinite number of subcategories. Nevertheless, it is held together by a common purpose, the purpose of getting readers to take a certain course of action, and perhaps explaining how to take it.

The category of persuasive/prescriptive/normative genres has also undergone immense proliferation, thanks not only to the growth of bureaucracy, technology and education, but also to the modern escalation in advertising. Some of the genres within this group are characteristically marked by the oral feature of direct address to receivers.

The reason why this classification is useful for translation methodology is that differences in approach to subject matter entail fundamental differences in the way a text is formally constructed. In other words, differences in genre tend to correspond to characteristic differences in the use of textual variables. So – to take a simple example – sound-symbolism and the deliberate use of connotative meanings are inappropriate in English empirical/descriptive texts. Nevertheless, 'hybrid' texts and genres that cut across categories are common and provide clear illustration of the importance of genre distinctions for the practice of translation. There are three main ways in which a particular text can cut across basic genre distinctions. Either it can belong by subject matter to one category but borrow the stylistic form of another (as in Norman Mailer's *The Armies of the Night*, or Goethe's scientific treatises in verse): hybrids of this type have a double purpose, such as providing literary enjoyment along with empirical description. Or a text may comprise several sections allocated to subject matters falling into different genres (as in many newspapers and magazines). The Bible is a good example of such a hybrid text, in which different books represent different genre categories: the Song of Songs represents a literary genre, Paul's Epistle to the Romans a religious/devotional genre, the Acts of the Apostles a historical/descriptive genre, and Leviticus a prescriptive one.

Alternatively, a text can use genre-imitative subsections as a conscious stylistic device. A good example is this descriptive passage from Juan Goytisolo's *Señas de identidad* parodying the style of a certain type of travel guide:

> Situada a 2 grados 9 minutos de longitud Este del meridiano de Greenwich y a 41 grados 21 minutos de latitud Norte, Barcelona se extiende en el llano que, entre los ríos Besós y Llobregat, baja en suave pendiente desde el anfiteatro de montañas que la limitan y protegen por septentrión hasta el viejo Mare Nostrum. Nuestra Ciudad goza de un clima templado cuyas temperaturas extremas rara vez alcanzan los 30 grados ni descienden bajo cero, lo cual da una temperatura media ideal que para estos últimos cinco años ha resultado ser de 16,12 grados centígrados. En el mismo período de tiempo la presión atmosférica ha oscilado entre 769,5 mm. y 730 mm. La humedad, quizá el factor más acusado de nuestro clima, ha dado un promedio para los mismos años del 70 por ciento. [. . .]
>
> El anfiteatro de montañas que rodea a Barcelona por el Norte se está repoblando totalmente como parque forestal. El punto más alto, la cumbre del Tibidabo (532 metros sobre el nivel del mar) es el mirador ideal de la Ciudad, punto turístico de fácil acceso, en el que se erige la basílica, aún sin terminar, dedicada al Sagrado Corazón, cuya fundación inició San Juan Bosco. Otro mirador de la ciudad es la cumbre y ladera de Montjuich, el monte en que se inició su historia, coronado por la fortaleza que, perdido hoy su carácter militar, vuelve a la ciudad como museo.
>
> (Goytisolo 1976: 400–1)

This passage repays discussion in class. It is also very instructive to compare it with real tourist guides such as the following:

> Sin duda uno de los mejores lugares del Mediterráneo es Barcelona. La capital de Cataluña se encuentra en una posición privilegiada en la costa noreste de la península Ibérica. Su ubicación junto al mar Mediterráneo, al noreste de la costa española, la convierte en la ciudad más cosmopolita y activa del país. Barcelona se encuentra a 160km al sur de los Pirineos,

entre las desembocaduras de los ríos Llobregat y Bes y la costa mediterránea. Se eleva a 4m del nivel del mar y se encuentra a 98km de Tarragona, 100km de Girona, 156km de Lleida, 274km de Huesca, 284km de Castellón, 296km de Zaragoza y 621 de Madrid. Situada en la comarca del mismo nombre, Barcelona es la segunda ciudad más grande de España, tanto en tamaño como en población. Acoge a una población de 1.510.000 hab., pero este número aumenta en más de 4 millones, si se incluye la periferia. En 2005 se estimaba que la población de la ciudad ascendía a 1.593.075 hab., mientras que la del área metropolitana era de 4.686.701. [. . .]

A 542m el Tibidabo es la cumbre más alta de la línea boscosa que forma el telón de Barcelona. Puede llegar a la cumbre de esta montaña por el único teleférico que todavía existe en Barcelona, y encontrar ahí uno de los parques de entretenimiento más espectaculares y famosos de Europa. Los barceloneses vienen para disfrutar de las atracciones del Parc d'Atraccions, que cuenta con atracciones y una casa de los horrores. Una de las mayores atracciones es el levantamiento de un vaso que se eleva 115m hasta una zona de observación para los visitantes en la Torre de Collserola, una torre de comunicaciones. Uno puede encontrar consuelo en el Temple del Sagrat Cor, en recuerdo al Sacré Coeur de París. El Tibidabo mantiene el aire limpio y sigue siendo un gran lugar para contemplar la ciudad

(Barcelona Turismo 2006)

Hybrid texts, especially literary ones, illustrate why translators need to have a clear view of available genres and of their linguistic and stylistic characteristics. For instance, the point of the text from *Señas de identidad* would be lost if the typical style of TL tourist guides were not used (with appropriate adaptation) in the TT. A sense of genre characteristics enables translators to set themselves clearly formulated targets before they start producing TTs. It also forewarns them about any special needs in translating a particular text, such as finding the necessary dictionaries and source materials, doing the necessary background reading, and so on. No translation can be undertaken without due preparation, and identifying the genre of the ST is the first step towards adequate preparation.

There is another parameter on which genres can be compared in a way relevant to translation. This parameter can be visualized as a scale or continuum defined by the relative textual importance of explicit literal meaning at one extreme, and of implicitly conveyed connotative and/or stylistic meaning at the other. At one end of the scale are texts like scientific or legal documents, or textbooks, that require maximum attention to precision in literal meaning and minimum attention to aesthetic effects. They purport to be transparent vehicles for the communication of meaning, which does not mean that meaning is not influenced by stylistic features to which the translator needs to pay attention; what the translator can assume, though, is that whatever connotative nuances or overtones do exist in these texts will usually constitute a low priority for translation – indeed, care must be taken not to let such effects creep into the TT inadvertently, as they could be a distraction from the literal meaning.

At the opposite end of the scale are texts that depend maximally on subtle nuances of non-literal meaning and aesthetic effect, and minimally on the explicit, literal meaning. Poetry tends towards this extreme – towards opacity as opposed to transparency, drawing attention to its own textual fabric, feel and sound. Jakobson defines the 'poetic function of language' as 'focus on the message for its own sake', which has the effect of 'promoting the palpability of signs' (Jakobson 1960: 356). In poetry, understanding the literal content of sentences is often no more than perceiving the framework of a more subtle textual meaning dependent upon a range of linguistic effects (rhythm and metre, patterns of sound and metaphor, structural arrangement). A lyric poem may have relatively slight content in literal meaning and yet be both a serious poem and a very rich one. Poetry may, simply because it has words, tempt the inexperienced translator to identify its meaning with its literal content, whereas, in fact, to reproduce the total import of a poem in a TT would require recreating the whole unique bundle of meanings and sounds presented in the ST. That is the prime reason why poetry is often said to be untranslatable. In our view, however, if one accepts that translation loss is inevitable, and that the translator's role is to reduce it as much as possible, then it is feasible to envisage at least a highly honourable failure in translating poetry.

Translators can usefully gauge the genre of a ST, and also of their own TT, by rating its position on this scale between textbook and poetry. Obviously, this cannot be done objectively or accurately, but it is possible to assess roughly the proportions in which literal meanings and connotative resonances contribute to the overall meaning of a given text. So, for example, poetry can be taken as increasingly 'poetic' the less important literal meaning is in proportion to connotative resonances; and it can be taken as increasingly prosaic the more important literal meaning is relative to connotative reson-ances. Everyday conversation can also be invested with a poetic quality by the non-literal, often inventive, sometimes rhythmic nature of phatic elements and idiomatic expressions (savour, for example, the Australian expression 'a few kangaroos loose in the top paddock'). At the other end of the scale, scientific texts represent the extreme point of meaning in directly expressed and logically structured form. But the translator must be on the alert for the pseudo-scientific text, in which apparent objectivity is a consciously adopted register, and therefore constitutes a stylistic device requiring attention in translating.

In conclusion, then, we can say that even a rough-and-ready typology of oral and written genres pays dividends by concentrating the translator's mind on four vital strategic questions:

1   What genre is represented by the ST and what problems are expected in connection with this genre?

2   Given the genre of the ST, what ST features should be given priority in translation? Does the ST have recognizable, perhaps clichéd, genre-specific characteristics that require special attention?
3   What genre(s) in the TL provide(s) a match for the ST genre? What can a scrutiny of available specimens of these TL genres suggest about the manner in which the TT should be formulated?
4   What genre should the TT be couched in, and what genre-specific linguistic and stylistic features should it have?

Genre marking

Making a TT fit a particular genre means not only tailoring it to the standard grammar of the TL genre, but also giving it features that conform to typical stylistic properties of that genre. Some of these features may be simply formulaic. For instance, in translating a traditional folk tale told by a Spanish story-teller, it would be reasonable to open the TT with the phrase 'Once upon a time . . .'. This is a genuine choice, since one could translate the formulaic Spanish beginning 'Érase una vez . . .' more literally as 'There was once . . .'. Choosing 'Once upon a time' is an autonomous TL-biased decision motivated by the fact that English folk tales typically begin with this standard formula and that this opening therefore instantly signals the genre of the TT. Formulaic expressions such as 'Once upon a time . . .', '. . . they lived happily ever after', 'Érase una vez . . .' and '. . . y vivieron felices y comieron perdices' are simple genre-marking features, and good examples of genre-marking as a significant option for the translator. Similarly, TL linguistic etiquette suggests that the Spanish expression '¡Diputados!' should, in the genre of a parliamentary address, be rendered by the English formula 'Honourable Members'.

Ordinary conversation, too, has its share of genre-marking formulas, such as ritualized greetings, to which interpreters need to be sensitive and where the choice of a given formula is a matter of TL etiquette. So, for example, whether to render 'Buenos días' by 'How do you do', 'Good morning' or 'Hello', and, conversely, whether to render 'Hello. How are you?' as 'Buenos días. ¿Cómo está?' or '¡Hola! ¿Qué hay?', has in each case to be an autonomous decision made in the light of target-culture etiquette, with ST tonal register acting as a guideline. Note also that differences in linguistic etiquette may lead native speakers of English to overuse the expression 'por favor', particularly from the perspective of conventions in Spain (though the influence of Anglo-American culture is leading to its increased usage among native Spanish speakers).

The past decade has seen a massive expansion of written text production in electronic media, much of it comprising conversation-like communication taking place (especially among young people) by means of rapidly-written text exchanged through SMS text messaging, e-mail, online social networks, blogs and forums. The types of language typically used in these media are heavily marked by features imitating the spontaneity of oral conversation, even incorporating phatic and intonational features with emoticons (;-)). Simplification of spelling, punctuation and grammar is to some extent merely a reflection of this orality, but often also constitutes deliberate playing with conventions of writing and quirks of homophony, following patterns particular to the pronunciation and orthography of each language ('u no wot i men nu no it 2 hehe! cu l8r eh?'; 'pue x mi q se jodan jejeje. sabes lo q kiero decir?').

As these simple examples show, genre-marking a TT influences the process of translation in the direction of TL orientation. This may affect small details or general translation strategy; both types of effect are illustrated in the following extract from Alfonso Sastre's play *Escuadra hacia la muerte*. (*Contextual information*: the play was written in 1953 and is set in a military context. Here the 'Cabo' is addressing a motley squad of recruits who have been sent as a punishment to an isolated posting where they are almost certain to be killed):

> Éste es mi verdadero traje. Y vuestro 'verdadero traje' ya para siempre. El traje con el que vais a morir. [. . .] Este es el traje de los hombres: un uniforme de soldado. Los hombres hemos vestido siempre así, ásperas camisas y ropas que dan frío en el invierno y calor en el verano . . . Correajes . . . El fusil al hombro . . . Lo demás son ropas afeminadas . . ., la vergüenza de la especie. [. . .] Pero no basta con vestir este traje . . ., hay que merecerlo . . . Esto es lo que yo voy a conseguir de vosotros . . ., que alcancéis el grado de soldados, para que seáis capaces de morir como hombres. Un soldado no es más que un hombre que sabe morir, y vosotros vais a aprenderlo conmigo. Es lo único que os queda, morir como hombres. Y a eso enseñamos en el Ejército.
>
> (Sastre 1969: 13–14)

This text is clearly intended for oral delivery in the social register of the stereotypical 'drill sergeant' and in a bullying, contemptuous tonal register. Sastre's text is not, of course, a transcript – that is, it does not represent and record a pre-existing oral text. Nevertheless, Sastre has included enough features drawn from an appropriate genre of oral address to act as genre-marking cues. Whatever other components there are in the genre to which this monologue belongs (theatre; military setting; social and political critique), an essential feature is use of a genre of oral address. In the following literal TT, there is no allowance made for these genre-marking features of the ST; this strategy yields an accurate rendering of the meaning of the ST but a poor script for stage performance:

> This is my true garb. And your 'true garb' henceforth. The garb in which you are going to die. This is the garb of men: a soldier's uniform. Men have always dressed like this: rough shirts and clothes that let you freeze in the winter and swelter in the summer, with leather straps and a rifle over your shoulder . . . Anything else is effeminate clothing . . ., a disgrace

to mankind. But it is not sufficient to put on this garb . . . you have to earn it . . . And that is what I am going to make sure you do . . . that you attain the rank of soldiers, so you become capable of dying like men. A soldier is nothing more than a man who knows how to die, and you are going to learn this with me. That is the only thing which remains to you, to die like men. And that is what we teach in the Army.

Compare this TT with one that, in strategic approach, resembles the ST in being a script – that is, a written text designed for oral performance. In detail, this TT makes plausible use of communicative translation, clichés, **illocutionary particles**, contracted forms and vulgarisms, all as genre-marking features:

These clothes make me what I am. And that goes for you lot too from now on. Your togs 'til you're six feet under, get it? An Army uniform: that's what real men wear, I tell you. Real men 'ave always worn kit like this: rough shirt, gear that freezes you in winter and makes you sweat in summer . . . boots you can see yer face in . . . rifle over your shoulder . . . Anything else is for pansies . . ., the scum of the earth. But it's no good you just putting this uniform on . . . you've got to earn it . . . and I'll make bloody sure that's what you do . . . I'm going to make soldiers of you lot . . . teach you how to die like men, right? 'Cos that's all a soldier is, a man that knows how to die, and that's what you're going to learn, got it? It's all about dying like men . . . And you can forget the rest. That's what we teach you in the Army.

TL genre-marking characteristics can be overused, of course. Compare, for example, these lines from Violeta Parra's song 'Gracias a la vida' with the student TT that follows:

Me dio dos luceros que, cuando los abro,
perfecto distingo lo negro del blanco,
y en el alto cielo su fondo estrellado
y en las multitudes el hombre que yo amo.
                    (Reproduced in Pring-Mill, 1990)

As my eyes I open
I can see so clearly
The distant from the nearly
In the heav'ns above
Among shimmering stars awaits the man I love.

Unlike the ST, the TT is heavily marked for some kind of sentimental or lyrical 'poetic' genre. This is done through lexical items ('distant', 'heav'ns', 'shimmering', 'awaits'); contrived syntax ('my eyes I open'); hackneyed rhymes (one of which is achieved at the cost of the ungrammatical 'from the nearly'); clichéd pseudo-poetic collocations ('heav'ns above', 'shimmering stars'); and the line filler 'so' in line 2.

The lesson to be learnt from these examples is simple but important: there is a middle course to be steered between undermarking genre features, as in the literal translation of the Sastre extract, and overmarking them, as in the song TT.

Practical 4

4.1 Genre and skopos

Assignment

(i)   Working in groups, analyse the three short extracts below. For each ST, identify the genre as specifically as possible, invent a concrete skopos (i.e., a purpose for translating it and specifications for the precise form in which the TT would be published), and consider the strategic translation priorities imposed by that skopos.

(ii)   Translate one of the texts into English according to the strategy developed.

Contextual information

The STs are all taken from the Real Academia Española's online *Corpus de referencia del español actual* (www.rae.es), using the search term 'lenguaje'.

Source text 1

Pero entonces ¿qué es lo que ocurre exactamente? ¿Que es que la sociedad ya no entiende el mensaje que transmite la Iglesia, su lenguaje? ¿Qué es lo que ocurre? Porque, es decir, la . . . la . . . les preocupa la sociedad que discurre por unos caminos de abandono moral, por decirlo de alguna manera, o de desmoralización, por decirlo de alguna manera. Pero ahora   5
dice usted una cosa que me permite a mí pensar, ¿no será que es que la sociedad tampoco entiende ya un determinado lenguaje? Yo creo que el lenguaje, mire, sí que el lenguaje vale, claro, pero más que nada es tener las ideas claras. Cuando uno las tiene claras las transmite de alguna forma. Puesto que seguimos hablando de la sociedad, de la sociedad y de   10
la Iglesia . . . Y de su lenguaje y de su mensaje hablamos. Pero sí voy a hablar también de la Iglesia, pero sí quisiera añadir que la sociedad, nosotros, nos quejamos de la sociedad que no cree en Cristo, luego de la sociedad que diciéndose católica no practica el catolicismo, no va a las prácticas elementales del catolici . . . de . . . de rituales del catolicismo.   15

Source text 2

En el análisis cualitativo se aplica una metodología específica para captar
el origen, el proceso y la naturaleza de los significados que surgen en la
interacción simbólica de los individuos. Su objetivo es la captación y
reconstrucción de significados, su lenguaje es básicamente conceptual y
metafórico, su método de captar información es flexible y no estructurado,   5
su procedimiento es más inductivo que deductivo y su orientación es
holística y concretizadora. Con esta metodología los datos son extraídos
a través de observaciones lentas, prolongadas y sistemáticas, con base en
notas, libros de registros y grabaciones entre otros, en un diálogo constante
con la unidad de información observada; en este contexto se habla de una   10
flexibilidad completa en el trabajo de investigación, es decir, se puede
cambiar en cualquier momento la hipótesis de trabajo, la fuente de
información y la línea de interpretación.

Source text 3

La tendencia ultrasexy lanzada por los gurús de la pasarela milanesa
durante los desfiles para esta primavera-verano se ha instalado de forma
meteórica en las áreas comerciales. Londres, París, Nueva York, Bruselas,
Madrid o Barcelona experimentan ya este argumento estético en sus
mejores escaparates, mostrando un avance de las colecciones femeninas   5
más extremado que en temporadas pasadas. Salpicado por la crisis política
internacional, el fenómeno encuentra su mejor vehículo de comunicación
en las campañas publicitarias más influyentes con el rostro y medidas
explosivas de las tops del momento: Anna Kournikova para Valentino,
Gisèle Bundchen para Dolce & Gabbana, Carmen Kass para Gucci,   10
Natalia Vodianova para Calvin Klein . . . La moda muestra su mejor coraza
ante un futuro incierto estimulando las ventas a golpe de sexo, deseo y
descaro masivos. Traducido al lenguaje de las prendas: mínimo metraje
de tejido para su confección, escotes y aberturas de vértigo que reivindican
la piel al descubierto en las zonas más eróticas, combinaciones atrevidas   15
en todas las piezas de un mismo look, y líneas más que cercanas a una
silueta que se presupone curvilínea y apta para albergar diseños que en
muchos casos traspasan la frontera del concepto de estilo urbano.

4.2 Consecutive interpreting: a basic exercise

Assignment

(i)   Your teacher will provide an oral source text, either by reading aloud or
by playing a recording. Since this is an introductory exercise assuming
no previous experience of interpreting, you will only need to deal with
short sections of about 120 words. As you listen to each section, make

notes to help you to remember as much as possible of what you have heard and allow you to reconstruct in English the key elements of the message. Do not attempt to write down every word: the aim is to convey the ideas and connections between them (essentially an oral gist translation), together with specific factual information such as numbers and names. Professional interpreters learn and develop systems of symbolic annotation which allow them to capture the key ideas and data in long stretches of discourse and reconstruct them in a coherent oral TT. For the purposes of this exercise, you will need to improvise ways of condensing the content of the ST, jotting down whatever comes to you most immediately (as SL or TL words and abbreviations, or as symbols). There are some obvious universal symbols you might use: = (equivalence or similarity) and $\neq$ (not the same); + (in addition); > (more than) and < (less than); $\rightarrow$ (one thing leading to another); $\uparrow$ (rise) and $\downarrow$ (fall); / (alternatives); α (beginning). Spread your notes out, putting just a single idea or phrase on each line and moving vertically (or diagonally) down the page. Draw a horizontal line across the page to mark the end of each stretch of speech (sentence or paragraph). Numbers, names and technical terms need to be written down as soon as you hear them, so that you do not have to try to remember them. Some interpreters find using landscape rather than portrait orientation helpful.

(ii)   Working in pairs, take turns to interpret as soon as you have finished listening to each section of the ST (i.e., deliver to your partner an oral TT based on notes you have taken while listening to that section). Attempt to produce a clear, coherent version in English of an appropriate register, summarizing the ideas and including specific names and figures.

(iii)   Compare your notes and review how much of the message each of you managed to convey.

(iv)   Finally, you will be given a printed copy of the ST. Discuss the kinds of information you were able to capture in your notes or your memory, and whether what got left out was significant. Make additions to your notes, still trying to put down only just enough to prompt your memory, and deliver your oral TT(s) again (without looking at the ST).

4.3 Genre: textual markers of orality

Assignment

(i)   Working in groups, analyse the genre characteristics of the following ST, especially how the second part of it mimics spontaneous spoken language. Focus on the overall coherence of the extract; on the linking of sentences; on the choice of vocabulary, and on deictic and phatic elements.

(ii)   Translate the section of the ST that is not in italics, assuming that the TT would be in an English version of the novel published in an English-speaking country (specify which one).

Contextual information

The ST is an extract from the beginning of a chapter of Miguel Delibes's novel *Cinco horas con Mario* (first published in 1966). Apart from a prologue and an epilogue, the entire novel is composed of a monologue spoken (or perhaps only thought) by Carmen as she sits through the night with the body of her recently deceased husband. Each chapter begins with a brief quotation from the Bible – passages underlined by Mario, presumably because they were of special significance for him – followed by the rambling recollections and recriminations of his widow. A profound gulf emerges between the small-minded, sanctimonious traditionalist, Carmen, and the frustrated liberal intellectual, Mario. The biblical text in italics here is from the First Epistle of John (1 John 3: 16–17 and 4: 20). In the King James Version, these verses read as follows:

> Hereby perceive we the love of God, because he laid down his life for us: and we ought to lay down our lives for the brethren. But whoso hath this world's good, and seeth his brother have need, and shutteth up his bowels of compassion from him, how dwelleth the love of God in him? [. . .] If a man say, I love God, and hateth his brother, he is a liar: for he that loveth not his brother whom he hath seen, how can he love God whom he hath not seen?

Source text

En esto hemos conocido la caridad, en que él dio su vida por nosotros y nosotros debemos dar nuestra vida por nuestros hermanos. El que tuviere bienes de este mundo y viendo a su hermano pasar necesidad le cierra sus entrañas, ¿cómo mora en él la caridad de Dios? . . . Si alguno dijere: «Amo a Dios» pero aborrece a su hermano, miente. Pues el que no 5
ama a su hermano a quien ve, no ama a Dios a quien no ve, que es precisamente lo que siempre he sostenido, cariño, que tus ideas sobre la caridad son como para recogerlas en un libro, y no te enfades, que todavía me acuerdo de tu conferencia, ¡vaya un trago!, hijo mío, que te pones a mirar, y no hay quién te entienda, que te metías conmigo cada vez que 10
iba a los suburbios a repartir naranjas y chocolate como si a los críos de los suburbios les sobrasen, ¡válgame Dios!, y no digamos la tarde que se me ocurrió ir con Valen al Ropero. ¿Puede saberse qué es lo que te pasa? Siempre hubo pobres y ricos, Mario, y obligación de los que, a Dios gracias, tenemos suficiente, es socorrer a los que no lo tienen, pero tú en 15
seguida a enmendar la plana, que encuentras defectos hasta en el Evangelio, hijo, si a saber si tus teorías son tuyas o del Perret ese de mis pecados, o de don Nicolás, o de cualquiera otro de la cuadrilla que son todos a cual más retorcido, no me vengas ahora. «Aceptar eso es aceptar que la distribución de la riqueza es justa», habráse visto, que cada vez me 20
dabas un mitin, cariño, con que si la caridad solamente debe llenar las grietas de la justicia pero no los abismos de la injusticia . . .

(Delibes 2002: 70–1)

5   Cultural issues in translation

In a general sense, all translation issues are cultural. That is, translation is as much to do with mediation between cultures as with transfer of meaning between languages. By 'culture', we mean the whole physical, social, historical and ideological environment within which any use of language occurs. Texts and utterances are produced in particular places at particular times, are shaped by particular conventions, precedents and ideological constraints, and are aimed at particular receivers; they deploy forms of language to refer to aspects of their surrounding environment in ways designed to be understood by those receivers, assuming shared knowledge and experiences. Some texts refer more concretely and specifically to aspects of their environment than others, and may reflect this in the choice of varieties of language – particular dialects or sociolects.

Although the terms 'SL culture' and 'TL culture' are routinely used in translation studies, they are inevitably over-simplifications, since it is impossible to map languages and cultures onto one another with clear boundaries or at a fixed scale. One extremely broad way of defining a TL culture at which a translation is aimed might be, for example, what all speakers of English could be assumed to have in common; more narrowly, the customs, values, physical environment and life experiences shared by English speakers in England or one of its regions; or at the very specialized end of the scale, the specific kinds of knowledge and professional experience possessed by scientists and industrialists working on Process Analytical Technology, who may perhaps have different first languages but use English as a scientific or commercial lingua franca.

In some respects, the target readers in the UK of a translation of a Spanish-language ST published in Spain could be regarded as sharing with SL readers elements of the same European culture which they do not share with people in the USA: constitutional monarchy, the EU, highly developed welfare states, football, castles, a history of colonizing. In parallel, there are cultural elements that target readers in the USA could be assumed to have in common with the readers of a ST published in Mexico, albeit modulated in this case by a much greater imbalance in political and economic power: republicanism, the NAFTA, limited welfare states, baseball, suppressed indigenous cultures, a history of resisting colonization, as well as the major factor of the presence of a large Spanish-speaking population in the USA. Moreover, cultural differences and boundaries – and the ways in which they are reflected in language – are never static and are becoming ever more fluid as a result of economic and technological globalization. The culture within which a translation is intended to be received should therefore never be taken for granted: every translation task demands its own assessment of the likely gaps and overlaps between SL and TL cultures, and between the different knowledges that readers are assumed to possess. Students carrying out translation assignments for learning purposes should always postulate a target readership if the instructions for the assignment have not prescribed one, and make assumptions about what that readership could be expected to recognize.

Despite all these caveats about separating the cultural from the linguistic, for the purposes of planning a particular translation task it is important to identify those aspects of a ST that create problems primarily to do with cultural reference and knowledge rather than linguistic structures and usage, and to develop an appropriate strategy for dealing with them. For example, the fact that a motor vehicle is usually referred to as 'coche' in Spain but 'carro' in most parts of Latin America is in a sense a 'cultural' feature, but in practice can be considered simply as language variation within the SL culture (which is discussed in Chapter 11). The object referred to is the same in both areas, corresponds to very similar objects in use in the UK or USA, and both terms can be translated straightforwardly as 'car'. On the other hand, some of the many words used around Latin America for buses – 'colectivo', 'bondi', 'rapidito', 'trucho', 'guagua', 'combi' and 'pesero', among others – refer to particular kinds of vehicles with regional peculiarities and, in some cases, a special place in local cultural history (read about the *colectivos* of Buenos Aires at www.la-floresta.com.ar/colectivo.htm). As a result, they generate specifically cultural problems in translation: translating them simply as 'bus' may cause substantial translation loss, yet TL readers would not understand the untranslated SL terms (unless accompanied by some explanation), and it is unlikely that similarly specific variations on the theme of collective public road transport can be found in the TL.

Reference to objects and features of the physical environment which exist (or have distinctive characteristics) in one location but not in another creates the most obvious kind of cultural gap. Similar problems are generated by a range of less concrete phenomena, though: social customs and institutions; cultural traditions and conventions; names of people, places and organizations; knowledge of national or local histories; attitudes and values shaped by circumstances and environment. Many of the linguistic items involved tend to be single nouns or verbs, but the issue of cultural transfer may arise from more extended expressions or general features of complete texts. The individual components of the saying 'llamar al pan, pan y al vino, vino' pose no problem of intercultural recognition, but the use of the expression in Spain to mean something like 'to call a spade a spade' depends upon the long-established status of wine in Spain as a staple commodity, as basic and necessary as bread, while for most British English speakers wine has traditionally been regarded as more of a luxury commodity. Similarly, the Spanish habit of ordering food, drink or other goods in bars and shops with a rather brusque imperative ('Póngame un coñac') poses a translation problem that is not primarily linguistic but the result of cultural difference, forcing a choice between the following alternatives:

(a) retaining the brusqueness by translating literally, at the cost of cultural appropriateness in English ('Give me a brandy');
(b) losing the cultural feel of the SL expression and translating more idiomatically ('Can I have a brandy, please?');
(c) a compromise that attempts to combine brevity with politeness ('Brandy, please'), or a degree of assertiveness with colloquial familiarity ('Gimme a brandy, love').

The use of expletives and taboo expressions is also influenced by cultural differences. Not only are different swearwords prevalent in different parts of the world in which a particular language is spoken, but different levels of acceptability of taboo language apply within and between SL and TL cultures. Most Spaniards have long been more comfortable with sex-related terms such as 'coño' and 'joder' (and Mexicans with 'chingar') than many British people are with similar terms in English, although remaining resistance to 'fuck/fucking' has been eroded in recent years by its increasingly routine use on television. On the other hand, Spaniards are likely to identify 'hostia' or 'hostias' (literally, the host in holy communion) as their strongest taboo word, whereas few English speakers would place such importance on religious associations in gauging extreme offensiveness. The most culturally accurate translation of '¡Hostias!' into English, then, could be 'Fuck!'; and of '¿Qué coño haces aquí?' could be 'What the hell are you doing here?'

One of the most complex forms of cultural specificity is **intertextuality**, where a ST echoes or refers to other texts in the same language and SL readers are expected to recognize the connection. In a general sense, implicit intertextuality is an inevitable feature of all communication, as no text exists in total isolation from other texts. In specialized fields, a high proportion of the language used will be formulaic and convention-bound, but even an extremely innovative text cannot fail to form part of an overall body of literature by which the impact and originality of individual texts are defined: the originality of Joyce's *Ulysses*, for instance, is measured by reference to (and contrast with) a whole body of literature from Homer onwards. Intertextuality, moreover, is built into the process of translating texts of any genre, which must take account explicitly or implicitly of existing textual models from the TL culture. Translators need to develop a wide-ranging awareness of textual traditions and conventions in both source and target cultures, so as to be able to recognize intertextuality in a ST and build a comparable degree of intertextuality into the TT.

More specific and detailed action is required of the translator when a ST directly invokes, by allusion or quotation, parts of other texts which its author assumes will be familiar to SL readers, such as Cervantes, the Bible or a well-known advertising slogan. For instance, in Pérez Galdós's *Miau* (1971b: 318) the phrase 'en aquella ciudad provinciana, cuyo nombre no hace al caso' contains a clear allusion to a famous line from the beginning of *Don Quixote*: 'En un lugar de la Mancha, de cuyo nombre no quiero acordarme . . .'. Postmodernist writers in Spain and Latin America have made multifarious intertextuality, parody and pastiche key ingredients of their aesthetic practice. Ana Rossetti's poetry, for example, refers to Greek myth, the Bible, English Romantic poetry, nineteenth-century French culture, Lindsay Kemp, and advertisements for Calvin Klein and Wrangler.

The translator must always be on the look-out for such echoes. What to do with them depends on the circumstances. Some cases, when TL readers can be assumed to be capable of recognizing the allusion, will simply necessitate finding appropriate TL versions of the passages and integrating them into the TT (although, in the case of the Bible or ancient classics, thought will have to be given to which version to choose). Reference in a Spanish ST to a text written in English (translating a line from Shakespeare or Bob Dylan, for example, both of whom are more familiar to reasonably well-educated Spaniards or Latin Americans than Cervantes or, say, Víctor Jara to a reasonably well-educated person in the UK or USA), will almost always require retrieval of the original quotation. Failure to spot the allusion may result in the loss of a crucial link in a network of associations. In other cases, the echoes may be too abstruse, or unimportant from the point of view of a TL audience, to be worth building into the TT, though some way of compensating for this loss may be achievable.

Another significant mode of intertextuality is imitation. An entire text may be designed specifically as an imitation of another text or texts, as in pastiche or parody. (An example is the pastiche of Ortega y Gasset's famous perspectives speech in Luis Martín-Santos's *Tiempo de silencio* (1973: 133).) Alternatively, sections of a text may deliberately imitate different texts or genres – an example is David Lodge's *The British Museum Is Falling Down,* in which each chapter parodies a different author. Here the overall effect is of a text contrived as a mixture of styles that recall the various genres from which they are copied. A Spanish example is the merging of *novela rosa* and *novela política* in Isabel Allende's *De amor y de sombra* (1984). This aspect of inter-textuality has to be borne in mind, because there are STs that can only be fully appreciated if one is aware that they use the device of imitating other texts or genres. Furthermore, to recreate this device in the TT, the translator must be familiar with target culture genres, and have the skill to imitate them. Some STs may belong to or imitate a textual genre that is itself culture-specific, with its own distinctive structure and historical associations, such as a Spanish *libro de familia* document, the libretto of a *zarzuela*, or a Mexican *corrido*. Similar text types may be found in the TL culture on which to base a translation, but the particular cultural resonance of the SL form will be less easy to transfer, occasioning translation loss.

The cultural dimension can therefore pose some of the trickiest challenges facing the translator. TL readers can never have the same cultural knowledge and experiences as SL readers, which means that some degree of translation loss in this respect is inevitable. As always, though, the aim is not to seek exact equivalence or perfect solutions but to minimize translation loss and find stylistically appropriate ways of compensating for it. And as always, the translation decisions made in pursuit of this aim need to be guided by an overall strategy for each assignment informed by the characteristics of the particular ST, the assumed needs of the TT readership and the purpose of the translation.

Domesticating translation and exoticizing translation

Strategies for dealing with cultural issues in translation can be visualized as being located along a spectrum between two extremes. The tendency in one direction is towards maximum retention or conservation of elements of the SL culture by means of one or more of the following procedures:

(a) transferring SL terms and names into the TT without changing them (exoticism or cultural borrowing), or else translating them very literally (calque);
(b) not providing additional information to explain culture-specific references, or providing it outside the main TT, for example in footnotes or an introduction;
(c) translating idiomatic expressions literally, allowing the style of the TT to retain a feeling of exoticism;
(d) retaining intertextual elements (possibly leaving them in the SL) and culture-specific genre features without clarifying their cultural resonance;
(e) not making adjustments for differences in values, customs or expectations.

The tendency in the other direction is towards making the SL culture understandable by TL readers, or replacing it with elements from the TL culture. The procedures used represent various forms of **cultural transposition**, including the following:

(a) translating or finding rough cultural equivalents for all SL terms and names;
(b) integrating into the TT additional information to explain culture-specific references;
(c) translating idiomatic expressions communicatively, aiming for a fluent, coherent TT style;
(d) clarifying (within the TT) the significance of intertextual elements and culture-specific genre features, or even replacing them with comparable elements from the TL culture;

(e) aligning language indicating values, customs or expectations to TL cultural patterns;

(f) deleting any elements judged to be untranslatable, not of interest to TL readers, or undesirable.

The range of specific choices between the extremes of **exoticism** (leaving ST elements in their original form) and **cultural transplantation** (replacing them with elements from the TL culture) can be placed on a scale as in the following diagram:

Bias towards SL culture   Bias towards TL culture

◄──►

| Exoticism | Cultural borrowing | Calque | Communicative translation | Deletion | Cultural transplantation |

The first of the strategies outlined above – biased towards the conservation of SL culture features – can be termed **'exoticizing'** (or **'foreignizing'**). It can be regarded as bringing the readers of the translation towards the SL culture, offering them some sense of how that culture sounds and feels but not reading like a text originally written in the TL. The second strategy – biased towards adaptation to the TL culture – can be termed **'domesticating'** (or **'naturalizing'**). It has the effect of moving the text towards the readers of the translation, making it more accessible and familiar but blurring or even erasing cultural difference. One of the most influential studies of the implications of this dichotomy is Lawrence Venuti's *The Translator's Invisibility*, in which he sums up the two methods as follows:

> A **domesticating method**, an ethnocentric reduction of the foreign text to target-language cultural values, bringing the author back home, and a **foreignizing method**, an ethnodeviant pressure on those values to register the linguistic and cultural difference of the foreign text, sending the reader abroad.
>
> (Venuti 1995: 20)

Venuti and other theorists underline the ideological implications of approaches to translation, especially when dealing with translation into an economically and politically powerful language (such as English) from a less powerful one. Venuti argues that 'translation wields enormous power in the construction of national identities for foreign cultures' (1995: 19). Niranjana examines the role of translation in colonialism, concluding that a preference for domesticating translation of texts in the languages of colonized peoples tends to contribute to the representation of colonized cultures in a fixed, static way, constructing an image of the colonized 'other' as viewed by the colonizers 'in such a manner as to justify colonial domination' (1992: 2). In opposition to this, an exoticizing translation method is proposed in order to make the SL culture visible and audible, and allow elements of it to penetrate the hegemonic TL culture.

The current imbalances of power between English and Spanish are not directly comparable with a colonial situation, but they certainly have an impact on the amount of translation carried out in each direction and how the market for translation operates. In the area of audiovisual translation (dubbing and subtitling of films and television programmes), the amount of translation being carried out into English is tiny compared with the huge global demand for the dubbing and subtitling of US (and some British) media products. The situation with regard to book publishing is similar, if not quite so heavily tilted towards English. Between 2002 and 2006, the average number of titles published in Spain per year was around 75,800, of which 19,600 (26 per cent) were translations; half of the translations (9,800) were from English, with some of the other translations being from one of the official languages of Spain to another (Ministerio de Cultura 2007). UK publishers produced 115,500 titles in 2006 (Publishers Association 2007), of which only about 2 per cent were translations (as estimated in Lea 2007; Venuti 1992 gives figures of 2.5 per cent in the UK and 3.5 per cent in the USA for the period 1984–1990).

Foreign-language films and translated books distributed in the UK or USA are likely to be targeted at a relatively specialist, highbrow audience, which is usually assumed to value them as being typical or significant products of the source culture. The translation strategies applied to them therefore tend to be relatively favourable to the retention of 'exotic' features, but may at the same time emphasize and perpetuate stereotypical perceptions of the SL culture. On the other hand, English-language films and translations of books from English are much more likely to be distributed overseas as mass-market products, sold on the strength of their generic characteristics (as action movie, thriller, historical romance, detective story or marketing manual) rather than the insight they provide into the SL culture. They are correspondingly more likely to be subject to various kinds of domesticating translation, including the suppression of content, values and types of language judged to be of no interest to readers, or else politically or morally unacceptable in the TL culture. In the Spanish context, the Franco dictatorship offers a well-documented example of translation being used as a key part of a system of censorship (see Merino and Rabadán 2002 with reference to novels and theatre, and Vandaele 2007 for some revealing cinematic examples). The aim was to restrict the kinds of foreign texts and films made available and to ensure that they conformed not only to the reactionary political and moral values of the regime and the Catholic Church but also to chauvinistic ideals of linguistic purity and decorum – not only deleting references to Marx or adultery, for example, but also tidying up and toning down racy or coarse language.

While users of this book are unlikely to be working within a context as politically polarized as a colonial situation or a dictatorship, it is important to bear in mind that any translation decision on the cultural level has ideological implications – reinforcing or challenging cultural stereotypes; respecting, undervaluing or manipulating cultural difference; expanding or restricting TL readers' intercultural awareness; working with otherness or attempting to suppress or distort it. A domesticating approach to the translation of any text may have the positive effect of making the SL culture more accessible and comprehensible or the negative effect of erasing cultural difference, while an exoticizing approach may make the SL culture more visible and audible in its own terms or have a patronizing effect of fixing and exaggerating cultural difference. Exoticizing translation 'sends readers abroad' and thereby broadens their horizons, but has an impact on them which the ST could never have on a SL audience, for whom the text has none of the features of an alien culture. It is also worth remembering that strategies for dealing with the cultural dimension of translation need not in all cases be entirely homogeneous: an exoticizing treatment of specific sociocultural phenomena may be combined with a communicative, domesticating approach to idiomatic style and register.

Degrees of cultural transposition

The following sections examine in more detail some of the practicalities of the range of translation tactics on the scale between exoticism and cultural transplantation set out on p. 73.

Exoticism

The extreme option of leaving in the original language elements of the ST for which suitable TL equivalents are not available may have various motivations: a simplistic desire to retain 'local colour', a more ideologically aware aim of resisting the erasure of cultural difference; or an educational objective of encouraging TL readers to inform themselves about the SL culture and adapt their expectations. The translator of a non-fiction text about, for example, Madrid – or a fictional text set there and relying heavily upon evocation of its setting – might decide to refer in the TT to the Museo del Prado, the Parque del Retiro and the Barrio de Salamanca; to describe *madrileños* taking part in the traditional Fiesta de San Isidro, dressing up as *chulapos* and *chulapas*, munching *barquillos* and dancing the *chotis*; to report on clashes between *okupas* and *seguratas*; to reproduce snatches of dialogue in which people say things like 'Hasta luego', 'Vale' or 'Dame una caña, nena'. Incorporating such elements without any additional explanation may be a valid and productive strategy, stimulating the reader to work out meanings from the context or even through independent investigation, yet it obviously risks causing confusion or irritation. The risk may be mitigated by the provision of information in an introduction, footnotes or glossary, but this kind of extratextual apparatus may not be compatible with the conventions of many types of publication or with the expectations of readers. A term used repeatedly in a text may be accompanied by an explanation on its first appearance and subsequently used routinely in its SL form.

Insisting on rendering as exoticisms terms that have well-established conventional renderings in the TL, or are not culture-specific and can very easily be translated, could also prove counterproductive: for example, including in the hypothetical text about Madrid a reference to being in 'España' or ordering a *vino*, or to the *policía* breaking up an *antifascista* demonstration. However, there can be no hard-and-fast rules in this area, and what constitutes cultural specificity is not always easy to pin down. The 'chotis' referred to above as typical of Madrid folklore is itself borrowed from other cultures: the word and the dance are German in origin, a kind of polka supposedly in a Scottish style which became very popular throughout Europe in the second half of the nineteenth century, so using the hispanicized form 'chotis' in an English TT rather than 'Schottische' or 'Scottish' may be considered pointless. On the other hand, the particular form of the Schottische established in Spain (and then popularized via France as the 'Schottish Espagnole') has its own rhythm and steps and occupies a distinctive place in the popular traditions of Madrid, so the exoticism 'chotis' may be entirely justified in a foreignizing translation. As a strategic option, therefore, exoticism needs to be carefully handled, be based on a clear overall aim, and be informed by a clear awareness of its potential implications.

Cultural borrowing

The examples given in the previous section could be described as instances of 'cultural borrowing', that is, the transfer of a linguistic item from one culture to another without translating it (exactly in its original form, transliterated into a different alphabet or with the spelling modified to conform to TL patterns). What we have classified as 'exoticism' is primarily the kind of ad hoc borrowing that a translator carries out in a particular TT knowing that readers are unlikely to be familiar with the SL term. However, translators can often make use of loan-words from the SL that are already established in the TL, retaining a degree of exoticism but combining it with familiarity and incurring a much lower risk of incomprehensibility. The translator of our hypothetical text about Madrid could transfer terms such as 'flamenco', 'fiesta', 'siesta', 'plaza' and 'paella' without any risk of leaving English-speaking readers in the dark. Established loan-words may sometimes be used as replacements for unfamiliar exoticisms: 'tapas' for 'pinchos'; 'canyon' (from Spanish 'cañón') for 'barranca'; or 'guerrilla' for 'guerrillero' ('guerrilla' in Spanish refers to a kind of warfare or a group of people engaged in it, not to an individual fighter).

Of course, cultural borrowing only presents translators with an entirely open and free choice in cases where usage has not already set up a precedent for the verbatim borrowing of the ST expression. Where SL terms have become established loan-words in the TL without significant change of meaning, thus constituting standard equivalents of the original SL terms borrowed, the translator may not be faced with a significant decision at all. Unless special considerations of style can be invoked, there is little reason not to render such terms verbatim in an English TT. On occasion it may even seem perverse not to do so. The convenience of borrowings and their synonymy with the source terms should not be taken for granted, though, as the example of 'guerrilla' demonstrates. Loan-words come and go over time, depending upon different kinds and degrees of cultural contact (sometimes via a third language), and may not be assimilated to the same extent in all parts of the English-speaking world: unsurprisingly, there has been more borrowing from Spanish, historically and recently, in US English than in British English (see Rodríguez González 1996). A shift in spelling or meaning often takes place in the course of transfer, usually a narrowing – only one of a range of possible senses is transferred. For example, the RAE dictionary lists five senses of the term 'pueblo':

1 Ciudad o villa [town].
2 Población de menor categoría [village].
3 Conjunto de personas de un lugar, región o país [a people, the people].
4 Gente común y humilde de una población [the (common) people].
5 País con gobierno independiente [country, nation, people].

(Real Academia Española 2001–2008)

Only the second of these, used in a particular context, has been assimilated into English (mostly in the USA): 'A village or community in Spain or Spanish America; *spec.* a settlement or communal dwelling of Pueblo Indians, typically a multistorey, flat-roofed structure of adobe or stone' (OED 1989–2008). 'Salsa' was first borrowed for use in culinary contexts ('sauce' in a generic sense, dating back to 1846 in the OED), more recently (becoming established in the 1970s) as a broad genre of 'Latin' dance music, and even more recently, universally recognized as a kind of spicy, chilli-and-tomato-based sauce of Mexican origin used as a condiment, a dip or an ingredient in fusion cuisine.

Calque

A less radical form of foreignization is to translate ST material into the TL without making it fully convincing as discourse produced by a native speaker of the TL; that is, to subject it to calque – literal translation generating expressions that consist of TL words and respect TL syntax, but are unidiomatic in the TL because they are modelled on the structure of SL expressions. For most purposes and text types, especially in informal registers, calque is a form of translation to be avoided, tending to produce unidiomatic collocations and clumsy syntax. It is, however, a common feature of borrowing between languages: 'world-view' is calqued on German 'Weltanschauung'; French 'pot-pourri', borrowed directly by English, is originally a calque of Spanish 'olla podrida'; Spanish 'peso mosca' and 'hombre rana' are calqued on English 'flyweight' and 'frogman'. 'Balompié' was coined in Spain in an unsuccessful nationalistic attempt to displace the direct borrowing 'fútbol' ('baloncesto' has proved more durable as an alternative to 'básquet/básquetbol').

As a way of conveying the basic meaning of a phrase designating a person, institution, place or culturally specific object while at the same time retaining some of its foreignness, calque may have its uses – as long as the results are not ridiculous or incomprehensible. A British translator of the list of ministries in the Chilean government, for example, need not hesitate over 'Ministerio del Interior' ('Ministry of the Interior') or 'Ministerio de Planificación' ('Ministry of Planning'), despite the fact that there are no ministries with these names in the UK. The 'Ministerio de Relaciones Exteriores' offers a choice between the acceptable calque 'Ministry of Exterior Relations' and the more communicative 'Ministry of Foreign Affairs', which is what appears on the English version of the official website. If 'Ministerio de Bienes Nacionales' is calqued as 'Ministry of National Goods', however, TT readers will have little chance of working out that it deals with the administration of public property and national heritage.

There may also be good reasons for calquing idiomatic expressions rooted in cultural specificity. The most appropriate translation of 'llamar al pan, pan y al vino, vino' is likely in most circumstances to be the communicative rendering 'to call a spade a spade'; yet it may sometimes be desirable to retain some of the saying's cultural flavour by translating it literally as 'to call bread bread and wine wine'. To ensure that this is recognized as a deliberate tactic, one might add something like 'as they say around here'. Clearly, there are dangers in using calque as a translation device. The major one is that the meaning of calqued phrases may not be clear in the TT. In the worst cases, calques are not even recognizable for what they are, but are merely puzzling bits of gibberish for the reader or listener. The translation needs not only to make it clear that a particular phrase is an intentional calque, but the meaning of the calqued phrase must also be transparent in the TT context. The most successful calques need no explanation; less successful ones may need to be explained, perhaps in a footnote or a glossary.

Communicative translation

In general, communicative translation involves selecting those features of the TL that will convey the meanings and reproduce the textual effects of the ST in ways designed to strike the reader of the TT as idiomatic, stylistically coherent and in line with how the content would naturally be expressed by a native speaker, even if that means quite radical departures from literal translation (as set out in Chapter 2). It is a frequent and important aim in the translation of many text types, especially where the register is relatively informal or the content subjective, and can be more or less mandatory for

culturally conventional formulas where a literal rendering would be meaningless or absurd. Where a ST uses a cliché, idiom or proverb, or a standard
expression for a familiar situation, sentiment or object, particular reasons would
be needed to go against the grain by not choosing communicatively equivalent
formulas. If the use of conventional idioms is part and parcel of the stylistic
effect of the ST and the TT does not use corresponding TL idioms, this stylistic
effect will be lost. Nevertheless, communicativeness should not be taken for
granted as a requirement for all translations; it is a relative, variable quality,
not an absolute one, and there may be several ways of achieving it. Where an
obvious TL equivalent is not available, or the one that is available is judged
to be stylistically inappropriate, a paraphrase that does not have the same status
as a stock phrase but is convincingly idiomatic within the TT may be the best
solution. The bread and wine example could be communicatively translated
as 'he tells it like it is' or 'he's a straight-talking kinda guy' rather than 'he
calls a spade a spade'.

As a means of dealing with culture-specific elements of a ST according to
a domesticating strategy, communicative translation sacrifices exoticism and
specificity for comprehensibility, accessibility and familiarity, often by means
of generalization or expansion. To return to our hypothetical example of the
text about Madrid, instead of retaining 'siesta' as a borrowing, one could
choose 'afternoon nap' (or more precisely but pretentiously, 'postprandial
nap'); a copy of *El País* could be generalized as 'a newspaper', and the 'Cortes'
could become simply 'the parliament building'. 'Madrileños' out for their
'paseo' having 'cañas' and 'tapas' could be 'the locals out for their customary
early-evening stroll, stopping off at bars for glasses of beer and nibbles'.
Alternatively, the communicative option may consist of retaining some
exoticisms but building explanation or expansion into the flow of the TT
(providing an intratextual gloss):

> ST: A la gente de este barrio le encanta la Fiesta de San Isidro. Todos
> los vecinos se disfrazan de chulapos y chulapas. En la plaza se monta una
> pista de baile y todo el mundo baila el chotis. Los niños se atiborran de
> barquillos.

> Exoticizing TT: People in this *barrio* love the Fiesta de San Isidro. All
> the *vecinos* dress up as *chulapos* and *chulapas*. They set up a dance floor
> in the *plaza* and everybody dances the *chotis*. The kids stuff themselves
> with *barquillos*.

> Domesticating TT: People in this neighbourhood love the San Isidro Fair.
> All the locals put on traditional *chulapo* outfits, the men in waistcoat and
> flat cap and the women with a headscarf, a carnation in their hair and a
> shawl. They set up a dance floor in the square and everybody dances the
> Madrid version of the Schottische, a kind of slow polka. The kids stuff
> themselves with sweet, crunchy *barquillo* cones.

Deletion

In principle, we would not advocate the complete omission from a TT of any culture-specific elements of a ST. However alien or untranslatable an expression may be, the translator should be able to find some way of compensating for the translation loss and conveying something of the textual function of the reference. In practice, though, deletion may form part of some translation strategies for pragmatic or ideological reasons. When translation is subject to official censorship, deletion is frequently resorted to; the people controlling the process may see this as entirely justified in the interests of protecting their cultural values from contamination. Censorship of a less formal kind may be imposed by publishers or translators themselves: translations of sexually explicit texts such as Catullus's poetry have frequently left out material considered indecent. Other factors influencing the purpose of a particular translation task (its skopos) may result in the removal of ST elements judged to be irrelevant to that purpose. For example, a speech made by a high-profile South American politician (Hugo Chávez, perhaps), aimed at a specific audience and incorporating local references to people, places, events and texts, might be translated for publication in overseas media or on an English-language website with many of the culture-specific elements removed, on the grounds that what the international audience is interested in is not the means by which the orator appealed to that particular audience but his overall message and the general flavour of his rhetoric.

Franco Aixelá (1996) provides very revealing examples of the deletion of culture-specific items for marketing reasons in his detailed analysis of Spanish translations of Dashiel Hammett's classic detective novel, *The Maltese Falcon* (first published in 1930). A 1933 translation, clearly designed to appeal to a mass market on the basis of its generic narrative appeal as a detective story, dispenses with a large number of the 'spatial details which are so characteristic in the type of detective fiction created by Hammett' (Franco Aixelá 1996: 71), and deletes 18.8 per cent of the proper names that appear in the ST. A 'dark Cadillac sedan' is translated as 'un Cadillac oscuro' (Franco Aixelá 1996: 64), and the description of the package in which the figure of the falcon appears is simplified from 'an ellipsoid somewhat larger than an American football' to 'un paquete de forma ovalada' (76). In contrast, translations published in 1969 and 1992 are pitched at a more highbrow literary market in which Hammett's work has become canonical: they appear with prefatory material referring to the author's reputation and conserve much more of the cultural information written into the ST.

Cultural transplantation

At the opposite end of the scale from exoticism is cultural transplantation, a radical form of domestication in which culture-specific elements in the ST are replaced in the TT by elements that are specific to the TL culture. A low priority may be given to retaining the ST references as exoticisms or clarifying their cultural resonance, either because they are judged to have an incidental function within the ST or because they are not relevant to the purpose of the translation. There may be no point in retaining units of currency, for instance, even in a TT that in other respects adopts a relatively foreignizing approach: a text about Mexico aimed at US tourists might routinely convert all prices into US dollars without mentioning the original amounts in pesos. An intertextual allusion used in a ST for its articulation of a general idea rather than for its specific cultural relevance might be replaced by an intertextual element from the TL culture which expresses something similar. If a text dealing primarily with objects and experiences assumed to be familiar to the TL readership and emphasizing their universality (living in a city, going to work on the bus, using a computer, watching television) introduces an isolated reference to something culturally specific (buying *elote* from a street vendor on the way home), transplantation (buying fish and chips) may be justified in order to maintain the appeal to familiarity. An advertising campaign selling the same product in several countries with more or less the same message might vary certain culture-specific textual elements from one country to another in order to appeal to different cultural stereotypes or avoid unwanted associations.

Even names of people or institutions – especially those that are semantically motivated in some way – may be culturally transposed if their SL form is not textually significant. The 'Ministerio del Interior' in a Hispanic country could be rendered as 'the Home Office' to bring it closer to a British readership, and the 'Primera División' of the Liga Nacional de Fútbol Profesional in Spain could be referred to as 'Spain's Premier League' (not 'First Division'). The standard Spanish expression 'don Fulano', used to refer to an unspecified person, should be transposed to 'Joe Bloggs' or 'Mr Average' in a British context, or to 'John Doe' in an American one. Taking a different kind of example, careful consideration would need to be given in an English TT of Rosa Montero's novel *Te trataré como a una reina* (1983) to the translation of 'Isabel López', chosen as a stereotypical name for a *bolero* singer in a nightclub, as well as of 'Antonio and Antonia Ortiz' used for comic effect as stereotypical names for a civil servant and his sister. Should, for instance, 'Isabel López' become, by cultural transplantation, 'Liza Johnson', and 'Antonio and Antonia Ortiz' be transformed into 'Julian and Julia Smythe'? These solutions would allow some of the stereotyping, and comic effect, to be preserved in the TT, at the expense of the characters' inherent Spanishness. The examples show clearly why cultural transplantation of names is such a risky option. For example, if 'Liza Johnson' continued to be nicknamed as 'La Bella' (as she is in the ST), and if Julian Smythe were portrayed as having lived all his life in Madrid, or as a keen *aficionado* of bullfighting, the effect would be incongruous.

Cultural transplantation can be carried out on complete texts, resulting in the ST being completely reinvented in an indigenous target culture setting.

This is not uncommon in translation for the theatre, where the need to engage the interest of a live audience is a powerful stimulus for naturalization. Examples include *Carmen Jones,* the American version of Bizet's *Carmen* (which in turn is a reworking of Mérimée's novella), the musical *Man of the Mancha*, based on *Don Quixote*, and Lou Stein's *Salsa Celestina* (1993), which reenacts Rojas's tragicomedy in a modern Cuban nightclub setting. Valle-Inclán's play *Luces de Bohemia* (1921) is full of references – some of which were obscure even at the time and most of which are unfamiliar to Spanish audiences now – to places in Madrid, real people of the period, customs, texts and artistic genres. John Lyon's translation, written primarily for publication, adopts an effective communicative approach to the flavour of the dialogue but retains most of the cultural references, relying upon a substantial apparatus of introduction and notes to keep the reader on board (Valle-Inclán 1993). David Johnston's version (Johnston 1993), written for performance by the Gate Theatre (London) in 1993, transplants the whole play to Dublin in 1915, changing names, locations, references to events and intertextual elements, and radically adapting the dialogue accordingly. Max's drunken last night is mapped onto the streets of Dublin, including dinner at the Shelbourne Hotel with W. B. Yeats. There is, in a sense, enormous translation loss in such a procedure, but what was gained in this case was a dazzling revivification of the linguistic, political and theatrical power of the ST (see the translator's own discussion of the process in Johnston 1998 and 2000).

It may be argued that transplantation on this scale is, strictly speaking, not translation at all but adaptation – the production of an original TL text based loosely on a SL model. In practice, most work carried out by translators does not approach this end of the cultural transposition scale, and the theatrical examples above belong to a rather specialized field. Nevertheless, like exoticism at the other end of the scale, cultural transplantation is an option available to the translator to be used carefully and deliberately as part of a coherent overall strategy appropriate for the type of ST and, crucially, for the purpose of the TT.

Practical 5

5.1 Cultural issues in translation: exoticizing and domesticating strategies

Assignment

(i)   Working in groups, examine the ST and TT below, identifying elements of the ST that create problems of cultural specificity; discuss the approach taken in the TT to dealing with these elements and analyse the TT in terms of the degree of SL/TL culture bias ('exoticizing' or 'domesticating' translation). The translator is identified simply as 'irlandesa': discuss who this person might be, what her attitude towards the subject matter and the producers of the ST might be, and what assumptions she seems to have made about her target readers.

(ii)   Each group should produce an alternative translation of a section of the ST, following a different strategy from the one identified in the TT below. The suggested length of sections is marked in the ST with //.

Contextual information

The ST consists of extracts from the 'Sexta Declaración de la Selva Lacandona': a manifesto published by the Zapatistas in June 2005. The text is available online at http://palabra.ezln.org.mx. The English version is available online at www.anarkismo.net. You may need to carry out some research on the Zapatistas: you could start at http://flag.blackened.net/revolt/mexico/begindx.html.

Turn to pp. 84–5 for source text and target text.

Source text

Sexta Declaración de la Selva Lacandona
Ejército Zapatista de Liberación Nacional

Ahora vamos a explicarles cómo es que vemos nosotros los zapatistas lo que pasa en el mundo. Pues vemos que el capitalismo es el que está más fuerte ahorita. El capitalismo es un sistema social, o sea una forma como en una sociedad están   5
organizadas las cosas y las personas, y quien tiene y quien no tiene, y quien manda y quien obedece. En el capitalismo hay unos que tienen dinero o sea capital y fábricas y tiendas y campos y muchas cosas, y hay otros que no tienen nada sino que sólo tienen su fuerza y su conocimiento para trabajar; y en el capitalismo mandan los que tienen el dinero y las cosas, y obedecen los que nomás tienen su capacidad de trabajo. //   10
    Y entonces el capitalismo quiere decir que hay unos pocos que tienen grandes riquezas, pero no es que se sacaron un premio, o que se encontraron un tesoro, o que heredaron de un pariente, sino que esas riquezas las obtienen de explotar el trabajo de muchos. O sea que el capitalismo se basa en la explotación de los trabajadores, que quiere decir que como que exprimen a los trabajadores y les sacan todo lo que pueden de ganancias.   15
    [...]
    Al capitalismo lo que más le interesa son las mercancías, porque cuando se compran y se venden dan ganancias. Y entonces el capitalismo todo lo convierte en mercancías, hace mercancías a las personas, a la naturaleza, a la cultura, a la historia, a la conciencia. Según el capitalismo, todo se tiene que poder comprar y vender. Y todo   20
lo esconde detrás de las mercancías para que no vemos la explotación que hace. Y entonces las mercancías se compran y se venden en un mercado. // Y resulta que el mercado, además de servir para comprar y vender, también sirve para esconder la explotación de los trabajadores. Por ejemplo, en el mercado vemos el café ya empaquetado, en su bolsita o frasco muy bonitillo, pero no vemos al campesino que   25
sufrió para cosechar el café, y no vemos al coyote que le pagó muy barato su trabajo, y no vemos a los trabajadores en la gran empresa dale y dale para empaquetar el café. O vemos un aparato para escuchar música como cumbias, rancheras o corridos o según cada quien, y lo vemos que está muy bueno porque tiene buen sonido, pero no vemos a la obrera de la maquiladora que batalló muchas horas para pegar los cables y las   30
partes del aparato, y apenas le pagaron una miseria de dinero, y ella vive retirado del trabajo y gasta un buen en el pasaje, y además corre peligro que la secuestran, la violan y la matan como pasa en Ciudad Juárez, en México. //
    [...]
    Entonces, como quien dice que resumiendo, el capitalismo de la globalización   35
neoliberal se basa en la explotación, el despojo, el desprecio y la represión a los que no se dejan. O sea igual que antes, pero ahora globalizado, mundial.
    Pero no es tan fácil para la globalización neoliberal, porque los explotados de cada país pues no se conforman y no dicen que ya ni modo, sino que se rebelan; y los que sobran y estorban pues se resisten y no se dejan ser eliminados. Y entonces   40
por eso vemos que en todo el mundo los que están jodidos se hacen resistencias para no dejarse, o sea que se rebelan, y no sólo en un país sino que donde quiera abundan, o sea que, así como hay una globalización neoliberal, hay una globalización de la rebeldía.

(Ejército Zapatista de Liberación Nacional 2005a)

Target text

Sixth Declaration of the Selva Lacandona
Zapatista Army of National Liberation

Now we are going to explain to you how we, the zapatistas, see what is going on in
the world. We see that capitalism is the strongest right now. Capitalism is a social
system, a way in which a society goes about organizing things and people, and who   5
has and who has not, and who gives orders and who obeys. In capitalism, there are
some people who have money, or capital, and factories and stores and fields and many
things, and there are others who have nothing but their strength and knowledge in order
to work. In capitalism, those who have money and things give the orders, and those
who only have their ability to work obey.   10
    Then capitalism means that there a few who have great wealth, but they did not
win a prize, or find a treasure, or inherited from a parent. They obtained that wealth,
rather, by exploiting the work of the many. So capitalism is based on the exploitation
of the workers, which means they exploit the workers and take out all the profits they
can.   15
    [. . .]
    Capitalism is most interested in merchandise, because when it is bought or sold,
profits are made. And then capitalism turns everything into merchandise, it makes
merchandise of people, of nature, of culture, of history, of conscience. According to
capitalism, everything must be able to be bought and sold. And it hides everything   20
behind the merchandise, so we don't see the exploitation that exists. And then the
merchandise is bought and sold in a market. And the market, in addition to being used
for buying and selling, is also used to hide the exploitation of the workers. In the market,
for example, we see coffee in its little package or its pretty little jar, but we do not see
the campesino who suffered in order to harvest the coffee, and we do not see the coyote 25
who paid him so cheaply for his work, and we do not see the workers in the large
company working their hearts out to package the coffee. Or we see an appliance for
listening to music like cumbias, rancheras or corridos, or whatever, and we see that it
is very good because it has a good sound, but we do not see the worker in the
maquiladora who struggled for many hours, putting the cables and the parts of the   30
appliance together, and they barely paid her a pittance of money, and she lives far
away from work and spends a lot on the trip, and, in addition, she runs the risk of
being kidnapped, raped and killed as happens in Ciudad Juárez in Mexico.
    [. . .]
    Then, in short, the capitalism of global neoliberalism is based on exploitation,   35
plunder, contempt and repression of those who refuse. The same as before, but now
globalized, worldwide.
    But it is not so easy for neoliberal globalization, because the exploited of each
country become discontented, and they will not say well, too bad, instead they rebel.
And those who remain and who are in the way resist, and they don't allow themselves   40
to be eliminated. And that is why we see, all over the world, those who are being
screwed over making resistances, not putting up with it, in other words, they rebel,
and not just in one country but wherever they abound. And so, as there is a neoliberal
globalization, there is a globalization of rebellion.

(Ejército Zapatista de Liberación Nacional 2005b)

5.2   Cultural issues in translation: balancing style and culture-specific information

Assignment

(i)   With particular reference to cultural issues, discuss the strategic problems confronting the translator of the following text, and outline your own strategy for translating it.

(ii)   Produce a TT in English suitable for publication in an English-speaking country (specify which one). Assume that your TT would be a chapter in a book containing an introduction that describes the general context and purpose of the book from which the ST is taken but does not explain all the detailed historical and cultural references in the chapters that follow.

(iii)   Select a few examples from your TT that show your strategy for dealing with cultural issues being put into practice, and compare them with examples produced by other students/groups.

Contextual information

The ST is the beginning of a chapter in *El florido pensil: memoria de la escuela nacionalcatólica* by Andrés Sopeña Monsalve (Barcelona: Crítica, 1994). The book offers a parodic account, from the point of view of a mischievous schoolboy, of the methods and texts used in primary schools in Franco's Spain. It includes an introduction by a historian describing the religious and political indoctrination supervised by the Catholic Church and the Falange, and confirming the accuracy of Sopeña Monsalve's parody. There has also been a hugely successful theatrical adaptation (1997) and a film version (2002, directed by Juan José Porto). The title of this chapter is based on the child's misunderstanding of a line from the Falange's wartime anthem 'Cara al sol':

> Cara al sol con la camisa nueva
> que tú bordaste rojo ayer,
> me hallará la muerte si me lleva
> y no te vuelvo a ver.

> Formaré junto a los compañeros
> que hacen guardia sobre los luceros,
> impasible el ademán,
> y están presentes en nuestro afán.

Source text

Imposible el alemán

La última lección de la Historia de España trataba del Alzamiento Nacional, otra guerra. Esta vez era porque: 'En España había ya muchos

socialistas y muchos masones y muy poco temor de Dios. Los socialistas
excitaban a los pobres contra los ricos. Los masones querían que hubiera   5
revolución' (Serrano de Haro, *Yo soy español*, p. 83). Yo le tuve que
explicar al Briones que masones eran los que iban con las masas, que es
que no se entera de nada. Y a esta gente, por lo visto, lo que le pasaba es
que estaban envenenados por lecturas perniciosas y por eso renegaban de
su Patria. El Ruiz lleva una lectura perniciosa de esas en la cartera, y la   10
enseña si le das una perra gorda; pero ninguno de los que la ha visto
reniega. Claro que otro efecto de esas lecturas es que olvidas la religión
sacrosanta, y eso sí pasa mucho, la verdad; que ahora mismo, por ejemplo,
no recuerdo la diferencia entre Bienaventuranzas y Dones, que con unos
obrabas con facilidad y expedición, pero no caigo con cuál. Con las   15
mismas, el rey cogía y se marchaba para que tuviésemos la fiesta en paz,
que ganó las elecciones por veintidós mil a cinco mil, pero fue una última
generosidad de la monarquía; y las calles se llenaban de camiones llenos
de mujeres alegres y de malos estudiantes, que encima que no estudian
se montan en camión. Y cantaban coplas chabacanas. Los socialistas,   20
los masones, los separatistas, las mujeres alegres y los estudiantes eran
un puñado de infames. Y los mineros revolucionarios de Asturias, que
también salían.

Pero esta vez no ponía que la culpa era de Inglaterra, que vete tú a
saber . . .   25

> Rusia había soñado con clavar la hoz ensangrentada de su emblema
> en este hermoso pedazo de Europa, y todas las masas comunistas y
> socialistas de la tierra, unidas con masones y judíos, anhelaban
> triunfar en España, tomándola como peldaño de oro para triunfar en
> el mundo (Serrano de Haro, *España es así*, p. 289).   30

Y todos juntos, querían acabar con el respeto de los hijos a los padres,
con la unidad de la Patria y con la propiedad, oye. Lo cual que mataron
a José Antonio, que con verbo profético iluminaba con luces de Imperio
a una Patria en trance de ruina; que los verbos proféticos no los hemos
dado todavía, que yo recuerde. Y a Calvo Sotelo también lo mataban, que   35
era un genial estadista y protomártir que dirigía enérgicos apóstrofes al
Gobierno y debió de darle a alguien. Además querían imponer una
bandera que no era la roja y gualda por la que habían muerto los héroes,
fíjate qué brutos, que eso es como cambiar de madre.

(Sopeña Monsalve 1994: 197–8)

6   The formal properties of texts

Phonic, graphic and prosodic issues

Chapters 6 to 11 focus more concretely on the ST as a linguistic object that uses particular forms of language in order to achieve particular effects. Any text is the product of a series of choices made at every level, from the smallest linguistic units – individual speech-sounds or letters – to the largest – distinct textual genres. All the points of detail, no matter how large or small, where a text could have been different (that is, where it could have been *another* text) can be designated as **textual variables**: the form of a parliamentary speech rather than that of a marketing presentation; an allusion to the Bible instead of a quotation from Shakespeare; the Spanish preterite tense rather than the imperfect; a colloquial term preferred to a more formal one; a question mark where there might have been an exclamation mark (compare 'Was he drinking?' and 'Was he drinking!'); or differences signalled by a single letter or change of intonation or stress ('a French teacher' – 'un profesor francés' or 'un profesor de francés'?). A successful translation strategy, having established the generic characteristics of the ST and assessed its cultural implications, must be based upon pinning down as precisely as possible what the textual variables are and how they are designed to achieve their effects on SL readers or listeners. Identification of the relative importance of each of the different formal properties of the ST then enables the setting of priorities for translation, informed by an understanding of the different linguistic resources available in the source and target languages.

The translator's aim is not necessarily to find equivalent linguistic forms in the TL but to achieve comparable effects, and where there is a gap between these objectives, the most effective compensation strategies will often be those that focus on the kind of process at work in the ST rather than on the particular linguistic features that generate it. An effect created in the ST by a particular kind of textual variable may be reproduced by means of a different kind of textual variable in the TT. A ST may be characterized, for example, by the repetition of certain sounds: even if the same speech-sounds exist in the phonological system of the TL, reproducing the structural effect of repetition may be more important than retaining those particular sounds. If a ST makes conspicuous use of certain syntactical or morphological features, precise analysis of the function of those features within the ST should lead to the identification of the most appropriate TL structures to fulfil comparable functions within the TT (for example, passive constructions in English to replace pronominal verb forms in Spanish). Some of the ST features that fall prey to translation loss may not be significant enough as ST variables to be worth the effort of compensation. It is, therefore, excellent strategy to decide which of the textual variables are indispensable, and which can be ignored, for the purpose of formulating a good TT. In general, as we shall see, the more prominently a particular textual variable contributes to triggering effects and meanings in a text, and the more it coincides in this with other textual variables in conveying related meanings and effects, the more important it is.

In order to assess textual variables in a systematic way, one can usefully turn to some of the fundamental organizational principles of linguistics. There is no need here for a detailed incursion into linguistic theory, but linguistics does offer a systematic, hierarchically ordered series of levels on which the formal properties of texts can be located for the purposes of a methodical discussion. Taking the linguistic levels one at a time has two main advantages. First, looking at textual variables on an organized series of isolated levels enables one to see which textual variables are important in the ST and which are less important. Second, one can assess a TT, whether one's own or somebody else's, by isolating and comparing the formal variables of both ST and TT. This enables the translator to identify what textual variables of the ST are absent from the TT, and vice versa. That is, although translation loss is by definition not ultimately quantifiable, it is possible to make a relatively precise accounting of translation losses on each level. This also permits a more self-aware and methodical way of evaluating TTs and of reducing details of translation loss.

Conventional analysis of the components of language organizes them into four basic levels as follows, in general working from the smallest unit up to the largest but recognizing that the four levels are always interconnected and influence one another:

1 *Speech-sounds and the graphs (written symbols) that represent them in written texts.* Phonology describes not only the characteristics of individual speech-sounds but also each language's distinctive system for contrasting and combining sounds to produce meaning, using the concept of the phoneme to pinpoint the ways in which certain differences are significant and others are insignificant in a given language. For example, English distinguishes consistently between the bilabial sound written **b** and the labiodental sound written **v** ('bat' and 'vat' are always recognized as different words), so these constitute two distinct phonemes, /b/ and /v/. In most varieties of Spanish, on the other hand, the graphs **b** and **v** represent the same phoneme, pronounced slightly differently according to the linguistic context: either a plosive [b] (as in 'Bien, gracias' or 'Voy a cantar') or a fricative [β] (as in 'Está bien' or 'Yo voy a cantar'). Phonology also works with larger units of analysis, all of which function in different ways in different languages: the grouping of sounds into

syllables; breath-groups formed by sequences of syllables separated by pauses; variations of pitch and intonation, and patterns of stress. Some of these features of spoken language are marked in written text by means of punctuation, diacritics (accents and other marks showing variations and nuances of pronunciation) and text formatting (for instance, italics to indicate emphasis).

2   *Words and the morphemes of which they are composed.* A word has both a lexical function (as the basic unit of meaning) and a grammatical one (playing a particular structural role in relation to other words). Individual morphemes also carry lexical and grammatical information but do not stand on their own as independent units. For example, the word 'proponíamos' consists of four morphemes: the root *pon* (expressing the basic idea of putting), modified by the prefix *pro* ('forward') and the conjugational suffixes *ía* (indicating past tense, imperfective) and *mos* (third person plural). Semantics refers to the production of meaning in language, focusing primarily on words as signs but never considering them in isolation, since every time a word is used its precise meaning is conditioned by its relationship to the other words around it, to the whole text or utterance in which it appears, and to the social context in which it is used. That is, a sign has no fixed or inherent meaning but is defined by its difference from other signs, and each language maps out those semantic differences in its own way. For instance, English usually distinguishes clearly between 'city', 'town' and 'village', primarily with reference to size. In Spanish, on the other hand, 'ciudad' can refer to anything from a small town up to the largest city, while 'pueblo' tends to have a narrower meaning comparable to 'village' (and 'aldea' is a very small village, corresponding roughly to 'hamlet'). Each language also attaches different figurative meanings and connotations to its respective terms.

3   *Sentences.* Strictly speaking, a sentence is a group of words that forms a single grammatically complete structure (a statement, question or instruction) comprising a subject (someone or something that does or is something) and a predicate (what the subject does or is). It may consist of a single word – 'Go!' or 'Hablaron', in both of which the subject is implied in the morphology of the verb – or any number of words grouped into interconnected phrases and clauses. Of course, it is perfectly possible in any language to make meaningful utterances that do not conform to this strict definition, but the concept of the logically complete sentence is a fundamental organizational principle of language. Syntax describes the arrangement of words into sentences and the rules operating in each language to govern the relationships between sentence components. It focuses on factors such as word order; the marking of the functions of subject, direct object and indirect object; the expression of verbal tense and mood, and the embedding of subordinate clauses within a compound sentence. An understanding of the different ways in which these structural features are articulated in the languages with which a translator is working is crucial to the accurate analysis of STs and the productive formulation of

translation strategies. In written texts, syntax is reinforced by punctuation, which clarifies groupings of words and phrases and marks the ends of sentences and paragraphs.

4 *Discourse.* In its basic linguistic sense, a **discourse** is a collection of sentences or utterances forming a complete text: a conversation, a speech, a letter, an instruction leaflet, an advertisement, a poem, a novel. Analysis at this level is partly syntactical, focusing on how sentences are combined and linked to one another and how textual **cohesion** is achieved. Cohesion refers to the transparent linking of sentences and larger sections of text by the apt deployment of explicit discourse connectors like 'then', 'so', 'however' and so on, and by the appropriate use of **anaphoric** elements (expressions referring back to something already mentioned – 'this', 'she', 'the first one'). Discourse connectors need careful attention in translating, not just because they are more liberally used in some languages than in others, but because they can be *faux amis* (for instance, 'en absoluto', often wrongly rendered as 'absolutely' where the appropriate rendering would be 'not at all'). The term 'syntax' can also be applied to the larger-scale organization of a text into paragraphs, chapters or sections, as well as to the relationship between different kinds of textual components – for example, between the slogan, image and body text of an advertisement. The overall syntactical and semantic structure of a written text is reinforced graphically by the layout of text on the page, the use of different font designs and sizes, and the combination of text with other visual elements.

Discourse analysis also tends to take account of the pragmatic dimension of the use of language: the relationship between, on the one hand, the form of a text and, on the other, the intentions of its producer, its purpose within a given situation or context, and the social and cultural conditions influencing its production. **Pragmatics** is concerned with the conventions followed by speakers and writers in order to carry out particular kinds of communicative acts, especially those which do not have a referential function (that is, their primary purpose is not to convey information). The most widely used classification of these non-referential functions of language is Roman Jakobson's (1960): **expressive**, conveying the feelings of the speaker ('I don't believe it!'); **conative**, aiming to get the listener to do something ('Do what you're told'); **phatic**, helping to maintain the communicative and emotional relationship between speaker and listener ('Know what I mean?'); **metalingual**, referring to language itself ('That's an interesting way of putting it'); and **poetic**, focusing on the formal qualities of the language being used, more or less independently of any referential or other function ('Hey diddle diddle, the cat and the fiddle'). Any particular piece of discourse may fulfil more than one of these functions at the same time. An emphasis on pragmatics can be useful in linking formal issues with cultural ones, and in ensuring that language is seen not as an abstract system but as an instrument of communication fine-tuned by its users according to their purposes and the circumstances in which they are using it. A translator's failure to recognize the pragmatic functions of a phrase, sentence or complete discourse within the SL culture is likely to result in literal translation of the ST where a communicative approach would be more productive. For example, the Spanish expression 'oye' is hardly ever used with real imperative force (the conative function of telling someone to hear something) but tends to be phatic, for the purpose of attracting or refocusing attention ('Oye, Daniel, ¿por qué no me contestas?'), or, combined with an expressive element, of signalling annoyance at the direction an exchange is taking ('Oye, no te me pongas así'): in both cases, the most suitable phatic expression in English is likely to be 'Hey', though various alternatives might be considered for the second ('Whoa', 'Hang on', 'Look').

Finally, the translator's analysis of a ST and planning of a TT need to take into account overall textual **coherence**. Coherence is a more difficult concept than cohesion, because it is, by definition, not explicitly marked in a text, but is rather a question of tacit thematic and intentional development running through the text, the product of a combination of syntax, semantics and pragmatics. In the text used for Practical 6.2 ('Himno', p. 109), cohesion is marked largely by connectors with a simple narrative function ('y', 'entonces', 'más tarde'), together with anaphoric elements to identify who is doing what ('el de la máquina', 'este mozo', 'éste', 'él'). The overall coherence is reinforced by the interweaving of two extended metaphors, one musical and the other military, as well as the emphasis on phonic effects and an ironic contrast of styles. The first paragraph, consisting of four unconnected sentences, is deliberately undermarked for cohesion but creates coherence by building up a series of elements that link noise and patriotic fervour.

This chapter deals with Spanish–English translation issues related primarily to the first of the categories set out above. In a sense, this is the most basic level of textual variables, referring to the smallest units of structure – individual sounds and letters. As we have seen, though, phonological and graphical considerations also come into play at word, sentence and discourse levels. The discussion examines two kinds of translation issue: first, those arising from phonic and graphic particularities of STs, and second, those concerned with rhythmic features.

Phonic/graphic issues

Taking a text on the phonic/graphic level means looking at it as a sequence of sound segments (phonemes) if it is an oral text, or as a sequence of letters (graphemes) if it is a written one. Although phonemes and graphemes function in different ways, they can be considered as being situated on the same level of textual variables. To help keep this in mind, we shall refer to the 'phonic/graphic level' regardless of whether the text in question is an oral one or a written one.

Every text is a unique configuration of phonemes or graphemes structured according to the specific phonological or orthographical system of a particular language. This is why, in general, no text in a given language can reproduce exactly the same sequence of sound segments or letters as any text in another language. Occasional coincidences apart (which may be cited as curiosities, such as the sequence 'I VITELLI DEI ROMANI SONO BELLI', which can be read alternatively, and with two completely different meanings, in either Latin or Italian, as 'Go, Vitellus, to the martial sound of the god of Rome' or as 'the calves of the Romans are beautiful', respectively), an ST and a corresponding TT will always consist of markedly different sequences. This always and automatically constitutes a source of translation loss. The real question for the translator, however, is whether this loss matters at all. Could we not simply put it down as a necessary consequence of the transition from one language to another, and forget about it?

The suggestion that the translator has no need to pay attention to the specific sound/letter sequences in texts echoes Lewis Carroll's jocular translation maxim: 'Take care of the sense and the sounds will take care of themselves.' However, we should argue that the possibility of prioritizing the recreation of phonic/graphic effects of the ST, even to the detriment of the sense, should not be rejected out of hand. Some texts, such as the extract from Valenzuela's *La cola del lagaritijo* discussed in Chapter 3, make significant and self-conscious use of patterns of phonic/graphic variables to create special effects that reinforce semantic and syntactical features, and would lose much of their point (and meaning) if deprived of these properties when translated. Poetic texts contain obvious examples, but phonic/graphic effects may also play a significant role in non-literary text types – advertisements or newspaper headlines, for example.

The simplest example of a special phonic effect is **onomatopoeia**. Onomatopoeia is either directly iconic – that is, the phonic form of a word impressionistically imitates a sound which is the referent of the word ('pop', 'splash') – or iconically motivated – that is, the phonic form of the word imitates a sound associated with the referent of the word (for example, 'cuckoo'). The apparently obvious correspondence between the form of such words and their meaning is not, however, natural or universal but dependent upon cultural conventions and the phonological system of each language. Neither the initial combination 'spl' nor the final 'sh' of 'splash' is pronounceable within the normal phonological parameters of Spanish; the closest workable approximation might be 'esplás', but this is not used to represent the sound of something falling into a liquid (this is usually done with '¡zas!' or '¡plaf!'). In fact, cross-cultural variations in onomatopoeia are common and onomatopoeic words in a SL often do not have one-to-one TL counterparts. Verbal representations of sounds made by animals, for instance, can vary markedly between one language and another: while the sound made by a cat is almost universally rendered as something close to 'miaow' (UK spelling), 'meow' (US spelling) or 'miau' (Spanish), a dog goes either 'bow-wow' or 'woof' in English but 'guau' in Spanish and 'гав гав' ('gav gav') in Russian, and only in English does a cock go 'cock-a-doodle-do' ('quiquiriquí' in Spanish).

Especially if it has a thematically important function, onomatopoeia may require careful choice between various alternatives in translation. When the form and the conventional semantic function of an onomatopoeic word more or less coincide across the two languages, the opportunity to reduce translation loss to a minimum is likely to be irresistible: 'boom!' in English can be translated as '¡bum!' in Spanish (though the difference between the long English vowel sound and the short Spanish one prevents a precise match). On the other hand, the form '¡pum!' is probably used more often in Spanish to represent the sound of an explosion or loud impact, overlapping with the sharper, less resonant kind of sound rendered in English with 'bang!' and with the lighter impact of 'pop!'. '¡Zas!' is used very frequently in Spanish to represent a variety of sudden, unexpected, sharp or violent sounds or occurrences, corresponding to 'bang!', 'wham!', 'whack!', 'splash!', 'smack!', 'whoa!', or even 'hey presto!', as in 'Y ¡zas! por arte de magia desapareció todo'. The translator needs, therefore, to compare the range of options available in the SL and the TL, assess to what extent they coincide, and weigh up the effect that different choices may produce in the TT.

The examples above are onomatopoeia at its most basic: sound-imitative interjections, without a real syntactical function. In English, most interjections of this kind can be turned very easily into nouns or verbs: to pop, a splash, to miaow, a bang. In Spanish, on the other hand, it is not so easy to retain the direct onomatopoeic effect in nouns and verbs. Consider, for example, these three alternative sentences in English: 'And suddenly, splash, someone fell into the pool'; 'And suddenly there was a splash as someone fell into the pool'; 'And suddenly someone splashed into the pool'. The first can easily be rendered in Spanish as 'Y de pronto, ¡zas! cayó alguien en la piscina', whereas the second and third occasion greater translation loss: 'Y de pronto se oyó el ruido de alguien que caía en la piscina'; 'Y de pronto cayó alguien ruidosamente en la piscina' or 'Y de pronto se oyó a alguien caer ruidosamente en la piscina'. The scope for investing actions with an onomatopoeic quality in English by means of phrasal verbs is a very useful resource for the translator: 'se estrelló contra el muro' could be translated as 'smashed/crashed/slammed/whacked into the wall'.

Onomatopoeia may become a translation problem when the nearest semantic counterparts to an onomatopoeic SL word in the TL are not onomatopoeic. For instance, English 'peewit' is onomatopoeic, but its Spanish rendering as 'avefría' is clearly not. Conversely, Spanish 'búho' has an onomatopoeic quality, but its English rendering 'long-eared owl' does not. 'Cuclillo' is an indirectly onomatopoeic noun; translating it as 'cuckoo' involves very little translation loss. Translating 'zumbador' (in a Central American context) as 'humming-bird', on the other hand, involves a greater degree of phonic translation loss, which could be significant in certain contexts. To the extent that the very fact of onomatopoeia is an effect contributing to textual meaning, its loss in the TT is a translation loss that the translator may have reason to regret.

Let us consider a more extended example of translation issues arising at the phonic level. The following extract from a book offering advice to parents discusses the development of a baby's awareness of different sounds and consequently pays attention to certain onomatopoeic qualities of its own language:

> El taconeo de mamá precede a mamá; los pasos de papá son diferentes. El bebé dispone de mucho tiempo para aprender los sonidos que le resultan familiares, desde el chorro de agua con que se entibia el biberón hasta el ruido que hace la puerta cuando llega papá. Cuando hace buen tiempo, podemos aprovechar el paseo por el parque para hacerle escuchar el trino de los pájaros, el parloteo de la gente o la algarabía de los niños que juegan.
>
> (Penella 1995: 138–9)

'Taconeo', carefully contrasted with the more neutral 'pasos', neatly combines the reference to high heels with the sound that they make on a hard floor in a way that cannot be reproduced so economically in English. Translating the first sentence as 'Mum's footsteps precede the arrival of Mum; Dad's are different' would be semantically adequate but the loss of the phonic effect of 'taconeo' is serious. The effect can be retained by means of expansion: 'The clicking of Mum's heels precedes the arrival of Mum; Dad's footsteps sound different' (although the translator will at the same time have to make a decision about whether it is appropriate to transfer into the TT the cultural assumptions about women wearing high heels and babies' cots being in rooms with hard floors). In the third sentence of the extract, the author has deliberately chosen 'trino' rather than 'canto', 'parloteo' rather than 'hablar', and 'algarabía' rather than 'ruido' in order to convey something of the acoustic quality of the sounds being referred to. Consequently, 'twittering' or 'chir-rupping', 'chattering' or 'chit-chat', and 'happy hubbub' might be the best lexical choices.

Even something as apparently simple as onomatopoeia, then, may need careful attention in translating. Translation problems at this level highlight in miniature some of the key issues encountered at all textual levels: the importance of not taking for granted what may appear to be close equivalences between SL and TL, and the need to analyse as fully as possible the nature and function of a given element of a ST in relation to its linguistic and cultural contexts, in order to find a TT element that reproduces (as far as possible) its most important and relevant feature. The same is true, in fact, of any type of word-play that hinges on phonic/graphic similarities between expressions with different meanings. For example, the more obviously a pun or a spoonerism is not accidental or incidental in the ST, the more it is in need of explicit recognition in the process of translation. A major strategic decision will then be whether to seek appropriate puns or spoonerisms for the TT, or whether to resort to some form of compensation.

The most common way in which phonic/graphic special effects acquire textual significance is by forming patterns of repetition or contrast, especially alliteration, assonance and rhyme, thus generating sound symbolism – the reinforcement of the literal sense and the mood of a text by the creation of a pattern in its phonic qualities. Alliteration can be defined as the recurrence of the same sound/letter or sound/letter cluster at the beginning of adjacent words (for example, 'many mighty midgets'), and assonance as the recurrence within adjacent words of the same sound/letter or sound/letter cluster (for example, 'their crafty history-master's bathtub'). Assonantal rhyme is frequently used in Spanish verse, comprising a match of vowel sounds at the ends of lines: 'hermano . . . caballos . . . terminado'. It is important to remember a vital difference between alliteration and assonance on the one hand and onomatopoeia on the other: alliteration and assonance do not involve an imitation of non-speech sounds, unless they happen to coincide with onomatopoeia, as would be the case in 'ten tall clocks tock'.

Effects of sound symbolism may depend to a large extent on the subjective response of the reader or listener and may be overlooked by the casual or unsophisticated reader. The important thing to keep in mind is that, onomatopoeia aside, the sound-symbolic effect of words is not intrinsic to them, but operates in conjunction with their literal and connotative meanings in the context. For example, persistent repetition of the sound [1] does not, in and of itself, suggest a sudden burst of spiritual illumination, or a flood of bright daylight, or a cacophony of voices instrumental in ridiculing petty officialdom. Yet it may be said to suggest the first of these things in the opening lines of Jorge Guillén's *Cántico*:

> (El alma vuelve al cuerpo,
> Se dirige a los ojos
> Y choca.) – ¡Luz! Me invade . . .
>   (Guillén 1950: 16)

It may be said to connote the second in the opening lines of Jorge Guillén's 'Del alba a la aurora':

> ¿Luz de luna? No es la luna
> Quien va azulando la calle . . .
>   (Guillén 1950: 460)

And it has been noted as carrying the third set of connotations in the same author's 'Coro de burocracia':

> La ley levanta
> Frente al oficial cacumen
> La sacrosanta

Letra que todos consumen.
    (Guillén 1968: 576)

In each case, [1] draws its suggestive power from four things in particular: first, the lexical meanings of the words in which it occurs; second, the lexical meanings of the words associated with those in which it occurs; third, other phonetic qualities of both those groups of words; and, fourth, the many other types of connotative meaning at work in these texts, as in any other. (We shall discuss connotative meaning as such in Chapter 9.)

In the last of these examples, sound symbolism clearly has such an important textual role that to translate the texts without some attempt at producing appropriate sound-symbolic effects in the TT would be to incur severe translation loss. The more a text depends for its very existence on the interplay of onomatopoeia, alliteration and assonance, the more true this is – and the more difficult the translator's task becomes, because, as our examples show, sound symbolism is not only largely language-specific, but a very subjective matter as well.

By far the most widespread textual effects arising from the use of phonic/graphic variables involve the exploitation of recurrences. Apart from alliteration and assonance, rhyme is the most obvious example. When such recurrences are organized into recognizable patterns on a large scale, for example in a regularly repeated rhyme scheme, they are clearly not accidental or incidental. At this point, the translator is forced to take the resulting phonic/graphic special effects into serious consideration. However, this does not mean that one is obliged, or even well advised, to reproduce the exact patterns of recurrence found in the ST. In fact, opinions are divided among translators of verse about the extent to which even such obvious devices as rhyme scheme should be reproduced in the TT. In English, for example, blank verse is a widespread form that has long had at least as high a prestige as rhyming verse, so that there is often a case for translating rhyming STs from other languages into blank verse in English. This is a particularly attractive option when translating verse from Spanish, in which most words end in an open syllable (consonant+vowel) and are stressed on the penultimate syllable, into English, which has many more closed syllables (consonant + vowel + consonant) and words stressed on the last syllable, often making rhyme feel more conspicuous or even clumsy by comparison. In the end, this is a decision for individual translators to make in individual cases; often the genre of the ST and the availability of TL genres as 'models' will be a crucial factor in the decision.

We can conclude so far that the phonic/graphic level of textual variables *may* merit being given priority by the translator, and that translation losses on this level *may* be serious. There is no suggestion here that attention to sounds should be to the detriment of sense; on the contrary, it is where ignoring the contribution of phonic/graphic features would damage the sense of the text that they are considered important. There is, however, a style of translation that actually more or less reverses the maxim quoted from Lewis Carroll; that is, it concentrates on taking care of the sounds and allows the sense to emerge as a kind of vaguely suggested impression. This technique is generally known as **phonemic translation**. An extraordinary example, whose authors seem to take their method perfectly seriously, is a translation of Catullus's poetry by Celia and Louis Zukovsky. Here is part of one poem, followed by (i) the phonemic translation and (ii) a literal prose translation:

> Ille mi par esse deo videtur,
> Ille, si fas est, superare divos,
> qui sedens adversus identidem te
> spectat et audit
> dulce ridentem, misero quod omnis
> eripit sensus mihi; [. . .]

> (i) He'll hie me, par *is* he? the God divide her,
> he'll hie, see fastest, superior deity,
> quiz – sitting adverse identity – mate, in-
> spect it and audit –
> you'll care ridden then, misery holds omens,
> air rip the senses from me; [. . .]
>   (Catullus 1969, poem 51)

> (ii) He seems to me to be equal to a god, he seems to me, if it is lawful, to surpass the gods, who, sitting opposite to you, keeps looking at you and hearing you sweetly laugh; but this tears away all my senses, wretch that I am.

We shall not dwell on this example, beyond saying that it perfectly illustrates the technique of phonemic translation: to imitate as closely as possible the actual phonic sequence of the ST, while suggesting in a vague and impressionistic way something of its literal content.

As a matter of fact, it is difficult, if not impossible, for a TT to retain a close similarity to the actual phonic sequences of the ST and still retain anything more than a tenuous connection with any kind of coherent meaning, let alone the meaning of the ST. This difficulty is ensured by the classic 'arbitrariness' of languages, not to mention the language-specific and contextual factors which, as we have seen in discussing onomatopoeia, alliteration and assonance, make phonic effect such a relative and subjective matter.

Entertaining illustrations of the way phonic imitation in a TT can render the sense of the ST unrecognizable are Van Rooten's *Mots d'heures: gousses, rames (Mother Goose Rhymes!)* and John Hulme's *Mörder Guss Reims*, which consist in a playful imitation of English nursery rhymes in French and in German, respectively. Here, for example, the text of 'Humpty-Dumpty' is reproduced in French as:

Un petit d'un petit
S'étonne aux Halles,
Un petit d'un petit
Ah! degrés te fallent.
(Van Rooten 1968, poem 1)

and in German as 'Um die Dumm' die Saturn Aval;/ Um die Dumm' die Ader Grät' fahl' (Hulme 1981: 4). While providing an entertaining pastiche, for which we have unfortunately found no exact counterpart in Spanish (though there have been various attempts to translate 'Humpty Dumpty' into Spanish), *Mots d'heures: gousses, rames* and *Mörder Guss Reims* do not really count as phonemic translation proper: there is no attempt at all to render anything of the literal meaning of the ST. What we have here is a form of humorous pastiche which consists in the cross-linguistic phonic imitation of a well-known text.

Although phonemic translation as a consistent overall strategy can rarely be adopted with any seriousness, there are texts that are not intended to be sensible in the original and which qualify as suitable objects for a degree of phonemic translation. Nonsense rhymes, such as Lewis Carroll's 'Jabberwocky', are a good example. Here, by way of illustration, is the first stanza of 'Jabberwocky' followed by two of the many versions that exist in Spanish:

'Twas brillig, and the slithy toves
Did gyre and gimble in the wabe;
All mimsy were the borogoves,
And the mome raths outgrabe.
(Carroll 1954: 129)

GALIMATAZO (Jaime de Ojeda)

Brillaba, brumeando negro, el sol;
agiliscosos giroscaban los limazones
banerrando por las váparas lejanas;
mimosos se fruncían los borogobios
mientras el momio rantas murgiflaba.
(Carroll 1973: 9)

BEMBOGUABA (Enrique Sacerio-Garí)

Jamasardecía y las inquiejosas tojías
girascaban y garrateaban en las guaguanturas.
Tan misefuácatas estaban las cototías
y las jicotumbas con sus chilladuras.
(Sacerio-Garí 2006)

On reading the poem, Alice remarks astutely: 'Somehow it seems to fill my head with ideas – only I don't exactly know what they are!' (Carroll 1954: 130).

The explanations offered later by Humpty Dumpty offer her some rational clues ('slithy' being a combination of 'lithe' and 'slimy') but essentially emphasize subjective interpretation and semantic arbitrariness, encouraging her to make up her own meanings for the words according to how they sound and what lexical associations they suggest to her. The translator in this case is free, like Humpty Dumpty, to make words mean whatever he wants – to show them who is master. However, a clearly defined translation strategy based on systematic analysis of the ST is just as necessary here as for a more serious text, since the aim should be not to generate entirely meaningless *galimatías* (gibberish) but to fill TL readers' heads with possible meanings and associations, even if they are not sure exactly what they are.

Both Spanish versions incorporate a range of compensation manoeuvres to deal with the challenges of Carroll's inventiveness and allusiveness, making use of 'portmanteau' coinings and vaguely onomatopoeic effects comparable to those in the original, but with greater dependence on alliteration and assonance while creating a more self-consciously literary style with a prolifera-tion of polysyllabic words and longer lines of verse. De Ojeda's language is closer to recognizable words than either Carroll's or Sacerio-Garí's, achieving some of its effects by combining terms in incongruous ways ('mimosos se fruncían'). Sacerio-Garí's is an explicitly Cuban version, drawing on an exotic range of colloquial vocabulary from Cuba and other parts of Latin America: *bembo/bemba* (thick lips or snout), *guagua* (bus or baby, according to the region), *fuácata* (an onomatopoeic Cuban interjection similar to 'whack!' or 'kapow!'), *cototo* (big, difficult, or as a noun, a bruise or bump on the head) and *jicote* (a large wasp found in Central America, or its nest). Sacerio-Garí may even have picked up on the Germanic roots of some of Carroll's words: 'jicotumbas' seems to echo both 'wabe' (*Wabe* means 'honeycomb' in German) and 'outgrabe' (*ausgraben* is 'to dig up, excavate, disinter').

Finally, though they are less common than sound symbolism, special effects may also be contrived through the spatial layout of written texts. Such cases illustrate the potential importance of specifically graphic textual variables. An obvious example is the acrostic, a text in which, say, reading the first letter of each line spells out, vertically, a hidden word. Another is concrete poetry, where the visual form of the text is used to convey meaning. A simple example of this is the calligram 'Cabellera' by Guillermo de Torre (1900–71), see Figure 6.1 on p. 101.

While the graphic layout of this poem does not in itself pose a translation problem, the relationship between the graphic, phonic and semantic levels in such a text needs to be carefully evaluated. The example that appears in *Alice's Adventures in Wonderland* (the poem about the mouse and the cat, laid out to form a long, winding, tapering shape) would require greater ingenuity on the part of a translator, since its inclusion in the narrative is prompted by Alice's confusion of 'tale' with 'tail'. Just as onomatopoeia is iconic phonically, these texts, like much concrete poetry, are iconic graphically, imitating visually what they describe referentially.

Figure 6.1 'Cabellera' by Guillermo de Torre
Source: González Muela and Rozas 1986: 353

Prosodic issues

We have seen that on the phonic/graphic level, translators often have to pay special attention to patterns of recurrence in a text. The same is true on the **prosodic level**, which considers utterances as metrically structured stretches of speech, within which syllables have varying degrees of prominence according to stress and emphasis, varying melodic qualities in terms of pitch modulation, and differing qualities of rhythm, length and tempo. Groups of syllables may, on this level, form contrastive prosodic patterns (for example, the alternation of a short, staccato, fast section with a long, slow, smooth one), or recurrent ones, or both.

In texts not designed to be read aloud, such prosodic patterns, if they are discernible at all, are relatively unlikely to have any textual importance. However, in texts intended for oral performance (or intended to evoke oral performance), such as plays, speeches, poetry or songs, prosodic features can have a considerable theme-reinforcing and mood-creating function. In texts where prosodic special effects play a vital role, the translator may have to pay special attention to the prosodic level of the TT. A humorous example is found in Goscinny and Uderzo (1965), where an Alexandrian says 'Je suis, mon cher ami, très heureux de te voir', and this flowery greeting, which has a metrical pattern common in the classical alexandrine (2 + 4 / 3 + 3 syllables), is explained by someone else with the punning observation 'C'est un Alexandrin' (He's an Alexandrian/That's an alexandrine).

In most cases, it is not possible to construct a TT that both sounds natural in the TL and reproduces in exact detail the metrical structure of the ST. This is because languages often function in fundamentally different ways from one another on the prosodic level, just as they do on the phonic/graphic level. In this respect translating between Spanish and English is inevitably problematic, since the prosodic structures of the two languages are substantially different. The characteristic rhythm of English is often described as 'stress-timed' in contrast to the more 'syllable-timed' rhythm of Spanish: that is, English tends to sound more varied in terms of stress, with a greater contrast between stressed and unstressed syllables and more compression of the latter, while Spanish sounds more even and regular, with unstressed vowels pronounced in more or less the same way as stressed ones.

In English, patterns of stress are largely unpredictable, distributed idiosyncratically over the syllables of words, with each polysyllabic word having one maximally prominent and a number of less prominent syllables in a certain configuration: for example, the word '^{1}un^{2}na^{1}tu^{1}ral^{0}ly' (the numbers denoting a greater or lesser degree of stress on the syllable to which they are prefixed). This is known as *free word accent*. Only by knowing the word can one be sure what its prosodic pattern is, though this rarely causes comprehension problems as there are few instances of pairs of words distinguished from one another purely by stress.

In modern Spanish, in contrast, the word accent is mostly fixed, generally falling on the penultimate syllable of words ending in a vowel (paroxytone stress – '^{1}tor^{1}ce^{2}du^{1}ra') and the last syllable of words ending in a consonant (oxytone stress – '^{1}ca^{1}pi^{2}tal'). There is, however, an element of free word accent in Spanish, in that there is a fairly large number of words that do not follow the norm: words ending in a vowel but stressed on the last or antepenultimate syllable ('^{1}can^{2}té', '^{2}tó^{1}ni^{1}ca'), and words ending in a consonant but stressed on the penultimate syllable ('^{2}lá^{1}piz'). Departures from the norm are marked with a written accent and can, much more frequently than in English, comprise the difference between otherwise identical words ('ánimo/animo/animó'). These differences between the English and Spanish prosodic systems may in themselves sometimes give rise to translation problems in prose and verse alike. They are not, however, the main source of difficulties in verse translation: these stem rather from the fact that the metrical structure of Spanish verse is strictly syllabic while English verse is constructed out of units ('feet') consisting of two or more syllables each, with particular sequences of stressed and unstressed syllables.

Verse translation

Many students of translation may consider the translation of poetry an esoteric pursuit with little relevance to the real world of practising translators (unless they are planning to carve out a specialized career niche as translators of the lyrics of popular songs). In our view, however, it is worth paying attention to the special challenges of verse translation as a formative exercise because metrically controlled poetic STs offer examples, in a highly condensed, almost abstract form, of the possibilities of the SL being self-consciously explored, stretched and reflected upon. Each poem or song creates its own style and its own unique relationship between its phonic, graphic, semantic, syntactical and discourse dimensions. The translation problems thrown up by special sound effects, inventive metaphor, unfamiliar collocations, deliberate ambiguity and unusual syntax are all conditioned by the fundamental underlying issue of metrical structure, and the difference between Spanish and English versification constitutes a major problem in verse translation. We shall deal here in elementary terms with the basics of the two systems so that they can be compared. Such metrical structure is the main feature of the patterned use of recurrences on the prosodic level. (It does not, however, exhaust the entire field of prosody, since it ignores tempo and melodic pitch, which may also constitute vital textual variables in an oral text.) We shall not discuss free verse, which would need too detailed a study for the purposes of this course. However, in so far as free verse is defined by its difference from fixed form verse, our analysis will help translators isolate the relevant features of STs in free verse.

One of the first strategic decisions to be made about the translation of a text in verse is on the prosodic level: assuming (and this is a big assumption) that the TT is to be in verse, should it attempt to reproduce the metrical structure of the ST? This decision will depend ultimately on the textual function of metre in the ST, on whether creating metric recurrences in the TT would lead to unacceptable translation losses on other levels, and on the purpose of the translation. For some purposes, giving a high priority to the sense of the ST and a low priority to its form may be entirely valid, producing a prose TT that may be either a literal translation of the lexis of the ST or a communicative paraphrase of the translator's interpretation of its overall meaning. A very different approach is to carry out a kind of cultural/generic transposition, giving a high priority to the prosodic level, adapting the content of the ST to fit a metrical form native to the TL culture (for example, turning Spanish *ende-casílabos* into iambic pentameters), and allowing the demands of rhyme to determine lexical and syntactical choices. Between these two extremes there can be a range of compromises – using a regular metre comparable to that of the ST but without reproducing its rhyme scheme, for example; or translating metaphor literally and attempting to reproduce phonic effects directly but within a very different structure of rhythm and rhyme.

In discussing decisions on this level, it is useful to have a basic notation for describing metric structure. For English, there is a well-tried system, which we adopt here. For Spanish, we suggest a simple notation below. The notation brings out clearly and concisely the metric patterns, and the variations in them, which are so fertile a source of special textual effects. Only when these patterns have been identified in a ST, and their effects pinpointed, can the translator begin to face the decision as to what – if any – TL prosodic patterns might be appropriate in the TT. That there will need to be prosodic patterns in the translation of a prosodically patterned ST is usually certain; that they will hardly ever replicate those of the ST is even more certain. The challenge to the translator is to find appropriate compromises and forms of compensation.

Spanish versification

Spanish verse is *syllabic*. That is, the writer does not have to choose among conventional configurations of stressed and unstressed syllables, as is the case in traditional English or German verse. A line of verse in Spanish is defined in terms of the number of syllables it contains, and the pattern of stresses may vary greatly within that framework. However, syllable counting is not an entirely straightforward matter, since one needs to know how to deal with combinations of vowels within and between words. To some extent, the rules by which this is governed reflect the patterns of natural speech, but some aspects are simply conventions that can be manipulated by poets as they please.

Within a word, the basic rule is that **a**, **e** and **o** act as 'strong' vowels that are not normally combined into a single syllable. So 'poeta' and 'maestro' are normally treated as having three syllables: **po/e/ta**, **ma/es/tro**. Just as in rapid speech these words may in practice be pronounced as bisyllabic, it is possible for a poet to treat them, exceptionally, as **poe/ta** and **maes/tro**. This is particularly likely to happen when the two vowels are the same: **le/e/re/mos** > **lee/re/mos**. The phonetically 'close' vowels **i** and **u** are treated as 'weak': that is, they combine with another vowel to form a single syllable (a diphthong). So **tiem/po**, **rei/na**, **fue/go** and **deu/da** are all normally bisyllabic. When **i** and **u** come together, the first is 'weak' and the second 'strong': **ciu/dad**, **cui/da/do**. Again, though, it is possible for poets to override the normal process at times, producing diaeresis (sometimes marked with two dots over the **i** or **u**): **in/sa/cia/ble** > **in/sa/cï/a/ble**. A stressed **i** or **u** in combination with another vowel is treated as 'strong' (and bears a written accent): **ha/cia** has two syllables, **ha/cí/a** has three.

In normal speech, when a word ending in a vowel is followed by a word beginning with a vowel (or **h**, which is not pronounced in modern Spanish), the two vowels are usually elided into a single syllable: the normal pronunciation of 'no está aquí tu hermano' would be represented in phonetic form as **[noes-tá-kí-twer-má-no]**, with what appear to be nine syllables reduced in phonetic reality to six. This process, known in Spanish as *sinalefa*, operates within lines of verse, often even disregarding any punctuation that there may be, though as with the rules applying within words, poets may ignore it in order to produce the required number of syllables or to influence the way a line should be read aloud. *Sinalefa* can be shown in the notation used here with the symbol ‿:

A/quí‿es/tu/ve/ yo/ pues/to	= 7
o/ por/ me/jor/ de/ci/llo	= 7
pre/so‿y/ for/za/do‿y/ so/lo‿en/ tie/rra‿a/je/na	= 11

One further factor affects the syllable count. When the last word of a line has a stressed final syllable (**cor/tés**), an additional syllable is counted, and when the last word is stressed on the antepenultimate syllable (**fo/tó/gra/fo**), one less is counted. This has nothing to do with normal pronunciation of spoken language but is a metrical convention hardly ever broken by poets:

La/ muer/te/ no/ res/pon/dió [+ 1]	= 8
A/mor,/ tus/ fuer/zas/ rí/gi/das [− 1]	= 7

Although lines of Spanish verse can have virtually any number of syllables, certain patterns are more common than others. Lines of eight syllables or less are known as 'versos de arte menor' and have traditionally been considered more appropriate for light, popular subjects and styles. Octosyllabic lines are particularly common, especially in the *romance* form (with assonantal rhyme on even-numbered lines). Lines of more than eight syllables are known as 'versos de arte mayor', often considered more formal or weighty, allowing for more elaborate development of ideas. The eleven-syllable line (hendecasyllable) is the other staple ingredient of Spanish poetry, used in sonnets and a number of other traditional verse-forms, sometimes in com-bination with seven-syllable lines. Hendecasyllables normally conform to a set range of stress patterns, with the first primary stress on the first, second, third or fourth syllable, followed by stresses on the sixth and tenth syllables (with 4–8–10 as an alternative). The Spanish version of the alexandrine usually has fourteen syllables, divided into two hemistichs of seven syllables each with a caesura (a break, often but not necessarily matching a pause when the line is read aloud) in between; the syllable count is carried out for each hemistich independently, applying the rules for the last stressed syllable before the caesura as well as at the end of the line:

Mi/ so/li/lo/quio‿es/ plá/ti/ca [− 1] // co/n es/te/ bue/n a/mi/go = 7 + 7

The rules of scansion should not be seen as some kind of immutable straitjacket, either for the original poet or for the translator. They provide a familiar framework to be used by the poet to achieve a variety of rhythmic effects, and a guide for the reader as to how the lines should be read aloud. Once the rules have been assimilated, it is a fairly easy matter to read quickly through a piece of verse counting the syllables on one's fingers in order to establish first whether it has a regular metrical structure at all, then to determine what that structure is and how it relates to the lexical content and phonic characteristics of the poem. If almost all the lines fit a particular pattern, it will usually turn out that any that appear not to fit will do so if one of the 'tricks' mentioned above is involved: making sure that the line-end rule is applied, diaeresis imposed where there would normally be a diphthong, or a pause resulting in the suppression of *sinalefa*. If a line cannot be made to fit the pattern even when these factors are taken into account, the anomaly may have structural and thematic significance which should be reflected in translation.

English versification

Whereas a line of modern Spanish verse is defined in terms of a syllable count, lines in English verse are conventionally defined in terms of feet. A **foot** is a group of stressed and/or unstressed syllables occurring in a specific order, and a line of traditional verse consists of a fixed (conventional) number of particular feet. Take for example:

⏑   −   ⏑   −   ⏑   −   ⏑   −   ⏑   −

The cur | few tolls | the knell | of par | ting day

This line is a *pentameter:* that is, it consists of five feet. Each of the feet in this case is made up of one unstressed syllable followed by one stressed syllable. A foot of this type is an *iamb,* represented as |⏑ −|. A line consisting of five iambic feet is an iambic pentameter. It is the most common English line, found in the work of great playwrights and poets such as Shakespeare, Milton and Wordsworth.

A line consisting of three iambs is an iambic *trimeter;* one consisting of four iambs is an iambic *tetrameter;* one consisting of six iambs is an iambic *hexameter.* The shorter lines are more usual than the pentameter in songs, ballads and light verse.

Besides the iamb, the commonest other types of feet are:

− ⏑   −   ⏑   − ⏑   −   ⏑

trochee: Present | mirth brings | present | laughter *(trochaic tetrameter)*

⏑ ⏑ −   ⏑   ⏑ −   ⏑   ⏑   −   ⏑ ⏑   −

anapest: With a leap | and a bound | the swift A | napests throng
(anapestic tetrameter)

− ⏑ ⏑   −   ⏑   ⏑   − ⏑   ⏑   − ⏑ ⏑

dactyl: Ever to | come up with | Dactyl tri | syllable *(dactylic tetrameter)*

−   −   −   −   −   −

spondee: Slow spon | dee stalks | strong foot *(spondaic trimeter)*

Naturally, following a single rhythmic pattern without variation would quickly become tedious. Hence the sort of variation typified in lines 1 and 6 of Wordsworth's 'Composed upon Westminster Bridge':

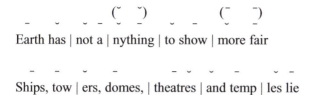

Earth has | not a | nything | to show | more fair

Ships, tow | ers, domes, | theatres | and temp | les lie

Like the rest of the poem, these lines may be described as iambic, because their rhythm is predominantly iambic; but within this overriding pattern there is considerable variation.

One other sort of English metre is worth mentioning, strong-stress metre. This is different from the syllable-and-stress metre described above. Only the stresses count in the scanning, the number of weak syllables being variable. Much modern verse uses this metre, most frequently with four stresses in a line, often in combination with syllable-and-stress metre.

Exact metrical analysis and scansion in English and in Spanish are a more complex and subtle issue than the simple summaries we have given here. However, for the purposes of an introduction to translation methodology, only three things are required: a simple method of identifying and notating rhythmic recurrences and variations; a way of assessing their expressive function in the ST; and a means of deciding, in the light of these things, what TL verse form (if any) to adopt. The main lesson for the translator of Spanish verse into English is not to attempt to reproduce precise numbers of syllables in lines or exact rhyme sequences, but rather to find structural patterns that work according to the conventions of English verse and approximate in some way to the most significant general features and effects of the original. For example, Spanish hendecasyllables with full rhyme may be turned into English iambic pentameter with half rhyme. The way that Spanish alexandrines fall into two balanced or contrasting halves may be reproduced in English alexandrines (usually iambic hexameter with a caesura in the middle). Variations in TT metre (between iambs and trochees, for instance) may be used to reflect other types of variation in the ST (between heptasyllables and hendecasyllables). As always, the success of the product depends crucially upon the accuracy with which the translator analyses the formal characteristics of the ST, assesses their function within the SL culture and identifies a coherent set of priorities to guide the process of translation.

Translators who become proficient enough in these skills to want to specialize in verse translation are recommended to consult the books by Malof (1970) and Navarro Tomás (1991) listed in the References. Walters (2002: 15–17) provides an accessible summary in English of the principles of Spanish versification. On English poetry and metre, see Wolosky (2001).

Practical 6

6.1 The formal properties of texts: onomatopoeia

Assignment

(i)   Working in groups, assess the textual effect of each of the occurrences of 'zas' in the following extracts, which are all taken from the Real Academia Española's online *Corpus de Referencia del Español Actual* (CREA) (at www.rae.es).

(ii)   Find a suitable English equivalent for each occurrence of 'zas'. (There is no need to translate the complete extracts.)

(iii) Review the range of possible uses of the word 'zas'. In your own time, try a search in the CREA for some other onomatopoeic term, such as 'pum'.

Examples

1   Vender medicinas vencidas, narcotráfico, trata de blancas y fabricación de chorizos de carne de gato, perro o burro. ¡Y hasta eventualmente salir victoriosos y transformarse en un zas en inefables miembros de comisiones de alto nivel para investigar nada menos que la corrupción! [Newspaper editorial: *El Salvador Hoy*, 28/02/1997]

2   —¡Gitanucas!—gritaba Maribel—. ¡Tom! ¡Jerry! Rápidamente, llegaban al arco y, ¡zas!, ¡zas!, cada una saltaba al hombro de uno de nosotros, para lamernos la cara . . . y ¡los ojos! [Non-fiction book: Pardo de Santayana, J.I. (2001), *El beso del chimpancé: divertidas e insólitas historias de la vida cotidiana en un zoo*, Madrid: Aguilar]

3   Os instaláis tan ricamente en cualquiera de las cafeterías de Barajas y de pronto, ¡zas!, se va la luz; cambiáis a tientas de cafetería y de repente, ¡zas! viene la luz. [Newspaper opinion article: Mendicutti, E. (1996), 'Vacaciones inolvidables', *El Mundo*, 15/12/1996]

4   Los lazos son endebles y poco seguros. Aunque no lo creas, son los nudos marineros los que aguantan más. Son mucho más resistentes, y además tienen la ventaja de que, a pesar de su aguante, en un momento dado se deshacen rápido, ¡zas!, de un solo golpe, para bien del marino, que se juega la vida en ellos. [Novel: Beccaria, L. (2001), *La luna en Jorge*, Barcelona: Destino]

5   [A student talking about running a marathon.] De eso, bueno, pues yo lo hice. Y pasó el período de . . . de crisis, porque tuve un momento de crisis que . . . que . . . que creía que . . . que tenía que abandonar, que me abandonaban las fuerzas. Y lo superé y zas, zas, zas, zas, zas, zas, zas y contando los pasos, pues claro, mil artimañas, mil . . . mil cosas, decir: 'Cien, diez pasos más y y me paro, otros diez pasos más y me paro.' [Oral text, Alcalá de Henares, no date given]

6   Un día fue a su vecina, la Amparo, a pedirle una miaja de aceite. La Amparo creía que sería para unas patas o unas carillas y le dio mitad de cuartillo. Pues, ¡zas!, a la cabeza. 'Pero ¿qué haces?', le dijo la Amparo. Y ella: 'Brillantina.' [Novel: Chamorro, V. (1984), *El muerto resucitado*, Madrid: Albia].

7   Solamente el jefe de contabilidad tiene éxito: logra introducir las cuentas en la terminal informática. Como el número de horas extraordinarias aumenta, se acuerda recurrir a contratar eventuales. Pero al final de mes, ¡zas!, todas las cuentas tienen errores y los contables tienen que trabajar todo el fin de semana para restablecer la situación. [Non-fiction book: Anon. (1991), *Cómo resolver los pequeños conflictos en el trabajo*, Bilbao: Deusto]

8   ¡Madre mía! No me vuelves a meter a mí en una película del tío ese ni atado. ¡Venga a matar rusos malísimos, y ni una mujer en toda la película! [. . .] Si al menos hubiera podido dormir algo . . . Pero no: es una película hecha con ruidos y más ruidos: ¡Pam, pum, plaf, zas! Bombazos, misiles, flechazos . . . [Drama: Alonso de Santos, J.L. (1989), *Pares y nines*, Madrid: Primer Acto]

9   Metí la mano en la caja, y ¡zas, me mordió un caimán! [Drama: Wolff, E. (1984), *La balsa de la Medusa*. Boulder, CO: Society of Spanish & Spanish-American Studies]

10 Recorrió una trocha bordeada de cañizal y descabalgó a la orilla de una encharcada. [. . .] Se contempló en las aguas verdinosas y creyó percibir leves arrugas en su frente. [. . .] De pronto, zas, metió la mano en el agua y atrapó un jaramugo de plata. El pececillo comenzó a crecer y se convirtió en tritón. [Novel: Faner, P. (1986), *Flor de sal*, Barcelona: Destino]

(Real Academia Española 1975–2008)

6.2 The formal properties of texts: phonic effects

Assignment

(i)   With particular reference to the phonic level of textual variables and overall textual coherence, discuss the strategic problems confronting the translator of the following text, and outline your own strategy for translating it.

(ii)   Translate the text into English as if for publication in a similar newspaper in an English-speaking country (specify which one).

(iii) Compare examples of strategy being put into practice.

Contextual information

The ST, written by Ignacio Carrión, is one of the short feature articles printed on the back page of the Spanish newspaper *El País*. They offer personal, often humorous commentaries on current affairs or everyday life.

Source text

Himno

El himno nacional español es el ruido. La gente oye ruido y se pone firmes. Se pone en trance patriótico. Saluda la enseña del decibelio y sangra de gusto por las orejas.

Vas a una hermosa cafetería de lujo y si no hay ruido no hay ambiente.   5
El camarero llega con un montón de platos y los suelta con estruendo sobre la barra, ya rebosante de otros melódicos ruidos. Te mira con cara de do de pecho y pregunta qué va a ser. Y tú respondes:

– Póngame una de ruido en taza mediana, con el asa atada a un badajo, y la leche fría de vaca mugiendo.   10

– ¡Una hecatombe en taza de bombardeo con la leche que le eche! – transmite el mozo al otro mozo de la máquina.

Entonces, el de la máquina maneja el manubrio y mientras el público consumidor se desgañita para aumentar el nivel ruidoso del local, cuyo fondo es *rock* duro, este mozo maquinista suelta el vapor para calentar la   15
leche y hasta las banquetas chirrían sin necesidad de rieles.

Más tarde entra el cliente fijo de las cinco. Éste no parece amante del follón, sino más bien protector de la sociedad de los animales mudos. El caballero avanza entre disparos de ruido –cucharillas tintineantes, berridos de tapas variadas, sartenazos de cocina– y alcanza su meta, que no es otra   20
que el diabólico juego de los marcianitos. Mete moneda y empiezan el gorgoteo, los pitidos, la traca y el reventón sin premio, aunque sí con rotura de tímpano y desgarro de las trompas de Eustaquio.

No puedes más. En la terraza atrona el tráfico y por encima de él se ríe de todos un helicóptero que ensordece. Alzas la voz, ya que no el puño,   25
y llamas al camarero: '¡La cuenta! ¡Traiga la cuenta!'

Y él se vuelve, herido en su pentagrama íntimo. Responde: '¡Jodé, jodé, no grite, que uno no está sordo!'

(Carrión 1989)

6.3 The formal properties of texts: poetry

Assignment

Working in groups:

(i)   Assess the salient formal properties – especially on the phonic and prosodic levels – of the following ST and discuss the strategic problems confronting the translator.

(ii) Compare the three versions in English in terms of the strategy that each has followed. Focus on metre, graphic layout, imagery, phonic effects and sense, and on how they are all brought together. Consider whether the TTs have different aims and target audiences.

Contextual information

The ST is a sonnet by Federico García Lorca from the *Sonetos del amor oscuro*, written in 1935–36. The TTs were composed for a festival held in 1998 at the Newcastle Playhouse in Newcastle upon Tyne (England) to mark the centenary of Lorca's birth. They were published, along with the ST and thirteen other versions of the poem, in S. Doggart and M. Thompson (eds), *Fire, Blood and the Alphabet: One Hundred Years of Lorca*, Durham: Durham Modern Languages Series, 1999.

Source text

Llagas de amor

Esta luz, este fuego que devora.
Este paisaje gris que me rodea.
Este dolor por una sola idea.
Esta angustia de cielo, mundo y hora.   5

Este llanto de sangre que decora
lira sin pulso ya, lúbrica tea.
Este peso del mar que me golpea.
Este alacrán que por mi pecho mora.

Son guirnaldas de amor, cama de herido,   10
donde sin sueño, sueño tu presencia
entre las ruinas de mi pecho hundido.

Y aunque busco la cumbre de prudencia
me da tu corazón valle tendido
con cicuta y pasión de amarga ciencia.   15

(García Lorca 1995: 29)

Target text 1

'The wounds of love' (John Kerr)

This brilliant light and fire which devour.
This grey expanse by which I am surrounded.
This sorrow which on one idea is founded.
This agony of heaven, world and hour.   5

These tears of blood with which is dressed
a lyre silent still, a torch of lust.
This sea of which I feel the thrust.
This scorpion which in my heart makes its nest.

They are love's garland, and the wounded's rest,   10
where, sleepless, I create you in a dream
amongst the ruins of my crushed-in breast;

and though I seek discretion's height supreme
your heart now gives me this vast vale oppressed
by passion's bitter skill, where hemlocks teem.   15

Target text 2

'The wounds of love' (Nicholas Round)

This light, and this consuming flame,
and this grey land on every side,
this grieving for a single thought,
this agony of earth and sky and time,   5
these tears of blood that fall like jewels on
my pulseless lyre, now made the torch of lust,
this pounding of me in the heavy seas,
this scorpion that lurks about my breast,
are the rewards love brings: a bed where I   10
wounded and sleepless, dream that you are here,
among the fragments of my shattered loving,
and though I struggle towards wisdom's height,
your heart has spread a valley at my feet
– hemlock and passion, bred of bitter knowing.   15

Target text 3

'You put a bomb in my heart' (Colin Teevan)

First a flash, then a fireball, which like a fash-
        ionable
new ism, swept all before it before,
Having only itself left to devour, did just that.   5
The sky, seeing the general distress,
Spat down tears of blood; the earth, for its part,
Through a million ruptured pipes, did its
Damnedest to piss the height of heaven and,
Needless to say, my Apollonian lyre   10
Was completely banjaxed in the blast.
It was a time for snakes and scorpions.
Yet, though this detritus was the only crop
Gathered from the ruins of our attrition,
And, though I should, in truth, have had more cop   15
Than to fall for such sweet ammunition,
From the second you blew me all over this shop,
It's been this kamikaze love, that's given me my definition.

(Doggart and Thompson 1999: 262–77)

7 The formal properties of texts
Syntactical, morphological and discourse issues

The textual variables considered in this chapter are grammatical, occurring at the levels of word morphology (inflection expressing grammatical function), sentence syntax and discourse syntax. Any utterance in any language – other than a basic, isolated interjection – requires the hearer or reader to interpret the words in it both as lexical items conveying meaning and as sentence components fulfilling syntactical functions. A native speaker of a language acquires a partly intuitive, partly explicit knowledge of a hugely complex system of general rules and particular patterns governing how words can be combined in that language to make meaning and generate discourses. Producers of discourses do not necessarily plan all the syntactical features of their texts: they make more or less conscious use of their knowledge of the resources available in their language, constructing relatively simple or complex sentences, linking them together in ways appropriate for different genres, choosing grammatical forms suitable for different registers or language varieties, being more or less careful according to the purpose of the communication and how it is being produced. The translator, however, must be able to make explicit what is built into a ST and to analyse exactly how it works in order to construct a TT that works in a comparable way for TL readers. As with other aspects of the translation process, this is above all a matter of determining priorities, reaching compromises, and finding the best ways of compensating for the inevitable translation loss caused by the systemic differences between languages.

The translator therefore needs an excellent grasp of the morphosyntactical systems of both of the languages involved, so as to form a clear understanding of the choices made by the producer of the ST and the choices available to the translator in the TL. The structural differences between Spanish and English are greater than those between Spanish and its fellow Romance languages, though not enormous in comparison with non-European languages. On the other hand, the similarities between two languages may pose just as many dangers for the translator, as choosing the closest equivalent in syntactical terms will often result in an undesirable degree of literal translation.

The most important part of the mindset required by the translator is an awareness of the need to take nothing for granted. Even when the TL appears to offer a close equivalent to a given grammatical feature of the ST, it is unlikely to function in the same way and may create a markedly different effect on TL readers. Consider, for instance, the sentence 'Me gusta este libro'. It is important for the translator to understand how this construction works in Spanish: strictly speaking, 'este libro' is the grammatical subject, 'gusta' is an intransitive verb and 'me' is the indirect object. 'Gustar', then, does not really mean 'to like' but 'to please', or more precisely, 'to be pleasing'. A similar construction is available in English – 'this book pleases me' or 'is pleasing to me' – but is likely to sound dated or unidiomatic in comparison with the evident familiarity of the Spanish expression, and therefore unsuitable for almost all translation purposes and text types. An idiomatic, balanced or communicative translation demands that the translator give the reproduction of the syntactical structure a lower priority than finding the expression that would normally be used by English speakers to convey what a Spanish-speaker means by saying 'me gusta este libro', which is, of course, 'I like this book'. This sentence has an entirely different syntactical structure and consequently represents the process as viewed from a different perspective: 'I' is now the subject, actively doing something rather than receiving an impression; 'like' is a transitive verb and 'this book' is the direct object. The change of perspective constitutes translation loss on the **syntactical level**, but this will nearly always be less important than the pragmatic priority of using a form that works as idiomatically in the TT as 'me gusta' does in the ST.

Translating 'me gusta . . .' as 'I like . . .' is an example of **grammatical (or syntactical) transposition**. By grammatical transposition we mean the replacement of a type of structure containing given parts of speech in the ST by some other type of structure containing different parts of speech in the TT. Many other writers designate this phenomenon simply as 'transposition'; we have used the full term 'grammatical transposition' in order to prevent confusion with 'cultural transposition' (discussed in Chapter 5). In some cases, grammatical transposition is obligatory: 'tengo sueño' cannot be translated into English with an equivalent structure (transitive verb + direct object noun) but must be transposed into 'I'm sleepy' or 'I feel sleepy' (subject pronoun + copulative verb + adjective). In other cases, grammatical transposition is an option to be used or not used by the translator depending upon the type of text and the overall strategy being followed. In most translation assignments, semantic and stylistic considerations are likely to override considerations of syntactical translation loss, priority usually being given to constructing grammatically well-formed, idiomatic TL sentences appropriate to the register and genre of the ST.

Nevertheless, translators need to be aware of grammatical differences between SL and TL as potential sources of translation loss, for there are exceptions to the norm described above, namely STs with salient textual properties manifestly resulting from the manipulation of grammatical structure: for example, a political speech using particular structures for rhetorical effect, or a literary text creating a distinctive style based on unusual or deliberately difficult syntax. A prestigious author's hallmark may partly consist in characteristic grammatical structuring. For example, drastic streamlining of syntax characterizes Lorca's rural tragedies, whereas Góngora's poetic style is known for its extreme syntactical complexity. Luis Martín-Santos's *Tiempo de silencio* is a challenging virtuoso performance in syntactical density and complexity, demanding that a high priority should be given to these formal properties in translation, if necessary at the expense of capturing the sense in idiomatic English. The impact of simpler texts may depend crucially upon carefully configured contrasts and recurrences in syntactical patterning, as in the well-known children's rhyme about magpies:

> One for sorrow,
> Two for joy,
> Three for a girl,
> Four for a boy,
> Five for silver,
> Six for gold,
> Seven for a secret
> Never to be told.

The grammatical patterns underlying this rhyme can be schematized as follows:

	number	preposition	abstract noun	} antonyms
	number	preposition	abstract noun	
(ascending	number	preposition	article + common noun	} antonyms
series)	number	preposition	article + common noun	
↓	number	preposition	mass noun	} ascending
	number	preposition	mass noun	series
	number	preposition	article + abstract noun + relative phrase	

To translate the rhyme into another language, one would have to give careful consideration to the grammatical patterning as schematized above, because the loss of its effects would deprive the text of much of its point; in effect, the structural scheme would be the basis for formulating a TT.

Mapping the grammatical differences between Spanish and English

We offer here a summary, focused on the implications for translation from Spanish into English, of the main morphosyntactical differences between the two languages. The table provides a basic checklist of features, which are expanded and explained in the text that follows. More comprehensive descriptions in English of Spanish syntax can be found in Butt and Benjamin (2004) and Mackenzie (2001). The definitive official account in Spanish is Demonte Barreto and Bosque (1999). López Guix and Minett Wilkinson (1997), and Beeby Lonsdale (1996) include useful discussions of contrasts, the first from the point of view of translation from English into Spanish and the second aimed at those translating from Spanish into English as a foreign language. Steel (2006) offers a wealth of comparative examples and translation exercises.

Spanish	English
Sentences and discourse structure	
1 Tendency to construct relatively long, complex sentences (especially in formal registers)	Tendency to use shorter, more simple sentences (even in quite formal registers)
2 Preference for **hypotaxis**, paying more attention to the use of explicit discourse connectors	Preference for **parataxis**, more frequent use of juxtaposition without conjunctions
3 Word order is very flexible, influenced by context and rhythm	Word order is relatively inflexible (Subject–Verb–Object)
Adjectives	
4 Inflected for number and gender	Invariable in form
5 Position variable	Nearly always placed before the noun
6 Limited use of nouns as attributive adjectives; instead, adjectives are formed by modification of a noun ('curso universitario') or replaced by a phrase ('de' + noun)	Nouns frequently used as attributive adjectives ('university course')
Articles	
7 Definite article is used with abstract concepts ('Luchamos por la libertad') and mass nouns ('Me gusta el vino chileno'), and can be used with people's names	Definite article is not normally used with abstract concepts, ('We're fighting for freedom'), mass nouns ('I like Chilean wine') or names
Demonstratives	
8 'Esto' is not used as often as English 'this' to refer back to an idea expressed in the previous sentence; instead, there is more of a tendency to link the sentences hypotactically	'This' (pronoun) is often used as an anaphoric device, acting as a loose paratactic connector between sentences
Possessives	
9 Ownership frequently marked with a definite article and/or dative personal pronoun, especially with clothing and parts of the body ('Se lavó las manos')	Ownership always marked with possessive adjectives ('He washed his hands')
Personal pronouns	
10 As the subject of a verb is indicated by its morphology, subject pronouns are normally not expressed ('Hablo español')	The subject is always expressed ('I speak Spanish')
11 Distinction between familiar ('tú, vosotros, vos') and formal ('usted, ustedes') second-person forms	Distinction between 'thou' and 'you' no longer used except in some British English dialects
12 Functions of subject and object are never confused	Tendency to blur subject/object distinctions ('I/me, who/whom')

Spanish	English
13 Extensive use of **ethic datives** ('El niño no me come')	Less extensive use of ethic datives

Prepositions

| 14 'Personal *a*': use of the preposition 'a' to mark human direct objects (as well as indirect objects) | Only indirect objects are marked with a preposition ('to') |

Adverbs

| 15 Infrequent use of adverbs formed by the addition of '-mente' to an adjective (replaced by other kinds of adverbial phrase, e.g. 'con' + noun) | Frequent use of adverbs formed by addition of '-ly' to an adjective |

Verbs: tense

16 A more elaborate system than in English: 11 tenses of the indicative (+ 9 progressive forms) and complete conjugation	The system is relatively simple: 8 tenses of the indicative (+ 8 progressive forms) and minimal inflection
17 Clear aspectual difference between the preterite tense (perfective) and the imperfect (imperfective)	The simple past is used for both perfective and imperfective aspects
18 Limited use of continuous/ progressive forms ('Estoy trabajando')	Frequent use of progressive forms ('I'm working'), even with a future sense ('We're going tomorrow')

Verbs: mood

| 19 Extensive use in all registers of all tenses of the subjunctive except the future | Subjunctive forms little used (or often not recognized as such); preference for modal auxiliaries to express mood |

Verbs: passive voice

| 20 Tendency to use alternatives to passive constructions ('se' phrases or active constructions, sometimes with an impersonal 3rd-person subject) | Frequent use of the passive, often in order to highlight the object of the action or place it before the verb |

Copulative verbs

| 21 Clear differentiation between 'ser' and 'estar' in terms of meaning and aspect | 'To be' has a wide semantic range, covering the meanings of both 'ser' and 'estar' |

Phrasal verbs

| 22 The effects achieved with **phrasal verbs** in English are expressed in Spanish by a variety of means, including verbs that contain the movement indicated ('go down' = 'bajar') and basic verbs of motion expanded by the addition of a gerund ('limp out' = 'salir cojeando') | Frequency and expressiveness of use of phrases consisting of verb + preposition/adverb of movement |

1–2 Sentence and discourse structure: length and complexity of sentences; hypotaxis and parataxis

The idea that Spanish favours long, complex sentences and more cohesively articulated discourse while English favours shorter, simpler sentences and fewer discourse connectors should be taken not as a hard-and-fast rule but as a general difference of tendency, mostly with reference to planned discourse – written texts and formal oral language. Colloquial spoken Spanish can be markedly laconic and concise, often making do with fewer phatic components and **illocutionary particles** than colloquial English, but written and planned oral discourse in Spanish is likely to consist of more complex syntactical structures than discourse in English, especially – but not only – when the social register is formal. This tendency can be described in terms of Spanish favouring hypotaxis and English being more inclined towards parataxis. **Hypotaxis** (in syntax) means the use of compound sentences containing subordinate clauses, so that the relationship between one part of a sentence and another is hierarchical: a main clause is modified or added to by one or more subordinate clauses, each of which plays a syntactical role within the structure of the main clause (that is, they are embedded within it). **Parataxis**, on the other hand, refers to phrases, clauses and sentences being placed next to one another without subordinating relationships or explicit connecting elements. Paratactic discourse features coordinated (rather than subordinate) clauses and **asyndeton** (the omission of conjunctions). The difference is shown in the following examples:

(i)   He gave me a blue book. (A simple sentence.)

(ii)   He gave me a book. The book was blue. (Two simple sentences not explicitly connected in any way.)

(iii)   He gave me a book. It was blue. (Two simple sentences linked only by the anaphoric function of the pronoun 'it'.)

(iv)   He gave me a book; it was blue. (A compound sentence consisting of two coordinated clauses in an asyndetic relationship. The semicolon suggests more of a logical connection between the two statements than there is in (iii), a distinction that would be marked in speech by a difference of intonation and pause length.)

(v)   He gave me a book and it was blue. (A compound sentence consisting of two coordinated clauses linked by a conjunction.)

(vi)   He gave me a book that was blue. (A compound sentence consisting of a main clause with a subordinate clause embedded in it.)

(vii)   He gave me a book, which was blue. (Also a compound sentence consisting of a main clause with a subordinate clause embedded in it, but here the relative clause is non-restrictive – an added comment rather than a specification of what kind of book was given.)

Examples (ii), (iii), (iv) and (v) are all paratactic to some degree, while (vi) and (vii) are hypotactic. All seven can be reproduced in more or less the same form in Spanish:

(i)   Me dio un libro azul.
(ii) Me dio un libro. El libro era azul.
(iii) Me dio un libro. Era azul.
(iv) Me dio un libro; era azul.
(v)   Me dio un libro y era azul.
(vi) Me dio un libro que era azul.
(vii) Me dio un libro, que era azul.

What we are proposing, then, is that a higher priority tends to be given in written Spanish to making syntactical cohesion and logical connections clear and explicit. In other words, a Spanish text is more likely than an English one to feature the kind of structure exemplified by (vi) and (vii) above in preference to (ii), (iii), (iv) or (v). A writer in Spanish is also more likely to prefer (iv) to (iii). Even when hypotactic structures are used in English, the subordinating conjunction or relative pronoun is often omitted in informal registers: 'He said [that] he'd come later'; 'I want the car [that] we looked at yesterday'. This kind of asyndetic formation of subordinate clauses hardly ever occurs in Spanish, even in colloquial language: it would be unthinkable to leave out 'que' in 'dijo que vendría más tarde' or 'quiero el coche que vimos ayer'. (The exceptions are 'rogar' and 'temer', which can be used – in relatively formal language – without the conjunction: 'Le ruego me disculpe'; 'Sigue subiendo el petróleo, que se teme pueda llegar hasta 40 dólares el barril'.) Consequently, it may often be justifiable to translate a hypotactic ST in Spanish into a more paratactic TT in English. In the examples above, this would mean transposing Spanish (vi) or (vii) into English (iii) or (iv); or Spanish (iv) into English (iii). Some literary, academic or professional texts in Spanish contain elaborately hypotactic passages which, if reproduced in English, will strike TL readers as more marked (contrived, awkward or high-register) than the ST does for its readers. Let us consider a more extended example, from an academic essay in a volume dedicated to the playwright Antonio Buero Vallejo:

Era Buero Vallejo, como no podía ser de otra forma, un poeta muy original, singular en sus formas de construir un poema y clásico en sus aportaciones formales, clásico o neoclásico, excelente conjuntador de sonetos y, sobre todo, inspirado autor de estructuras sólidas y cohesionadas en las que nada falta ni sobra, que esto es muy importante en poesía, variado en cuanto a sus temas, y rico en matices que van desde la emoción a la ternura, desde el recuerdo sobrio del amigo a la estampa leve, irónica y sabia de intelectual riguroso y sencillo al mismo tiempo.

(Díez de Revenga 2001: 23)

This paragraph comprises a single sentence containing five subordinate clauses and numerous adjectival, adverbial and noun phrases that expand upon the key elements. Although this is a complex, rather contrived sentence, it remains cohesive and is not particularly unusual for writing of this genre in Spanish. An English version retaining the same sentential structures would, however, strike most TL readers as unworkably convoluted and perhaps dated or excessively formal. Consequently, a certain amount of restructuring along the following lines to produce a more paratactic and more easily digestible TT would be entirely justified:

> As a poet, Buero Vallejo could not be other than highly original, unique in his approach to the construction of a poem and classical – or perhaps neoclassical – in his formal innovations. He was an excellent constructor of sonnets and, above all, an inspired creator of solid, cohesive structures lacking nothing and with nothing superfluous, an extremely important factor in poetry. His themes were varied and he was capable of a rich range of tones, from passion to tenderness, from the sober recollection of a friend to the light, ironic, judicious touch of a rigorous yet at the same time straightforward intellectual.

This does not mean that it will always be necessary or desirable to simplify the sentence and discourse syntax when translating from Spanish to English. As we have argued earlier in this chapter, syntactical complexity may be identified as a distinctive stylistic feature of a ST and priority given to retaining it, at least to the extent that it is noticeable in the TT without risking incomprehensibility or clumsiness. On the other hand, of course, not all texts in Spanish use elaborate syntax. Short sentences and parataxis are perfectly workable in Spanish and can be stylistically effective – in some cases perhaps feeling more marked than in English precisely because of the contrast with the general tendency towards complexity. The contribution that precedes the piece by Díez de Revenga in the volume cited above is by the playwright and TV scriptwriter Ignacio Amestoy, and contains much more punchy, paratactic language:

> No huye Buero del moderno, del esperpento, no huyó nunca. Su primera obra, *En la ardiente oscuridad*, es moderna. Pero su moderno siempre tuvo unas pautas. Los personajes *en pie*, con emociones – ¿quién teme al melodrama? – y en una estructura. ¡La estructura! En la estructura estará el Buero moderno.
>
> (Amestoy 2001: 18)

A relatively staccato style of this kind should be achievable without great difficulty in English and should not be turned into more flowing, hypotactic discourse:

> Buero does not shy away from modernity, the *esperpento*. He never did shy away from it. His very first play, *En la ardiente oscuridad*, is modern.

But his modernness was always subject to some basic rules. Characters seen on the same level as the spectator, with emotions (why be afraid of melodrama?) and within a structure. Structure – that is where the modern in Buero will be found.

3 *Word order*

The differences in word order between Spanish and English are numerous and the patterns of flexibility possible in Spanish are too complex to set out in full here. The most significant features of Spanish word order for the purposes of comparing with English, however, are: (a) that a subject can be placed after the verb; (b) that a direct or indirect object can be placed before the verb; (c) that adverbial elements tend to be placed immediately before or after the verb phrase they modify. The order of elements in a sentence in Spanish is not a crucial factor in determining meaning. Instead, word order is influenced by considerations of rhythm, emphasis, relevance and cohesion, especially the principle that an existing topic tends to come first, followed by new information or expansion. These differences pose more serious problems (or offer a wider range of possibilities) for the English-to-Spanish translator than for the translator into English. The first clause of the Amestoy quotation above, for example, could have been arranged in four different ways, the first three all equally idiomatic in themselves and the fourth slightly awkward in this context but still workable:

(i)   Buero no huye del moderno [subject – verb – complement]
(ii) No huye Buero del moderno [verb – subject – complement]
(iii) Del moderno no huye Buero [complement – verb – subject]
(iv) No huye del moderno Buero [verb – complement – subject]

The translation we have offered, 'Buero does not shy away from modernity', is the only idiomatically viable configuration in the TT. To translate 'Buero does not shy away from modernity' into Spanish is a trickier task: the translator must not take word order for granted – automatically choosing option (i) above – but must choose from multiple alternatives, each of which has different stylistic consequences. The Spanish-to-English translator also needs to understand the principles of Spanish word order, though, so as to be able to assess the effect of a particular choice made by a ST author and perhaps find a way of compensating for the translation loss occasioned by the inability to imitate the flexibility of Spanish.

All these factors mean that verb–subject and object–verb configurations can be produced routinely in Spanish without being marked for special emphasis. When this is the case, the translator need not do anything to reproduce – or compensate for not reproducing – the word order of the ST but should simply find the most idiomatically appropriate word order in English. However, the flexibility of Spanish allows further manipulation of word order to produce emphatic or poetic effects, which may need special attention in translation. In the quotation used in the previous section of this chapter to illustrate hypotactic discourse, the word order of the opening clause, which is at the beginning of the article, is not influenced by any of the factors listed above: 'Era Buero Vallejo [. . .] un poeta muy original' could have been 'Buero Vallejo era [. . .] un poeta muy original'. The latter would sound more normal and straightforward, but the author has used slightly unusual word order as a rhetorical device to attract attention at the beginning of his article – not taking 'Buero Vallejo' for granted as the theme but highlighting it. While 'Buero Vallejo was [. . .] a very original poet' would be a satisfactory translation, the TT we offered above ('As a poet, Buero Vallejo . . .') ensures that the name is not the first element.

Unexpected word order with emphatic effect can be an expressive feature of colloquial language, and may sometimes be reproduced in English:

> Está muy rico este vino. ['It's very nice, this wine.']
>
> A mí no me culpes. Lo ha hecho él. ['Don't blame *me*. *He* did it.']
>
> Vaya, vaya, vaya. Menudos cambios hemos visto. ['My, my, my, what changes we've seen.']

For poets, the possibilities of hyperbaton (disruption of word order) are much richer in Spanish than in English, possibilities that were explored with particular relish in the sixteenth and seventeenth centuries. Here is an example from Garcilaso's 'Égloga I' (as a classroom exercise, try turning this into Spanish prose with more normal word order):

> El dulce lamentar de dos pastores,
> Salicio juntamente y Nemoroso,
> he de contar, sus quejas imitando;
> cuyas ovejas al cantar sabroso
> estaban muy atentas, los amores,
> de pacer olvidadas, escuchando.
>
> (Garcilaso de la Vega 1996: 129)

4 Inflection of adjectives

The fact that in Spanish an adjective agrees in number and gender with the noun it modifies should not cause major problems for the translator, but is another example of a distinction being made in one language and not the other, which does inevitably cause a degree of translation loss. A narrative text in Spanish might, for example, make a point of not specifying the sex of a character for some time, using a series of verbs without expressing the subject, then finally revealing that it is a woman by saying 'se puso nerviosa' (also see the extract from 'Estación de la mano' used for Practical 2.1). Care would need to be taken to maintain the uncertainty in the TT, if possible avoiding the use of the subject pronoun 'she' until the point at which 'nerviosa' appears in the ST, thereby compensating for the absence of gender marking in the TL.

5 *Position of adjectives*

As with other aspects of word order in English, the positioning of an adjective in relation to the noun it qualifies is generally inflexible: both determiners and descriptive adjectives precede the noun ('your house, the first house, many houses, the white house, an enormous house'). Spanish, in contrast, makes nuances possible through adjective positioning which are difficult to capture in translation. The basic principle that governs this in Spanish is that the normal position for a descriptive adjective is after the noun, where it has a differentiating function: 'la casa blanca' as opposed to the blue or pink one; 'una casa enorme' as opposed to a small one. A prenominal adjective, on the other hand, does not differentiate the noun from others but expresses a quality that it is assumed to have: 'la blanca nieve'; 'la enorme cruz del Valle de los Caídos'. In some cases, this distinction means that a postnominal adjective has a literal sense and a prenominal one is figurative: 'el hombre pobre' is on a low income, whilst 'el pobre hombre' is pitiable.

In some instances of prenominal adjective positioning, the differentiating/ non-differentiating distinction is not clear-cut, since writers may simply choose to pre-position an adjective to achieve stylistic emphasis. In the following extract, both 'intensos' and 'blanca' could have been placed after the noun but are highlighted by appearing before it:

> Sorprende que a pesar de su proximidad al litoral central, Los Roques aún sigan siendo un remanso de paz donde el visitante entra en comunión con los intensos azules de sus profundidades marinas y la blanca arena.
>
> (Araujo 1997)

Perhaps the only compensation possible here would be to expand each of the adjectives: 'the intense, vivid blues' and 'the dazzlingly white sand'. The author of the following text exaggerates the effect of pre-positioning by putting two adjectives before a noun:

> Los trágicos hechos acaecidos en Nueva York y en Washington, que han conmovido hasta los cimientos las estructuras de este mundo globalizado con sus insistentes imágenes penetrando una y otra vez en nuestras intimidades domésticas [. . .], lo primero que han estandarizado es el miedo. Han globalizado vertical y horizontalmente la ancestral, filosófica

angustia de sabernos finitos. Sin garantías, ni avales, ni contratos. Han institucionalizado, en un democrático manto mundial, sin exclusiones, la antiquísima y posmoderna condición humana de la inestabilidad, de la crisis, del peligro indiscriminado.

(Suárez 2001)

This overwrought effect cannot be imitated in English by the same means, but should prompt the translator to seek to create a comparable style in other ways.

6 Use of nouns as attributive adjectives

Although English does not go as far as German in its facility for forming compound nouns (such as 'Kinderreisebett' – 'child's travel cot'), the way in which two nouns can be collocated so that one qualifies the other as if it were an adjective is one of the key features that differentiates English from the Romance languages. Some well-established pairings form compound or hyphenated words ('bookshop, fireplace, campsite, bath-house'), but virtually any noun can be used in apposition like an attributive adjective: 'bank statement, statement book, book cover, cover design, design agency', and so on.

Compound words formed from a verb with a noun have long existed in Spanish: 'limpiabotas, parabrisas, sacacorchos, matamoros'. A small number of noun + noun collocations have become established and this kind of construction is becoming more common under the influence of English: 'un coche bomba, una casa cuartel, el tema clave, la atracción estrella, nuestro producto líder, el diseño web' (note that the second noun is invariable – 'productos líder'). In general, though, Spanish does not function in this way, instead using adjectives of the type 'bancario, estatal, universitario', or forming a phrase with a preposition, usually 'de': 'cuna de viaje', 'agencia de diseño'.

The consequences for translation are not likely to be serious, since transpositions such as 'cuna de viaje' – 'travel cot' – are obvious enough. There may at times be choices to be made, however. 'Turismo enológico' could be calqued as 'oenological tourism' but would bring in more business if billed as 'wine tours'. 'Infantil' may mean 'like a child' ('infantile, childlike, childish') or 'for a child', as in 'asiento infantil' ('child seat'). 'El desempleo rural' is 'rural unemployment' but 'casas rurales' are 'country cottages'.

7 Articles

Different patterns in the use of definite and indefinite articles pose frequent problems for English-speakers learning Spanish and Spanish-speakers learning English, giving rise to calqued expressions such as 'soy un estudiante' or 'the President Bush spoke about the terrorism'. While translators working into their own first language should not encounter such problems, an explicit awareness of the differences helps to avoid unintended calque.

In addition, Spanish allows certain idiomatic uses of articles with no counterparts in English. Any adjective can be turned into a noun by adding a definite article ('el nuevo, la nueva, los nuevos, las nuevas'), and into an abstract concept with the neuter article 'lo', a formulation that can be translated in various ways depending upon the particular collocation and the context: 'newness', 'the new thing', 'the new dimension' or 'what is new'. The colloquial habit of using a definite article with a person's name may have subtle effects on tonal and social register which can only be translatable indirectly, by means of some form of compensation. Reference to a person as 'el Manolo' or 'la Pepa' will usually be a marker of informal register and oral language, and may imply affection; while referring to the character as simply 'Manolo' or 'Pepa', the translator will need to ensure that the informality, orality and tone are brought out in other ways in the TT. A ST referring to Hillary Clinton as 'la Clinton' may be merely jocular, but may also imply hostility towards her and a sexist attitude towards high-profile women in politics.

8 Demonstratives: anaphora

Anaphoric use of the pronoun 'this' – economically reproducing an idea mentioned in the preceding clause or sentence – is one of the ways in which English tends to work more paratactically than Spanish. The way in which the following text links the last part of the sentence ('significa que el músculo . . .') causally to the preceding clause ('predomina la síntesis sobre la degradación') is characteristic of the greater prevalence of hypotaxis in Spanish:

> Tras la ingestión de una dieta que contenga proteínas o un suplemento de las mismas, en el músculo se produce el efecto contrario a lo que sucede en ayunas, es decir, en este caso, predomina la síntesis sobre la degradación, lo que significa que el músculo aumenta su contenido en a.a. para compensar los perdidos durante el ayuno.
>
> (Palavecino 2004)

This could be translated with a relative clause easily enough: 'Synthesis predominates over degradation, which means that the muscle . . .' However, even in this relatively formal register, an English writer may be reluctant to construct a sentence as elaborate as the Spanish one above. A convenient way of making the discourse feel more manageable in English is to break the sentence after 'degradation' and begin a new one with 'this', removing the hypotactic link and relying on simple anaphora:

> After the ingestion of a diet containing proteins or a protein supplement, the muscle is subject to an effect opposite to that which takes place during

fasting, that is, synthesis now predominates over degradation. This means that the muscle increases its amino acid content to compensate for the depletion caused by fasting.

Of course, the same formula is available in Spanish, using 'esto' or 'ello' (both to be translated as 'this'). Our argument, though, is that this is done less often in Spanish than in English, making the translation offered above justifiable on the grounds of equivalence of register – that is, because the hypotactic approach would feel more formal and elaborate to a TL reader than the ST does to a Spanish-language reader.

9 Possessive adjectives

Expressions of the type 'se lavó las manos' (literally, 'he washed the hands to himself'), 'se le cayó el pelo' or 'me quitaron los zapatos' are so common in Spanish that they are unlikely to confuse many translators into English. The trap they pose is for the unwary translator from English into Spanish, who may opt too easily for calque with a possessive adjective, producing 'lavó sus manos', 'se cayó su pelo' or 'quitaron mis zapatos', which make sense but would be unidiomatic in most contexts. The indirect object pronoun in these sentences ('se, le, me') is known as an **ethic dative** or 'dative of interest': it indicates that the person referred to is associated with the direct object ('his hands, his hair, my shoes'). What may become interesting from the point of view of translation into English is the way in which this kind of structure with an ethic dative, especially in colloquial language, can be used in more surprising ways, some of which can be translated with a possessive:

> El niño no me come. [Not 'The child isn't eating me' but 'My child isn't eating'.]

> En mi vida ha habido de todo, bueno y malo. Tres hijos se me murieron, y el marido. Los dos hijos que me viven están lejos, muy lejos. ['Three of my children died on me ... The two children of mine who're still alive ...'.]

> (Montero 1981: 12)

10 Subject pronouns

The translation problem most likely to arise from the fact that a verb can be used in Spanish without specifying its subject is that a Spanish speaker has a choice about whether to use a subject pronoun, while an English speaker does not. It is sometimes necessary to distinguish between possible third-person subjects ('él/ella/usted tiene') and between the first and third persons of the imperfect tense ('yo/él/ella/usted tenía'). This simple disambiguating function of the subject pronoun needs no special action on the part of the translator, unless one is dealing with a ST in which uncertainty is deliberately created by the omission of pronouns needed to make clear who is doing what – uncertainty that would be difficult to reproduce in English. When there is a need to distinguish repeatedly between two different subjects, texts in Spanish may avoid overusing 'él/ella', introducing instead a demonstrative pronoun ('éste/ésta') or a noun phrase specifying more fully who is referred to, such as 'el hombre', 'el otro', 'el marido'. None of these would need to be translated literally, as repeated use of subject pronouns in English is perfectly normal. In the following example, both 'el otro' and 'éste' should be translated simply as 'he':

> Una mujer acude a un día de campo con su familia. [. . .] Mientras los niños juegan, ella y él deciden sacar la comida de la canasta. Él destapa una botella de gaseosa. Ella comienza a sacar los sandwiches. Él destapa la misma botella de gaseosa . . . Ella simplemente no lo comprende. ¿No acabás de hacer eso?, le pregunta. ¿Hacer qué?, responde el otro mientras sigue acomodando las cosas. ¡Abrir la botella!, replica ella. Él ya no presta atención a sus palabras. [. . .] Ella se da vuelta aterrada hacia su marido. Éste la mira fijo y balbucea algo romántico en cámara lenta.
>
> (Yablon 2003)

The other common reason for expressing subject pronouns in Spanish is emphasis. English tends to express such emphasis by means of intonation, which can be represented in print with italics, or by some kind of expansion:

> Yo no he hecho nada. Pregúntale a Martín. Lo rompió él.

> *I* haven't done anything. Ask Martin. *He* broke it/He's the one who broke it.

11 Distinction between formal and familiar second-person forms

The pattern of forms of address has been drastically simplified in modern English, with 'you' generally serving as singular and plural, formal and familiar. 'Thou/thee' survives as a singular form in parts of England, 'yous' has developed as a plural in some English, Irish, US and Australian dialects, and 'y'all' is available in southern USA. Spanish, in contrast, retains the capacity to distinguish between singular and plural 'you', as well as various ways of signalling formal and familiar address: 'tú/usted/vosotros/ustedes' in most of Spain; 'tú/usted/ustedes' in parts of Spain and Latin America; 'vos/usted/ustedes' or 'tú/vos/usted/ustedes' in other parts of Latin America. Forms of address therefore play an important role in the pragmatics of Spanish, with implications for social register and regional variation which will often call for deft compensation manoeuvres on the part of the translator.

The singular/plural distinction can be conveyed easily enough by expansion in English: 'you lot', 'all of you', 'you guys', or even 'yous' if carrying out cultural transplantation into a TL setting featuring a particular dialect. The formal/familiar distinction will usually prove much more problematic, especially if there is a mixture of 'tú' and 'usted' in the same text, or a shift from one to the other. A variety of solutions may be needed: reflecting the overall effect of formality or familiarity in other ways of marking register; adding phatic elements to signal the intimacy of 'tú' or 'vos' ('mate', 'my friend', 'darling', 'man'); using an analogous distinction between surnames and Christian names ('tutéame, por favor' – 'call me Joe, please'); retaining the exoticism and glossing it ('insistía en llamarme de usted' – 'he insisted on addressing me respectfully as *usted*'). In Ernest Hemingway's novel *For Whom the Bell Tolls*, Spanish dialogue is represented as if translated literally into English, as part of which 'thou/thee' is used for 'tú'. A translator could imitate this exoticizing device for some texts, as long as it was consistent with an overall translation strategy.

We offer below an example of 'tú' and 'usted' being explicitly contrasted with one another as part of an exploration of an intimate relationship complicated by a difference of social status. Consider the implications for translation:

–Es ridículo, ¿no?, que me llames de usted . . . [. . .]
–Es que si empiezo a llamarle de tú, a estas alturas, me voy a acostumbrar porque, claro, eso pasa siempre, [. . .] y si se entera mi madre
. . .
–¿Qué?
Ella no quiso contestarle, pero le miró [. . .]. Ésta no es una historia fácil, le dijeron sus ojos, no puede serlo porque fuera de esta cama tú y yo no somos iguales, y si se entera mi madre, empezará a sospechar enseguida por qué me ha dado por tutearte, y acabaré metiendo la pata y todo el mundo lo sabrá, [. . .] por eso esta historia que es tan fácil aquí dentro, se vuelve tan difícil fuera de esta cama, porque aquí dentro tú y yo somos iguales, pero fuera no lo somos, y tú eres usted, pero yo sigo siendo yo, y soy muy poco.
–Yo, la verdad, si no le importa . . . –dijo por fin, después de un rato –. Yo preferiría seguir llamándole de usted.

(Grandes 2002: 358)

12 Confusion of subject and object pronouns

One of the characteristic features of colloquial English is a lack of precision in marking syntactical function. The relative pronoun 'whom' is rarely used, and subject pronouns are often replaced by object forms when paired with another pronoun or in an 'it is/was . . .' construction: 'Me and Claire are going out later'; 'It was them who started it.' Such confusion of categories is rare in Spanish, even in colloquial spoken language. The ability to distinguish between formal and informal discourse in English by being more or less careful with grammar offers the Spanish-to-English translator idiomatic ways of marking register which are not available in Spanish. To take a simple example, 'usted y yo' might be translated as 'you and I' while 'tú y yo' might be 'me and you'. In conjunction with decisions about whether to use contractions in English, the varying of grammatical precision according to social and tonal register can be a useful resource for the purposes of compensation.

13 Ethic datives

The Spanish ethic dative was introduced in section 11. Its use, especially in colloquial language, extends far beyond the function of indicating possession. The most common type of ethic dative indicates the person *for whom* something is done, and in some cases this can be expressed in the same way in English: 'Hazme un bocadillo y échame un poco de vino' – 'Make me a sandwich and pour me some wine'. In other cases, the sense is neither *to* nor *for* but a looser association between the action being carried out and the person referred to as indirect object, which may be reflexive. These pronouns need not always be translated: 'Ponte esto' – 'Put this on'; 'No me lo creo' – 'I don't believe it'; 'Se sabía toda la lección' – 'He knew the whole lesson (by heart)'. The following examples play self-consciously with ethic datives:

> Póntelo. Pónselo. ['Get it on. Get it on him.'] (Slogan for a Spanish government campaign promoting the use of condoms, 1989)

> 'Vale, vale, no te me pongas borde,' dijo ella en tono conciliador; y sirvió para apaciguarme ese 'me', porque me hizo sentirme un poco suyo. ['All right, all right, don't get difficult with me.']
> (Marías 1994: 219)

> Estuve enamorado de ella hasta que descubrí que ella también. ¿Me acariciaba, o es que – como un gato – se me acariciaba? ['Was it me she was caressing, or herself, rubbing up against me like a cat?']
> (Xavier Rubert de Ventós in a television programme on TVE, 1991)

14 Prepositions: 'personal a'

One of the ways in which cohesion is ensured in Spanish despite variable word order is the use of the preposition 'a' to mark a human direct object:

Pedro vio la casa. ['Peter saw the house.']
La casa la vio Pedro. ['Peter saw the house' or 'The house was seen by
Peter.']
Pedro vio a mi hijo. ['Peter saw my son.']
A mi hijo lo vio Pedro. ['Peter saw my son' or 'My son was seen by Peter.']

In the fourth example, the possibility of interpreting 'mi hijo' as subject ('My
son saw Pedro') is avoided by the 'personal *a*' and the pleonastic pronoun 'lo'.
In general, the translator does not need to pay special attention to this feature,
since word order is decisive in English. The use of a passive construction in
two of the TTs above ('was seen by Peter') is the only way of retaining the
order in which the sentence components are presented in the ST. Interesting
translation problems may arise, however, when the human/non-human
distinction is blurred – that is, when a human direct object is not marked with
'a' or a non-human one is:

Una de esas noches Marina regresó muy asustada, porque había visto un
hombre vestido de negro y con una máscara negra, que la miraba en la
oscuridad desde el lavadero. [The masked man is dehumanized by the
omission of the preposition, so 'figure' could be chosen instead of 'man'.]
(García Márquez 1996: 149)

El antiguo niño ingenuo y aristocrático se ha vuelto áspero, astuto, veloz,
sufrido, un verdadero experto en flaquezas humanas y en saber sacar
provecho de ellas. Ve a la muerte de cerca, tanto la de personas próximas
como la de pueblos enteros [Death is personified by the inclusion of the
preposition, so perhaps 've' could be expanded in translation: 'comes face
to face with death'.]
(Cabrera 1999: 166)

15 Adverbs

The Spanish tendency to find alternatives to adverbs formed by adding '-mente'
to an adjective need not be reflected in translation into English. The fact
that a Spanish writer has chosen, for example, 'con alegría' rather than
'alegremente' does not necessarily make 'with joy/happiness' preferable to
'joyfully/happily' in the TT. Even a longer Spanish formula such as 'de una
manera' may in some cases be rendered most satisfactorily with a simple
adverb in English: 'Hay que hacerlo de una manera muy lenta' – 'You have
to do it very slowly.'

16–17 Past tenses

In general, the tense systems of Spanish and English are similar. The action
designated by a verb is located in the past, the present or the future, indicated
by inflection of the basic form of the verb ('talk > talked') or the addition of

an auxiliary verb ('will', 'have', 'had'). Both languages complicate the basic past–present–future scheme in more or less the same ways (considering, for the moment, only the indicative forms):

1   Pluperfect – past prior to another past action ('had talked', 'había/hubo hablado').
2   Simple past ('talked', 'habló/hablaba').
3   Perfect – past still relevant to the present ('has talked', 'ha hablado').
4   Present ('talks', 'habla').
5   Future ('will talk', 'hablará').
6   Future perfect – perfect from the point of view of the future ('will have talked', 'habrá hablado').
7   Conditional – future from the point of view of the past ('would talk', 'hablaría').
8   Conditional perfect – future perfect from the point of view of the past ('would have talked', 'habría hablado').

Alert readers will have noticed that item 2 in the list above (the simple past in English) refers to two different tenses in Spanish – the preterite ('pretérito indefinido') and the imperfect ('pretérito imperfecto'). This is the most significant difference between the two tense systems, and therefore offers interesting challenges for translation. When referring to past actions in Spanish, it is compulsory to distinguish between perfective aspect (a single, complete event or an activity carried out for a defined amount of time, usually expressed by the preterite) and imperfective aspect (continuous activity or events repeated indefinitely, usually expressed by the imperfect). 'Leyó' is clearly different from 'leía'. In the case of verbs whose meaning is closer to the imperfective idea of continuity than the perfective idea of suddenness or completion (knowing, loving, wanting, being able), the perfectivity expressed by the preterite tense may be inchoative, indicating the beginning of the action: 'supe' – 'I discovered/ found out'; 'pude' – 'I managed/succeeded'. In English, it is possible to specify imperfectivity by various means – 'was reading, used to read, would read' – but this is not required, since the simple past tense covers both aspects: both 'leyó' and 'leía' may be translated as 'she read'. The translation loss arising from the gap between the precision of Spanish and the vagueness of English in this respect may not matter a great deal in many cases, since the context supplied by adjacent adverbs and other sentence components is likely to clarify the sense. However, the difference between the tenses in Spanish can be exploited in subtle ways that create nuances difficult to capture in English. The suggestions for compensation in translating the following examples aim to ensure that the point of the aspectual distinction is acknowledged in some way in the TT:

> Él percibía una gran diferencia, medida en espacios entre navidades, del niño que fue y el anciano que era. ['between the child he once was and the old man he was now'.]
>
> (Arias 2004)

Eso fue un equipo encabezado por Víctor García de la Concha, que era el secretario y fue un impulsor maravilloso. ['who was the Secretary and did a marvellous job of generating initiatives.']

(Lázaro Carreter 2003)

Sacó un chicle de su bolso, el coche olió a menta. ['the car was filled with the smell of mint.']

(Marías 1994: 216)

The text used in Practical 2.1 ('Estación de la mano') includes some interesting shifts between the preterite and the imperfect. As a classroom exercise, trace these shifts and discuss the implications for translation.

The division into two forms, perfective and imperfective, of item 2 in the list of tenses means that item 1, the pluperfect, also has a variant in Spanish: the 'pretérito anterior' ('hubo hablado'). The existence of this tense is a logical consequence of the availability of two past-tense forms into which 'haber' can be put, yet in practice there is virtually no difference in meaning between 'había hablado' and 'hubo hablado', and the latter is rarely used. Technically, its function is to indicate an immediate succession of events: 'No bien hubo terminado la frase, se escuchó una fuerte detonación' (Álvarez Gil 2002: 57). However, the notion of one event being immediately followed by the other is not always present, and in some cases this form seems to be used in written language simply as an alternative to the pluperfect: 'Don Ricardo Urgoiti logró salir de España y se fue a América, donde residió hasta que hubo terminado nuestra guerra civil' (Díaz 1993: 142). Consequently, there is no reason for the translator to attempt to reflect the minimal difference between the two pluperfects, though the presence of the past anterior in a text is an indicator of a literary register and a careful, even pretentious or pedantic style, which may be signalled in other ways in the TT.

Our checklist at the beginning of this chapter mentioned eleven indicative tense forms in Spanish. The eleventh is yet another version of the pluperfect, used only in written language, only in relative clauses and, like the past anterior, indicating a certain pretentiousness of style: 'hablara', sometimes referred to in Spanish as the 'subjuntivo mayestático' even though in this role it is indicative (in contrast to 'hablase', which is exclusively subjunctive). As used by journalists, it sometimes loses its pluperfect sense and becomes an alternative for the preterite – translatable by the simple past tense:

En el suelo, desmochados y resecos, estaban los oscuros muñones de lo que antaño fueran árboles frutales. ['what had once been fruit trees.']

(Montero 2000: 214–15)

Pero la primera parte del ensayo, la que escribiera el autor en la inmediatez de los hechos, basándose casi exclusivamente en las palabras del secuestrado, permite advertir la capacidad analítica del autor. ['which the author wrote in the immediate aftermath of the events.']

(ABC Cultural 1996)

This function of the *-ra* verb form does not create serious translation problems, but the translator needs to recognize what is going on in such examples and ensure that a comparable register is maintained in the TT.

18 Continuous forms of verbs

A translator working from English into Spanish needs to be careful not to use the continuous (progressive) forms of verbs as frequently as English does, especially in spoken discourse. 'I am/was/will be working' should normally be translated as simply 'trabajo/trabajaba/trabajaré'. It is only necessary to specify 'estoy/estaba/estaré trabajando' if there is an emphasis on the action being under way at the moment of speaking: 'No, no puedo salir ahora. ¿No ves que estoy trabajando?' If a Spanish ST to be translated into English uses a continuous form, it may be a good idea to make the emphasis explicit in the TT: 'No, I can't go out. Can't you see I'm working right now?' A degree of inventiveness may also be needed to capture the nuances conveyed by other continuous constructions in Spanish: 'ir' + gerund implies extended continuity or increasing intensity; 'venir' + gerund refers to continuous activity up to the present moment; 'andar' + gerund indicates habitual activity.

19 The subjunctive mood

For most native speakers of Spanish, the subjunctive mood does not a represent a difficulty or confine itself to a restricted, formal range of registers. All tenses of the subjunctive except the future ('hablare') are routinely and instinctively used in both planned and unplanned discourse, both written and oral. While subordinate clauses are in general more likely to appear in relatively formal or planned language, the presence of the subjunctive does not in itself indicate high register or formality. In contrast, most native speakers of English have little awareness of the existence of subjunctive forms, which are often the same as the indicative forms, or can be avoided or replaced by modal auxiliaries ('may', 'might', 'should'). The subjunctive may find its way into careful or formal language, but is rarely felt to be required: 'If I were/was prime minister . . .'; 'It is essential that the ministry be/is/should be informed promptly of any infringement of these regulations.' Consequently, the translation of Spanish subjunctive constructions into English involves choices determined by register. 'Mira, quiero que te vayas ahora mismo' requires a simple infinitive ('Look, I want you to leave right now'), while 'La Presidencia ruega que se respete al orador en uso de la palabra' could be translated with a more elaborate construction including a subjunctive ('The Chair requests that due respect be accorded to the member who has the floor').

When dealing with the kinds of constructions in which the use of the subjunctive in Spanish is optional, the translator needs to be alert to the differences conveyed by mood. In relative clauses, for instance, there may be ways of reflecting in English the sometimes subtle difference in sense between the Spanish indicative (referring to a concrete, existing antecedent) and subjunctive (referring to a hypothetical, required or non-existent antecedent). Consider this sentence from an interview with a theatre director: 'El director debe tener una gran empatía que le haga capaz de extraer lo mejor de cada uno de sus colaboradores' (Serrano Cueto 2002). The subjunctive 'haga' is prompted by 'debe tener' – compare 'aquel director tiene una gran empatía que le hace capaz . . .'. Both options could be rendered as 'a great sense of empathy that makes him capable of . . .', but it is possible to retain some of the effect of the subjunctive: 'a great sense of empathy that can make him capable of . . .'.

Adverbial clauses introduced by conjunctions such as 'cuando', 'como', 'de modo que', 'así que', 'porque', 'aunque' frequently offer an indicative/ subjunctive choice, sometimes producing clearly differentiated meanings: 'así que' with the indicative means 'so', while with the subjunctive it usually means 'as soon as'; 'como' + indicative means 'as', while 'como' + subjunctive means 'if' ('Como digas una sola palabra, te mato'); and 'aunque' can be translated as either 'although' (indicative) or 'even if' (subjunctive). Compare the following sentences using 'de modo que':

> Costa de Marfil se vio inmersa en un círculo vicioso que la llevó a cortar cada vez más y más árboles, de modo que acabó con el 90 por ciento de sus selvas, y su crecimiento se estancó. ['with the result that'.]
>
> (Delibes de Castro 2001: 271)

> Imaginemos por un momento que nos regalan un planeta ideal para vivir [. . .]. Aparte de trasladarnos nosotros mismos, con nuestra familia, nuestros amigos, nuestros libros y nuestras bicicletas, ¿qué especies llevaríamos, como mínimo, para hacerlo habitable, de modo que pudiera ser ocupado de forma permanente? ['so that it could be occupied', or 'so that it might be made suitable for permanent occupation'.]
>
> (Delibes de Castro 2001: 290)

20 The passive voice

Comparison of the passive voice in Spanish and English is complicated by various factors. Firstly, both 'ser' and 'estar' can be used with a past participle to express in different ways what is expressed by 'to be' + past participle in English, with further nuances added by the difference between the preterite and imperfect tenses. All three of the following sentences can be translated simply as 'The houses were built of stone':

Las casas fueron construidas de piedra.
Las casas eran construidas de piedra.
Las casas estaban construidas de piedra.

However, this obscures the clear distinction made in the Spanish constructions. The first two (with 'ser') refer to the action taking place, the process of
building: they got built by someone at a particular time ('fueron construidas'),
or were being built at a particular time or habitually used to be built ('eran
construidas'). The third (with 'estar') refers to the result of the building work,
describing of what material the houses were made. Since 'estaban construidas'
represents the outcome of 'habían sido construidas', it might be translated as
'had been built' – and 'están construidas' as 'have been built'. The 'ser/estar'
distinction may become semantically significant with particular verbs: 'fue
detenido' means 'he got arrested', while 'estuvo detenido' means 'he was held
under arrest [for a certain amount of time]'. Another variation to be taken
into account is that in some cases a past participle used with 'ser' may be
functioning as an adjective or noun: 'Soy casado' is most likely to mean 'I am
a married man.'

A second complicating factor is that the frequency of use of both the
'ser' and 'estar' constructions varies according to tense. The passive with 'ser'
(referred to from here on as SP passive) is used much more frequently in the
preterite than in any other tense, narrating events taking place. In many of the
instances in which it appears in the present tense, it functions as a 'historic
present': 'En junio de 1985 es detenido de nuevo.' The 'estar' + past participle
construction (EP passive) is used extensively in the present and imperfect
tenses, describing the state of the subject, while in the preterite its function is
rather specialized, conveying the idea that the subject remained in that state
for a given amount of time: 'Etelvina dejó su verdadera estela en Raúl de
Cárdenas, un estudiante eterno que estuvo enamorado de ella' (Cabrera Infante
1993: 57) ['who was in love with her for a while'].

The third factor influencing the use of the SP passive in Spanish is the
availability of several alternative means of expressing a passive idea:

(a) The placing of a direct object before the verb without resorting to a passive
     construction ('Esta película la dirigió Medem' – 'This film was directed
     by Medem').
(b) The use (more frequent than in English) of an unspecified third-person
     plural subject ('Me han despedido' – 'I've been fired' or 'They've fired me').
(c) An apparently reflexive expression understood as passive, either with the
     agreement that would be expected in a true reflexive construction ('Se han
     construido demasiadas casas' – 'Too many houses have been built'), or,
     where there might be confusion with a true reflexive, with 'se' functioning
     as if it were an impersonal subject pronoun, a singular verb and the
     preposition 'a' marking the direct object ('Se detuvo a los ladrones' –
     'The robbers were arrested').

While use of the SP passive has increased in both Peninsular and Latin American Spanish in recent decades, especially in journalistic writing (often influenced by English-language journalism), translators should still bear in mind that it is less common than the passive construction in English. Verbs that are likely to be employed in relatively formal registers may appear more frequently in SP constructions than in 'se' phrases. For example, the CREA database produces a large number of examples of 'es/fue/era nombrado', mostly from books and the press but including a few from oral sources; verbs that are used in a wider range of registers, however, will appear more often in 'se' phrases: examples of 'es/fue/era construido' in CREA are heavily out-numbered by 'se construye/construyó/construía' in both oral and written sources (Real Academia Española 1975–2008).

From the point of view of translation, the main consequence of this is that a variety of structures in Spanish STs – the SP and EP passives as well as the three alternatives listed above – can normally be translated into passive constructions in English:

> La casa estaba valorada en mil millones de pesetas. Se importaron piedras de África para adornar el jardín. El techo de palma lo tejieron indios Yanomami traídos del Amazonas. Le colocaron un equipo de aire acondicionado de 120 toneladas. Fue construido un muro de contención de 60 metros en el cauce de una quebrada.
>
> (Adapted from a news report of 1994)

> The house was valued at 1000 million pesetas. Stones were imported from Africa to decorate the garden. The palm roof was woven by Yanomami Indians brought from the Amazon. A 120-tonne air-conditioning system was installed. A 60-metre containing wall was constructed in a ravine.

21 *'Ser' and 'estar'*

If the correct use of 'ser' and 'estar' constitutes one of the trickiest conceptual problems faced by learners of Spanish, the problem largely disappears when translating into English, since both verbs can in many cases be translated simply as 'to be'. Nevertheless, the translator needs to be aware of the essential differences between them and to be alert to opportunities for bringing out those differences or making them explicit. Since 'ser' is the verb that means 'to be' in the purest, most straightforward sense of essence, existence or identity, it is the more likely of the two to be translated simply as 'to be'. This essential, defining function may be underlined in translation by turning a 'ser' + adjective construction into 'ser' + noun phrase: 'Es bueno tu hijo' – 'He's a good boy, your son.'

'Estar', on the other hand, has a more complex function, meaning literally 'to stand' or 'to be located' and figuratively 'to have arrived at a state, situation or condition' (it implies perfective aspect, expressing the result of an action having taken place). Consequently, the translation of 'estar', especially when explicitly contrasted with 'ser', may at times require a verb other than 'to be' ('look, feel, taste'), or adaptation of the following adjective:

Este vino es muy bueno > This wine is very good/a very good wine [An observation based on looking at the label].

Este vino está muy bueno > This wine tastes very good/is very tasty/is in very good condition [An observation based on taking a sip].

¿Ves aquellas chicas? Qué buenas están, ¿no? > See those girls? Hot, aren't they?

The following example from a play offers a simple and elegant contrast between the two notions of being:

Aún es joven, pero no tiene solución porque está vieja por dentro.
(Buero Vallejo 1964: 71)

She's still young really, but there's no hope for her because she's grown old inside.

As a classroom exercise, discuss the contrast between the two verbs developed in the following extract and possible translations of the phrase 'estar y ser' used in it:

Aparentemente estoy libre, mas la verdad es que soy mi propia cárcel. Nunca como ahora he comprendido mejor la diferencia entre estar y ser. Cuando estaba presa, aún era alguien, pues Pepe vivía, vivíamos, aunque humillados y envilecidos. Ahora, convertida en mi propia prisión perpetua, no soy nada; casi casi ni estoy tampoco en ninguna parte.
(Espinosa 1995: 110)

22 Phrasal verbs

The way in which a verb in English can be combined with a preposition or adverb (or even a combination of the two) to form a compound expression, modulating or completely transforming the basic meaning of the verb, provides a flexible and idiomatically expressive resource that has no counterpart in Spanish. For example, each of the following phrases based on 'to put' corresponds to various verbs in Spanish, which may have analogues in English that belong to a more formal register:

put on	poner(se), asumir, fingir, encender
put off	posponer, distraer, desanimar, apagar
put up (with)	subir, soportar, tolerar, hospedar, colgar
put down (for)	dejar, sofocar, rebajar, anotar, alistar(se)

put in (for)	meter, instalar, dedicar, solicitar
put out	sacar, extinguir, molestar, difundir

The choice between a phrasal verb and a more formal (often Latinate) single verb may therefore be crucial in conditioning social and tonal register when translating from Spanish into English: 'entrar' > 'to enter' or 'to go into'; 'atravesar' > 'to cross/traverse' or 'to go/walk/travel across'; 'inventar' > 'to invent' or 'to make up', and so on. Taking advantage of opportunities to introduce phrasal verbs into a TT can make a valuable contribution to achieving an idiomatic style and conveying spatial relationships or dynamics of movement. As a quick group exercise, identify the phrasal verbs in the TT below and consider possible alternatives to them:

ST

> Leonardo Villalba se despertó sobresaltado, una hora antes de que el tren llegara a su destino, y se sentó en la litera, entre periódicos arrugados y ropas revueltas. Dio la luz. La calefacción estaba demasiado alta. Acababa de soñar que viajaba a gran velocidad en una apisonadora gigantesca con aspecto de portaaviones, que arrasaba a su paso bosques y casas. Desde   5
> una especie de cabina alta de mandos, blindada en cristal, contemplaba el estrago que él mismo iba provocando, incapaz de atajarlo ni de salir de allí, a pesar de que buscaba afanosamente al tacto alguna puerta o ranura en aquellas paredes herméticas.
>
> (Martín Gaite 1994: 309)

TT

> An hour before the train was due to arrive, Leonardo Villalba woke up with a start and sat up on his bunk amidst crumpled newspapers and tangled clothes. He switched on the light. The heating was turned up too high. He had just been dreaming that he was tearing along in a gigantic steamroller that was rather like an aircraft carrier, flattening forests and   5
> houses as it went. Sitting high up in a kind of reinforced glass cockpit, he gazed down at the devastation he was bringing about, unable to prevent it or to get out, despite frantically groping around for a door or an opening of any kind in the airtight walls.

Practical 7

7.1 The formal properties of texts: syntax and discourse

Assignment

(i)   Working in groups, examine the ST and TT below, identifying examples of the types of syntactical difference set out in the table on pp. 116–17 and discussing the implications for translation.

(ii) Suggest alternative translations of phrases or sentences where appropriate.

Contextual information

The first part of the ST is the beginning of Javier Marías's best-selling novel, *Corazón tan blanco* (first published in 1992). The second part is from further on in the same extended paragraph that takes up the first eight pages of the book. The publisher's blurb for the Alfaguara edition describes the work as 'una novela hipnótica sobre el secreto y su conveniencia posible, sobre el matrimonio, el asesinato y la instigación, sobre la sospecha, el hablar y el callar y la persuasión: sobre los corazones tan blancos que poco a poco se van tiñendo y acaban siendo lo que nunca quisieron ser'. The TT is Margaret Jull Costa's translation, *A Heart So White* (New York: New Directions, 2000). This edition describes the novel as 'a sort of anti-detective story of human nature' and suggests that 'Marías elegantly sends shafts of inquisitory light into shadows'.

Turn to pp. 140–1 for source text and target text.

Source text

No he querido saber, pero he sabido que una de las niñas, cuando ya no
era niña y no hacía mucho que había regresado de su viaje de bodas, entró
en el cuarto de baño, se puso frente al espejo, se abrió la blusa, se quitó
el sostén y se buscó el corazón con la punta de la pistola de su propio
padre, que estaba en el comedor con parte de la familia y tres invitados.   5
Cuando se oyó la detonación, unos cinco minutos después de que la niña
hubiera abandonado la mesa, el padre no se levantó enseguida, sino que
se quedó durante algunos segundos paralizado con la boca llena, sin
atreverse a masticar ni a tragar ni menos aún a devolver el bocado al plato;
y cuando por fin se alzó y corrió hacia el cuarto de baño, los que lo   10
siguieron vieron cómo mientras descubría el cuerpo ensangrentado de su
hija y se echaba las manos a la cabeza iba pasando el bocado de carne de
un lado a otro de la boca, sin saber todavía qué hacer con él. Llevaba la
servilleta en la mano, y no la soltó hasta que al cabo de un rato reparó en
el sostén tirado sobre el bidet, y entonces lo cubrió con el paño que tenía   15
a mano o tenía en la mano y sus labios habían manchado, como si le diera
más vergüenza la visión de la prenda íntima que la del cuerpo derribado
y semidesnudo con el que la prenda había estado en contacto hasta hacía
muy poco: el cuerpo sentado a la mesa o alejándose por el pasillo o también
de pie. Antes, con gesto automático, el padre había cerrado el grifo del   20
lavabo, el del agua fría, que estaba abierto con mucha presión. [. . .] La
doncella, que en el momento del disparo había soltado sobre la mesa de
mármol del office las fuentes vacías que acababa de traer, y por eso lo
había confundido con su propio y simultáneo estrépito, había estado
colocando luego en una bandeja, con mucho tiento y poca mano – 25
mientras el chico vaciaba sus cajas con ruido también –, la tarta helada
que le habían mandado comprar aquella mañana por haber invitados; y
una vez lista y montada la tarta, y cuando hubo calculado que en el
comedor habrían terminado el segundo plato, la había llevado hasta allí y
la había depositado sobre una mesa en la que, para su desconcierto, aún   30
había restos de carne y cubiertos y servilletas soltados de cualquier manera
sobre el mantel y ningún comensal (sólo había un plato totalmente limpio,
como si uno de ellos, la hija mayor, hubiera comido más rápido y lo hubiera
rebañado además, o bien ni siquiera se hubiera servido carne).

(Marías 1999: 11, 16)

Target text

I did not want to know but I have since come to know that one of the girls, when she wasn't a girl anymore and hadn't long been back from her honeymoon, went into the bathroom, stood in front of the mirror, unbuttoned her blouse, took off her bra and aimed her own father's gun at her heart, her father at the time was in the dining room with other 5 members of the family and three guests. When they heard the shot, some five minutes after the girl had left the table, her father didn't get up at once, but stayed there for a few seconds, paralysed, his mouth still full of food, not daring to chew or swallow, far less to spit the food out on to his plate; and when he finally did get up and run to the bathroom, those who followed 10 him noticed that when he discovered the blood-spattered body of his daughter and clutched his head in his hands, he kept passing the mouthful of meat from one cheek to the other, still not knowing what to do with it. He was carrying his napkin in one hand and he didn't let go of it until, after a few moments, he noticed the bra that had been flung into the bidet 15 and he covered it with the one piece of cloth that he had to hand or rather in his hand and which his lips had sullied, as if he were more ashamed of the sight of her underwear than of her fallen, half-naked body with which, until only a short time before, the article of underwear had been in contact: the same body that had been sitting at the table, that had walked down the 20 corridor, that had stood there. Before that, with an automatic gesture, the father had turned off the tap in the basin, the cold tap, which had been turned full on. [. . .] The maid who, at the precise moment when the shot rang out, had been setting down on the marble table in the scullery the empty dishes she'd just brought through and had thus confused the noise 25 of the shot with the clatter she herself was making, had since been arranging on another dish, with enormous care but little skill – the errand boy meanwhile was making just as much noise unpacking his boxes – the ice-cream cake she'd been told to buy that morning because there would be guests for lunch; and once the cake was ready and duly arrayed on the 30 plate, and when she judged that the people in the dining room would have finished their second course, she'd carried it through and placed it on the table on which, much to her bewilderment, there were still bits of meat on the plates and knives and forks and napkins scattered randomly about the tablecloth, and not a single guest (there was only one absolutely clean 35 plate, as if one of them, the eldest daughter, had eaten more quickly than the others and had even wiped her plate clean, or rather hadn't even served herself with any meat).

(Marías 2000: 3, 6)

7.2 The formal properties of texts: syntax and discourse

Assignment

(i)   Discuss the strategic problems confronting the translator of the ST below, paying particular attention to its salient formal properties on the sentential and discourse levels, especially constructions featuring 'se'.

(ii) Translate the extract as if for publication in a series of European Classics produced by a UK or US publisher.

(iii) Explain the main decisions of detail you made in producing your TT.

Contextual information

The ST is from *La Regenta,* by Leopoldo Alas ('Clarín'), first published in 1885. The novel is a satirical exploration of the mores of a dilapidated provincial town. The extract is part of an extended scene set in the Casino, which is the regular meeting place and club of the town worthies.

Source text

De los periódicos e ilustraciones se hacía más uso; tanto que aquéllos desaparecían casi todas las noches y los grabados de mérito eran cuidadosamente arrancados. Esta cuestión del hurto de periódicos era de las difíciles que tenían que resolver las juntas. ¿Qué se hacía? ¿Se les ponía grillete a los papeles? Los socios arrancaban las hojas o se llevaban papel   5
y hierro. Se resolvió últimamente dejar los periódicos libres, pero ejercer una gran vigilancia. Era inútil. Don Frutos Redondo, el más rico americano, no podía dormirse sin leer en la cama el *Imparcial* del Casino. Y no había de trasladar su lecho al gabinete de lectura. Se llevaba el periódico. Aquellos cinco céntimos que ahorraba de esta manera, le sabían   10
a gloria. En cuanto al papel de cartas que desaparecía también, y era más caro, se tomó la resolución de dar un pliego, y gracias, al socio que lo pedía con mucha necesidad. El conserje había adquirido un humor de alcaide de presidio en este trato. Miraba a los socios que leían como a gente de sospechosa probidad; les guardaba escasas consideraciones. No   15
siempre que se le llamaba acudía, y solía negarse a mudar las plumas oxidadas.

(Alas 1991, vol. 1: 327–8)

8   Literal (denotative) meaning and translation issues

In Chapter 2 we raised objections to using the concept of 'equivalence' in assessing the relationship between a ST and a corresponding TT. This is because it does not seem helpful to say that good translation produces a TT that has 'the same meaning' as the corresponding ST, when such a claim rests on the comparison of two virtually imponderable and indeterminable qualities. The term 'meaning' is especially elastic and indeterminate when applied to an entire text. At one end of the scale, the 'meaning' of a text might designate its putative sociocultural significance, importance and impact – a historian might define the meaning of *Mein Kampf* in such terms. At the other end of the scale, the 'meaning' might designate the personal, private and emotional impact the text has on a unique individual at a unique point in time – say, the impact of *Mein Kampf* on a German bride presented with a copy of it at her wedding in 1938. Between these two extremes lie many shades of shared conventional meaning intrinsic to the text because of its internal structure and explicit contents, and the relation these bear to the semantic conventions and tendencies of the SL in its ordinary, everyday usage.

Meanings in a text that are fully supported by ordinary semantic conventions (such as the lexical convention that 'window' refers to a particular kind of aperture in a wall or roof) are normally known as **literal** (or 'denotative' or 'cognitive') meanings. In the case of words, it is this basic literal meaning that is given in dictionary definitions. However, even the dictionary definition of a word, which is meant to crystallize exactly that range of 'things' that a particular word can denote in everyday usage, is not without its problems. This is because the intuitive understanding that native language-users have of the literal meanings of individual words does itself tend to be rather fluid. That is, a dictionary definition imposes, by abstraction and crystallization of a 'core' meaning, a rigidity of meaning that words do not often show in reality. In addition, dictionaries very often differ from one another in defining literal meanings, especially of words denoting abstractions. As an example for class discussion, here are the abridged *Merriam-Webster OnLine* and the online *Oxford English Dictionary* definitions of 'theology':

Merriam-Webster: 'theology'

1   the study of religious faith, practice, and experience; *especially*: the study of God and of God's relation to the world
2a   a theological theory or system <Thomist *theology*> <a *theology* of atonement>
b   a distinctive body of theological opinion <Catholic *theology*>
3   a usually 4-year course of specialized religious training in a Roman Catholic major seminary

dogmatic theology: DOGMATICS
liberation theology: a religious movement especially among Roman Catholic clergy in Latin America that combines political philosophy usually of a Marxist orientation with a theology of salvation as liberation from injustice
natural theology: theology deriving its knowledge of God from the study of nature independent of special revelation
practical theology: the study of the institutional activities of religion (as preaching, church administration, pastoral care, and liturgics)
systematic theology: a branch of theology concerned with summarizing the doctrinal traditions of a religion (as Christianity) especially with a view to relating the traditions convincingly to the religion's present-day setting

                        (Merriam-Webster 2007–2008)

OED: 'theology'

1a   The study or science which treats of God, His nature and attributes, and His relations with man and the universe; 'the science of things divine' (Hooker); divinity.

Biblical theology: orig. theology as a non-dogmatic description of the religious doctrines contained in the Bible, following J. P. Gabler's distinction, in 1787, between biblical and dogmatic theology; now usu. the exposition of biblical texts (both O.T. and N.T.), based on the presupposition that there is a common biblical way of thinking which informs the Bible as a whole.

dogmatic theology, theology as authoritatively held and taught by the church; a scientific statement of Christian dogma. *natural theology*, theology based upon reasoning from natural facts apart from revelation. *pastoral theology*, that branch of theology which deals with religious truth in its relation to the spiritual needs of men, and the 'cure of souls': see PASTORAL *a.* 4.

b   A particular theological system or theory. Also *fig. liberation theology, theology of liberation*: see LIBERATION THEOLOGY.
c   Applied to pagan or non-Christian systems.
d   In trivial or disparaging use: a system of theoretical principles; an (impractical or rigid) ideology. Cf. THEOLOGICAL *a. (n.)* 3.

2a   Rarely used for Holy Scripture. So late Gr. Θεολογία (Pseudo-Dion. *De Cæl. Hier.* 9 §3), med.L. *theologia. Obs.*
b   Hence, *virtues of theology* (also *vertues theologyes*, (?) *theologycs*) = 'theological virtues': see THEOLOGICAL 1. *Obs.*
3   Metaphysics. *Obs.*
      Addition 1993: [1.] [b.] *theology of hope* [tr. G. *Theologie der Hoffnung*], a theory popularized by West German theologians in the 1960s, emphasizing Christian hope as the basis for human action and realized eschatology; cf. LIBERATION THEOLOGY *n.*

                        (OED 1989–2008)

We shall return to these definitions in discussing possible translations of 'teología'.

Further to all of this, once words are put into different contexts, their literal meanings become even more flexible. These two facts make it infinitely difficult to pin down the specific literal meaning of any text of any complexity. This difficulty is still further compounded by the fact that literal meanings supported by a consensus of semantic conventions are not the only types of meaning that can function in a text and nuance its interpretations. As we shall see in Chapter 9, there are various connotative tendencies – not sufficiently cut and dried to qualify as conventional meanings accepted by consensus – which can play an important role in how a text is to be interpreted and translated.

Synonymy

Although the apparent fixity of literal meaning is something of an illusion, a narrow concept of 'semantic equivalence' is still useful as a measure of correspondence between the literal meanings of isolated linguistic expressions (words or phrases) figuring in texts. If one is prepared to isolate such expressions, one can talk about semantic equivalence as a possible, and fairly objective, relationship between linguistic items that have identical literal meanings, such as 'hoover' and 'vacuum cleaner', or 'peewit' and 'lapwing' in British English (in some parts of the US peewit refers to flycatchers). In what follows, we shall discuss ways of comparing degrees of correspondence in literal meaning between STs and TTs, and our discussion will presuppose the type of semantic equivalence defined here.

We make one further basic supposition: that literal meaning is a matter of *categories* into which, through a complex interplay of inclusion and exclusion, a language divides the totality of communicable experience. So, for example, the literal meaning of the word 'page' does not consist in the fact that one can use the word to denote the object you are staring at as you read this. It consists rather in the fact that all over the world (in past, present and future) one may find 'similar' objects each of which is *included in* the category of 'page', as well as countless other objects that are, of course, *excluded from* it. To define a literal meaning, then, is to specify the 'range' covered by a word or phrase in such a way that one knows what items are included in that range or category and what items are excluded from it. The most useful way to visualize literal meanings is by thinking of them as circles, because in this way we can represent intersections between categories, and thus reflect overlaps in literal meaning between different expressions. In exploring correspondence in literal meaning, it is particularly the intersections between categories that are significant; they provide, as it were, a measure of semantic equivalence.

Comparisons of literal meaning made possible by considering overlaps between categories, and visualized as intersections between circles, are usually drawn between linguistic expressions in the same language. They allow, in the semantic description of a language, for an assessment of types and degrees of semantic correspondence between items (for example, lexical items). There is, however, no reason why analogous comparisons may not be made between expressions from two or more different languages, as a way of assessing and representing types and degrees of cross-linguistic semantic equivalence.

To take a simple example of our suggested way of visualizing literal meanings, the expressions 'my mother's father' and 'my maternal grandfather' may be represented as two separate circles. Their two ranges of literal meaning, however, coincide perfectly. This can be visualized as moving the two circles on top of each other and finding that they cover one another exactly, as in Figure 8.1.

Both in general and in every specific instance of use, 'my mother's father' and 'my maternal grandfather' include and exclude exactly the same referents; that is, their literal meanings are identical in range. This exemplifies the strongest form of semantic equivalence: full **synonymy**. Note, however, that in different contexts the two formulations may not be used in the same way, and are unlikely to be interchangeable. 'My maternal grandfather', for example, is likely to be deemed more formal.

Just as alternative expressions in the same language may be full synonyms, so, in principle at least, there may be full synonymy across two different languages. As one might expect, the closer the SL and the TL are in the way they process and categorize speakers' experiences of the world, the more likely it is that there will be full cross-linguistic synonyms between the two languages. Thus, one can fairly confidently say that 'un vaso de agua' and 'a glass of water' cover exactly the same range of situations, and are, therefore, fully synonymous in their literal meanings, as is seen in Figure 8.2.

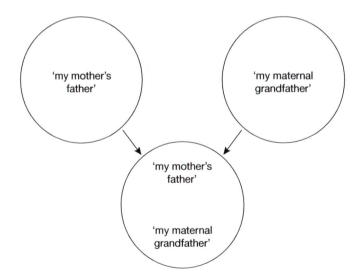

Figure 8.1

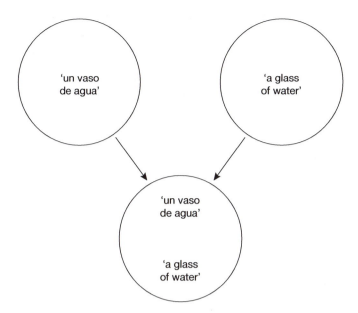

Figure 8.2

Hypernymy–hyponymy

Unfortunately, full cross-linguistic synonymy is more the exception than the rule, even between historically and culturally related languages. More often than not, the apparent 'nearest equivalent' for translating the literal meaning of a ST expression falls short of being a full TL synonym. Compare, for example, 'el chico abre la ventana' with 'the boy opens the window'. It is at least possible that the Spanish phrase refers to a progressive event reported by the speaker. This would have to be expressed in English by 'the boy *is opening* the window'. That is, 'el chico abre la ventana' and 'the boy opens the window' are not full synonyms, but have non-identical ranges of literal meaning. There is a common element between the two phrases, but the Spanish one covers a wider range of situations, a range that is necessarily covered by at least two different expressions in English. This can be shown diagrammatically, as in Figure 8.3.

The type of relationship between these two phrases can also be instanced within a single language. For example, 'I bought a boat' and 'I bought a dinghy' have a common element of literal meaning, but show a discrepancy in the fact that 'I bought a boat' covers a wider range of situations, including in its literal meaning situations that are excluded from 'I bought a dinghy' – such as 'I bought a yacht', 'I bought a punt', and so on. This is seen diagrammatically in Figure 8.4.

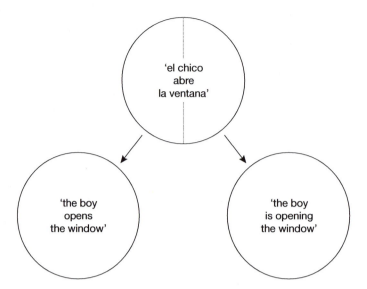

Figure 8.3

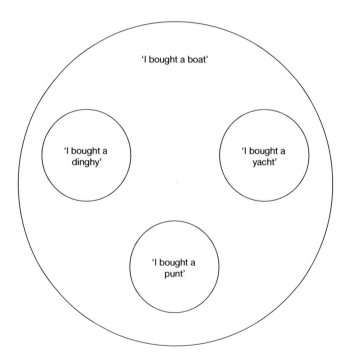

Figure 8.4

The relationship between 'I bought a boat' and 'I bought a dinghy' is known as hypernymy–hyponymy. The expression with the wider, less specific, range of literal meaning is a **hypernym** of the one with the narrower and more specific literal meaning. Conversely, the narrower one is a **hyponym** of the wider one. So, 'I bought a boat' is a hypernym of each of the other three phases, while these are hyponyms of 'I bought a boat'. Each of the small circles above could have smaller circles within them: in relation to 'I bought a *sailing* dinghy', 'I bought a dinghy' is hypernymic (and 'sailing dinghy' is now the hyponym). Similarly, 'el chico abre la ventana' is a hypernym of both 'the boy opens the window' and 'the boy is opening the window', while these two are hyponyms of the Spanish expression.

Hypernymy–hyponymy is so widespread in any given language that one can say that the entire fabric of linguistic reference is built up on such relationships. Take, for example, some of the alternative ways in which one can refer to an object – say, a particular pen. If there is a need to particularize, one can use a phrase with a fairly narrow and specific meaning, such as 'the black pen in my hand'. If such detail is unnecessary and one wants to generalize, one can call it 'a writing implement', 'an implement', 'an object' or, even more vaguely, just 'something'.

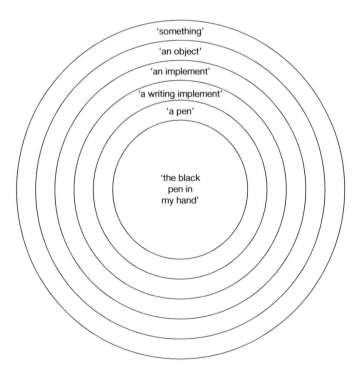

Figure 8.5

It is in the very essence of the richness of all languages that they offer a whole set of different expressions, each with a different range of inclusiveness, for designating any object, any situation, anything whatsoever. Thus the series 'the black pen in my hand', 'a pen', 'a writing implement', 'an implement', 'an object', 'something' is a series organized on the basis of successively larger, wider inclusiveness – that is, on the basis of hypernymy–hyponymy. The series can be visualized as a set of increasingly large concentric circles, larger circles representing hypernyms, smaller ones hyponyms, as in Figure 8.5. As this example shows, the same external reality can be described in an indefinite number of ways, depending on how precise or vague one needs to be.

By its very nature, translation is concerned with rephrasing, and in particular with rephrasing so as to preserve to best advantage the integrity of a ST message, including its degree of precision or vagueness. Therefore, the fact that both a hypernym and a hyponym can serve for conveying a given message is of great importance to translation practice. It means that, as soon as one acknowledges that there is no full TL synonym for a particular ST expression (for example, 'el chico abre la ventana'), one must start looking for an appropriate TL hypernym or hyponym. In fact, translators do this automatically, which is why they may see 'the boy opens the window' as the 'nearest' semantic equivalent to 'el chico abre la ventana'; but they do not always do it carefully or successfully. For example, in most contexts, particularly if the person referred to is present at the time of utterance, 'aquella es mi prima' is effectively translated as 'that's my cousin'. Yet the English

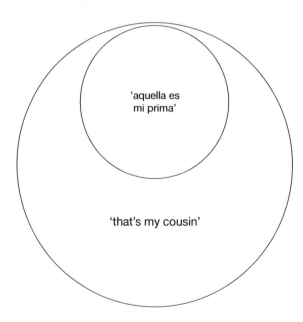

Figure 8.6

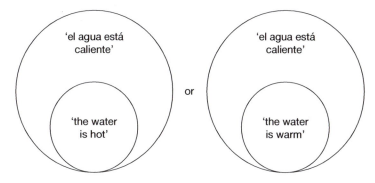

Figure 8.7

expression is wider and less specific in literal meaning than the Spanish one, since 'cousin' could also mean 'primo'. In other words, a SL hyponym is unhesitatingly translated by a TL hypernym as its nearest semantic equivalent, as shown in Figure 8.6.

Conversely, translating 'el agua está caliente' into English necessarily implies choosing between 'the water is hot' and 'the water is warm'. Of course, contextual and situational clues will normally determine which of the alternatives is appropriate in a given TT. The point, however, is that each of the English phrases designates a different set of circumstances and has a literal meaning distinct from the other. Whichever alternative is chosen, the translator is rendering a SL hypernym by a TL hyponym. This can be represented as shown in Figure 8.7.

Where plausible cross-linguistic synonyms are not available, translating by a hypernym or a hyponym is standard practice and entirely unremarkable. Indeed, choosing a hypernym or hyponym even where a synonym does exist may actually be the mark of a good translation. For instance, the term 'toro bravo' is sufficiently current in Spanish usage to be used with discrimination even in non-specialized and non-technical narrative contexts; yet in English, translating it literally as 'wild bull' would seem implausible in the TL, and rendering it 'fighting bull', rather than simply using the generic term 'bull', would in some cases be unduly pedantic and cumbersome. Although not a precise synonym, in most contexts, except technical ones, the hypernym 'bull' is the appropriate translation of 'toro bravo'. It is, then, only when using a TL hypernym or hyponym is unnecessary, or unnecessarily extreme, or misleading, that a TT can be criticized on this basis.

Particularizing translation and generalizing translation

Translating by a hyponym implies that the TT expression has a narrower and more specific literal meaning than the ST expression. That is, the TT gives *particulars* that are not given by the ST. We shall therefore call this **particularizing translation**, or **particularization** for short. Thus, in our earlier example, 'the water is warm' is a particularizing translation of 'el agua está caliente'.

Conversely, translating by a hypernym implies that the TT expression has a wider and less specific literal meaning than the ST expression. That is, the TT is more *general,* omitting details that are given by the ST. We shall call this **generalizing translation**, or **generalization** for short. Our example of translating 'prima' as 'cousin' is a case of generalizing translation.

Particularization and generalization both imply a degree of translation loss as we defined it in Chapter 2: detail is either added to, or omitted from, the ST meaning. However, neither the addition nor the omission of detail is necessarily a matter for criticism, or even comment, in evaluating a TT. We outline here a set of criteria under which particularizing and generalizing translation can be judged acceptable or unacceptable.

Particularizing translation is acceptable on two conditions: first, that the TL offers no suitable alternative in the form of an idiomatic and textually appropriate synonym; second, that the added detail is implicit in the ST and fits in with the overall context of the ST. For instance, translating 'patrona' (which has a range of meanings including 'patroness, female employer, landlady') as 'madam' is evidently the appropriate particularization in a TT that is set in a brothel.

Particularizing translation is *not* acceptable where one or more of the following three conditions hold: first, if the TL does offer a suitable alternative to the addition of unnecessary detail; second, if the added detail creates discrepancies in the TT; third, if the added detail contributes to a misinterpretation of the overall context of the ST. As an example, one may take the following extract from the section on 'Ética' in one of Gaspar Melchor de Jovellanos's essays on public education, 'Humanidades' (first published in 1794): 'Si volvemos los ojos a nuestras escuelas generales, vemos que [. . .] la enseñanza de la teología abraza muchas cuestiones de la ética cristiana [. . .]' (Jovellanos 1840: 116). Rendering 'teología as 'theology' instead of 'religious education' or 'religious studies' would be unacceptable in this context for all three reasons: first, 'religious studies' offers a more exact alternative to the unduly particularizing term 'theology'; second, the specification of 'theology' in an educational context tends to imply a narrower curriculum than one which includes faith-based moral issues at the education under discussion ('escuelas generales'); third, the specification of 'theology' creates a misleading impression of the educational system described in the overall context of the essay.

Generalizing translation is acceptable on two conditions: first, that the TL offers no suitable alternative; second, that the omitted detail either is clear and can be recovered from the overall context of the TT, or is unimportant to the ST. For example, in the context of the Cortázar passage in Practical 2.1 (pp. 26–7), translating 'brasero' as 'heater' occasions a harmless, insignificant translation loss.

Generalizing translation is *not* acceptable where one or more of the following three conditions hold: first, if the omitted details are important to the ST; second, if the TL does offer suitable alternatives to the omission of this detail; third, if the omitted detail is not compensated for elsewhere in the TT, and cannot be recovered from the overall context of the TT. Thus, translating Spanish 'hoja de laurel' by the botanically generic term 'laurel', rather than as 'bay leaf', may be relatively harmless in the context of a novel, but it may occasion potentially lethal translation loss in a recipe book.

Partially overlapping translation

As well as particularizing and generalizing translation, there is another type of semantic near-equivalence. This is more easily illustrated in phrases than in single words. Take the phrase 'The teacher treated brother and sister differently'. 'La profesora trató a los hermanos de un modo distinto' is probably as close a literal rendering into Spanish as possible. Yet in the English phrase the sex of the teacher is not explicitly specified, whereas the Spanish text makes this literally explicit. In respect to the sex of the teacher, the Spanish TT *particularizes* (just as it would have done in specifying 'el profesor'). Conversely, in the English phrase the gender difference between the two siblings is specified unambiguously, whereas the Spanish TT leaves this ambiguous: the Spanish TT *generalizes* here, in that 'los hermanos' is a gender-neutral term, more or less equivalent in its literal meaning to 'siblings'.

In other words, this TT combines particularization with generalization, adding a detail not found in the ST and omitting a detail that is given in the ST. This is best visualized as two partially overlapping circles, as shown in Figure 8.8.

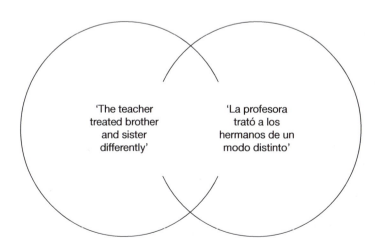

'The teacher treated brother and sister differently'

'La profesora trató a los hermanos de un modo distinto'

Figure 8.8

This type of case is a further category of degree in the translation of literal meaning: along with synonymic, particularizing and generalizing translation, there is **partially overlapping translation**, or **overlapping translation** for short. The concept of overlapping translation applies less obviously, but more importantly, in the case of individual words (as distinct from phrases). For example, if in a particular context Spanish 'profesora' were to be rendered as 'professor', this would constitute a case of overlapping translation: the common element between ST and TT is the reference to a member of the teaching profession, but the TT *loses* the detail of female gender reference, while it *adds* explicit reference to the teacher's level of employment, British and American uses of 'professor' being limited to tertiary (in particular, university) education.

Once again, overlapping translation may or may not invite comment when one is evaluating a TT. The conditions under which it is acceptable and the criteria for criticizing it are similar to those for particularization and generalization. Overlapping translation is acceptable on two conditions: first, if the TL offers no suitable alternatives in the form of closer semantic equivalents; second, if the *omitted* detail is either unimportant or can be recovered from the overall TT context, and the *added* detail is implicit in, or at least not contradictory to, the overall ST context. For example, 'bullfighter' is an accurate idiomatic rendering of 'matador', but it does *add* explicit reference to bullfighting, and *lose* the reference to 'killing', which is explicit in the ST.

Overlapping translation is *not* acceptable when one or more of the following three conditions hold: first, if the omitted detail is important to the ST but cannot be recovered from the overall context of the TT; second, if the added detail creates discrepancies in the TT; third, if the TL does offer suitable alternatives to avoiding either the omissions or the additions or both. For an example, see the translation of 'ruin' by 'wicked' in the TT used in Practical 8.1 and our comments on p. 160.

Translating gender

In this chapter, and in our discussion of compensation in Chapter 3, we have used several examples in which what is at stake in literal meaning is the expression of gender. Translation issues relating to gender arise in the transfer of texts from Spanish to English because the two languages mark grammatical gender differently: Spanish marks grammatical gender across nouns, adjectives, articles and pronouns, and English only through the third-person singular personal and possessive pronouns, that is 'she', 'his', etc. Grammatical gender is a linguistic category of nouns, on which agreement with adjectives (and pronouns and articles in Spanish) depends, and which forms two (feminine, masculine) or more classes (Corbett 1991: 2–6). There is no natural link between grammatical gender and the category of the object described, as is evident if we consider the various Spanish nouns by which 'the chair' might be translated. There is nothing intrinsically male or female about the broadly overlapping terms 'silla' or 'asiento' nor about the hyponyms of chair, 'el sillón' and 'la butaca' ('armchair'). Consequently, the grammatical gender of inanimate objects can usually be considered accidental. Although animals have two sexes, names for many animals other than the most common are grammatically fixed as either masculine or feminine, such as 'el búfalo' or 'la hiena', and qualified by 'macho' or 'hembra' as necessary. Some studies suggest that native speakers associate stronger and more positive attributes more readily with masculine nouns than feminine ones (i.e. strong and solid buffalo versus hysterical, hypocritical hyena). Domestic pets and farmed animals are likely to be referred to by gender-specific nouns, 'la gata', 'el buey', 'el cerdito', 'las ovejas' but, unless it is conventional in the TL to attribute a gender to them or the ST emphasizes gender characteristics, neuter pronouns are more likely to be appropriate than he or she.

However, many linguists agree that, when referring to humans, there is a tendency for feminine nouns to refer to women, and masculine ones to refer to men; as in 'la secretaria', 'el secretario' or 'el cocinero', 'la cocinera'. The artificiality of this correlation is implicitly acknowledged by a few words that can be used generically without variation according to the sex of the people referred to: 'el ser', 'el individuo' (although 'la individua' does sometimes appear in colloquial language), 'la persona', 'la gente', 'la víctima'. In English, the feminist argument that forms such as 'manageress' and 'poetess' are unnecessary and patronizing has largely won the day, but in Spanish debates about the use of feminine forms of nouns denoting professions or status are still very much alive: 'la jefa' or 'la jefe'; 'el abogado' (man or woman), 'la abogado' or 'la abogada'? The translator needs to be alert to the implications of such choices and make sensible decisions about whether they need to be reflected in the TT. These decisions may be straightforward in some cases; for example, to translate 'la abogada' as unmarked 'the lawyer' but compensate by ensuring that her sex is indicated somewhere by a subject pronoun ('she') not present in the ST. One also needs to be careful not to introduce unjustified connotations when translating such terms, by, for instance, assuming that 'cocinero' should be 'chef' (a high-status professional role) but 'cocinera' should be 'cook' (a lower-status, more domestic role). Note, however, that until relatively recently the feminine form of professions referred primarily to the wife of the male post-holder. For example, the title of Leopoldo Alas's novel *La Regenta* (1884–5; translated by John Rutherford as *La Regenta* (1984; corrected version 2005)) refers to the protagonist, Ana Ozores, spouse of the retired city magistrate ('el regente').

In lower registers in Spanish, women's names are more frequently preceded by the definite article – 'la Carmen', 'la Refugio', 'la Rosalía' – than men's, and its use adds a nuance of gossip or tittle-tattle, except in Chile and Catalonia where it appears frequently, even in educated speech. Very famous women's (but not men's) surnames may also be introduced by the definite article: la Callas, la Pardo Bazán, la Monroe. The context will determine whether or not the translator needs to compensate for loss of the definite article, that is 'Carmen' versus 'that Carmen woman' or 'Monroe' versus 'Monroe herself'. Another gender imbalance arises from the fact that, whereas in Britain and the USA, married women have traditionally chosen to adopt their husband's surname and the nubility title 'Mrs', in Spain, married women keep both of their own surnames, but may choose to be known as 'la (señora) de'. An example of translation issues arising from conventional use of titles occurs in Benito Pérez Galdós's novel, *La de Bringas* (first published in 1884). The novel's protagonist has an aristocratic and illustrious sounding name: Rosalía Pipaón de la Barca (where de la Barca recalls the famous Golden Age playwright Pedro Calderón de la Barca), and the novel's title alludes to her status as wife of Francisco de Bringas. In the preface to her translation, Catherine Jagoe observes that Galdós frequently uses the article 'la' + first name or + an adjective to refer to his female characters to convey varied attitudinal connotations (Pérez Galdós 1996: xxxv). Consequently, she has translated the novel's title as *That Bringas Woman* to convey a familiar and derogatory tinge. Jagoe is undoubtedly right that the narrator conveys just such an attitude to Rosalía in the novel, but by adding this nuance to its title considerable loss is occasioned since the ST expression is actually attitudinally neutral, and a cultural equivalent is available in the TL: Mrs.

The generic masculine may be used in singular or plural forms: 'Los alumnos aventajados recibieron un diploma'; 'El trabajador debe exigir sus derechos'. The **generic** or **androcentric masculine** refers to the use of the masculine gender to refer to male and female referents, or to describe a mixed-sex group regardless of the proportion of women and men comprising it. 'Los alumnos' could refer to a mixed-sex group of students or to an all-male group, and 'el trabajador' could refer to a single-sex or mixed-sex work force. These examples show that translators should give careful attention to context when translating gender. Consider, for example, that 'Outstanding schoolboys received diplomas' and 'The worker ought to demand his rights' would be inappropriate for STs set in all-girl boarding schools or a female-staffed tobacco factory, respectively. Where appropriate, there is an increased tendency to use splitting or gender neutral terms (particularly in legal and administrative contexts), and these solutions should be borne in mind when translating documents of this type: 'Gifted boy and girls . . .' or 'Gifted pupils . . .' or 'Workers . . . they . . .'.

This issue is a matter of concern for campaigners against sexist language. For example, the Ayuntamiento de Málaga's *Manual del lenguaje administrativo no sexista* recommends that a group of people of both sexes should not be referred to as if they were all male ('los alumnos') but in a way that explicitly embraces both sexes ('los alumnos y las alumnas') or is gender-neutral ('el alumnado'), and furthermore that each gender-specific term should be qualified by its own adjective in the appropriate form: 'Los trabajadores y trabajadoras de esta empresa son habilidosos y habilidosas' (Ayala Castro *et al.* 2002: 38). Such scrupulously careful language becomes very difficult to translate without either losing the effect altogether or making the TT even more cumbersome than the ST. 'Los trabajadores y trabajadoras' could be translated as 'male and female workers' but it would not be obvious to readers of the TT why this was being specified; and there is no way of imitating in English the duplication of the adjective in masculine and feminine forms. The translator would therefore need to accept the double translation loss at this point ('workers in this company are highly skilled') and compensate elsewhere by introducing other kinds of markedly non-sexist language, such as specifying 'he or she'. In British English it is acceptable to use a plural anaphoric pronoun ('they') with generic singular antecedents in informal registers only: 'everyone should leave without putting on their coat'. A typical problem experienced by translators of Spanish to English, therefore, is that gender information is either lost or overstated. Suzanne Romaine has argued that the structure of languages like Spanish obliges the speaker to give information about gender and status, which English does not require:

> To say *estás cansada* means not simply you are tired, but that the addressee is female (compare masculine *cansado*) and the speaker knows her well enough to address her in the intimate second-person singular form (compare the polite form *está*). Spanish grammaticalizes distinctions of status and gender.
>
> (Romaine 1999: 21)

We should argue that the translator of any ST ought to evaluate the role of the linguistic marking of gender (male or female). Consider for example, the following pair of STs and TTs:

ST1 Le he pedido muchas veces que me lleve con ella. Pero siempre me rechaza diciendo que soy demasiado pequeña para entender las cosas y que me hace daño madrugar.

(Castellanos 1961: 27)

TT1 I've asked her many times to take me with her. But she always refuses; saying that I am too young to understand things and that getting up early is bad for me.

ST2 Cuando todavía es temprano para una noche porteña, pero el loquerío está que arde en la Divine, batiendo las caderas al son fatal de la Grace Jones. Esa africana de lengua ardiente que nos lleva por 'la vida en rosa' de la costa francesa.

(Lemebel 2001: 119)

TT2 When the Porteña night is still young, but the gay crowd is really heating up at the Divine, thrusting their hips to the inevitable sound of Grace Jones herself; that hot-tongued African woman who carries us through the French coast's 'vie en rose'.

In ST1, the sex of the narrator is made explicit through the adjective 'pequeña', but that information is lost in TT1. If the information that the narrator was female were recoverable elsewhere in the TT then the loss might be considered incidental, but if this is the only instance in which explicit reference is made to the gender of the narrator, and that detail is significant in some way to the message or themes of the ST, then loss is unacceptable, and should be compensated for. In ST2, 'esa africana' is nominalized in the TT as 'African *woman*' thereby overstating Jones's sex in comparison with the ST. Likewise, preceding a name with a definite article is part of normal usage in Lemebel's native Chile, and to introduce the emphatic pronoun 'herself' overstates the significance of Jones as a figure mentioned in the narrative, and again overemphasizes her sex.

The gender of nouns with non-human referents may also pose a challenge to the translator. Consider the Cortázar ST in Practical 2.1 (pp. 26–7), which concerns the visit of a mysterious hand to the narrator. Our students have frequently identified the biological sex of Dg as female simply on the basis of grammatical gender in the SL. These are two typical student TTs of the opening phrase:

> I gave her names; I used to like calling her Dg . . .
> I named her; I liked to call her Dg . . .

When we ask them to defend this viewpoint with textual evidence, they argue that the hand must be female because it is vain, and adorns itself with jewellery; despite the fact that the jewellery is provided by the (male) narrator. His sex is not revealed until the third paragraph, through the use of a masculine adjective, 'cansado'. Our students are applying British assumptions about social gender; that is, women are vain, men do not wear jewellery, and so on. In fact, as we have argued in the strategy and tried to show in our translation of the TT in the *Teachers' Handbook*, the narrator's attitude does not remain constant, but shifts through marvelling, to companionship, and finally to scientific curiosity. Using 'she' throughout the TT overmarks the gender of an absurd and amazing but essentially genderless creature, and may even add a degree of (sexual) intimacy that is not present in the TT. In the ST, Cortázar does not fully personify the hand, which he treats as more like a curious animal. In personification, an inanimate object or concept is portrayed as if it were a person, and the thing personified *may* take on characteristics associated with the social gender with which its grammatical class aligns it in the target culture; however, great care should be taken. Social gender refers to the expectation of the adoption of some of a range of behavioural conventions and speech styles considered typical of men and women, and qualified by other factors such as ethnicity, class affiliation, sexual orientation, age, historical factors, context, and so on. In contrast biological sex is defined as the physiological differences between the two sexes. We shall consider translation issues related to social gender further under the heading of social register in Chapter 10.

In discussions of the translation of gender, the personification of death is frequently raised since it is very often personified, and the assignation of gender varies among languages; for example, in German it is a masculine noun 'der Tod', and in English it is conceptually male (consider such collocations as The Grim Reaper, Death the Hunter, and so on). In contrast, in Spanish, French, and Russian, for example, it is a feminine noun. The fifteenth-century Castilian verse *Dança de la Muerte* represents the grammatically feminine 'La Muerte' as engaging in the stereotypically male-gendered activities of hunting and warfare, but also as inviting the Abbot, 'Abraçadme agora: seredes mi esposo, / pues que deseastes plazeres e vicios' (Álvarez Pellitero 1990: 304) ('Embrace me now, you shall be my husband / since [in life] you desired pleasure and delight'). In other words, in the *Dança*, despite being grammatically feminine, 'La Muerte', is neuter. The grammatical gender of Death has posed particular issues for translators of Terry Pratchett's Discworld series. Early in the series, Death was referred to as 'it'; however, the publication of *The Reaper Man* (1991) assigned a masculine social gender to the personified character. Despite the noun being feminine, Death had nonetheless been represented as male in Czech, Polish and Russian (i.e. through masculine agreements) so there was no problem. In Spanish and French, however, the translators had opted for the feminine nouns 'La Muerte', and 'La Mort'. Cristina Macía, translator of the Discomundo series, opted to change the gender of Death, with an explanatory footnote for her Spanish TT, *El segador* (2003).

To sum up, translators should give particular attention to gender in translation from Spanish to English in order to avoid either overstating or losing gender information. As a general guideline, loss of gender information is acceptable where what information is lost is either insignificant in the ST in question or where the information is recoverable from the context. It is unacceptable where gender is important and that information cannot be recovered from the context or where sex or gender is rendered inaccurately in the transfer. Where unacceptable loss is occasioned compensation or splitting is a necessary tool to prevent loss. The overstatement of gender information is only acceptable if it is the only way to avoid making explicit significant gender information which would otherwise be lost. (For a useful study of specifically linguistic problems in translating gender, see Nissen 2002; for a theoretical discussion of broader ideological and cultural implications, see Simon 1996.)

Practical 8

8.1 Particularizing, generalizing and partially overlapping translation

Assignment

(i)   Starting at line 6 of the ST below ('Era mi padre aficionado . . .'), make a detailed analysis of particularizing, generalizing, and overlapping translation in the TT printed opposite the ST.

(ii)   Where possible, give an edited TT that is a more exact translation, and explain your decisions.

Contextual information

The passage is taken from the autobiography of St Teresa of Avila (1515–82), *Su vida.* The extract is the opening section of the first chapter in which St Teresa tells of her early childhood. The translation, published in 1957 under the title *The Life of Saint Teresa of Avila by Herself,* is by J.M. Cohen.

NB: Here is an example of how to lay out your material for this exercise:

ST2–4: 'En que trata . . . los padres'

1   The omission of a rendering for 'en que trata' constitutes an unnecessary generalization in the TT, losing the element of self-reference by the narrator.
2   'rouse' is a particularization of 'despertar' ('wake'/'awaken'/'stir up'/ 'arouse'), introducing an element of intensity to the TT which is not present in the ST; 'rouse' is an intensified hyponym of the more neutral 'awaken', which is a more exact, and contextually more appropriate, literal rendering.
3   'her' is an idiomatically necessary particularization of 'esta'; using the literally exact demonstrative pronoun 'this' would have made the TT grammatically stilted.
4   'soul' is a necessary particularization of 'alma' ('soul'/'spirit'/'heart') and is contextually appropriate.
5   'in childhood' is an apt generalization of 'en su niñez'.
6   'to a love of virtue' is an overlapping translation of 'a cosas virtuosas'; the TT loses the reference to individuated objects ('cosas'), but adds the notion of 'love', which is not explicit in the ST. (A contextually plausible solution might be the literally more exact 'to a love of things virtuous'.)
7   'to have good parents' is a generalizing translation of 'ser [virtuosos] los padres'; the TL cannot replicate the economy of the ST's anaphorical use of 'lo', and the translator has decided to avoid repetition of 'virtue/ virtuous' (repetition that could be regarded as desirable).

Edited TT: In which is told how the Lord started to awaken her soul to virtue in childhood, and how helpful it is in this respect to have virtuous parents.

ST5–6: 'El tener padres . . . ser buena.'

1   'wicked' is an inexact, partially overlapping rendering of 'ruin'; suitable more literally exact alternatives are available, for instance 'base'.
2   'devout' is an unnecessarily narrow particularization of 'virtuosos'; the ST refers to 'moral rectitude' in general, not to its specifically religious forms designated by 'being devout'.

3 'el Señor me favorecía' rendered as 'the favour of God's grace' contains two instances of particularization: the unnecessary duplication of 'grace' and 'favour' renders the TT over-particularized to the point of tautology (as well as grammatically stilted); the unnecessary particularizing of 'Señor' as 'God', where the more literally exact 'Lord' is also more contextually apt.

4 'make me good' is a partially overlapping rendering of 'ser buena'; the TT has lost the element of personal responsibility for good behaviour contained in the ST 'ser' (and the explicit gender reference in 'buena'), but at the same time it has added the notion of a permanent quality of 'goodness', which is not expressed in the ST's reference to good behaviour.

Edited TT: Having virtuous and God-fearing parents, together with the grace of the Lord, should have been enough to ensure that I was good – had I not been so base.

Turn to pp. 162–3 for source text and target text.

Source text

CAPÍTULO I

EN QUE TRATA CÓMO COMENZÓ EL SEÑOR A DESPERTAR ESTA ALMA EN SU NIÑEZ A COSAS VIRTUOSAS, Y LA AYUDA QUE ES PARA ESTO SERLO LOS PADRES

El tener padres virtuosos y temerosos de Dios me bastara, si yo no fuera   5
tan ruin, con lo que el Señor me favorecía, para ser buena. Era mi padre
aficionado a leer buenos libros, y ansí los tenía de romance para que
leyesen sus hijos. Éstos, con el cuidado que mi madre tenía de hacernos
rezar, y ponernos en ser devotos de Nuestra Señora y de algunos Santos,
comenzó a despertarme, de edad, a mi parecer, de seis o siete años.   10
Ayudábame, no ver en mis padres favor sino para la virtud. Tenían
muchas. Era mi padre hombre de mucha caridad con los pobres y piadad
con los enfermos, y aun con los criados; tanta, que jamás se pudo acabar
con él tuviese esclavos, porque los había gran piadad; y estando una vez
en casa una de un su hermano, la regalaba como a sus hijos; decía, que   15
de que no era libre, no lo podía sufrir de piadad. Era de gran verdad, jamás
nadie le oyó jurar ni murmurar. Muy honesto en gran manera.

(Teresa de Jesús 1978: 21)

Target text

CHAPTER 1

How the Lord began to rouse her soul in childhood to a love of virtue, and what a help it is in this respect to have good parents

If I had not been so been so wicked, the possession of devout and God-fearing parents, together with the favour of God's grace, would have been   5
enough to make me good. My father was fond of reading holy books, and
had some in Spanish so that his children might read them too. These, and
the pains my mother took in teaching us to pray and educating us in
devotion to Our Lady and certain Saints, began to rouse me at the age, I
think, of six or seven. It was a help to me that I never saw my parents 10
inclined to anything but virtue, and many virtues they had. My father was
most charitable to the poor, and most compassionate to the sick, also to
his servants; so much so that he could never be persuaded to keep slaves.
He felt such pity for them that when a slave-girl of his brother's was, on
one occasion, staying in his house, he treated her like one of his own 15
children. He said that he could not bear the pain of seeing her not free.
He was an extremely truthful man and was never heard to swear or speak
slander. He was also most rigid in his chastity.

(Teresa de Jesús 1957: 23)

8.2   *Literal meaning: particularizing, generalizing and partially overlapping translation; translation and gender*

Assignment

(i)   Consider the treatment of grammatical gender in the ST.
(ii)   Consider how the contrast between the two characters is conveyed through the kinds of language used.
(iii) Develop a strategy for translating the ST, paying particular attention to gender.
(iv)   Translate the whole extract as if for inclusion in a volume of Latin American short stories published in an English-speaking country.
(v)   Explain the decisions of detail you made in translating the TT.
(vi)   Compare your TT with the published TT, which your tutor will distribute in class.

Contextual information

The ST is from a short story, 'La palabra asesino' by the Argentinian writer Luisa Valenzuela. The story appears in a collection, *Cambio de armas* (1982). The series of five stories which comprise *Cambio de armas* deals with the links between the artistic, socio-political and sexual oppression of women in Argentina during the military dictatorship of 1976 to 1983. Valenzuela is generally concerned with exposing the mechanisms of power. The anonymous female protagonist of 'La palabra asesino' is overwhelmed by a morbid desire for a violent man but repulsed by her knowledge that he has killed in Vietnam (including his Vietnamese wife) and at home and in peacetime until – driven to the brink of suicide by the conflict between her desire and repulsion – she shouts out 'asesino'.

Source text

Ella merodea por la vida en busca de una respuesta. Las respuestas no existen. Ella sólo logra preguntas pésimamente formuladas que al final la dejan en carne viva. Ella comprende que para saber hay que dejarse herir, hay que aceptar lo que venga en material de información, no negar la evidencia, conocer y conocer y meterse en profundidades de las que quizá   5
no se vuelva. Allí donde no caben las vacilaciones. Cabe el deseo.
    El deseo cabe en todas partes y se manifiesta de las maneras más insospechables, cuando se manifiesta, y cuando no se manifiesta – las más de las veces – es una pulsión interna, un latido de ansiedad incontenible.
    Él no oculta nada, más bien revela en exceso. De entrada no más le dijo   10
    —Tengo 28 años y he vivido 6. El resto del tiempo lo pasé en instituciones. Ahora espero recuperar los años de verdadera vida que la vida me debe.

Otras cosas también dijo en ese primer encuentro, después de haberse mirado demasiado intensamente si nos atenemos a las normas sociales en 15 vigencia. Ojo a ojo, un mirar hacia dentro que ambos tuvieron el coraje de sostener sin agachadas. Pero sin desafíos. Un reconocimiento mutuo.

Después la aclaración: instituciones, es decir, hospitales, reformatorios, cárceles, el ejército; esas barreras. Y ella no sintió la necesidad de preguntarle por qué le estaba contando precisamente eso precisamente a 20 ella durante una amable fiesta, lejos de toda barrera.

Ella tomó la información como una entrega de pedacitos de él y bastante más adelante, después de reiteradas dudas y retiros, lo tomó a él de cuerpo entero y supo de sus líneas perfectas y de su piel. Esa piel.

Él, oscuro. De oscuro pasado y piel oscura. Ella apenas opaca. Él, en 25 comparación, oscuro y transparente. Ella, siempre dispuesta a ver a través, con él negándose a ir más allá de esa piel impecable y tersa, infinitamente acariciable.

(Valenzuela 1982: 67–8)

8.3 Literal meaning: particularizing, generalizing and partially overlapping translation

Assignment

(i)   Develop a strategy for translating the ST below. (You may find it useful to research sports articles, especially those dealing with basketball.) Assume that your TT will be circulated by e-mail to a newsgroup of English-language basketball fans interested in the Spanish league.

(ii)   Your teacher will allocate you a half of the passage to translate. Both halves will be discussed in class.

(iii) Explain the decisions of detail you made in your TT, with particular attention to the need to use particularizing, generalizing and partially overlapping translation.

Contextual information

The Malagan basketball team (sponsored by Unicaja) are set to play against MMT Estudiantes at 8.00 pm in Madrid on 12 May 2007. Unicaja have played well but at the physical cost of its players in the semifinal round of the Euroleague (known as the Final Four), and in matches against ViveMenorca and C.B. Granada. The two teams are contesting for a place in the quarter finals. At the same time Real Madrid (*los blancos*) is playing DKV Joventut in Badalona, also in the final phase of qualifying matches. Real Madrid is currently top of the ACB league, but the opposition (DKV Joventut) in the match is jostling to maintain its third-place position. Tau Cerámica of Vitoria is currently second, and still has a match pending. Everything is to play for. Real Madrid will maintain their top position if they win against DKV or if

Tau loses, but will fall to second place if they lose and Tau wins its match thereby moving to the top of the league. DKV currently will maintain its position if it beats Madrid or the fourth-place team (not mentioned in the article) loses its match, but will cede third place if it loses and the fourth-place team wins.

Source text

Unicaja cumple el trámite pendiente de la enfermería

Loncar peligra por una lesión. Berni, Tusek y Jiménez, bajas

ANTONIO GALLARDO/LA PREVIA

Hace unas semanas Sergio Scariolo y
5 su Unicaja hubieran firmado con ojos cerrados un partido en el Telefónica Arena como el que van a abordar esta tarde. Sin nada en juego. Un trámite. Las quinielas deparaban un Estudiantes-
10 Unicaja a cara de perro esta tarde. Pero nada de eso. Menorca y Granada se encargaron de endulzar el festín europeo del Unicaja y prepararon una cómoda resaca post-Final Four a los malagueños.
15 Eso sí, el precio a pagar ha sido muy alto. Berni Rodríguez, Marko Tusek, Carlos Jiménez, Faverani y el descartado Santiago se han quedado en Málaga por diferentes motives físicos. Carlos Salas
20 (médico del club) tiene la enfermería a rebosar. Scariolo ha podido utilizar la semana para dar un respiro físico y mental a sus hombres. El playoff arranca el jueves y el rival no concederá la más
25 mínima tregua. Pero la preocupación ahora no está en la pista. Además de los que se han quedado en Málaga, Kresimir Loncar, pívot croata del Lokomoitiv de Rostov ruso que estaba casi fichado, se
30 lesionó una rodilla en el último partido de playoff de su equipo y su fichaje está en el aire. Ayre se hizo una resonancia, de cuyos resultados dependerá su llegado o no a la Costa del Sol. Enésima lesión y enésimo revés para el Unicaja y Sergio 35 Scariolo, que se han pasado la temporada parcheando y buscando soluciones de emergencia a tanto maleficio físico.

Unicaja B. La única premisa hoy no es engordar la lista de bajas. Para 40 evitar riesgos innecesarios, Scariolo se ha llevado a Madrid a cuatro jugadores el equipo filial. Los cuatro se tomarán el partido como si de él dependiesen sus opciones futuras de triunfar en la élite 45 del baloncesto español. No es Scariolo un técnico dado a regalar segundas oportunidades. El otro aliciente que presenta la jornada es conocer al rival para el playoff. Real Madrid o Tau se las 50 verán en cuatros con el actual campeón. Hace una semana, todos hubiesen elegido a los blancos. A día de hoy, con Maljkovic cuestionado y tras lo sucedido en la final de consolación en Atenas, los hay que no 55 hacen ningún asco a los vitorianos.

(Gallardo 2007: 48)

8.4 Literal meaning: particularizing, generalizing and partially overlapping translation

Assignment

(i)   Compare the Spanish and English texts given below. Consider the extent to which particularization, generalization, partially overlapping translation, and grammatical transposition will be necessary to prepare a translation of the Spanish ST.

(ii) With particular attention to literal meaning, prepare a strategy for translating lines 9–32 ('Los servicios de correos . . . 10 mayo 1995') of the Spanish ST. Your TT is to appear on an English-language version of the webpages.

(iii) Translate the section identified above into English, assuming that the TT is aimed at English-speaking residents in Spain.

(iv) Explain the decisions of detail you made in your TT, with particular attention to the need to use particularizing, generalizing, and partially overlapping translation.

Contextual information

The Spanish text appears on a site dedicated to democratic participation in the 2007 local elections on the webpages of the Dirección General de Política Interior of the Spanish Ministerio del Interior. It aims to give accurate information about the electoral process, the timetable for different stages of the elections, and answers frequently asked questions. The English text comes from the British Electoral Commission's webpages developed for the May 2007 local elections, and which continue to provide information relevant to the next set of elections (London Mayor, Greater London Authority, some district councils), and for a future general election. It provides information about the elections, registration and the democratic institutions in which elected representatives work.

Spanish text

VOTO POR CORREO

¿Cómo se vota por Correo desde España?

El elector que quiera votar por correo debe hacer lo siguiente:

Ir – entre el 3 de abril y el 17 de mayo – personalmente y con su D.N.I., a cualquier Oficina de Correos y solicitar el impreso para votar por correo.   5

Rellenar y firmar el impreso de solicitud. El funcionario de Correos comprobará la coincidencia de la firma. En ningún caso se admitirá fotocopia del DNI.

Los servicios de Correos remitirán toda la documentación a la Oficina del Censo Electoral. Ésta anota en las Listas del Censo que se ha 10 solicitado votar por correo – de modo que YA NO PUEDA VOTAR PERSONALMENTE – y remite al elector por correo certificado al domicilio que le haya indicado o, en su defecto, al que figure en el Censo:

- Una papeleta de cada una de las formaciones políticas que se presente a las elecciones y un sobre de votación, en el que se introducirá la 15 papeleta correspondiente.
- el certificado de inscripción en el censo.
- un sobre en el que figurará la dirección de la Mesa donde le correspondería votar.
- una hoja explicativa.   20

Esta documentación también debe ser recogida personalmente por el elector previa acreditación de su identidad. Si no estuviese en su domicilio, tendrá que ir personalmente a recogerla a la Oficina de Correos correspondiente.

Una vez que el elector haya escogido la papeleta de voto, la introducirá 25 en el sobre de votación y lo cerrará, y siguiendo las instrucciones correspondientes, lo remitirá junto con el certificado de inscripción en el censo en otro sobre que remitirá por correo certificado antes del día 23 de mayo. Debe tenerse en cuenta que no es necesario que el elector acuda personalmente a la Oficina de Correos a certificar el sobre de votación, 30 sino que podrá hacerlo otra persona en su nombre (Acuerdo JEC 10 mayo 1995).

El Servicio de Correos conservará hasta el día de la votación toda la correspondencia dirigida a las Mesas Electorales y la trasladará a dichas Mesas a las nueve de la mañana.   35

Asimismo, seguirá dando traslado de la que pueda recibirse en dicho día, hasta las veinte horas del mismo. El Servicio de Correos llevará un registro de toda la documentación recibida, que estará a disposición de las Juntas Electorales.

Los sobres recibidos después de las veinte horas del día fijado para la 40 votación se remitirán a la Junta Electoral de Zona (y se destruirán).

Más información:

Artículos 72 y 73 de la Ley Orgánica 5/1985, de 19 de junio, del Régimen Electoral General.

¿Cómo se mezclan los votos recibidos por Correo con los que se han 45 *depositado personalmente en la urna?*

El 27 de mayo, a las 20 horas, una vez que haya votado el último elector, en la Mesa Electoral, se procederá a introducir en la urna respectiva los sobres que contengan las papeletas del voto remitidos por correo.

Para ello, deben seguirse los siguientes pasos: 50

1) Abrir, de uno en uno, los sobres remitidos al Presidente de la Mesa y comprobar que contienen el Certificado de Inscripción en el Censo del elector y el sobre o sobres de voto por correo.
2) Comprobar que el elector está inscrito en el Censo de la Mesa.
3) Introducir en la urna correspondiente el sobre o sobres de votación.   55
4) Anotar al elector en la Lista Numerada de Votantes (Los Vocales anotarán el nombre del elector en la Lista Numerada de Votantes).

Más información:

Manual de Miembros de Mesa.

(Ministerio del Interior 2007)

English text

aboutmyvote.co.uk   *The Electoral Commission*

Please note that the deadline for applying for a postal vote for the 3 May elections has now passed. However, you can still apply to have a postal vote in future elections.

Who can apply for a postal vote?   5
Anyone who is registered to vote.

How do I get a postal vote?
You can download a postal vote application form here. Fill it in and return it to the local electoral registration office.

For what period does my postal vote last?   10
You can apply for just one election, for a specific time period, or for a permanent postal vote.

Why do I need to give my date of birth and signature to get a postal or proxy vote?
The Electoral Administration Act 2006 introduced new measures to   15 improve the security of postal and proxy votes. From 1 January 2007 all postal and proxy voters in England and Wales will be required to give their date of birth and signature when applying for a postal or proxy vote.

  During January 2007 each local authority will write to all existing   20 postal/proxy voters and request their date of birth and signature on a form. If you do not return the form, with the requested details, your postal or proxy vote will be cancelled. You will not be removed from the electoral roll though, and can re-apply for a postal or proxy vote, but will still need to provide your date of birth and signature. Special provision can   25 be made for those who are unable to sign the form. For more information please contact your local Electoral Registration Officer for more information.

How secure is a postal vote?
It is an offence to complete a postal vote that is not your own, and to 30
influence how others complete their postal vote. If you have any
allegations of fraud, they should be referred to the police.

Why haven't I received my postal ballot paper?
You'll receive it one to two weeks before the elections. If it doesn't arrive,
you can get a replacement ballot paper in person from your <u>Electoral</u> 35
<u>Registration Officer</u> up until 5pm on election day.

I've spoiled my ballot paper/postal voting statement. What do I do?
You can get a replacement up until 5pm on election day. You must pick
it up in person from your <u>Electoral Registration Officer</u>. You will also need
to return your spoilt ballot paper and the other parts of the ballot pack that 40
were sent to you.

I've lost my postal ballot paper. What do I do?
You can get a replacement ballot paper in person from your <u>Electoral</u>
<u>Registration Officer</u> up until 5pm on election day.

If I have applied for a postal vote, can I still vote at the polling station? 45
If you have applied to vote by post, you cannot vote in person at the polling
station. However, on election day you can return you postal vote to the
polling station (before 10pm) or to your <u>the Electoral Registration Officer</u>
<u>at your local council</u> (before they close) if you do not want to post it or it
is too late to post it. Contact <u>the Electoral Registration Officer at your local</u> 50
<u>council</u> to find out where your polling station is.

(Electoral Commission 2007)

9 Connotative meaning and translation problems

As was pointed out in Chapter 8, literal meaning is only one aspect of textual meaning. Understanding the literal reference conventionally attached to verbal signs is a necessary part of unravelling the complex meaning of a text, but it is not, in itself, enough. In actual fact, the meaning of a text comprises a number of different layers: referential content, emotional colouring, cultural associations, social and personal connotations, and so on. The many-layered nature of meaning is something translators must never forget.

Even within a single language, so-called referential synonyms are as a rule different in their overall semantic effects. For instance, in contemporary English, 'homosexual', 'queer' and 'gay' must be rated as synonyms in terms of referential content, but they clearly have different overall meanings. This is because, while 'homosexual' is a neutral expression, 'queer' is often understood to carry pejorative overtones, and 'gay' meliorative ones. These overtones are not part of literal meaning, but it is evident that to refer to someone as 'queer' could be taken as hostile in a way that the designations 'homosexual' or 'gay' could not. However, in academic and cultural contexts 'queer' has been rehabilitated. It is impossible to ignore such overtones in responding to messages in one's own language, and one certainly cannot afford to overlook them when it comes to translating. For example, a speaker who refers to a man as 'un maricón' or 'una loca' does not merely designate a person with certain sexual preferences, but also conveys a certain attitude to him. Consequently, while translating 'maricón' as 'homosexual' would accurately render the literal meaning of the ST, it would fail to render the denigrating attitude connoted by 'maricón' (better translated as 'queer' or 'pansy'). Conversely, translating a reference to a man as 'una loca' denotatively as 'mad' entirely loses its connection with homosexual identity ('queen' would be a better option).

We shall call such overtones connotative meanings – that is, associations which, over and above the literal meaning of an expression, form part of its overall meaning. In fact, of course, connotative meanings are many and varied, and it is common for a single piece of text or a single expression to combine several kinds into a single overall effect. Nevertheless, there are six major types of commonly recognized connotative meaning (some of them are adapted from Leech 1974: 26), which we will examine in turn. We should perhaps add that, by definition, we are only concerned with socially widespread connotations, not private ones – as long as private connotations are recognized for what they are, and not allowed unduly to influence the production of a TT, they are the translator's own affair. Translators do not normally let personal connotations influence a TT if they can help it.

Attitudinal meaning

Attitudinal meaning is that part of the overall meaning of an expression which consists of some widespread attitude to the referent. That is, the expression does not merely denote the referent in a neutral way, but, in addition, hints at some attitude to it on the part of the speaker.

Our example of 'queer' versus 'homosexual' versus 'gay', and 'homosexual' versus 'maricón', are clear cases of attitudinal connotations. As these examples show, attitudinal meanings can be hard to pin down. (For instance, just how hostile is the expression 'queer'? Is it more or less pejorative than 'pansy'? Is 'maricón' less pejorative than 'queer', or perhaps even affectionately derogatory, say as used between teenage boys? How is the pejorative connotation of 'queer' to be reconciled with the contemporary appropriation of that term in queer ideology? How pejorative is the expression 'That's so gay' when used in the schoolyard? When used by the homosexual protagonist of a situation comedy to describe his best friend's clothes? Connotations will vary from context to context.) For instance, in appropriate contexts, 'the police', 'the pigs', and 'the Old Bill' are synonyms in British English in terms of referential content, but they have different overall meanings. These attitudes are not part of the literal meaning of expressions, but it is impossible to ignore them in responding to the expressions. It is important therefore not to ignore them when translating. 'The police' for peninsular Spanish 'la poli' accurately conveys the literal meaning of the ST but loses the colloquial register, whereas it fails to depict the hostility reflected in the Chilean slang term 'los pacos' ('the filth', 'the pigs'). Conversely, the translator must be careful not to introduce significant connotations that are absent from the ST and clash with TT context, as in translating 'el cura' as 'the sky-pilot'.

There are two main reasons why attitudinal meanings are generally hard to define. First, being connotations, they are intrinsically intended to be suggestive: the moment they cease to be suggestive, and become fixed by convention, they cease to be connotations and become part of literal meaning. Second, being controlled by the vagaries of usage, they can change very rapidly. Both these factors are illustrated by the evolution of the word 'Tory', originally a term of abuse imported from Irish ('tóriadhe', meaning 'outlaw'), but later proudly adopted by the parties so labelled.

Associative meaning

Associative meaning is that part of the overall meaning of an expression which consists of stereotypical expectations – rightly or wrongly – associated with the referent of the expression. Any area of reference where prejudices and stereotypes, however innocuous, operate is likely to give examples of associative meaning. Even something as banal as a date may trigger an associative meaning, for example 24 June, 14 July or 5 November. Similarly, in Spain and England – though not in Scotland – 'golf' will automatically trigger associations of an upper- or middle-class milieu. Here are some examples. The noun 'autoridad' is strongly associated with governmental authority but in the title of the *Diccionario de Autoridades*, the first edition of the dictionary of the Real Academia Española de la Lengua, it refers to texts cited as linguistic authorities ('autoridades') in support of the dictionary's definitions; this association leads an ignorant character, the butt of humour, in Leopoldo Alas's *La Regenta*, to refer to it as 'el que manda. El diccionario del gobierno'. An article entitled, '¿Qué pasó el 24 de diciembre?' could reasonably be expected to deal with a topic linked to the birth of Christ or the Christmas festive season. In 'El rey de Harlem', Lorca uses oxymoron in phrases like 'rubor negro' and 'rojos oprimidos' to cancel the literal meaning (of colour reference) and bring the associative value of brightness to the fore.

The appreciation of associative meanings requires cultural knowledge, and the translator must constantly be on the look-out for them. Take, for instance, an ideologically loaded term in Spanish such as 'patria'. As the text used for Practical 5.2 ('Imposible el alemán') reminds us, it played a key role, usually with a capital P, in the right wing rhetoric of the Franco regime, associated with Catholicism, the legacy of empire and the authoritarian unification of the Spanish state. As a result, the word has not been easy to use in a positive way in the context of a democratic, secular and decentralized Spain, although attempts have been made to re-establish it, including the lyrics proposed in 2007 as a new national anthem for sporting events. Since its Latin origin connects it with 'pater' (father), 'fatherland' (or 'Fatherland') would seem to be the most obvious translation. However, this term may generate associations with Germany and cultural memories of the Second World War, which would be entirely appropriate for the translation of 'Imposible el alemán' but not for a text requiring a more neutral or unproblematically positive term. A range of alternatives should therefore be borne in mind: 'homeland', 'mother country' or 'native land' – even 'land of our fathers' or 'land of the free' to generate culture-specific mythical associations.

Affective meaning

Affective meaning is that part of the overall meaning of an expression which consists in an emotive effect worked on the addressee by the choice of that expression. The expression does not merely denote its referent, but also hints at some attitude of the speaker/writer to the addressee.

Features of linguistic politeness, flattery, rudeness or insult are typical examples of expressions carrying affective meanings. Compare, for instance, 'Hagan el favor de bajar la voz' with '¡Callaos!' These expressions share their literal meaning with English 'lower your voice', but their impact in terms of affective meaning is quite different: polite and deferential in one case, brusque and peremptory in the other. That is, the speaker's tacit or implied attitude to the listener produces a different emotive effect in each case.

Not only imperative forms, but also statements and questions, can have alternative forms identical in basic literal meaning yet totally different in affective meaning, as in 'Excuse me, Madam, I think that's my seat' versus 'Oi, you, I was sitting there'; or, in Spanish, 'Perdone señora, ¿podría usted sentarse en otro asiento?' versus '¡Oye, tú! ¡Quítate de allí!'

Clearly, translators must be able to recognize affective meanings in the ST. But they must also be sure not to introduce unwanted affective meanings into the TT. Take, for example, 'Mañana me lo devolverá usted' translated as 'You will give it back to me tomorrow'. Whereas the Spanish is formal and polite, the English sounds rude and peremptory. A better TT would cushion what sounds to English ears as excessively assertive: 'Could you give it back to me tomorrow?'

Reflected meaning

Reflected meaning is the meaning given to an expression over and above its literal meaning by the fact that its form is reminiscent of the completely different meaning of a homonymic or near-homonymic expression, that is, one that sounds or is spelled the same, or nearly the same.

An often-cited example of reflected meaning compares the connotative difference between the two synonyms 'Holy Spirit' and 'Holy Ghost' (Leech 1974: 19). Through homonymic association, the 'Ghost' part of 'Holy Ghost' is reminiscent of the reflected meaning of 'ghost' ('spook' or 'spectre'). Although such an association is not part of the literal meaning of 'Holy Ghost', it has a tendency to form part of the overall meaning of the expression, and therefore may actually interfere with its literal meaning. By another, near-homonymic, association, the 'Spirit' part of 'Holy Spirit' may call to mind the reflected meaning of 'spirits' ('alcoholic drinks'); here again, the association tends to interfere with the literal meaning. Clearly, then, while 'Holy Spirit' and 'Holy Ghost' are referential synonyms, their total semantic effects cannot be called identical, in so far as they evoke different images through different reflected meanings.

When a term is taken in isolation, its reflected meaning is usually merely latent – it is the *context* that triggers or reinforces latent reflected meanings. In the case of 'Holy Ghost' and 'Holy Spirit', if there is anything in the context that predisposes the hearer to think about 'spooks' or 'alcoholic drinks', reflected meaning may come across as a *double entendre*. If one were translating 'Espíritu Santo' (which, in writing, only shares the reflected meanings of its English synonyms when uncapitalized, 'espíritu santo'), one would have to take care that the TT context did not trigger the latent reflected meaning of whichever English expression was selected for the TT. Otherwise the TT could be marred by infelicitous innuendo, as for example if one wrote 'Holy Spirit' just after a reference to Communion wine. An example of this comes from a passage in Luis Martín-Santos's novel, *Tiempo de silencio* (first published in 1961). In a brothel scene, the drunken protagonist refers to 'las landas bordelesas' ('plains of Bordeaux') (Martín-Santos 1973: 105), which many of our students read as 'burdelesas'.

Similarly, infelicitous reflected meanings might be doubly obtrusive in a TT rendering of Gustavo Adolfo Bécquer's lines (from *Rima* XII), 'y verdes son las pupilas / de las hurís del profeta' (Bécquer 1961: 11) as 'and green are the pupils / of the Prophet's houris' (Bécquer 1985: 14) where the referent of 'green are the pupils' might equally be eyes or inexperienced students. Conversely, a ST may deliberately trade on reflected meaning and innuendo, using an expression primarily for its literal meaning, yet expressly, if implicitly, expecting the addressee to perceive a connotation echoing the meaning of some homonymic expression. A good example is the double entendre in Lorca's use of '¡Dale ya con el cuerno!' in Act III, scene 2 of his play *Yerma,* which refers to the actions of the dance of the archetypal *Macho* and *Hembra*, the horn's symbolic referent (the penis), but which also has connotations reflected from the expression 'poner los cuernos', 'to cuckold'. (It is very common for an expression to combine more than one type of connotative meaning, as in this example.) In such cases, a fully successful TT would be one which deliberately traded on innuendo similar to that in the ST; but such a TT may be extremely difficult to construct.

Collocative meaning

Collocative meaning is given to an expression over and above its literal meaning by the meaning of some other expression with which it collocates to form a commonly used phrase. Thus, in the clichéd expression 'a flash of lightning', the word 'flash' collocates regularly with the word 'lightning', forming such a strong stereotyped association that 'flash' by itself is capable of evoking the meaning of its collocative partner. This no doubt is why a collocation like 'a flash of moonlight' feels a little unusual – there is nothing in the literal meaning of 'flash' to prevent its qualifying 'moonlight', but the connotation it has through collocative association with 'lightning' (sudden bright light) is carried over and clashes with the literal meaning of 'moonlight' (steady muted light). Similarly, the well-known gender-specific connotations of 'pretty' and 'handsome' can be seen as collocative meanings, deriving from the tendency of 'pretty' to collocate with words denoting females ('girl', 'woman' and so on) and the tendency of 'handsome' to collocate with words denoting males ('boy', 'man' and so on). Each tends to have derogatory nuances when applied to a referent of the sex opposite from that which its collocative meaning implies.

Some collocative meanings are so strong that they need very little triggering by context. For example, in modern colloquial English the word 'intercourse' (literally 'mutual dealings') can hardly be used at all without evoking its collocative partner 'sexual', and is well on the way to becoming a synonym of 'sexual intercourse'. Other collocative meanings need to be activated by the context, as with the humorous innuendo in 'I rode shotgun on the way to the wedding', based on activating the collocative echo of 'shotgun wedding'.

Collocative meanings are important for the translator, not only because they can contribute significantly to the overall meaning of a ST, but also because of the need to avoid unwanted collocative clashes in a TT. For example, translating '¿Tienes las vacaciones reservadas?/¿Ya ha reservado usted las vacaciones?' as 'Have you reserved your holiday yet?' produces a collocative clash or infelicity – according to English collocative idiom, seats or tables in restaurants are reserved, but holidays are *booked*. An unfortunate collocative clash is also produced – partly as a result of miscollocation, the correct collocation being 'to reserve a book', and partly as a result of an infelicitous play on words – by translating 'Quisiera/Me gustaría reservar este libro para mañana' as 'I'd like to book this book for tomorrow'.

Collocative clashes are always a threat to idiomaticity when the TL offers an expression closely resembling the ST one. Compare, for instance, 'floods of tears' with 'an ocean of tears' as translations of 'un mar de lágrimas'; or 'to sweeten/sugar the pill' with 'to gild the pill' as translations of 'dorar la píldora'. In fact, collocative clashes are often produced by failure to spot the need for a communicative translation, as in rendering 'más blanco que la nieve' by 'whiter than snow' instead of 'as white as snow'. Worse still, translating 'es un chaval hermoso' as 'he is a pretty boy' produces a collocative clash that totally distorts the meaning of the ST (better rendered as 'he's a nice-looking/good-looking lad/guy').

Allusive meaning

Allusive meaning is present when an expression evokes, beyond its literal meaning, the meaning of some associated saying or quotation, in such a way that the meaning of that saying or quotation becomes part of the overall meaning of the expression.

Allusive meaning hinges on indirectly evoking sayings or quotations that an informed hearer can recognize, even though they are not fully spelt out. The evoked meaning of the quotation alluded to creates an added innuendo that modifies the literal meaning of what has explicitly been said. For example, saying that 'there are rather a lot of cooks involved' in organizing an event evokes the proverb 'too many cooks spoil the broth', and by this allusive meaning creates the innuendo that the event risks being spoilt by over-organization.

In the case of allusive meaning in STs, the translator's first problem is to recognize that the ST does contain an allusive suggestion. The second problem is to understand the allusive meaning by reference to the meaning of the saying or quotation evoked. The third problem is to convey the force of the allusion in the TT, ideally by using some appropriate allusive meaning based on a saying or quotation in the TL.

A simple example is from Pérez Galdós's *La de Bringas* (1991: 143) in which the phrase 'y aquí paz' is an allusive echo of the proverb 'Aquí paz y después gloria', meaning 'and that's that'. Similarly, in the same text (274), the sentence 'Y quién me había de decir que yo bebería de este [sic] agua' makes allusion to the proverb 'Nunca digas de esta agua no beberé' (literally 'Never say I shall not drink of this water'; implying 'Never say never'). Both these examples show how recognizing the proverbs alluded to is the key without which the meanings of the STs may remain obscure, even puzzling. Once these allusive meanings have been grasped, the translator's problem is whether they can be rendered by similarly allusive means in an English TT, or whether it is necessary to resort to compensation in kind. In the first example a communicative rendering, 'and that's that', with loss of a proverbial allusion, is probably the best option; in the second, a solution could perhaps be devised by some suitable use of a cliché such as 'Never say never' or 'There's no such word as "never"'.

Even these relatively simple examples, then, are potentially problematic, but really drastic difficulties can arise if an apparent allusive meaning in the ST is obscure. Considerable research may be necessary to track down the allusion; and even after it has been identified and understood, the translator faces another challenge if there is no parallel to it in the TL culture. The solution in such cases is usually to compensate by some other means for the absence of a suitable allusion.

A complex instance of allusion intricately woven into a text is found in Julio Cortázar's *Rayuela:*

> En setiembre del 80, pocos meses después del fallecimiento
> Y las cosas que lee, una novela, mal escrita, para colmo
> de mi padre, resolví apartarme de los negocios, cediéndolos
> una edición infecta, uno se pregunta cómo puede interesarle
> a otra casa extractora de Jerez tan acreditada como la mía;
> algo así.

(Cortázar 1984: 341)

This puzzling extract, and the entire section 34 of *Rayuela* from which it is drawn, is constructed as a confusing alternation between allusive segments (only some of which are textually marked by italics) quoted from Pérez Galdós's (1971a) *Lo prohibido* – the novel which Oliveira, the protagonist of section 34, has been leafing through – and Cortázar's elaboration of his musings. Even once the translator has cracked the code whereby section 34 can be rendered intelligible to the reader, the problem of translating the ST as a mixture of allusions and musings remains a particularly difficult and challenging one.

A different sort of example of the same problem of allusive meaning is afforded by the title of Gustavo Adolfo Bécquer's poem 'Es un sueño la vida'

(1961: 52). Here the allusion is, of course, to Calderón's classic *La vida es sueño* which forms the intertextual background to Bécquer's text. In order to build a recognizable literary allusion into the title of an English TT, a possible solution might be to base that title on an allusion to the Shakespearian lines 'We are such stuff as dreams are made on/And our little life is rounded with a sleep' (*The Tempest*), rendering it perhaps as 'Our little life'. This solution carries two main risks: the risk that, in the absence of an explicit mention of 'dream', the TT reader may miss the title's oblique allusion to dreams; and the risk that, embedded into the Shakespearian intertextual context, the resulting TT may come to connote a philosophy of life which distorts and falsifies the global impact of the ST. In either case the translator risks a form of translation loss which would vitiate the function of the allusion in the TT.

Allusive meaning can also play an important role in non-literary texts. For example, advertising often plays on allusions to other mass media products or popular sayings. A magazine advertisement for the Spanish rail network RENFE from 1990 is headed 'EL ULTIMO TALGO EN PARIS', over a photograph of part of a bed showing a pillow and a shirt laid out next to it. What is being promoted is a sleeper service offering an early arrival in Paris and a late return to Madrid. The suggestive reference to Bertolucci's 1973 film *Last Tango in Paris* is combined with the punning strapline 'RENFE: Mejora tu tren de vida' – 'tren de vida' is an expression defined by the RAE dictionary as 'lujo y comodidades con que vive una persona; ritmo de vida de una persona' (Real Academia Española 2001–2008). 'LAST TALGO IN PARIS' would be a workable translation into English as long as it was made immediately clear in the body text that a Talgo is an express train, but the impact of the slogan in the ST depends upon the familiarity of the Talgo in Spanish culture, and the effect of the word-play on 'tren de vida' would be very difficult to convey.

Practical 9

9.1 Connotative meaning

Assignment

Taking the expressions in bold type in the ST printed below,

(i)   Categorize and discuss those in which connotative meaning plays a part and discuss the translation of them in the TT printed opposite the ST. Where appropriate, give an edited TT, rendering the ST connotations more successfully into English.

(ii)   Identify and discuss expressions which have introduced unwanted connotative meanings into the published TT, give an edited TT in each case, and explain your decisions.

Contextual information

This extract is taken from Act III, scene 2 (the final scene) of Federico García Lorca's play *Yerma: poema trágico en tres actos y seis cuadros* (written in the early 1930s). The ST and TT appear as parallel texts, edited and translated by Ian Macpherson and Jacqueline Minett, published in 1987. The TT is intended as a performance text, developed in rehearsal with the cast of a production at the People's Theatre (Newcastle upon Tyne). Your target audience is readers interested in Lorca's poetry, and in the overlap between drama and poetry. The extract appears at the beginning of the ritual fertility dance of the *Hembra* and the *Macho*. (NB: Line numbers denote lines of *text*, not lines of verse.)

Turn to pp. 180–1 for source text and target text.

Source text

HEMBRA	En el río de la sierra
	la esposa triste se bañaba.
	Por el cuerpo le subían
	los caracoles del agua.
	La arena de las orillas
	y el aire de la mañana
	le daban fuego a su risa
	y temblor a sus espaldas
	¡Ay qué **desnuda** estaba
	la **doncella** en el agua!
NIÑO	¡Ay cómo **se quejaba!**
HOMBRE 1	¡Ay **marchita de amores!**
	¡Con el viento y el agua!
HOMBRE 2	¡Que diga a quién espera!
HOMBRE 1	¡Que diga a quién aguarda!
HOMBRE 2	¡Ay con **el vientre seco**
	y la color **quebrada!**
HEMBRA	Cuando llegue la noche lo diré,
	cuando llegue la noche clara.
	Cuando llegue la noche de la **romería**
	rasgaré los volantes de mi enagua.
NIÑO	Y en seguida vino la noche.
	¡Ay que la noche llegaba!
	Mirad qué oscuro se pone
	el **chorro** de la montaña.
	(*Empiezan a sonar unas guitarras.*)
MACHO	(*Se levanta y agita el cuerno.*)
	¡Ay qué blanca
	la triste casada!
	¡Ay cómo se queja entre las ramas!
	Amapola y clavel serás luego,
	cuando **el macho despliegue su capa.**
	(*Se acerca.*)
	Si tú vienes a la romería
	a pedir que **tu vientre se abra,**
	no te pongas **un velo de luto**
	sino **dulce camisa de holanda.**

Line numbers: 5, 10, 15, 20, 25, 30, 35

Target text

FEMALE	In the mountains, in the river,	
	the sad wife bathed.	
	Soft around her body	
	curled the water like a snail.	
	Sand from the banks by the river	5
	and the morning breeze:	
	her bare arms shivered	
	and her laugh flowed free.	
	How naked was that maiden,	
	the maiden of the stream!	10
BOY	O, how the maiden wept!	
1ST MAN	Pity the loveless in the water!	
	Pity the barren in the wind!	
2ND MAN	Let her say for whom she wants!	
1ST MAN	Let her say for whom she waits!	15
2ND MAN	Pity the wife with the barren womb!	
	Pity her face with colour flown!	
FEMALE	When night-tide falls I'll tell,	
	in night-tide's lucid drift,	
	when pilgrims walk by night,	20
	I'll tear my ruffled shift.	
BOY	Then quickly night-tide fell.	
	How fast that night did fall!	
	How dark, how dark as well,	
	the mountain waterfall.	25
	(*Sound of guitars.*)	
MALE	(*Gets up and brandishes his horn.*)	
	Oh, how white,	
	the sorrowful wife!	
	Oh, how she sighs in the shade!	30
	Carnation and poppy	
	you'll later be	
	when I unfold my cape.	
	(*He approaches.*)	
	If you come as a pilgrim	35
	to pray your womb flowers,	
	wear soft linen shift,	
	not sad widow's veil.	

(García Lorca 1987: 122–5)

9.2 Connotative meaning

Assignment

Working in groups:

(i)   Discuss the strategic problems confronting the translator of the following text, paying particular attention to connotation.

(ii) Translate a section of the text (e.g. four groups each translate two stanzas) into English as if for publication in a poetry anthology. You should pay some attention to prosodic features (refer back to Chapter 6 for guidance on this) and attempt to produce a TT in verse, but the main focus of the exercise is meant to be lexical.

(iii) Explain the main decisions of detail you made in producing your TT.

Contextual information

The text is Rubén Darío's poem 'Sinfonía en gris mayor'. The Nicaraguan poet Rubén Darío (1867–1916) has been described as the chief representative of the 'modernista' (a term he himself is said to have coined) movement in Spanish poetry. His post-Romantic poetry, written at the turn of the century, is often characterized by an idealization of the sensual: in 'Sinfonía en gris mayor', this idealization takes the form of a highly pictorial 'mood poem', aptly termed a kind of 'word-etching'.

Source text

SINFONÍA EN GRIS MAYOR

El mar como un vasto cristal azogado
refleja la lámina de un cielo de zinc;
lejanas bandadas de pájaros manchan
el fondo bruñido de pálido gris.   5

El sol como un vidrio redondo y opaco
con paso de enfermo camina al cenit;
el viento marino descansa en la sombra
teniendo de almohada su negro clarín.

Las ondas que mueven su vientre de plomo   10
debajo del muelle parecen gemir.
Sentado en un cable, fumando su pipa,
está un marinero pensando en las playas
de un vago, lejano, brumoso país.

Es viejo ese lobo. Tostaron su cara   15
los rayos de fuego del sol del Brasil;

los recios tifones del mar de la China
le han visto bebiendo su frasco de gin.

La espuma impregnada de yodo y salitre
ha tiempo conoce su roja nariz,   20
sus crespos cabellos, sus bíceps de atleta,
su gorra de lona, su blusa de dril.

En medio del humo que forma el tabaco
ve el viejo el lejano, brumoso país,
adonde una tarde caliente y dorada   25
tendidas las velas partió el bergantín . . .

La siesta del trópico. El lobo se aduerme.
Ya todo lo envuelve la gama del gris.
Parece que un suave y enorme esfumino
del curvo horizonte borrara el confín.   30

La siesta del trópico. La vieja cigarra
ensaya su ronca guitarra senil,
y el grillo preludia un solo monótono
en la única cuerda que está en su violín.

                              (Darío 1987: 138–9)

9.3 *Connotative meaning*

Assignment

Working in groups:

(i)   Discuss the strategic problems confronting the translator of the following
      text, paying particular attention to connotation.
(ii) Translate a section of the text into English, assuming that your TT will
      be published in a handbook of source materials for students of political
      science.
(iii) Explain the main decisions of detail you made in producing your TT.

Contextual information

The ST is drawn from a selection of speeches by Franco on his conception
of *democracia orgánica*. Although practised with different intentions now in
a number of Swiss Cantons and some North American towns, the concept
of organic democracy was a feature of fascist dictatorship in Spain and
Italy in the twentieth century. It holds the view that the leader represents the
identity of the nation's people, which is seen as a heterogeneous group sharing
core values embodied in patriotism, the family and religion. Government is
drawn from institutions which participate in organic democracy. The texts are
collected on a pro-Franco website.

Source text

22/11/1966: Presentación de la Ley Orgánica del Estado, Cortes Españolas

La democracia, que bien entendida es el más preciado legado civilizador de la cultura occidental, aparece en cada época ligada a circunstancias concretas, que se resuelven en fórmulas políticas y varias a lo largo de la   5
Historia. No hay democracia sin bienestar; no existe verdadera libertad sin capacidad del pueblo para la satisfacción de las necesidades morales y materiales; no hay representación auténtica sin verdadera ciudadanía, pues los hombres y las unidades naturales de la sociedad tienen que hacerse presentes ante el Estado, siendo plenamente dueños de sí mismos, única   10
forma de que el Estado pueda mantener la autoridad al servicio del Derecho, sin imponer servidumbres so pretexto de liberar a unos y a otros de otras disciplinas artificiales.

18/11/1971: Discurso en la X Legislatura de las Cortes

Frente a la democracia formal, nosotros oponemos la democracia práctica,   15
una democracia a través de los cauces naturales en que el hombre discurre y que por eso recibe el nombre de democracia orgánica. La Constitución política española, integrada por nuestras Leyes Fundamentales, se ha apartado en todo momento de la creación abstracta de normas y se caracteriza por la ausencia de unos marcos rígidos como los que con tan   20
poco éxito ilusionaron a los constitucionalistas del siglo XIX, sino que ha nacido de la propia realidad española, como respuesta concreta a nuestras peculiaridades y a nuestros problemas, que nos ha permitido un proceso de constante perfeccionamiento de nuestras estructuras políticas, que ofrecen un ejemplo de Estado social de derecho que las actuales naciones   25
del mundo, tan sujetas a profundas convulsiones, harían bien en considerar con mayor atención y menos doctrinarismos.

(Franco 2003–2008)

10 Language variety

Social and tonal register

In this chapter and Chapter 11, we discuss the principal implications for translation of language variety. There are four main ways in which oral and written language manifests variety (affecting textual variables on all levels – phonic, graphic, morphological, syntactical and lexical):

1 **Social register** – users choose forms of language appropriate for particular social situations or topics, with varying degrees of formality, different stylistic conventions and employing particular subsets of their vocabulary.
2 **Tonal register** – users choose forms of language designed to convey their attitude towards what is being expressed or towards their addressees (or to generate an emotional response from addressees).
3 **Dialect** – speakers use forms of language that are particular to specific geographical areas and act as markers of identity and origin (and which are perceived as related but distinct by speakers of other dialects of the same language).
4 **Sociolect** – speakers use forms of language that are particular to specific social groups (socio-economic classes, occupations, age-groups, sub-cultures) and which are often perceived as markers of social status.

All four categories operate simultaneously in any given piece of language and interact with one another. Different dialects and sociolects have different ways of marking social and tonal register; a particular effect of social or tonal register may be achieved by choosing a feature specific to a dialect or sociolect; a sociolect may cut across several dialects and vice versa. Categories 1 and 2 are primarily a matter of choices made by language users, though some are more conscious than others of the range of choices open to them. Category 1 is often referred to as simply 'register', but we prefer to distinguish between social and tonal registers. While categories 3 and 4 are more to do with instinctive language habits than conscious choices, most people are capable of adapting their language behaviour according to whether they are addressing fellow members of a language community or outsiders. Dialects and sociolects do not in principle have clear or fixed boundaries, often taking the form of a continuum of varieties shading into one another, although decisive dividing lines are imposed in some cases by politics or geography. Categories 1 and 4 may in practice be marked by many of the same linguistic features, but whereas social register is a temporary adaptation for particular communicative purposes, sociolect is an established habit.

By way of introduction to the notion of language variety, here is an extract from Luis Martín-Santos's *Tiempo de silencio* (1973) for discussion in class. The novel combines self-consciously literary language characterized by elaborate syntax, rich vocabulary and sophisticated cultural allusions with passages such as the one below. It consists of a monologue in which Cartucho, a resident of a shanty-town on the outskirts of Madrid, describes a knife-fight he has had with 'el Guapo' over a girl who has become pregnant and had an abortion.

> '¿Qué se había creído? Que yo me iba a amolar y a cargar con el crío. Ella, "que es tuyo", "que es tuyo". Y yo ya sabía que había estao con otros. Aunque fuera mío. ¿Y qué? Como si no hubiera estao con otros. Ya sabía yo que había estao con otros. Y ella, que era para mí, que era mío. Se lo tenía creído desde que le pinché al Guapo. Estaba el Guapo como si tal. Todos le tenían miedo. Yo también sin la navaja. Sabía que ella andaba conmigo y allí delante empieza a tocarla los achucháis. Ella, la muy zorra, poniendo cara de susto y mirando para mí. Sabía que yo estaba sin el corte. Me cago en el corazón de su madre, la muy zorra. Y luego "que es tuyo", "que es tuyo". Ya sé yo que es mío. Pero a mí qué. No me voy a amolar y a cargar con el crío. Que hubiera tenido cuidao la muy zorra. ¿Qué se habrá creído? Todo porque le pinché al Guapo se lo tenía creído. ¿Para qué anduvo con otros la muy zorra? Y ella "que no", "que no", que sólo conmigo. Pero ya no estaba estrecha cuando estuve con ella y me dije "Tate, Cartucho, aquí ha habido tomate". [. . .] Yo achaparrao y ella mirándome como si para decir que era marica. Y él: "Bueno, si no quiere priva, pañí de muelle." Y viene con el vaso de sifón y me lo pone en las napies y yo lo bebo. Mirándole a la jeta. Y él, riéndose: "Que me hinca los acáis." Y se va chamullando entre dientes. "No hay pelés."'
>
> (Martín-Santos 1973: 45)

Discussing this text and the problems of translating it will immediately highlight certain features: the markers of sociolect, the non-standard grammar, the slang vocabulary, the indicators of accent, and the aggressive, *machista* tone. The point of this extract (contrasted with the intellectually and linguistically more sophisticated passages preceding and following it) is to place and define Cartucho in terms of social, cultural and physical environments, as well as personal and emotional characteristics. It is, in fact, an excellent example of one of the most difficult aspects of textual 'meaning', namely the appreciation not of referential content, but of characteristics in the way the message is expressed that voluntarily or involuntarily reveal information about the speaker or writer; the communicative situation; the relationship between speaker/writer and listener/reader; or the protagonist and the setting in a work of fiction. Linguistic choices (expressing something in one way rather than another) reveal things about speakers/writers that they do not necessarily intend to reveal, notably social and regional affiliations, and tend to be associated by listeners/readers with social and cultural stereotypes. They also reveal things that are intended, notably the calculated effects they want their utterances to have on listeners/readers.

These stylistically conveyed meanings are components of connotation: they share with the types of connotation discussed in Chapter 9 the character of meanings 'read between the lines' on the basis of associations that are widespread, even if not enshrined in dictionaries.

We continue this chapter by considering translation problems arising from features of social and tonal register in STs; issues of dialect and sociolect will be discussed in Chapter 11.

Social register

The social register of language is most often measured in terms of degrees of formality. Extreme informality (colloquial, slangy, relaxed, personal and spontaneous, as in a chat between friends in a bar) is sometimes labelled as 'low register' and extreme formality (careful, decorous, impersonal, erudite and precise, as in an academic article or exchanges between a judge and lawyers in court) as 'high register', although the value judgements implied by 'high' and 'low' can be unhelpful. Another way of describing this is as a scale from familiarity (assuming you can say what you like because you're with your mates) to deference (being careful to acknowledge social status and avoid causing offence). The level of formality or deference may be determined by a number of factors: the situation in which the communication takes place, the topic referred to, the medium and textual genre, the (relative) social status of the speaker/writer and listener/reader, the level of education of the speaker/writer, or the assumed level of education of the people addressed. This list of factors points to a more nuanced way of talking about social register: it is not simply a matter of formality/deference as opposed to informality/familiarity, but a complex range of variations in style to suit different circumstances and purposes, which vary from one speech community to another and change in the course of time. A man may use more swear-words and make more offensive sexist remarks when drinking with fellow fans after a football match than he does when drinking with colleagues after work; a civil servant's briefing paper written for a government minister will have a different style from the public statement based on it and from the speech that the minister delivers as part of a debate in parliament; a teenager is likely to write an e-mail to her college tutor in more careful prose than she uses for chatting on Facebook.

Clearly, modes of social register are linked to the genre categories we discussed in Chapter 4 and the degree to which a particular piece of discourse is planned or unplanned. Oral conversation tends to be associated with informality, familiarity and spontaneity, oral address with a greater degree of formality, decorum and preparation; most forms of written language are in general likely to be more formal and controlled than most forms of oral language. However, genre does not determine register. Some kinds of conversation (such as giving evidence in court) are tightly constrained and formalized, while some kinds of oral address (a stand-up comedy act, for example) deliberately aim for the 'lowest' register they can get away with, as well as giving prepared material an air of spontaneity. When written texts aim for a relatively informal or familiar social register, they often do so by incorporating the linguistic markers of oral genres. An obvious and easy way of doing this in English is simply to use contractions in imitation of spoken language: the phrase 'because you're with your mates' in the previous paragraph stands out as signalling a different social register from the text around it thanks to the choice of 'you're' instead of 'you are' (as well as the lexical choice of 'mates').

For the translator, social register is therefore a crucial part of assessing what kind of language one is dealing with and how a ST is designed to be perceived by SL readers, and as a result planning effectively for how the TT is to be designed for its target audience. Where there are linguistic and cultural differences in the ways in which two languages mark register, the translator needs to be able to draw on extensive SL and TL resources in order to find effective forms of compensation. Since social register is generated by so many different linguistic resources and sometimes consists of very subtle nuances, it is difficult to pin it down specifically in one language, let alone make systematic comparisons between a SL and TL for translation purposes. Nevertheless, it is possible to identify some useful patterns of comparison between Spanish and English in this respect, for which we can refer back briefly to the analysis of grammatical differences set out in Chapter 7. The following items from the table on pp. 116–17 are of particular relevance:

1–2   Discourse structure and complexity of sentences (the often laconic nature of colloquial Spanish; the greater syntactical complexity of formal written Spanish).

11   Forms of second-person address (the distinction in Spanish between 'tú/vosotros' and 'usted/ustedes').

12   Blurring of distinctions between subject and object pronouns (the tendency in colloquial English to confuse 'I' with 'me', and even in relatively careful discourse not to use 'whom').

13   Ethic datives (not exclusive to informal registers in Spanish, but often a marker of familiarity and idiomatic language).

17   Tenses (the existence of three tenses in Spanish used only in formal or specialized registers – the past anterior, the indicative '-ra' form and the future subjunctive).

19   Subjunctive mood (subjunctive forms used only in relatively careful or formal English).

20   Passive voice (to some extent an indicator of formality and impersonality in both languages but more markedly so in Spanish; impersonal Spanish constructions with 'se' can be translated either with colloquial 'you' or formal 'one').

22   Phrasal verbs in English (the difference in register between a phrasal verb and a single-word verb of Latin origin with the same literal meaning – 'to make up' and 'to invent').

As an example of one of these factors, consider the implications for social register of the contrast between formal and familiar address in the following piece of dialogue from an Argentinian novel:

– Bueno, yo no quiero que vos entréis aquí.
– Y ¿qué le he hecho yo a usted?
– Nada, mijito, pero no podéis entrar.
– Y ¿por qué los demás sí pueden?
– Eso es distinto.
– ¿Cuál es la diferencia?
– Que vos sois vos.
– Y ¿quién carajo soy yo?
– No te sulfuréis.
– Sí me sulfuro. Yo también bobo, yo ando con mis amigos, déjeme entrar.
– No podéis, no veis cómo vos me tratáis distinto, tus amigos me llaman La Carbonera, me dicen vos y tú me llamas Señora Dorotea y me decís usted.

(Morón 1986: 291)

A range of other linguistic and paralinguistic features is involved in the marking of register in different ways in English and Spanish, including intonation, carefulness of articulation, gestures, choice of vocabulary, use of pragmatic formulas (for greeting, thanking, making requests, giving and accepting orders, and so on), and use of taboo expressions and euphemisms. The variations are too numerous to go into here. Stewart (1999, especially Chapters 6, 7 and 8) and Batchelor and Pountain (2005: 2–19) offer useful guides to register and types of discourse, and analyse textual examples in detail; Steel (2007) provides a comprehensive guide to colloquial Spanish with numerous examples.

We have emphasized that social register is to a large extent a conscious performance, the product of choices made by language users to match their discourse to communicative situations or to position themselves in terms of social status. This is true not only of spoken language but also of the styles adopted by writers, who may use specialized terminology, complex syntax and formal ways of addressing their readers to project themselves (or the narrative personae they are constructing) as experts or authorities, or else avoid jargon, use simple syntax and favour colloquialism and informality to construct the voice of an ordinary member of the community being addressed. On the other hand, many of those choices are not conscious, and one of the effects of the marking of social register in language is that listeners and readers tend to infer from it what kind of person is speaking or writing (or being represented in writing as a speaker), in the sense of associating him or her with a social stereotype to which expectations and preconceptions are attached. Such assumptions are distinct from those made on the basis of information carried specifically by dialectal features, though they may sometimes be confused with them. Perhaps less obviously, they are also distinct from those based on information carried specifically by sociolect. Although dialect and sociolect may be ingredients of a given social register, dialect only conveys regional affiliations, and sociolect corresponds to very broad conceptions of social grouping (mostly defined by sociological notions of 'class structure'), whereas social register tends to be interpreted as designating relatively narrow stereotypes of the sorts of people one expects to meet in a given society. (For example, the textual features in the extract from *Tiempo de silencio* on p. 186 indicate a social register more immediately than they do a sociolect.)

For instance, many people encountering a man given to using abundant expletives regardless of the social situation in which he finds himself, especially if they are the kind of people who do not do so, are likely to make assumptions about socio-economic class (low-income), level of education (limited) and personality (aggressive, insensitive). A British style full of 'thank you' and 'please' may prompt contrasting perceptions: 'middle-class', 'well brought up', 'educated', 'polite and considerate', 'stuck-up'. However inaccurate or imprecise such assumptions may be in practice (and however much traditional class structures and behavioural norms may have eroded in contemporary Western societies), inferences from social stereotype to linguistic stereotype and vice versa are virtually inevitable. For the translator, the point is to attempt to identify the inferences likely to be drawn by SL readers/listeners from the style of a ST and to anticipate those that will be generated by stylistic decisions made in the composition of a TT.

Another dimension of the reflection in language of people's self-projection and assumptions about one another is gender. The way Cartucho speaks in the *Tiempo de silencio* extract identifies him not only in terms of class and social environment but also as a man who behaves in a way typical of that environment, displaying stereotypically aggressive, patriarchal *machismo*. Many of the situations in which people consciously or unconsciously modify their style of discourse according to the social situation are at the same time being modulated by gender – whenever a universalized reference to human beings assumes that they are male; whenever a provider of a service takes it for granted that the male member of a group is the breadwinner, bill payer or decision maker; whenever a father, husband or son is treated more deferentially than a mother, wife or daughter; whenever a man puts his partner down by saying something like '¡Cállate, mujer! Qué sabes tú de esas cosas . . .'; whenever the talk among a group of friends is most relaxed precisely because no one of the other sex is present. Such effects are largely a product of the content of a piece of discourse and the vocabulary chosen, but there are also specific ways in which linguistic structures themselves affect this aspect of social register in different languages: this has been noted in Chapter 3 as part of the general discussion of compensation and in Chapter 7 with reference to the agreement of adjectives, and discussed in detail in Chapter 8. These patterns may in some respects be culture-specific, especially in the case of communities holding onto traditional values (involving formal constraints on relations between the sexes and different patterns of speech among men and women). Delibes's novel *Cinco horas con Mario* (an extract from which is used for Practical 4.3) is an extended and astute exploration of the gendered nature of the language of Carmen, a woman stuck in the social, moral and political values of the 1940s while Spanish society begins to change rapidly in the 1960s. The more distinct the modes of speech used by men and women in a given society are, the more they can be regarded not just as manifestations of different social registers but as different sociolects.

It will be clear by now that in translating a ST which has speaking characters in it, or in which the author uses a social register for self-projection, the construction of social register in the TT is a major concern. Equally clearly, in translating, say, P.G. Wodehouse into Spanish, one would have to do something about the fact that Jeeves speaks in the social register of the 'gentleman's gentleman', and Bertie Wooster in that of the aristocratic nitwit. The fundamental problem is this: how can essentially English stereotypes like Jeeves and Bertie be transplanted into a Spanish-speaking context, produce plausible dialogue in Spanish, and still remain linguistically stereotyped so as to hint at the caricatures of gentleman's gentleman and inane aristocrat? There are no obvious global answers to such questions. A choice of appropriate TL registers can, however, sometimes seem relatively easy when the translator is operating between similar cultures such as contemporary Britain and Spain, where certain social stereotypes (such as the plain-clothes detective or the teenage heavy-metal fan) and stereotypical situations (such as shopping in a supermarket or working in an office) do show some degree of cross-cultural similarity. It may well be that some social stereotypes can be fairly successfully matched from one culture to another. The translator is then left with a two-stage task. First, a ST stereotype must be converted into an appropriate target-culture stereotype; and second, a plausible social register must be selected and consistently applied for each of the target-culture stereotypes chosen.

Nevertheless, parallels in social stereotyping are in practice far from exact. There are obvious discrepancies between, for example, the stereotypes of British aristocrat and Spanish aristocrat, or British policeman and Spanish policeman. In any case, is it desirable for Bertie Wooster to become every inch the Spanish aristocrat in a Spanish TT? Is the translation not vitiated if the translator fails to convey to the Spanish reader a sense of Wooster's essential Britishness (or even Englishness)? (At this point considerations of register intersect with the cultural issues discussed in Chapter 5.)

Even greater difficulties arise when it comes to matching stereotypes that have no likely parallels in the target culture. For instance, there seem to be no close target-culture parallels for the British gentleman farmer from the shires, the first-generation Italian immigrant from Brooklyn, the Spanish *torero* or the Central American *cacique*. Given any of these types in a ST, what social register would be appropriate for the corresponding character in the TT? Or should their speech be rendered in a fairly neutral style, with very few marked features of social register? For that matter, should these characters be rendered as culturally exotic? After all, for Cartucho in *Tiempo de silencio* to lose all trace of Spanishness in an English translation would surely be as disappointing as for Bertie Wooster to come across as completely Spanish. Even once the strategic decisions have been taken, there remains the eternal double challenge to the translator's linguistic skill: to be familiar with the quirks and constraints of TL varieties, and to be able to produce a consistently plausible TL social register.

Tonal register

Tonal register is usually the most conscious of the four modes of language variation (though it is not uncommon for listeners and readers to perceive tonal implications unintended by speakers and writers), modulating effects of dialect, sociolect and social register in ways that indicate subjective attitudes or an intention to generate emotional responses. Whatever the social situation or genre, expressive choices can be made that suggest affability or aggressiveness, levity or solemnity, sincerity or irony, exultation or despair, objectivity or subjectivity, pomposity or directness. As with social register, the variables occur on all levels of analysis (phonic, grammatical and lexical) and are non-verbal as well as verbal. Markers of tonal register can be even more subtle and hard to pin down than indicators of social register, at times consisting only of intonation or emphasis, or perhaps a cumulative pattern of affective and associative meanings.

Tonal and social register overlap in practice and may be expressed by the same kinds of linguistic features, but the two constitute different ways of looking at communication. For example, forms of language signalling deferential social register and a genuine desire to be polite and respectful may often go together, yet to see that they are distinct phenomena one only has to imagine the following formula spoken with intonation suggesting irony, or in the context of a vicious attack on the addressee: 'Le hablo al señor senador con todo el respeto debido a su augusta persona . . .' Or to take a contrasting example, the extensive use of slang and expletives may function as a marker of social register (informal situation or low socio-economic status of the speaker) and as a marker of tonal register (friendliness or aggression, desire to be accepted or to offend).

For further illustration of the relationship between social and tonal register, let us return to the extract from *Tiempo de silencio* with which this chapter started. Various signals relating to the social status of both Cartucho and el Guapo, the dynamics of their relationships with the girl and the situation in which Cartucho was taunted are transmitted by pronunciation ('estao'); prosody (repetition and short, emphatic phrases); grammar ('la' as indirect object in 'tocarla' and the generally elliptical, paratactic, incohesive quality of the discourse structure); slang vocabulary, some of it dialect- or sociolect-specific ('amolarse', 'los achucháis', 'cagarse', 'achaparrao', 'marica', 'priva', 'pañí', 'napies', jeta', 'acáis', 'chamullar' and 'pelés'), and connotative meanings ('pinchar', 'estrecha', 'tomate'). At the same time, many of these linguistic features indicate attitudes, emotional states and ways of provoking emotional responses. Cartucho's tone is aggressive, boastful, contemptuous, but also obsessive, resentful and defensive. Whether he is actually delivering this monologue to a listener or muttering it to himself, he is simultaneously asserting status and prestige (a macho tough guy who walks the walk and talks the talk) and seeking sympathy and a sense of belonging. If the passage were a theatrical monologue, tonal register might be indicated with a series of stage directions: 'Con resentimiento . . . Agresivo . . . Dando un puntapié furioso a una botella en el suelo . . . Luchando con la desesperación.'

The implications of tonal register for the translator are essentially no different from those of dialect, sociolect and social register. Since tonal register is linked to intended effects on the listener/reader, interpreting the impact of a ST depends very heavily on identifying its tonal register. Once this has been done, care must be taken to match the tonal register of the TT, combined with other aspects of language variety, to the intended effect on the target audience. Depending upon the overall translation strategy being followed, this effect may or may not involve attempting to replicate exactly the tonal register of the ST (for example, a community interpreter helping a desperate immigrant to access maternity services will aim to communicate the woman's point of view and the urgency of her need but not necessarily the full range of emotions she is expressing). Inappropriateness or inconsistency in register can all too easily make a translation unfit for purpose. In the *Tiempo de silencio* example, there would be unacceptable translation loss in rendering 'Aunque fuera mío. ¿Y qué? Como si no hubiera estao con otros. Ya sabía yo que había estao con otros. Y ella, que era para mí, que era mío' as 'Even if it were mine. What of it? As if she had not been with other men. I already knew that she had been with others. And she insisted on saying that it was mine.' This fails to capture not only the right social register (slightly too formal and idiomatically unconvincing) but also the confused tone. Compare with the following: 'Even if it *was* mine, so what? Don't give a toss. It's not as if she 'adn't been with other blokes, innit? I knew that already, innit. And she was, like, it's yours, swear to God, it's yours.'

As with the other language varieties, looking for suitable renderings of tonal register puts translators on their mettle, giving ample scope for displaying knowledge of the SL and its culture, knowledge of the target culture, and, above all, flair and resourcefulness in the TL.

Practical 10

10.1 Language variety: social and tonal register

Assignment

(i) Working in groups, identify and discuss the salient features of social and tonal register in the following short extracts.

(ii) Each group should produce two translations of one of the STs, one aiming to reproduce register accurately and the other deliberately misjudging it. Compare and explain your decisions in each case.

Contextual information

ST1 is an extract from a play, Carlos Gallego's *Adelaida*. The action is set in a mining town in Spain.

ST2 is an extract from an online exchange in January 2008 in a 'Política y gobierno' forum on www.colombia.com ('El portal que une a los colombianos'). The topic is kidnappings by the guerrilla group FARC (two women had just been released, thanks to mediation by Hugo Chávez of Venezuela).

ST3 is the preamble of Law 52/2007, passed by the Spanish Cortes on 26 December 2007, 'por la que se reconocen y amplían derechos y se establecen medidas en favor de quienes padecieron persecución o violencia durante la guerra civil y la dictadura'.

Source text 1

SERVANDO. – Además, a mí no me trate de usted, hombre, que me dan remilgos. Yo soy para todo el mundo Servando, el hijo del peón caminero, y basta.
D. MATÍAS. – En eso tiene razón, a veces los tratamientos son embarazosos. Quizás de ahora en adelante nos tengamos que ver más a   5
menudo. No me importará que me llames Matías, eso facilitará las cosas.
SERVANDO. – (*Sorprendido.*) ¡Eh, eh . . . alto el carro!, vamos a dejar una cosa clara. El que usted a mí me trate de tú, no quiere decir que seamos amigos de toda la vida, no nos confundamos. Yo sería incapaz de tutearle, la verdad, no sé por qué, aunque para mí en el fondo no sea más que el   10
hijo de Matías 'el adulón'. Todos sabemos por qué usted es el Alcalde.
D. MATÍAS. – (*Colérico.*) ¡No le consiento que hable así de mi padre! Modere el lenguaje o me veré obligado a marcharme. No he venido aquí a aguantar impertinencias. [. . .]
SERVANDO. – Si no está a gusto ya sabe en donde tiene la puerta. ¡En   15
mi casa, el amo soy yo, nunca lo olvide, (*Irónico.*) señor Alcalde.

(Gallego 1990: 13–14)

Source text 2

Lucero08. el gobierno colombiano lo que deberia hacer es mandarle una
bomba atomica a la guerrilla y asi acabar con esa plaga. de nada sirve que
liberen a un par de secuestradas y luego secuestren a 6 todo esto es pura
vagamunderia.
Nacionalista radical. niña, eres comidilla para el psiquiatra. ve a que te   5
hagan un chequeo. y deja de estar abriendo tantos foros que nos perdemos,
lo poco util que tengas que decir puedes hacerlo en un unico cuadro.
Lucero08. ud esta igual que el loco chavez creyendo que es el unico que
tiene la razon. este foro es libre para todos los que quieran opinar de lo
que quieran y como quieran. el derecho ajeno es el principio de la paz. yo 10
lo que hago es plasmar el pensamiento y el deseo de muchos de acabar
con la doble moral y la curseria como la suya que cree que va a deslumbrar
a los usuarios de este foro con comentarios rebuscados y copiados de otros.
Nacionalista radical. lucerito, lucerito, de verdad que das pena. a todo
esto porque no respondes en los otros foros?   15

(Colombia.com 2008)

Source text 3

JUAN CARLOS I
REY DE ESPAÑA

A todos los que la presente vieren y entendieren.
Sabed: Que las Cortes Generales han aprobado y Yo vengo en sancionar
la siguiente ley.   5

EXPOSICIÓN DE MOTIVOS

El espíritu de reconciliación y concordia, y de respeto al pluralismo y a
la defensa pacífica de todas las ideas, que guió la Transición, nos permitió
dotarnos de una Constitución, la de 1978, que tradujo jurídicamente esa
voluntad de reencuentro de los españoles, articulando un Estado social y 10
democrático de derecho con clara vocación integradora.

El espíritu de la Transición da sentido al modelo constitucional de
convivencia más fecundo que hayamos disfrutado nunca y explica las
diversas medidas y derechos que se han ido reconociendo, desde el
origen mismo de todo el período democrático, en favor de las personas 15
que, durante los decenios anteriores a la Constitución, sufrieron las
consecuencias de la guerra civil y del régimen dictatorial que la sucedió.

(BOE 2007)

10.2 Language variety: social and tonal register

Assignment

(i)   Analyse the encounter dramatized in the ST below in terms of social and
       tonal register and discuss the strategic problems of translating it for
       performance in front of an audience in a specified part of the English-
       speaking world.

(ii)   Translate the ST into English in accordance with the strategy formulated.

(iii)   Explain the decisions of detail you made in producing your TT.

Contextual information

The ST is the beginning of a short play by the *madrileña* dramatist and actor Paloma Pedrero, *Solos esta noche* (1990). The piece is one of a series of one-act plays designed to be performed together under the collective title *Noches de amor efímero*, which all deal with brief encounters between men and women at night in urban settings. The opening stage direction describes Carmen ('una mujer de treinta y bastantes años', dressed elegantly but conventionally, with 'pelo de peluquería y uñas largas muy pintadas') arriving on the platform of a Metro station and sitting down. A moment later, José ('un joven moreno de piel y musculoso') turns up, sits on another bench and lights a cigarette.

Source text

> *Carmen pasea nerviosa por el andén. Después de un momento, el joven comienza a acercarse a la mujer. Carmen, asustada, se agarra el bolso y se dirige hacia la salida. El joven la llama con un «Eh, oye . . .». Carmen se para en seco. José llega hasta ella.*
>
> CARMEN. – (*Muy asustada. Hablando muy deprisa.*) No tengo nada. Me   5
> he metido en el metro porque me he quedado sin dinero. Ni un duro, te
> lo juro . . . Toma. (*Le da el bolso.*) Puedes quedarte con él. El reloj es
> caro. Toma, puedes venderlo . . . Los anillos . . . ¡No puedo sacármelos!
> Por favor, los dedos no. No me cortes los dedos . . .
> JOSÉ. – (*Interrumpiéndola perplejo.*) Pero, ¿qué dices? ¿Qué te pasa? ¿Te   10
> he pedido yo algo?
> CARMEN. – ¿Qué quieres? ¿Qué quieres de mí?
> JOSÉ. – Joder, qué miedo llevas encima, ¿no? ¿Tengo tan mala pinta?
> CARMEN. – No, no, es que . . . es muy tarde. No estoy acostumbrada a
> estar sola a estas horas . . . No cojo nunca el metro y . . .   15
> JOSÉ. – Ya. A estas horas estás en tu casa viendo la televisión. Toma tus
> cosas y relájate. (*Carmen asiente.*) Tranqui, ¿eh? tranqui . . .
> [. . .]
> JOSÉ. – Bueno, habrá que esperar. (*Saca un bocadillo.*) ¿Quieres?
> CARMEN. – (*Sin mirarle.*) No fumo, gracias.   20
> (*Carmen pasea nerviosa por el andén.*)
> JOSÉ. – Estáte quieta, chica, es que me estás mareando. ¿Tienes hambre?
> CARMEN. – No, gracias.
> JOSÉ. – Es de jamón. (*Carmen sigue paseando sin hacerle caso.*) Oye,
> que es de jamón.   25
> CARMEN. – ¿Y qué?
> JOSÉ. – Que es de jamón. ¿No quieres un cacho?
> CARMEN. – No, de verdad, gracias. He cenado hace un rato.
>
> (Pedrero 1999: 177–8)

11 Language variety

Dialect, sociolect and
code-switching

Chapter 10 introduced the topic of language variety, identifying four principal ways in which languages vary according to who is using them and in what circumstances, and went on to discuss translation issues arising from social and tonal register. This chapter considers the implications of texts being characterized by markers of dialect (geographical variation) and sociolect (variation between distinct social groups). Whereas register is largely the product of choices made by language users, dialect and sociolect are forms of language that define speech communities and are used mostly instinctively, although conscious and unconscious adjustments are made by speakers and (especially) writers as part of the production of social register.

The specific indicators of dialect and sociolect can be found at all levels of linguistic analysis, especially the phonic (accent and intonation) and lexical. They tend to be most conspicuous in unplanned oral discourse (and texts imitating speech), but are not limited to spoken language or informal registers. Producers of written texts aiming for a relatively high register may deliberately incorporate dialectal or sociolectal features in order to appeal to particular group loyalties or sympathies among their readers; this is most likely to be done with vocabulary and certain syntactical features, but may also involve variations of pronunciation being reproduced in writing. The more narrowly defined the target audience of a piece of oral or written discourse is, the more likely it is to incorporate distinctive markers of dialect or sociolect. However, even the 'standard' forms of language used to address wider audiences beyond the membership of a dialect or sociolect community are the product of certain dialects and sociolects acquiring elite status and becoming established as norms. The Real Academia Española, which has no counterpart in the English-speaking world, has had a powerful standardizing influence on Spanish worldwide, yet in the past decade it has focused more on descriptive functions and less on prescriptive ones, according greater recognition and validity to Latin American usage in its publications, and redefining its role as the coordinator of a collaborative effort by the various national Academias of the Spanish-speaking world, 'armonizando la unidad del idioma con la fecunda diversidad en que se realiza' (Real Academia Española 2007).

We do not intend to become embroiled here in problems of definition. For the purposes of analysing STs for translation and planning the kinds of language to be used in TTs, all that matters is the degree to which particular linguistic features signal specificity in terms of geographical area or social group. Any of the following levels of contrast within the Spanish-speaking world can be regarded as dialectal: Peninsular/Latin American, Mexican/Colombian, *andaluz/manchego*, *rioplatense/andino*, *chiapaneco/veracruzano*, *gaditano/ cordobés*. (For a concise survey in English of dialectal variation in Spanish, see Mackenzie 2001.) Sociolects, even more difficult to pin down than dialects, may correspond to broad socio-economic categories (upper/middle/working class) or other demographic dividing lines (young/old, male/female). They may be associated with occupations and lifestyles using specialized jargon (priests, soldiers, construction workers, jet-setting celebrities, school children), or with marginalized social groups (immigrants, vagrants). The term can also be applied to more narrowly-defined argots specific to particular places, such as *chilango* in Mexico City, *lunfardo* in Buenos Aires or *cheli* in Madrid. These might be regarded as dialects rather than sociolects, but their original function is more to do with signalling social affiliation than regional identity as such. Both dialects and sociolects change over time, and the distinctiveness of particular forms depends upon a range of geographical, social and cultural factors: for example, a speech community that is physically isolated will maintain greater stability and distinctiveness in its dialect; a society with traditional, hierarchical social structures will produce clearly-defined sociolects; and conversely, in industrialized countries with physically and socially mobile populations the boundaries between dialects and sociolects become increasingly fluid.

Dialect

To speak a particular dialect, with all its phonological, lexical and syntactical features, is to give away information about one's association with a particular geographical area. It is sometimes also possible to infer the degree of speakers' regional affiliations from the proportion of dialectal features in their speech; for instance, whether they are natives of the region and have little experience of other regions, or whether they are originally from the region, but retain only traces of that origin overlaid by speech habits acquired elsewhere; or whether they are incomers who have merely acquired a veneer of local speech habits. Furthermore, some speakers are notable for having a repertoire including several dialects between which they can alternate (that is, they are capable of 'code-switching'), or on which they can draw to produce a mixture of dialects.

As an example, let us consider Andalusian, the dialect (or rather set of dialects) spoken in an area of Spain roughly corresponding to the Comunidad Autónoma de Andalucía. There is little controversy surrounding its status as a dialect of Castilian or variant of Spanish, and no serious campaign to have it recognized as a language in its own right (with a status similar to that of Catalan or Galician). The new Statute of Autonomy for Andalucía, being very careful to refer to it neither as 'dialecto' nor as 'lengua', declares as one of the prime objectives of the Comunidad Autónoma 'la defensa, promoción, estudio y prestigio de la modalidad lingüística andaluza en todas sus variedades' (Junta de Andalucía, 2007, Art. 10), yet the Junta publicizes no specific programmes for pursuing this aim. The differences between Andalusian and Castilian are mostly phonological, with a few distinctive features of vocabulary and syntax (*lo* rather than *le* used as human masculine direct object pronoun, and *ustedes* used in place of *vosotros* in some areas with second-person plural conjugation – 'ustedes habláis').

The Andalusian accent, particularly its *ceceante* variant, has sometimes been stigmatized as an indicator of low social status or limited education, or at least disparaged for its tendency to blur many of the articulatory distinctions maintained in central and northern Castilian – though not in the same class-based way nor to the same extent as regional accents have been stigmatized in England. When features of Andalusian pronunciation are reproduced in writing (usually in plays or novels set in Andalucía or featuring Andalusian immigrants in Madrid or Barcelona), it has sometimes been with a comical, caricaturing intention, or at best constituting an element of folksy *costumbrismo*. There have, however, been attempts to have Andalusian taken more seriously as a vehicle for discourse on any level and to establish an orthographical system that represents its phonological features, an ambition that has recently been given new impetus by the World Wide Web. The *Andalú* online encyclopaedia, hampered somewhat by a lack of standardization of its own orthography, offers two parallel versions of a definition of Andalusian. (Use analysis of these extracts in class as a reminder of the key features of the accent.)

El andalú (también yamáo lengua andalusa o idioma andalú) ë el idioma qe s'abla en Andalusía, en er sú d'Ëpanha. Manqe sufre bariasionë heográficä, lö ablantë d'ëte idioma poseen muxä caräterîtikä en común.

El idioma andalúh (también yamáo lengua andaluza o zimplemente andaluh) eh er idioma ke ze abla en Andaluzía, en er zú dè la Penínzula Ibérika. Manke zufre bariazioneh heohráfikah, loh ablanteh d'ehte idioma pozéen muxah karahteríhtikah en común.

(Andalú 2008)

However well meaning initiatives like this may be, they are never likely to gain widespread support beyond or even within Andalucía. The deliberately non-Castilian appearance of these orthographies strikes many as perverse, and occasionally provokes hostility from Spanish nationalists:

Pero bueno, ¿vosotros qué queréis? ¿Que acabemos todos hablando suajili? ¿De dónde habéis salido, de una fumada colectiva o es un nuevo virus para el que aún no hay medicación? ¿Habéis consultado al médico si lo vuestro tiene cura? Hay que estar muy mal para escribir como vosotros que lo más que se parece es a algún artículo que he leído en indonesio. ¿Será que os da mucho el sol en Andalucía y estáis así? Venga dejad por un día de darle a la botella, que por 24 horas de abstinencia no se muere nadie y aprended a escribir en cristiano, que a este paso no va a hacer falta ya ni que vengan los moros.

('Uño que escribe con eñe' 2007)

All these aspects of dialectal usage are stylistic carriers of information about speakers and about the circumstances in which they produce utterances and texts, and no translator can afford to ignore them. They also contribute to the cultural specificity of the texts in which they appear, and therefore need to be dealt with as part of the translator's overall approach to the cultural dimension (as discussed in Chapter 5). Four main problems arise from taking account of them.

The first problem is easily defined: it is that of recognizing the peculiarities from which dialectal affiliation can be inferred in a ST. Clearly, the more familiar the translator is with SL dialects, the better.

The second is that of determining the textual relevance of the dialectal features and the information they convey: deciding how important they are to the overall effect and purpose of a ST and its representation of the SL culture, and on the basis of this, how important it is to reproduce them in the TT. The translator always has the option of rendering the ST into a neutral, standard version of the TL, with no distinctive dialectal traces. This may be appropriate if the dialectal style of the ST can be regarded as incidental, at least for the specific purposes of the TT. For example, in translating an eyewitness account of a murder for Interpol, one might be well advised to ignore all dialectal features and concentrate on getting the facts clear. In the extracts from *Andalú* above, the dialectal features are in one sense central, yet on the other hand, the point of the project is to present Andalusian as a standard language appropriate for a relatively high-register written text, which would point to a translation strategy based on largely ignoring the dialectal nature of the ST and treating it in the same way as a text using standard Castilian orthography (perhaps retaining the spelling of proper nouns as an exoticizing feature – Graná, Güerba). However, if the dialectal nature of the ST cannot be regarded as incidental – for example, in a novel where plot or characterization actually depend to some extent on dialect, or a political speech appealing to regional affiliations – the translator has to find means for indicating that the ST contains dialectal features. This creates some difficult practical problems.

For instance, suppose the ST is so full of broad dialectal features as to be virtually incomprehensible to a SL speaker from another region. The translator's first strategic decision is whether to produce a TT that is only mildly or imprecisely dialectal, and totally comprehensible to any TL speaker. There are features of spoken English common to various dialects which can be used selectively in a TT without attempting to create a consistent reproduction of the speech of a particular area: contractions such as 'I've', 'she's' and 'ain't';

unaspirated h ('on 'is 'ead'); the dropping of the final g in words ending in '-ing'; idioms that can be recognized as generally North American or broadly English. Arguments against this solution might be similar to those against 'improving' a ST that is badly written. However, there can be circumstances where this is the best alternative; depending, as any strategic decision does, on such factors as the nature and purpose of the ST, the purpose of the TT, its intended audience, the requirements of the person or organization paying for the translation, and so on. In some cases one may decide to inject a mere handful of TL dialectal features into the TT, just to remind the audience that it is based on a ST in dialect. On the other hand, the very obscurity of a piece of ST dialect may serve important textual purposes which would be vitiated in the TT if the piece were not rendered in an equally obscure TL dialect. In such a case – and probably only in such a case – it may be necessary for the translator to go all the way in the use of a TL dialect.

The third problem arises if the translator does opt for a broad TL dialect: just what dialect should the TT be in? Supposing that the ST is in Andalusian dialect, is there any dialect of English that in some way corresponds to it, having similar status and cultural associations among English dialects to those held by Andalusian among Spanish dialects? There is no obvious objective answer to this question – after all, what exactly is the position of Andalusian dialect among Spanish dialects at the time of translation, and is it similar to its relative position at the time the ST was produced? Of course, there may be certain stereotypical assumptions associated with given ST dialects which might be helpful in choosing a TT dialect (for instance, 'Andalusians have the reputation of being lazy', or 'Cockneys are cheeky and cheerful'). When a dialect is used in the ST specifically in order to tap into such stereotypes, it could conceivably be appropriate to select a TL dialect with similar popular connotations. In other cases, the choice of TL dialect may be influenced by geographical considerations. For instance, a northern dialect of Spanish (say, Asturian), in a ST containing references to 'northerners', might be plausibly rendered drawing on a northern dialect of English. Even more plausibly, a Spanish ST with a plot situated in an industrial setting, say Bilbao, might be rendered with elements of a TL dialect from Detroit or an industrial city in the Midlands or the North of England, perhaps Birmingham or Manchester.

A final difficulty, if one decides to adopt a specific TL dialect, is of course the problem of familiarity with its characteristics. If the translator does not have an accurate knowledge of the salient features of the TL dialect chosen, the TT will become as ludicrous as all the texts which, through ignorance, have Scots running around saying 'hoots mon' and 'och aye the noo'.

It will be clear by now that rendering ST dialect with TL dialect is a form of cultural transplantation. Like all cultural transplantations, it runs the risk of incongruity in the TT. For instance, having broad Norfolk on the lips of country folk from Valencia could have disastrous effects on the plausibility of the whole TT. The surest way of avoiding this would be to transplant the entire work – setting, plot, characters and all – into Norfolk; but, of course, this might be quite inappropriate in the light of the contents of the ST and the purpose of the translation. Short of this extreme solution, the safest decision may after all be to make relatively sparing use of TL features that are recognizably dialectal without being clearly recognizable as belonging to a specific dialect. Fortunately, there are many features of non-standard accent, vocabulary and grammar that are widespread in a number of British dialects. Nevertheless it would be even safer, with a ST containing direct speech, to translate dialogue into fairly neutral English, and, if necessary, to add after an appropriate piece of direct speech some such phrase as 'she said, in a broad Andalusian accent', rather than have a woman from Andalusia speaking Scouse or Glaswegian.

Sociolect

It has already been noted that the distinction between dialect and sociolect is not clear-cut. Some sociolects are contained within dialects (the speech of urban teenage gangs in Glasgow, for example), while others cut across them or are independent of them (the prestige sociolect of the English upper classes, or standardized forms of written language used for particular kinds of discourse). Users of a given sociolect may speak with different regional accents but share a distinctive set of lexical, intonational and grammatical features: for example, professional soldiers from various British regional and social backgrounds may tend to develop an authoritative tone, clipped delivery and a fondness for military metaphors. On the other hand, the term 'urban working-class sociolect' cannot designate a particular language variety of English unless it is qualified by geographical reference. While 'upper class' and 'public school' sociolects are not region-specific, the further down one goes on the socio-economic scale, the more necessary it is to take social and regional considerations together, thus creating concepts of mixed regional and sociolectal language varieties such as 'Norwich urban working class', 'Edinburgh "Morningside" urban middle class' and so on. Such mixed socio-dialectal designations are generally more meaningful labels for recognizable language variants than purely sociological ones.

The situation in a Spanish context is somewhat different from the situation in Britain: regional variations tend to cut across the social scale, with each regional dialect having sociolectally higher and lower forms. Nevertheless, as in Britain, regional dialects may sometimes be stigmatized and variations within the range of 'upper class' and 'upper-middle class' sociolects of Spanish (often identified as 'castellano culto') are limited. The situation is further complicated by Latin American varieties of Spanish, whose status is not necessarily comparable to that of non-British varieties of English (US, Canadian, Australian and so on). Unlike these sociolinguistically autonomous varieties of English, Latin American varieties of Spanish have often been perceived, even by Latin Americans themselves, as less prestigious than the supposedly 'pure' Spanish spoken in Castilla.

Whatever one's reservations about the usefulness and precision of the notion of sociolect, it remains true that sociolectal features can convey important information about a speaker or writer and about the social environment in which a piece of discourse is produced, or which is evoked by a text. If they are obtrusive in the ST (in the form of non-standard, non-prestigious or prestige-marked features of accent, grammar, vocabulary or sentential marking), the translator cannot afford to ignore them and needs to make the effort to identify as exactly as possible what they signal. The passage from *Tiempo de silencio* reproduced in Chapter 10 (p. 186) is the first time that Cartucho appears in the novel, but is later contextualized very fully in various sections, especially a lengthy description in which Cartucho is precisely placed in social, economic and cultural terms. It is worth reproducing substantial extracts from this, as an example of a close relationship between social environment and language:

> Cartucho pertenecía a la jurisdicción más lamentable de los distintos distritos de chabolas. Mientras que la mortuoria del Muecas había sido establecida del modo legal y digno que corresponde al inmigrante honrado, la de Cartucho (o más bien la de la anciana madre de Cartucho) era una chabola avinagrada, emprecariante y casi cueva. Estas chabolas marginales y sucias no pretendían ya como las otras tener siquiera apariencia de casitas, sino que se resignaban a su naturaleza de agujero maloliente sin pretensiones de dignidad ni de amor propio en estricta correlación con la vida de sus habitantes. [. . .] Los lamentables habitantes de estos barrios no mostraban en sus manos callosas los estigmas de los peones no calificados, sino que preferían ostentar sus cuerpos en actitudes graciales y favorecedoras con pretensiones de sexo ambidextramente establecido y comercialmente explotado. Usaban a este fin de pantalones ajustados con cremalleras en las pantorrillas y de los debidos cono-cimientos folklóricos y rítmicos. [. . .] Eran, pues, gentes de un bronce apenas moldeado los que, entre blasfemias y hasta con posibles fatigas retribuidas de tiempo en tiempo (como cargar camiones o descargar camiones o llevar carbón a un hotel), nunca conseguían un estatuto estable y permanecían exiliados tanto de la sociedad que sólo a sí misma se admite, como de las infrasociedades que bajo aquélla se constituyen inventándose códigos de honor ininteligibles, lenguajes, gestos y provis-orias asambleas constituyentes. Por aquí se veían gitanos de paso hacia la ciudad. Cuando llegaban a conquistarla aquí se detenían y luego avanzaban, casi respetuosamente, y se perdían en sus calles. Más tarde, se podía ver de nuevo a las gitanas viejas cuando ya la ciudad las volvía a dejar caer desde su falda, como quien se sacude las migajas de lo que ha estado merendando.
>
> (Martín-Santos 1973: 117–18)

The challenge facing a translator attempting to reproduce the effect of these factors in a translation of Cartucho's monologue is daunting. However, as with dialect, the textual and functional importance of sociolect varies and needs to be assessed case by case. The mere fact that the ST contains marked sociolectal features does not necessarily mean that the TT should be just as heavily marked for sociolect. As with translating dialects, there may be considerations militating against this, such as whether the sociolect has a decisive textual role in the ST, or the purposes for which the ST is being translated. In many cases it is sufficient for the translator to include just enough devices in the TT to remind the audience of the sociolectal character of the ST. Alternatively, there may be good reasons for producing a TT that is in a bland 'educated middle-class' sociolect of the TL – this is also a sociolect, but, for texts intended for general consumption, it is the least obtrusive one.

Once the translator has decided on a TT containing marked sociolectal features, the problems that arise parallel those created by dialect. The class structures of different societies, countries and nations never replicate one another. Consequently, there can be no exact matching between sociolectal varieties of one language and those of another. At best, something of the prestige or the stigma attached to the ST sociolect can be conveyed in the TT by a judicious choice of TL sociolect. The translator may therefore decide that a valid strategy would be to render, say, an 'urban working-class' SL sociolect by an 'urban working class' TL sociolect. But this does not solve the question of which 'urban working class' sociolect. The decision remains difficult, especially as the wrong choice of TL sociolect could make the TT narrative implausible for sociological or cultural reasons. This question of the socio-cultural plausibility of the TT is one of the translator's major considerations (assuming, of course, that the ST is not itself deliberately implausible). Finally, as with dialect, it goes without saying that the translator must actually be familiar enough with features of the chosen TL sociolect(s) to be able to use them accurately and convincingly; in general, it is safest to use them sparingly.

Code-switching

Passing mention was made above of **code-switching**. This well-known phenomenon occurs in the language use of speakers whose active repertoire includes several dialects and sociolects, and most conspicuously in bilingual speakers who switch between different languages. It consists of a rapid alternation from one moment to another – sometimes within sentences – between different language varieties. Code-switching is used, by ordinary speakers and writers, for two main strategic reasons: first, to fit the style of speech (consciously or unconsciously) to the changing social circumstances of the speech situation; and second, to impose a deliberate definition on the speech situation by the choice of a style of speech, especially to reinforce human relationships and group identities.

Since code-switching is a definite strategic device, and since its social-interactional function in a text cannot be denied, the translator of a ST containing code-switching should attempt to convey in the TT the effects it has in the ST. For written dialogue, the possibility of explaining the code-switch without reproducing it in the TT does exist, as in 'he said, suddenly relapsing into the local vernacular'. There is, of course, no such option for the text of a play or a film, except as an instruction in a stage direction. At all events, it would be more effective, if possible, to reproduce ST code-switching by code-switching in the TT. Such cases place even greater demands on the translator's mastery of the TL, two or more noticeably different varieties of the TL needing to be used in the TT.

There is no code-switching in the *Tiempo de silencio* passage, but it is clearly illustrated in the extract from Rodríguez Méndez's *Flor de Otoño* used for Practical 11.2.

Practical 11

11.1 Language variety: dialect and sociolect

Assignment

(i)   Working in groups, identify dialectal and sociolectal features in the three short extracts below, and discuss the strategic problems that they pose for the translator.
(ii)   Outline a strategy for translating each of the STs, assuming a particular purpose (skopos) for the translation. Compare conclusions and strategies between groups.
(iii)   Translate one of the texts into English according to the strategy developed.

Contextual information

Source text 1 is from the 'Suplemento de Humor' of a newspaper. Text 2 is from a novel first published in 1994. Text 3 is the opening of an academic research article. Details of where the texts were published are given in the bibliography, but we suggest that you do not look these up until you have completed part (i) of the exercise.

Source text 1

Un borracho entra en un ómnibus, se para en medio del pasillo al frente, y señalando a la derecha con su mano, grita:
– Los que están de este lado . . . ¡son todos putos!
Los pasajeros no salen de su asombro, pero el borracho, señalando para la izquierda, insiste:
– Y los que están de este lado . . . ¡son todos unos vagos de mierda!
Un tipo que estaba sentado a la derecha, le protesta:

5

– Pará, ché, que yo no soy puto ...
El borracho, tambaleándose, le contesta:
– Entonces pasá p'acá, hermano, que me la estás complicando ...   10
En eso el conductor – que ya no se banca más al choborra – se manda una
frenada que hace que todos los pasajeros se caigan al piso. El chofer se
para, y le grita al borracho:
– ¿Me podés repetir a quién le dijiste puto vos?
A lo que el borracho, desparramado por el piso, le dice: 15
– Ahora ya me perdí, vo ... Con esa frenada me entreveraste todo.

(Guambia 2003)

Source text 2

Me jode ir al Kronen los sábados por la tarde porque está siempre
hasta el culo de gente. No hay ni una puta mesa libre y hace un calor
insoportable. Manolo, que está currando en la barra, suda como un cerdo.
Tiene las pupilas dilatadas y nos da la mano, al vernos.
– Qué pasa, chavales. ¿Habéis visto el partido, troncos? – pregunta.   5
– Una puta mierda de equipo. Del uno al once, son todos una mierda –
dice Roberto.
– Me han jodido el baño en Cibeles, tronco. Si esto sigue así, acabaré
haciéndome del Atleti. A ver, ¿qué queréis?
Pillamos un mini y unas bravas.   10
Roberto echa una ojeada a nuestro alrededor para ver si Pedro ha llegado.
Luego, mira su reloj y dice: joder con el Pedro, desde que tiene novia pasa
de todo el mundo.
– ¿Hemos quedado con alguien más? – pregunto.
– Sí. Con Fierro, Raúl y con Yoni.   15
– ¿Quién es Yoni?
– Un amigo de Raúl. Un tío guay, nada que ver con el pesado de Raúl.

(Mañas 1998: 11)

Source text 3

Es ya ampliamente reconocido que las anomalías estructurales terminales
de los cromosomas son una importante causa de retraso mental (DeVries
y cols., 2003). Con el avance de las técnicas de citogenética y los cariotipos
de alta resolución, en la actualidad se pueden identificar anomalías que
no se reconocían con cariotipos de baja resolución, como es el caso de la   5
monosomía 1p36. Esta alteración se considera hoy como un síndrome de
genes contiguos (Slavotinek y cols., 1999). Sus características clínicas, si
bien no contienen rasgos específicos del síndrome, sí se manifiestan como
un patrón fenotípico que muchas veces permite sospechar la anomalía.
Reconocer este patrón clínico orientará al diagnóstico citogenético, ya que 10
la pequeña deleción involucrada se puede visualizar en un cariotipo de alta
resolución y con técnicas de FISH.

(López-Grondona *et al.* 2003: 11)

11.2 Language variety: dialect, sociolect and code-switching

Assignment

(i)   Working in groups, identify and discuss features of dialect, sociolect and code-switching in the ST. Discuss the strategic problems that they pose for the translator, bearing in mind the requirement that the TT should be designed for oral performance. You may also need to take account of social and tonal register.

(ii)   In the light of the conclusions arrived at in (i), discuss the TT and assess its success in dealing with problems of language variety.

(iii)   Outline a strategy for producing a TT different from the one given, and illustrate it with a few selected examples.

Contextual information

The ST is from the play *Flor de Otoño* (written in 1972 and first performed in 1982), by José María Rodríguez Méndez. There have been two productions in recent years: one at the small Sala Artenbrut in Barcelona and one at the Centro Dramático Nacional in Madrid (which translated all the Catalan dialogue into Spanish). The play is set in Barcelona in 1930. The protagonist, Lluiset, is a young gay lawyer from a wealthy and prestigious Catalan family who also performs as a drag artist with the stage name Flor de Otoño in a seedy cabaret in the red-light district, as well as leading an anarchist group of would-be terrorists. The text is a celebration of the linguistic, social and cultural diversity of Barcelona, combining Catalan with various dialects of Castilian spoken by immigrants from all over Spain. Lluiset moves effortlessly between various social classes and environments, from the *alta burguesía* in the Eixample to the *hampa* in the Barrio Chino. In this scene, set in the workers' cooperative in the suburbs in which Lluiset and his comrades are planning bombings, his boyfriend Ricard (also a middle-class lawyer) is briefing a group of burly market porters about a job that Lluiset wants carried out.

The TT is from *Autumn Flower*, a translation by Marion Peter Holt, published in the USA by Estreno in 2001.

Turn to pp. 208–9 for source text and target text.

Source text

RICARD – (*Levantándose.*) Aleshores . . . Ya les habrá dicho algo el
Sebastianet.
EL CAMÁLIC CATALÁ – Sí, señor. Pero si le place pot parlarhi catalá,
aunque éste es gallego, ése andaluz y el otro murciano, ho comprend. ¿Oi
que sí? (*Gruñidos del trío gallego-andaluz-murciano que no se pueden*   5
interpretar ni como sí, ni como no.)
RICARD – Es igual. Hablaremos en castellano, pa que todo quede bien
clarito. Se trata de suministrar un correctivo a un tipo, vamos, quiere
decirse, de dar una paliza a un gachó . . .
EL CAMÁLIC CATALÁ – Sí, señor, una panadera que diem en   10
catalá . . .
EL CAMÁLIC ANDALUZ – Amoo, una capuana que llaman en mi
tierra . . .
EL CAMÁLIC GALLEGO – Una güena soba . . .
EL CAMÁLIC MURCIANO – (*Orondo y efusivo como buen levantino.*)   15
Soba, tunda, zurra, panaera, curra, vaselina . . . (*Tienen que cortarle los*
otros.)
EL CAMÁLIC CATALÁ – Pues, señor, ens diu vusté de qui es tracta,
las condicions y queda el asunto finiquitao.
RICARD – (*Sacando una foto del bolsillo trasero del pantalón.*) Éste es   20
el gachó. ¿Acaso le conocéis?
EL CAMÁLIC CATALÁ – (*Sacando unos lentes y poniéndoselos, mira*
con solemnidad la foto.) De moment . . . (*La triada de cabezas se asoma*
para mirar la foto.)
RICARD – Es uno que andaba con «La Asturianita», una del Barrio Chino.   25
EL CAMÁLIC ANDALUZ – ¡Zí, zeñó . . .!, ¡zí, zeñó . . .! Un zervió
curreló pa ezte tipo . . . ¡Zí, zeñó! Un zervió maniobraba el organillo,
cuando ezte hijo e la gran puta ze dedicaba a la múzica.

(Rodríguez Méndez 1979: 175–6)

Target text

RICARD – Well, then . . . Sebastian has probably told you something . . .
CATALAN PORTER – Yeah, senyó. But if yuh don't mind, speak real
clear because these guys are from all over and they won't understand half
you say. Right? (*Grunts from the Andalusian-Galician-Murcian trio who
really are half out of it.*)   5
RICARD – Fine, I'll repeat everything if I have to, so it'll be clear to them.
It's all about administering a corrective to a certain individual, in everyday
language, beat up the guy.
CATALAN PORTER – What we call 'roughing up'.
ANDALUSIAN PORTER – Take the starch outta 'em.   10
GALICIAN PORTER – A good lickin'.
MURCIAN PORTER – (*Self-satisfied and effusive.*) All that stuff and beat
him to a pulp . . . yeah! Yeah!
CATALAN PORTER – Well, senyó, we get the idea, so give us the details
and the deal's done.   15
RICARD – (*Taking a photo from his back pant's pocket.*) This is the guy.
Any chance you know him?
CATALAN PORTER – (*Taking out some eyeglasses and putting them
on, he looks at the photo solemnly.*) At the moment . . . (*The triad of heads
leans over to see the photo.*)   20
RICARD – He's the one who ran around with La Asturianita, the one from
the Barrio Chino.
ANDALUSIAN PORTER – (*With a regional lisp.*) Yeah, senyó, sure. I
worked for the guy. Sure, yours truly was his organ grinder when this son
of a bitch was in the music business.   25

(Rodríguez Méndez 2001: 43–4)

11.3 Language variety: dialect and sociolect

Assignment

(i)   Discuss the strategic problems confronting the translator of the ST below, paying particular attention to features of dialect and sociolect. You may also need to take account of social and tonal register.

(ii) Translate the text into English, assuming that your target readership's primary interest is in sport (and celebrity) rather than Hispanic culture.

(iii) Explain the main decisions of detail you made in producing your TT.

Contextual information

The ST is the beginning of the autobiography of Diego Maradona, Argentina's most famous and controversial soccer star. A *líbero* (originally an Italian term) is a free-ranging defensive player who is expected to initiate counter-attacks.

Source text

Empiezo este libro en La Habana. Por fin me decidí a contar todo. No sé, pero siempre me parece que quedan cosas por decir. ¡Qué raro! Con todo lo que ya dije, no estoy seguro de haber contado lo importante, lo más importante.

Acá, por las noches, mientras aprendo a saborear un habano, empiezo   5
a recordar. Es lindo hacerlo cuando uno está bien y cuando a pesar de los errores no tiene de qué arrepentirse.

Es bárbaro recorrer el pasado cuando venís desde muy abajo y sabés que todo lo que fuiste, sos o serás, es nada más que lucha.

¿Saben de dónde vengo? ¿Saben cómo empezó esta historia?   10

Yo quería jugar, pero no sabía de qué quería jugar, no sabía . . . No tenía ni idea. Yo empecé de defensor. Me gustó siempre y todavía me seduce jugar de líbero, ahora que apenas me dejan tocar una pelota porque tienen miedo de que mi corazón explote. De líbero mirás todo desde atrás, la cancha entera está delante tuyo, tenés la pelota y decís, pim, salimos para   15
allá, pum, buscamos por el otro lado, sos el dueño del equipo. Pero en aquellos tiempos, ¡ma'qué líbero ni líbero! La cosa era correr atrás de la pelota, tenerla, jugar.

(Maradona 2000: 11)

12 Scientific and technical translation

In so far as all texts can be categorized in terms of genre, there is no reason why one particular genre should be singled out for special attention rather than any other. However, since technical translation is a far more marketable skill than literary translation, and since most language students are, owing to their lack of training in science or technology, in awe of 'technical' texts, we consider it worthwhile to devote a separate chapter to problems confronting the translator of texts in this genre. By 'technical' translation we mean especially the translation of empirical/descriptive texts written in the context of scientific or technological disciplines. As a matter of fact, any specialist field, from anthropology to zymurgy via banking, history, numismatics and yachting, has its own technical register, its own jargon, its own genre-marking characteristics, with which translators should be familiar if they are to produce convincing TTs in the appropriate field. This is as true of scientific and technical translation as it is of any other specialized field: a look at a hobby magazine, or a review of a rock concert, or the sport or business pages in the paper quickly confirms this. Take, for example, the opening sentence of an article from the leading Spanish press agency, EFE, published by the sports newspaper, *Diario As*:

> María José Rienda, la española que más pruebas ha ganado de la Copa del Mundo (seis), se mostró ayer 'orgullosa y feliz' por haber vuelto a esquiar seis meses y una semana después de lesionarse de gravedad la rodilla derecha.
>
> (EFE 2007: 53)

The general meaning of 'pruebas', 'proof/test/trial', could lead the translator unaware of the word's technical sense of 'race' to mistranslate it in this context.

Technical translation illustrates three points in the translation of all specialist texts particularly well. First, the translator must be just as familiar with technical terms and genre features in the TL as in the SL. Second, specialist and technical texts have clearly defined skopoi, as discussed in Chapter 4, and the identification of ST and TT skopos will influence the translator's priorities. ST and TT skopos may overlap, but will not by necessity do so. For example, technical manuals and even recipes give detailed information and instructions, and failure to convey these may lead to accident, malfunction or letdown. Legal STs, on the other hand, may be translated to have the full force of law – such as within the European Community – or merely for information. Third, the problems met in translating specialist texts are mostly no different from those met in translating in any other genre, specialized or not. Textual variables are textual variables, particularizations are particularizations, whatever the genre and whatever the subject matter; and the relative merits of literal and communicative translation need to be considered in translating any text. Nevertheless, the very fact that technical texts are at the far extreme of unfamiliarity for many language students makes them especially valuable illustrations of all these points. There are three reasons, then, for devoting a chapter to technical translation: first, because it probably offers the widest field of employment for translators; second, because it is often so unnerving for language students; and third, because it is so exemplary of issues crucial to translation methodology.

A notable generic property of technical texts is that they are seldom aimed at complete non-specialists. Thus, in subject matter and comprehension, the typical technical ST is not easily accessible to most native SL speakers, let alone to those who have learnt the SL as a foreign language. There are three main reasons for this relative inaccessibility. One is lexical and the other two are conceptual. All three can be illustrated from the following text, the abstract of an archaeological paper by Duccio Bonavia, to which we shall refer in our discussion:

> *La importancia de los restos de papas y camotes de época*
> *precerámica hallados en el valle de Casma*
>
> Se hace una revisión crítica de los datos existentes sobre el hallazgo de papa (Solanum tuberosum) y camote (Ipomoea batatas) en contexto precerámico del Área Andina Central. Se concluye que las únicas 5 evidencias a las que se puede dar validez científica, corresponden a los especímenes excavados en el yacimiento de Huaynuma del valle de Casma (costa Nor-central peruana), con una antigüedad aproximada de 2.000 años a. d. C.
>
> (Bonavia 1984: 20)

Lexical issues in technical translation

There are three sorts of lexical problem arising from the specialized use of technical terms. First, there is the obvious problem of terms not used in everyday, ordinary language, which are, therefore, unfamiliar to the lay translator. The text given above contains an example of this problem. A term such as 'precerámico' is instantly recognizable as belonging only to a specialized scientific context. Without specialist knowledge, therefore, translators cannot guess the exact meaning of the term or make a reliable guess at its correct TL rendering. Of course, 'preceramic' (or 'pre-ceramic') is a likely candidate, but its appropriateness, as well as whether the word should be written with or without a hyphen, can only be established by dictionary or database research, or by consultation with an archaeologist.

The second problem is that of terms that have ordinary uses familiar to the translator, but which in the ST are manifestly used in some other, technically specialized, way. That is, the familiar senses of the terms do not help, and may even hinder, the translator in finding an appropriate rendering of their technical senses. The ST above contains a simple example of this in the phrase 'revisión crítica'. In its ordinary usage, Spanish 'revisión' could easily be taken to mean simply English 'revision' (in the sense of 'modification'); however, in context this rendering is inappropriate and misleading. What is at issue is a critical reviewing of a certain body of evidence. Thus, 'revisión crítica' is more accurately rendered as 'critical review'.

Almost any science or technology has such lexical pitfalls. Medicine, for example, is rich in these. Anyone familiar with medical terminology will instantly gloss 'soplo cardíaco' as 'heart murmur', but the translator not used to medical texts may find the phrase puzzling at first sight. Similarly puzzling in a medical context is 'estenosis' (which has nothing whatever to do with shorthand typing), which is used as a technical term referring to 'narrowing of the arteries'.

Third, a term may have an ordinary, everyday sense that is not obviously wrong in the context. This is the most dangerous sort of case, because the translator may not even recognize the term as a technical one, and carelessly render it in its ordinary sense. For example, 'hallazgo', in the archaeological text above, is glossed in a standard 1988 dictionary as 'finding, discovery; find, thing found'. The right technical translation in the archaeological context (where reference is to vestiges indicating the former presence of potatoes and yams) certainly lies well within the range of meanings implied by the dictionary glosses; but the translator needs experience or advice in order to have the confidence to select 'traces', and in the present context this is clearly preferable to the available alternatives such as 'finding' or 'discovery'. Likewise, a translator in a hurry might (especially if arts-trained) translate 'las únicas evidencias' (in the same text) either as 'the only evidence' or as 'the only proofs', where an archaeologist might expect 'the only findings'.

As these examples show, access to technical dictionaries and up-to-date databanks is indispensable for translators of technical texts. However, not even these source materials can be guaranteed to keep the translator out of difficulties. For one thing, technical texts are liable to be innovative – why publish them unless they make some new contribution? This means that dictionaries and databanks must always lag slightly behind the most up-to-date use of technical terms. Second, even the best source materials do not necessarily give a single, unambiguous synonym for a particular technical term, so that the translator may still have to make an informed choice between alternatives. Finally, even established technical terms are sometimes used loosely or informally in technical texts, in which case it may be misleading to render them by their technical TL synonyms. All of this suggests that the normal limitations on the use of dictionaries apply also to technical translation, but in a particularly acute form. That is, translators can only select the appropriate TL terminology from a range of alternatives offered by the dictionary if they have a firm grasp of the immediate textual context and of the wider technical context. The problem is not lessened, of course, by the awkward fact that some of the context may remain obscure until the correct sense of the ST terms has been identified. This brings us to the two conceptual reasons why technical texts may be difficult to translate.

Conceptual issues in technical translation

The first type of conceptual problem is caused by failure to understand the background assumptions and knowledge taken for granted by experts in a science, but not shared by non-specialists and not explicit in the ST. This is a point that can be illustrated from the following: 'el ozono que en los cielos antárticos protege la vida de las letales radiaciones ultravioleta' (*Enciclopedia Universal Ilustrada* 1993: 45).

The phrase 'protege la vida de las letales radiaciones ultravioleta' is potentially ambiguous. Purely syntactically, it may be construed either as meaning 'protects the life of lethal ultraviolet rays' or as 'protects life from lethal ultraviolet rays'. This ambiguity is almost certainly not present for the author or for the informed SL reader who is aware of the function of the ozone layer. It is this awareness, that is to say a piece of technical knowledge, which effectively neutralizes the syntactic ambiguity in question. Yet the translator still has to choose between 'protects the life of' and 'protects life from'; the wrong choice would seriously mislead the TL reader, and would damage the translator's reputation (and possibly the author's too) in the eyes of an informed readership. In this instance, of course, few translators are likely to be so ill informed as to make the wrong choice. In short, translation problems like this are generally easily resolved by any TL speaker with a basic grasp of the technical discipline in question. In more difficult cases of a similar kind, however, non-specialist translators may reach a conceptual impasse from which no amount of attention to syntax or vocabulary can rescue them. In that case they have only two options: study the technical field in which they are translating, or work in close consultation with experts.

The most intractable problems in technical translation arise in translating the development of new ideas. In such an instance, even a basic grasp of background knowledge may be insufficient to save the translator from a conceptual impasse. This is the second conceptual reason for inaccessibility in technical texts. What one might call the 'logic' of a discipline – methods of argumentation, the development of relations between concepts – is normally specific to that discipline. There may therefore be translation problems that hinge crucially on that logic. It may transpire that the translator is quite unable to solve a conceptual problem of this nature, and that the only alternative is to consult either an expert or, if necessary (and if possible), the author of the ST.

Even in less advanced texts, the translator may face serious conceptual difficulties in grasping the 'logic' of a discipline, in particular the relationship between concepts. This is illustrated in the following extract drawn from a section of an article by Felipe Cantera Palacios on the pros and cons of using cooling to desalinate seawater: 'Uno de los mayores problemas que se plantean en este sistema de conversión reside en la separación de los cristales de hielo y la salmuera' (1971: 268).

Without a grasp of desalination processes in general, and of the particular refrigeration technique discussed in the text, student translators cannot be absolutely sure whether, in the above sentence, the problem is how to *prevent* the separation of ice crystals, or whether the problem is how to *achieve* this separation. What is more, the use of 'y' in the ST creates another uncertainty: do both the ice crystals and the brine (salmuera) need to be separately extracted from some third substance, or is the important thing to extract the crystals from the saline solution? According to different understandings of these issues, student translations vary between:

(a) One of the main problems posed by this conversion system resides in the fact of the separation of the ice crystals and the brine.
(b) One of the main problems requiring solution in this conversion system resides in the separation of the ice crystals from the brine.
(c) One of the main problems for this conversion system resides in separating off the ice crystals and the brine.

The decision as to which of these alternatives is the appropriate one hinges, of course, on one's understanding of how desalination systems work: the technical expert will know without hesitation that the problem referred to is how to find a way of extracting the ice crystals from the surrounding saline solution. (Indeed, a further reading of the article makes this relatively clear in context.)

Experience in Spanish will tell the translator two things: first, there is in general a strong chance that 'reside en la separación de' should not be literally rendered as 'resides in the separation of', but will require some form of particularization, while ST 'y' may need to be particularized as 'from'; second, the essential evidence for the appropriate particularizations must be sought in the wider context, more precisely in terms of the internal 'logic' of the ST and of its subject matter. (The only real internal evidence, a subsequent description in the ST of how the problem referred to has been solved, merely underlines the importance of context.) But, while the context strongly hints at a particular interpretation, the 'logic' of the ST is so dependent on technical knowledge that even the closest and most sensitive linguistic analysis is bound to be less reliable (and less cost-effective) than a brief consultation with a technical adviser. Trying to 'crack' a technical text on the basis of linguistic experience alone is valuable for honing one's translation skills, and fun as a challenge; but delivering a *dependable* technical TT usually requires consultation.

To summarize thus far: the non-specialist is not sufficiently equipped to produce reliable technical TTs guaranteed to be useful to technical experts in the target culture. Prospective technical translators must acquire as soon as possible some degree of technical competence in the field in which they intend to work. Training technical translators usually has this as its main target. Such training cannot be general, however: an academic degree in a science and a qualification in a foreign language is an ideal background for a technical translator. However, not even people with this kind of qualification can expect to keep abreast of research while at the same time earning their living as translators, and they will sooner or later come up against problems that can only be solved by consulting technical experts.

These remarks about the need for consultation are not to be taken lightly. They raise the important question of the responsibility – and perhaps the legal liability – of the translator. There is a difference here between literary translation and technical translation. It is not that literary translators are not held responsible for their published TTs, but that the practical implications of mistranslation are seldom as serious for them as for technical translators, whose mistakes could cause financial damage or loss of life and limb. This is another respect in which technical translation is exemplary, bringing out extremely clearly a golden rule which is in fact essential to all translation: *never be too proud or embarrassed to ask for help or advice.*

Even after every precaution has been taken in translating, it is often necessary for the translator to attach a legal disclaimer to the TT. Here is a disclaimer from the US Department of Education's translation of the 1997 Individuals with Disabilities Education Act (IDEA '97):

Spanish text

Salvedad en español

El Departamento ha hecho todo lo posible por garantizar la fidelidad de esta traducción de las regulaciones de la Ley de la Educación de Personas con Discapacidades de 1997 (1997 Individuals with Disabilities Education Act). En caso de existir una contradicción entre cualquiera de los términos de esta traducción en español y la versión en inglés de las regulaciones, regirá la versión oficial en inglés. La versión oficial de estas regulaciones es la versión que fue publicada por la Office of the Federal Register en el Código Federal de Regulaciones (Federal Code of Regulations) en 34 C.F.R., Partes 300 y 303 (1999).

English text

Disclaimer in English

The Department has made every effort to ensure the accuracy of this Spanish translation of the 1997 Individuals with Disabilities Education Act regulations. In the event of any inconsistency between any terms in this Spanish translation of the regulations and the English language version of these regulations, the official English language version of the regulations shall control. The official version of these regulations is the version published by the Office of the Federal Register in the Code of Federal Regulations at 34 C.F.R. Parts 300 and 303 (1999).

(US Department of Education 2003)

Interestingly, even the translation of the disclaimer from Spanish to English contains a grammatical error that could have legal consequences in certain situations: a legal disclaimer should read 'shall take precedence'. The spectre of legal liability is a reminder that even the minutest error of detail on any level of textual variables is typically magnified in a technical text. This is not surprising, given that matters of factual correctness rank maximally high in empirical/descriptive genres. Some such errors are in the category of *faux amis* – banal, but no less potentially embarrassing, like, for example, the DE's mistranslation of 'regirá', above; or when, in a financial text, translating 'acción' as 'lawsuit' or 'legal action', as opposed to 'share' or 'stock(s)', could at the very least cause confusion.

Much more dangerous (and more likely, if the translator is not a specialist) is confusion between closely similar technical names. Consider, for example, the many minutely differentiated prefixes and suffixes that can be attached to the root 'sulph':

per- bi- de- hypo- hydro-	sulph	-ate -ite -ide -onate

Obviously, the slightest error in affixation here will constitute a major factual error, whereas, in non-technical language, slight differences in affixation may often go unnoticed. For example, in Spanish, there is a fine but clear distinction of meaning between the verbs 'colorar' and 'colorear' or 'colorir'. 'Colorar' might well be used in the specific sense of 'to dye', whereas 'colorear/colorir' could mean 'to take on a colour/ colour up'. In translating technical texts, the difference between the two terms would have to be scrupulously observed. In non-technical texts, however, the translator may choose to render either term as (among other options) 'to colour', prompted more by considerations of idiomaticity, genre and register than by those of literal accuracy. Similarly, there is only a relatively subtle difference in English between 'defrock' and 'unfrock', between 'levitating' and 'levitation', or, in popular usage (increasingly, if confusingly), between 'disinterested' and 'uninterested'. In literary texts one can, to some extent, base such choices on questions of euphony or style. But that temptation must be resisted absolutely in translating technical terms.

Again, in a literary text, choosing the wrong synonym is, at worst, a stylistic infelicity; but in a technical text it might create a serious misnomer showing ignorance, thus undermining the reader's confidence in the text. For example, it is not immaterial, in a given chemical context, whether vanilla is referred to by its trivial name 'vanilla', its technical name 'vanillin', its old systematic name '4-hydroxy-3-methoxybenzaldehyde', or its empirical formula $C_8H_8O_3$. Similarly, 'heat' and 'thermal energy' are, to all intents and purposes, referentially synonymous: yet the choice of one or the other in technical contexts is not a matter of indifference to a physicist.

Some parts of technical texts may be expressed with mathematical precision. Indeed, they may actually be formulated in mathematical symbols, in which case they only need a modicum of effort in translation. Mathematical formulae cannot always be literally transcribed, however. Two of the elementary things to note in this respect are the mathematical use of the comma on the Continent, whereas US and British conventions require the use of a decimal point, and the use of a point or period to separate thousands, rather than the comma, employed in many Spanish-speaking countries (but not Mexico, Puerto Rico, the Dominican Republic, and some Central American countries.) In these cases, the important thing is for the TT to achieve, relative to the conventions of the TL, the same standard of mathematical precision as the ST.

Having said this, we should not forget that even the driest technical text is bound to have more informal passages – perhaps introductory, parenthetical or concluding remarks in ordinary, even colloquial, prose. Such passages pose another kind of problem for the technical translator, for it is here that the technical author may let personality intrude, or even deliberately cultivate a persona. Thus, although technical translators are chiefly accountable for the literal and factual content of the ST, they cannot always remain insensitive to such stylistic ploys as register, connotation, humour, polemic and so on. The TT should at least not spoil, cancel or contradict what is to be read between the lines in the ST. The overall register of the text – if only the question of pompous versus casual style – is also a matter of concern. To this extent at least, no text can avoid being the result of stylistic choices. In short, as we suggested at the beginning of this chapter, technical translators should not see themselves as having nothing in common with, for example, literary translators. On the contrary, because problems of style affect all texts, all translators have problems and methods in common. To this we must add that, while 'factuality' in a text may on the face of it appear antithetical to 'style', the cult of factuality is in itself a kind of style, and may on occasion even be a carefully cultivated pose manifested in excessive use of technical jargon.

The relationship between accuracy and style is not always straightforward. There is – as with any text – the problem of what to do if the ST is badly written, ungrammatical, or even factually deficient. Should the deficiencies of the ST be reflected in the TT or should they be ironed out? This is a general and controversial issue. In our view, translators are not in principle responsible for 'improving' defective STs, but it may be strongly advisable, perhaps even necessary, in the case of technical texts – or indeed any empirical/descriptive or prescriptive text – because the paramount concern is factual accuracy. If there is any ambiguity, obscurity or error in the ST, and it is potentially misleading or dangerous, there is every reason to keep it out of the TT – if necessary (as ever) after consultation with the author or an expert. Failing that, the translator may feel the need to append a translator's note to the TT calling attention to the deficiency in the ST.

The technical translator's paramount concerns, therefore, must be accuracy and conformity with the requirements of the genre. In so far as the requirements of the genre imply style, register is also important: the wrong tonal or social register may alienate the reader or undermine confidence in the TT or even in the author of the ST. Consider the following extract from an ST on the use of the polymerase chain reaction (PCR) method to identify the presence of DNA sequences from genetically modified organisms in food samples:

> En la PCR, los pequeños fragmentos de ADN complementario se llaman cebadores y se utilizan por pares. Estos cebadores se diseñan para hibridarse con sitios de reconocimiento de la secuencia complementaria en hebras opuestas del gen de interés.
>
> (Querci 2007a: 4)

Here is the published TT:

> In PCR, the small complementary DNA pieces are referred to as primers and used in pairs. These primers are designed to hybridize to complementary sequence recognition sites on opposite strands of the gene of interest.
>
> (Querci 2007b: 4)

The ST authors have chosen straightforward syntax to convey their message; an excellent strategy given the fact the ST is designed as a training manual. However, although their lexis also appears simple it is actually highly technical and convention bound. The translators have opted for a faithful approach rather than a communicative approach. Take, for example, the phrase 'los pequeños fragmentos de ADN complementario'. Although the TT rendering 'pieces' occurs in a limited proportion of the technical literature, more usual and accurate collocations include 'fragments' or 'specific regions'. Since 'fragments' is widely used in the technical literature, there is no clear argument against its use in this context. 'Fragments' needs no adjectival qualification, but if that were deemed necessary, 'short' not 'small' is the usual collocation. When qualifying ADN, 'complementario' has a specific technical meaning as English 'cDNA'. 'Complementary' or 'cDNA' is produced in a different reaction – reverse transcription PCR – whose starting material is RNA not DNA. In the ST, however, 'complementario' is used in its everyday adjectival sense of 'complementary/follow-up'. Here it simply refers to the presence of the target sequence on the DNA primer being described. The adjective is later used more clearly in its everyday sense in the phrase 'secuencia complementaria', 'the complementary sequence'. Given that the target readership is control laboratory personnel who need training and support to carry out PCR, an exegetical but technically phrased translation is required; such as 'short single-stranded DNA fragments'. Consequently, our edited first sentence reflects the straightforward syntax, realized through grammatical transposition, but achieves a convincing (and accurate) TL technical collocation: 'PCR uses pairs of short single-stranded DNA fragments, referred to as primers.'

The second sentence of the ST begins with the demonstrative adjective, 'estos', which is used in the SL to refer to something which is immediately relevant to the discussion, and has just happened or been mentioned. In the case of technical texts, it is used to ensure greater cohesion and prevent ambiguity. TL demonstrative adjectives may be used in a similar but not identical way to signal cohesion when two nouns or nominal phrases are referentially equivalent. Since the *cebadores* in each noun phrase are not identical but refer to type, there is a loss of cohesion, raising the questions: are the primers mentioned in the second sentence specific ones? Are they the same (also specific) primers described in the first sentence? Are they a second, as yet unmentioned, set of primers, or are they primers of this type in general? The replacement of the demonstrative adjective with the adjective 'such' signals that the identity between the two phrases is of type (this kind of primer, primers consisting of pairs of single-strands of DNA). 'To hybridize to target sites' is a calque on 'hibridizar con sitios de reconocimiento', which is inappropriate for the protocol being described. In the TL, it is employed to describe Northern Blotting, which uses radioactive probes. Further, in the TL the indirect object is not usually expressed explicitly, and the verb tends to be nominalized. By **nominalization** we mean the use of a noun which, in the same language or in a TT, could be replaced by an expression not containing a noun; in this instance, 'designed for hybridization to' is a nominalization of 'designed to hybridize to'. Nominalization is a typical feature of technical texts. Here, for discussion, is a sentence from the ST on DNA and an alternative formulation without nominalization:

> Por otra parte, la determinación de la identidad genética permite la segregación y la trazabilidad (preservación de la identidad) a lo largo de la cadena de distribución de las plantas GM.

Por otra parte, el determinar la identidad genética de las plantas GM permite segregarlas y trazarlas (preservar la identidad) a lo largo de la cadena de distribución de las plantas GM.

Returning to the two-sentence ST under discussion, the TL favours the technical verb 'to anneal' for 'hibridizar con sitios de reconocimiento'. 'Anneal' refers, in genetic engineering, to the whole process by which the primer strands bond with the template DNA to form a double strand. The ST is only accurately translated by a hyponym. This example points to the complexity of lexical issues in technical translation; even a technically trained translator who was not familiar with the protocol discussed in the text could easily produce an inaccurate TT without consultation with appropriately trained experts. The TT translator's rendering of the final phrase of the ST produces a banal calque whose technical sense is lost: 'de interés' is broadly equivalent to TL 'target'. If technical precision were called for then a translator of this passage might opt to employ the phrase 'the target DNA', or to avoid ambiguity 'the target sequence'. Consider two TTs of the second ST sentence:

> Such primers are designed for hybridization to complementary sequences on each of the strands of the target DNA.

> Such primers are designed to anneal to complementary sequences on each of the strands of the template DNA.

Earlier in this discussion, we suggested that in technical translation factual accuracy was a more important concern than stylistic considerations. From that point of view, each of the TTs given above offers a plausible version of the ST. The use of simple syntax, and occasionally less precise technical lexis does not undermine the ST, but rather conforms to its function as a teaching manual. In our opinion, assuming that the ST shares the specific purpose of the TT, that is to train laboratory staff, then stylistic considerations should be borne in mind when developing a strategy, and, consequently, we feel that the first of the two TTs offered above is preferable.

Before embarking on the Practical, it will be useful to note some of the characteristics of technical texts in English. First, the language is usually informative, and often includes expressions denoting purpose or role, and explanations of method or process. Second, in accounts of experiments or research programmes, the passive is used extensively, which keeps the style impersonal. The same is true of Spanish technical texts, although passive 'se' may be used instead of the true passive (structured on 'ser' + past participle) as in the DNA text cited above; both forms are generally rendered with the passive in English.

Another typical feature of technical texts is the frequent use of compound nouns (e.g. 'website design', 'stability problems', 'mouse port') and indeed of nominalization in general. English uses compound nouns (NNs) with a higher frequency than Spanish, which tends to use a preposition to couple two nouns (NPNs); for example, the appropriate technical translations of 'punto de fusión' and 'calor de evaporación' are 'melting point' and 'evaporation heat', respectively. However, care should be taken since translation of ST NPNs by TT NNs is often not mandatory and can even introduce ambiguity. Consider, for example, 'calor de fusión', which is conventionally translated as TL NPN 'heat of fusion' or 'heat of melting', depending on the processes being outlined. The context of the STs given here is the article by Felipe Cantera Palacios on cooling as a method of water desalination, mentioned above, and consequently 'melting' is indicated. Another example of such ambiguity can be found in the machine translation of 'difusión anual de resúmenes y documentos técnicos' as 'annual summary and technical document dissemination': are only the summaries annual? Are only the documents technical? (Aymerich 2001: 33).

The examples we have been looking at illustrate the features of scientific and technical language that Pinchuk neatly categorizes as follows:

1   [Technical language] is specialized and tends to become more and more specialized in contrast to the versatility of ordinary language. [Everyday] language tends towards liveliness and multiplicity of meaning, but the controlled language of science is manipulated in the direction of insipidity and colourlessness.
2   It seeks the most economic use of linguistic means to achieve standardization of terms and usage.
3   It seeks to avoid ordinary language associations and endeavours to define terms accurately.

(Pinchuk 1977: 165)

As Pinchuk points out (246–51), before embarking on a translation it is important to ascertain whether the work has already been translated. He provides a list of organizations that have registers of available translations, including Aslib (The Association of Special Libraries and Information Bureaux). And of course technical translation, like translation in any genre, requires familiarity with SL and TL material of a similar type, to serve as a source of information and as a stylistic model. The translator may well need some time to find the information sought (e.g. concepts or lexis). Useful sources of information include monographs, abstracting and indexing journals, periodicals, yearbooks, textbooks, encyclopaedias, standards and trade literature, theses and dissertations. Increasingly the internet is being used for up-to-date information. Some organizations keep databases containing centrally agreed translations of technical expressions; such as the European Commission's multilingual termbank, IATE (Interactive Terminology for Europe, http://iate. europa.eu). These databases are continually added to, and translators are expected to conform to the agreed renderings, in the interests of organization-wide consistency and clarity. Rapid innovation in science and technology means that there is often a time lag between the coining of a new term or the expansion in the meaning of an established one and its appearance in even the most rigorously maintained databases. Translators in all fields are also making increasing use of translation memory software, which allows rapid checking in their own records and in those of organizations for previous translations of similar material. And when all else fails, fellow translators can be consulted through online forums.

Some of our examples in this chapter were drawn from the text on p. 212 ('La importancia de los restos de papas'). In preparation for Practical 12, the problems it poses should be analysed, and a translation attempted. The exercises in Practical 12 will show that, apart from the lexical and conceptual problems outlined above, technical translation is not essentially different from most other sorts of prose translation: as long as specialist help can be called on (and students should be strongly encouraged to enlist the aid of their own technical advisers), there is no reason why technical translation in most fields should be more daunting than translation in any other genre.

Practical 12

12.1 Technical translation

Assignment

(i)   You are translating the following ST for publication in a survey of recent research on medical pedagogy.
(ii) Discuss the strategic decisions that you have to take before starting detailed translation of this ST, and outline the strategy you adopt.
(iii) Translate the second and third paragraphs of the ST ('Material y métodos' and 'Conclusiones') into English.
(iv) Explain the main decisions of detail which you took.
(v)   Discuss the published TT, which will be given to you by your tutor.

Source text

Estableciendo las bases del proceso Enseñanza/Aprendizaje de la Estomatología para alumnos del último nivel de la currícula de Odonto-logía, y en especial de la Asignatura Patología y Clínica Estomatológica, se ha diseñado este estudio. El mismo se ha llevado a cabo teniendo en cuenta los siguientes *Objetivos:* 1) La observación del desempeño de 5 los estudiantes en un hospital público, en donde han realizado su trabajo en terreno. 2) Un relevamiento de las lesiones y enfermedades que se han presentado con la observación y guía por el personal docente y la resolución de los casos clínicos.

Material y Métodos: los alumnos del nivel quinto de la Asignatura de 10 Patología y Clínica Estomatológica de la Facultad de Odontología de la

Plata, año tras año han sido citados, por comisiones pequeñas (no más de 7 alumnos por cada una) con el fin de observar y participar de la tarea hospitalaria que realiza un equipo docente de Estomatología dentro del funcionamiento del Servicio de Odontología de un Hospital de Agudos. 15 Se tomaron los datos correspondientes a un tiempo estimado en horas de 1.800 horas paciente/docente-alumno. De 495 pacientes fueron evaluados los datos de edad, sexo, ocupación, estado civil, hábitos y factores ambientales. Se registraron los datos correspondientes a las lesiones y enfermedades y se realizó el análisis estadístico de los mismos. 20

Conclusiones: 1) Se observa que el Hospital docente asistencial pareciera brindar al mecanismo de Enseñanza/ Aprendizaje, la posibilidad de insertar al alumno en la realidad de la salud pública del medio ambiente al cual pertenece. 2) Las demás especialidades, integradas al Servicio de Odontología/Estomatología, permitirían una acción en conjunto del 25 equipo sanitario, por un fenómeno de retroalimentación. 3) Coincidiendo con otros datos de diversos Servicios Asistenciales y otras Facultades del país, la Candidiasis oral resultó la lesión más frecuentemente observada. 4) La incidencia de Cáncer bucal nos lleva a insistir sobre su diagnóstico temprano y la importancia del reconocimiento de las enfermedades 30 precancerosa y establecer estrategias contra el hábito del tabaquismo, en nuestro medio de referencia.

(Mercado *et al.* 2006)

12.2 Technical translation

Assignment

(i)   Your task is to translate an article on the experimental analysis of behaviour into English for publication in an English-language journal on psychology and psychotherapy. Analyse the salient features of the ST, comparing it with the abstract in English, and formulate a strategy for translating it.
(ii)   Translate the ST into English.
(iii) Explain the main decisions of detail you took.

Contextual information

The ST is an academic article entitled 'Análisis experimental de la conducta en España' on the experimental analysis of behaviour. Its target audience is psychologists with an interest in experimental psychology. The article was originally published in a special issue of the learned journal *Avances en Psicología Latinoamericana*. Its authors are state-employed academics, Gabriel Ruiz, Ricardo Pellón and Andrés García. Here is the published SL abstract:

En este artículo se revisan los antecedentes y el estado actual del análisis experimental del comportamiento (AEC) en España. Se introduce con una explicación histórica sobre la psicología y el problema de la ciencia en España. Posteriormente se muestra el desarrollo de la psicología científica, en general, y del AEC, en particular. Se analiza "Lo que pudo ser" (1900–1936) y "Lo que fue" (1939–1953). Se reseña la importancia de "El Laboratori de Conducta" (1970–1980). Y se efectúa un recurrido del AEC después de 1980. Finalmente, se presentan algunos programas españoles actuales de investigación en AEC: conducta adjuntiva y regulación de la conducta, y formación de clases de estímulos.

Key words: Experimental analysis of behaviour (EAB), history of psychology, Spain.

(Ruiz *et al.* 2006a)

The ST comes from the section describing a current project on adjunctive behaviour and behaviour regulation, which has been supported by a grant from the Spanish Ministerio de Educación y Ciencia: Dirección General de Investigación.

Source text

La ingestión polidípsica de agua, así como otras conductas adjuntivas, depende críticamente de la frecuencia de presentación del reforzador comida. La cantidad de consumo por reforzador se relaciona como una función de U-invertida con la tasa de reforzamiento, pero la tasa de bebida adjuntiva decrece de forma lineal a medida que disminuye la frecuencia 5 de reforzamiento (Reid and Staddon, 1990; Pellón 1992). Es más, la cantidad de polidipsia inducida por programa depende de las variables que definen el valor de la comida, como puede ser la magnitud y calidad del alimento, además de su frecuencia de presentación; sin embargo, resulta bastante independiente de las manipulaciones que afecta a la naturaleza 10 del líquido disponible (*véase* la revisión de Pellón, 1992).

Hoy en día existe evidencia experimental suficiente para afirmar que la conducta adjuntiva es susceptible de modificación por sus consecuencias ambientales, lo que cumpliría con las características formales de la conducta operante. La polidipsia inducida por programa puede ser 15 aumentada por reforzamiento positivo y reducida por castigo.

(Ruiz *et al.* 2006b: 92)

Practical 12.3 Scientific translation

Assignment

(i) You have been commissioned by the United Kingdom Department for Food, the Environment and Rural Affairs to translate into English the

European Commission training course on the analysis of food samples for the presence of genetically modified organisms (GMOs), currently available only in Spanish on the EC website. Discuss the strategic decisions that you have to take before starting detailed translation of this ST, and outline the strategy you adopt.

(ii)   Make a list of ST technical terms and identify TT equivalents.

(iii) Translate the ST into Spanish. Do not translate the comparative chart at the end of ST ('Cuadro 2').

(iv)   Explain the main decisions of detail you took.

(v)   Discuss the published TT, which will be given to you by your tutor.

Contextual information

The training manual was produced by the Joint Research Centre of the European Commission and the World Health Organization's European Centre for the Environment and Health Food Safety Programme. The Joint Research Centre provides the EC with scientific and technical support. The aim of the manual is to provide training materials for control laboratory staff in developing skills in GMO detection and quantification techniques. The manual deals with DNA extraction from raw and processed foods, and the use of polymerase chain reactions (PCR) and enzyme-linked immunosorbent assay (ELISA) for the detection and quantification of GMOs.

Source text

El enfoque de las proteínas

El método de ensayo de proteínas utiliza anticuerpos de la proteína de interés. La técnica ELISA detecta o mide la cantidad de proteína de interés en una muestra que puede contener otras muchas proteínas diferentes. Utiliza un anticuerpo para ligar la proteína específica, un segundo   5
anticuerpo para amplificar la detección (fase optativa) y un conjugado de anticuerpo con una enzima, cuyo producto genera una reacción coloreada, que es fácil de observar y cuantificar comparando con una curva patrón de la proteína de interés.

Entre las características fundamentales de los ensayos con ELISA están   10
las siguientes:

- menor sensibilidad que la PCR, por lo que es más difícil que aparezcan «falsos positivos» debidos a pequeños niveles de contaminación;
- elevados costes iniciales para el desarrollo del ensayo y la obtención de anticuerpos y patrones de proteínas;   15
- reducidos costes por muestra, una vez elaborados los reactivos;
- no puede discriminar entre diferentes modos y modelos de expresión de diferentes productos transgénicos que expresan características proteínicas similares;

- los métodos de ensayo de proteínas son prácticos y eficaces cuando   20
se produce una proteína detectable. Sin embargo, es posible que los
productos modificados genéticamente se formen solo durante ciertas
fases del desarrollo o en determinadas partes de los vegetales, por lo
que resultaría poco probable que tales productos fueran detectados sin
problemas por ELISA. Por otra parte, las transformaciones industriales   25
desnaturalizan fácilmente las proteínas, lo que plantea dificultades para
el uso de métodos ELISA con fracciones de alimentos transformados.

Teniendo todo esto en cuenta, ha de quedar claro que el ELISA y la PCR
deben considerarse mutuamente complementarios y no se excluyen
entre sí.   25

Cuadro 2 Comparación resumida de los métodos ELISA y PCR

Método	Objeto	Duración	Facilidad de utilización	Resultados
ELISA	Proteínas	2–8 horas	Moderada; exige conocimiento de las prácticas de laboratorio; los ensayos son específicos de especie y de variedad.	Confirma una modificación genética específica y permite la cuantificación.
PCR	ADN	1–3 días	Escasa; requiere formación y material especializados.	Muy sensible; tiende a dar falsos positivos; confirma la presencia de ADN GM y permite la cuantificación.

(Querci 2007a: 34–5)

13 Legal and financial translation

For the lay translator, and especially the student translator following a Humanities or Arts programme, the many genres of legal and business text can be just as disconcerting as technical texts, and for exactly the same lexical and conceptual reasons. There is an added complication, however. Technical texts may be unfamiliar to the lay person, but at least they are talking about the same empirical set of phenomena, whatever the language – English *deoxyribonucleic acid* is Spanish *ácido desoxirribonucleico* is Romanian *acid dezoxiribonucleic*. But there are real differences between, say, the peninsular Spanish and British or Mexican Spanish and North American legal, financial and tax systems (not to mention the difference between Scottish and English law in Great Britain or between state law codes in the USA). Therefore, translators have not only to master SL and TL terminology, but also to familiarize themselves with the different systems and have a clear idea of the closest equivalences between them. Still, foreign trade does take place, British people do buy houses abroad, Europol does function, and so on. So, translation between systems is possible. The translator has two broad functions in enabling these things to happen. The first is to translate texts that have the force of law (e.g. legislation, constitutions, contracts) or are required by law (e.g. financial statements). The second is to translate legal or financial texts not as legally binding documents, but for other purposes, such as giving or requesting information.

We shall look first at translating texts that have the force of law. The vital things here are scrupulous accuracy and, usually, no matter how complex the ST may be, to produce a TT that respects the ST layout. Some Spanish and English genres have similar layouts in any case, but there is no question of large-scale textual reorganization in such texts. In the event of textual reorganization being necessary, it should always be carried out by an appropriately qualified legal practitioner. And, where an organization is multinational, such as the European Union, or Telefónica, S.A., it is especially important to keep the same format for the text in each language. Style, on the other hand, may need grammatical transposition and compensation. Both languages, for example, are highly formulaic but there may not be full synonymy between legal terms. In the English legal system, litigants are represented by solicitors and barristers, but only by *abogados* in Spain. Likewise, a *notario* administers oaths and attests to the authenticity of official documents whereas in England documents are usually notarized by a solicitor, who also represents clients in a limited number of law courts, like a North American attorney at law. English favours archaizing style and lexis with redundancy to obviate ambiguity, and tends to use minimal punctuation. Spanish favours nominalization, and a high incidence of relative clauses.

Contracts and legally binding agreements must be translated with similar considerations in mind to legislative or constitutional texts. Here, as samples, are excerpts from typical peninsular Spanish and English-language contracts for letting a house:

Spanish text

CONTRATO DE ARRENDAMIENTO DE VIVIENDA

En Madrid, a doce de diciembre de dos mil siete

R E U N I D O S

De una parte, D. MANOLO CARDONA MARTÍN, con domicilio en Madrid, c/ Mayor nº 72 y con D.N.I nº 88.888.888 X, actuando en nombre   5 propio como propietario y arrendador de la vivienda objeto del presente contrato.

Y de otra, Dª MARÍA SOLOMÉ RISCAL, mayor de edad, con domicilio en la c/Candelaria nº 34 y con D.N.I nº 77.777.777 Y, actuando en nombre propio como arrendataria.   10

Ambas partes tienen y se reconocen mutuamente plena capacidad para el otorgamiento del presente contrato, y a tal fin:

E X P O N E N

PRIMERO – Que D. MANOLO CARDONA MARTÍN es propietario de la finca urbana sita en Madrid, c/Justina, nº 52, piso 4º, escalera izquierda,   15 letra D. Inscrita en el Registro de la Propiedad Nº 35 de Madrid, Tomo 1.744, Libro 10, Folio 124, Finca 72.978. Con referencia catastral 244.312.

SEGUNDO – Que interesando a Dª MARÍA SOLOMÉ RISCAL, arrendar dicho inmueble para satisfacer su necesidad permanente de vivienda, y previas conversaciones mantenidas al efecto, ambas partes   20 llevan a cabo el presente CONTRATO DE ARRENDAMIENTO DE VIVIENDA, de conformidad con las siguientes:

C L Á U S U L A S

PRIMERA – Legislación aplicable.

El presente contrato se regirá por lo previsto en la Ley 29/1994, de 24 de   25 noviembre, de Arrendamientos Urbanos (en adelante LAU) y por lo establecido en este contrato.

En defecto de norma o pacto expreso, se regirá por lo previsto en el Código Civil.

SEGUNDA – Objeto.   30

Es objeto de este arrendamiento la finca urbana situada en Madrid, c/Justina, nº 52, piso 4º, escalera izquierda, letra D. Cuenta con una superficie construida de 80 m², y útil de 69 m². Consta de distribuidor, cocina, salón-comedor, dos dormitorios, dos baños y tendedero. Linda a la izquierda con el apartamento de puerta B, y a la derecha, con las 35 escaleras y su rellano.

[. . .]

El arrendatario declara conocer y aceptar el estado de la vivienda, recibiéndola en perfecto estado de conservación y con plena habitabilidad e idoneidad para servir al destino de vivienda permanente pactado en el 40 presente contrato.

CUARTA – Duración del contrato.

El plazo de duración de este contrato es de UN AÑO, a contar desde el otorgamiento del presente contrato, prorrogable, a voluntad de la arrendataria, por periodos anuales sucesivos hasta un periodo de cinco años 45 en total, conforme al régimen previsto en el artículo 9 de la LAU.

De conformidad con el artículo 10 de la LAU, una vez transcurrido este plazo de cinco años, si ninguna de las partes notifica a la otra, al menos con un mes de antelación, su voluntad de no renovarlo, el contrato se prorrogará obligatoriamente por plazos anuales hasta un máximo de tres 50 años más, salvo que el arrendatario manifieste al arrendador con un mes de antelación a la fecha de terminación de cualquiera de las anualidades, su voluntad de no renovar el contrato.

Al contrato prorrogado le seguirá siendo de aplicación el régimen establecido en el presente contrato.   55

Finalizada la duración pactada y, en su caso, la de las prórrogas sucesivas, el arrendatario deberá abandonar el inmueble, sin necesidad de requerimiento expreso del arrendador, dejándolo en el mismo estado que tenía cuando lo ocupó, con la excepción del desgaste normal derivado del uso habitual de la vivienda.   60

English text

An Agreement
Made the 6th Day of January 2007
BETWEEN
Leonard Rossiter
of   5
c/o Rupert Rigsby Chartered Surveyors, 28 Crawford Street,
London SE2 1ZZ

(hereinafter called "The Landlord" which expression shall where the context admits include the person or persons for the time being entitled to the reversion immediately expectant on the termination of the tenancy 10 hereby created) of the one part
and
Sherlock Holmes of 221B Baker Street, London NW1 6XE
and
Sirrius Black of 12 Grimmould Place, London SW1A 1AA 15
(herein called "The Tenant" which expression shall where the context admits include successors in title) of the other part

Whereby it is agreed as follows:
1 The Landlord lets and the tenant takes all that (*messuage or dwelling house with the appurtenances thereto belonging*)(*or flat*) situated at 20 and known as:
84 Charing Cross Road, London WC2H 0BN
hereinafter ("The Premises")
   Together with (the use of the entrance hall and lift (if any) staircase, vestibule and outer door of the building containing the premises in 25 common with the other occupiers of the building) and the Fixtures and Fittings now in or on the premises (*as more particularly described in the first schedule (hereinafter "the Fixtures and Fittings") (and the Furniture and Effects now in or on the premises (as more particularly described in the (second) Schedule (hereinafter "the Furniture and* 30 *Effects")*).
   TO HOLD the same unto the Tenant for the term of six months commencing on the 6th day of January 2007 and terminating on the 30th day of July 2008.
   [. . .] 35
2 THE TENANCY GRANTED UNDER THIS AGREEMENT IS AN ASSURED SHORTHOLD TENANCY UNDER section 20 of the Housing Act 1988.
[. . .]
4 THE Tenant hereby agrees with the Landlord as follows: 40
   [. . .]
   (vi) To keep during the tenancy hereby created the interior of said premises and the Fixtures and Fittings [. . .] (*and the Furniture and Effects*) in good clean and tenantable repair and condition (excepting any damage by accidental fire and any repairs for 45 which the Landlord may be responsible under the provisions of the Landlord and Tenant Act 1985 as amended) and to replace immediately any broken glass and to make good repair or restore or (at the option of the Landlord) to pay the cost of replacement of all or any part of the Fixtures and Fittings (*and* 50 *the Furniture and Effects*) which may be broken, lost or

damaged or destroyed by the Tenant or his family, servants or others and at the expiration or sooner determination of the said tenancy to deliver up to the Landlord the premises together with the Fixtures and Fittings (*and the Furniture and Effects and any 55 articles added to or substituted for the same*) in such repair and condition as aforesaid.

These two texts are organized very differently from each other. In part, this reflects differences between Spanish and English practice, and in part it shows that different legal frameworks call for things to be prioritized differently. As we have seen, in many genres, TL conventions imply that the TT should be arranged differently from the ST, to conform to TL genre requirements. But a contract normally only has legal force under source-culture law, and is translated essentially for information. There is thus no point in embarking on a rearrangement, especially given the differences between different landlords' priorities. The main thing, then, when translating a contract or agreement, is to respect the arrangement and detail of the ST, making sure that the content is clear.

Bearing these comments in mind, compare the two texts carefully, and then translate the last section of the Spanish text ('CUARTA – Duración del contrato') into English.

A particularity of contracts in English, as of constitutional texts, is the use of third-person 'shall' to signify a binding obligation or prescription. If 'will' is used in a contract, it signifies that the event is a matter of fact rather than of obligation.

A less traditionally formal genre is what might be called the 'summary of terms and conditions', such as might be sent with a credit card or a club card. Certainly, in English-speaking countries, these tend to use 'we' and 'you' rather than third-person forms, and to use everyday verbal tenses rather than 'shall'. But if one signs a declaration that one has read the terms and conditions and agrees to abide by them, these texts are just as binding as more formally drafted ones. In Spain and Latin America, even when they are purely informative and not binding, they are often less personal – 'el titular' is widely used, whilst the Banco Santander, for example, often employs a calque of the English 'cardholder', 'el tarjetahabiente'. Consequently, it would be prudent not to produce TTs as informal as the conventional English ones: too personal a text might be perceived as undermining the dignity of the company, or as trivializing the arrangement proposed. On the other hand, you may not want to make the company sound pompous to a target public; in that case, it is normally acceptable to avoid where possible the legal 'shall', even where the ST is in the third person.

We turn now to translating legal texts that purely and simply give or request information. Here, while accuracy is essential, there is sometimes more scope for flexibility in respect of layout and style in the TT. To take a hypothetical case, imagine that a *Jueza de menores* writes to competent legal authorities to make certain enquiries in connection with the guardianship or custody of a child.

The *Juzgado* is located in the autonomous community of Valencia. It is an official request, made with reference to certain Spanish national and autonomous community laws, listed in the letter. In Spain, the rights and legal obligations of the citizen are set out in the *Código civil*, and embodied in statute (*ley orgánica*), which is legislation of the highest level of jurisdiction, taking precedence over other types of law. Ordinary law (*leyes*) governs matters not protected by constitution, *decretos-leyes* are enacted for extraordinary matters (such as a sudden, unseasonal increase in forest fires) and must be ratified within thirty days, and *decretos legislativos* are dispositions on delegated legislation. *Reglamento* is of the lowest level of jurisdiction and controls and develops administrative functions and the rights and duties of citizens not otherwise regulated. As the laws do not apply as such outside of Spain, the judge encloses photocopies of the relevant parts of the *Código civil*, the *Ley de la Infancia*, and the *Reglamento de Medidas de Protección Jurídica del Menor* of the Generalitat Valenciana to show the basis on which she has made the request. These obviously need to be translated, and the translator must use appropriate legal terms where necessary, but there is no need to adopt the formal language of UK parliamentary acts in translating what is in any case a digest of a number of different documents. Here are three extracts, for class discussion and translation. The first is from the section of the *Código civil* dealing with minors, the second is from the section of the *Ley Orgánica* on the legal protection of minors, and the third from the Autonomous Valencian Government's *Reglamento de Medidas de Protección Jurídica del Menor en la Comunidad Valenciana*.

ST 1 (i)

TRANSCRIPCIÓN DE LOS ARTÍCULOS 156, 159 Y 172, 1º, DEL CÓDIGO CIVIL [. . .]

Art. 172, 1º La entidad pública a la que, en el respectivo territorio, esté encomendada la protección de los menores, cuando constate que un menor se encuentra en situación de desamparo, tiene por ministerio de la   5
Ley la tutela del mismo y deberá adoptar las medidas de protección necesarias para su guarda, poniéndolo en conocimiento del Ministerio Fiscal, y notificando en legal forma a los padres, tutores o guardadores, en un plazo de cuarenta y ocho horas. Siempre que sea posible, en el momento de la notificación se les informará de forma presencial y de modo   10
claro y comprensible de las causas que dieron lugar a la intervención de la Administración y de los posibles efectos de la decisión adoptada.

ST 1 (ii)

Ley Orgánica 1/1996, de 15 de enero, de Protección Jurídica del Menor

Art. 19. Guarda de menores. Además de la guarda de los menores tutelados por encontrarse en situación de desamparo, la entidad pública

podrá asumir la guarda en los términos previstos en el artículo 172 del
Código Civil, cuando los padres o tutores no puedan cuidar de un menor   5
o cuando así lo acuerde el Juez en los casos en que legalmente proceda.

ST 1 (iii)

*Reglamento de Medidas de Protección Jurídica del Menor en la
Comunidad Valenciana, aprobado por Decreto 93/2001, de 22 de
mayo, del Gobierno Valenciano.*

Art. 4. Menores objeto de protección. 3º. Al menor extranjero que se
encuentre en el territorio de la Comunidad Valenciana en situación de   5
riesgo o desamparo, se le aplicarán las medidas de protección contem-
pladas en el presente reglamento, de conformidad con lo dispuesto en la
legislación vigente en materia de protección jurídica del menor.

A common form of legal translation for information purposes concerns court
cases conducted, under Spanish law, between say, an Anglophone foreign
national or company and a Spanish company. The translator's job is typically
to translate the background information and the texts of any judgements and
appeals for the litigant's information so that they can take best counsel from
their legal advisors. So it is not unusual (although of course deeply alarming)
to be confronted with a sentence like:

PRIMERO La parte dispositiva de la sentencia apelada dice: «QUE
ESTIMANDO LA DEMANDA interpuesta por la entidad Cherubino
Valsangiacomo, SA representada por la Procuradora de los Tribunales
Doña Concepción Teschendorff Cerezo, contra la entidad Americana
Juice Import, INC, con representación procesal ostentada por la   5
Procuradora de los Tribunales Dª Gemma García Miquel, debo declarar
y declaro haber lugar a la misma, y, en consecuencia, declarando la
resolución contractual del que es objeto del presente procedimiento, con
remisión, a efectos de su identificación a los Fundamentos Jurídicos de la
misma, debo condenar y condeno a la citada demandada a que, firme que   10
sea la presente Sentencia, abone a la parte actora, o a quien legítimamente
le represente, la cantidad de DIECISIETE MILLONES QUINIENTAS
CINCUENTA Y DOS MIL CIENTO CINCUENTA Y OCHO (17.552.158
pesetas), que efectivamente le son adeudadas, con más los intereses
legales procedentes, todo ello con expresa imposición de costas a la parte   15
demandada, y, DESESTIMANDO LA DEMANDA interpuesta por la
entidad Americana Juice Import, INC, contra la entidad Cherubino
Valsangiacomo, SA, con las representaciones procesales indicadas, debo
declarar y declaro no haber lugar a la misma, y, en consecuencia debo de
absolver y absuelvo de los pedimentos deducidos contra la misma, con   20
expresa imposición de costas a la actora».

In this example, the translator is providing a TT of a legal ruling handed down from the Audiencia Provincial de Valencia on 7 June 2003, in which a Spanish company alleges a breach of contract against a North American supplier of grape must for wine production. The case is used to establish an accurate interpretation of the United Nations Convention on Contracts for the International Sale of Goods. Clearly, the translator has to know what the technical terms mean ('la parte dispositiva', 'la sentencia apelada', 'interpuesta por', 'ostentada por', etc.), but an even bigger problem is working out the structure of the sentence. Luckily, once this has been done, it is legitimate to recast the sentence or split it up, so that the message is instantly clearer. Certainly, as with the excerpts from legislative documents given in ST1, the TL barrister or advocate requires an accurate TT. But as the TT is for information only, there is every reason to produce a user-friendly combination of accuracy with clarity: the outcome of the case may depend on it.

This is one reason why, with texts of this type or with contracts, it is standard practice for the translator to add a disclaimer declining responsibility for the legal consequences of the TT, or for any obscurity arising from differences between the two legal systems. In fact, the safest thing is to do this with any legal translation. It is the responsibility of the end-user of the translation to find out the precise implications of source-culture bodies, courts and legal terms, and to act accordingly. Thus a typical disclaimer might read:

> This translation is not intended, and may not be interpreted, to constitute legal advice; only a lawyer admitted to practice in the jurisdiction in question can give advice about the meaning of this law. Nor can there be any assurance that a regulatory agency or court of law has not construed, or will not construe, the original statute/regulation in a way inconsistent with this translation.

Another commonly translated genre is the annual report and financial statements to shareholders. These may be in abbreviated or full form. The order of sections in the TL is fairly conventional (Chairman's Letter, followed by sections on shares and marketing, a 10-year financial summary, discussion of financial trends, auditor's report and financial statements, details about headquarters, subsidiaries and brands, with relevant addresses, and a list of directors and officers). SL 'Memorias' or 'Informes anuales' are less consistent about the order in which information is presented. A typical 'Informe Anual' might open with a description of annual performance (often 'Magnitudes'), and a letter from the Chairman of the Board followed by a description of management structures, 'Órganos de Gobierno' or 'de Gestión' (or the calque 'Estructura del grupo'), sections on shares and marketing, corporate social responsibility policy, auditor's report and accounts, report on corporate governance, and information about headquarters and subsidiaries. Whatever other headings are used in a particular company's accounts, they will always be accompanied by a statement, saying what accounting policies have been used and giving further disclosure relating to items in the statements. Finally, companies are required by law to have the accounts audited by an independent auditor (or two, in the case of publicly quoted companies); the document must include an 'auditor's report', stating that in the auditor's opinion the accounts present a true and fair view of the company's financial results.

The language of finance and accountancy is as esoteric in Spanish as in English: as with scientific and technological texts, translators have to familiarize themselves with the SL and TL terminology, partly with help from a mentor, partly by looking at representative TL texts. Once the terminology, conventions and different national systems have been mastered, there are three other factors that may come into play.

First, given the differences in accounting practice between Spanish- and English-speaking countries, the translator must decide how to lay out the TT. In fact, there is little choice: there are official internationally agreed translations of accounting captions, and these are normally used. It is usual to copy the ST arrangement in the TT. It is emphatically not the translator's job to supply more, or less, information than is given in the ST.

One thing translators do typically come up against is the request to use exactly the same headings and terminology as in the client company's previously translated annual reports. Even where the translator points out that a given TL rendering is inappropriate, the company will not agree to a change for fear of being flooded with phone calls from analysts wondering what they are trying to hide. One example of this is the frequent use of 'Magnitudes' as a title in SL annual reports. 'Magnitudes' typically deals with long-term results, market size, and geographical distribution of the company and its subsidiaries. Its rendering in the TL as a calque makes little sense whereas 'Achievements' might be a contextually appropriate solution.

Second, if the accounts are produced in conformity with different legal requirements from target-culture ones, a gist and/or exegetical translation may be in order. This is something to check with the company. We saw an extreme example on p. 13 (Chapter 1, 'Sin embargo . . .'), but it is really not uncommon to see TTs like the following:

ST	TT
Las cuentas anuales consolidadas correspondientes al ejercicio 2006 de XXX, S.A., se han elaborado a partir de los registros de la Sociedad, habiéndose aplicado las disposiciones legales vigentes en material contable, y se han elaborado de acuerdo con las normas de información financiera vigentes en la Unión Europea.	The consolidated financial statements corresponding to the financial year ending in 2006 of XXX, S.A. have been prepared from the accounting records of the Company, in accordance with legal 5 provisions in force on accounting matters in Spain, and in accordance with the International Financial Reporting Standards (IFRS) ratified by the European Union 10

In this case, both ST and TT have clearly been drafted on a need-to-know basis. Strictly speaking, the TT does not correspond to the ST (i.e. 'elaborado', 'habiéndose aplicado' etc); and the IFRS is only one option among international accounting principles (there is also, for example, the United States Generally Accepted Accounting Principles). What has probably happened in this case is that the translator had recognized the headings in the accounts as IFRS ones, verified this with the client, and indicated as much in their text. It is, however, also common to see faithful TTs, however esoteric the Spanish legal details may seem to TL readers, as here:

ST	*TT*	
Las cuentas anuales consolidadas de XXX, S.A., correspondientes al ejercicio anual terminado el 31 de diciembre de 2005 han sido elaboradas de acuerdo con las Normas Internacionales de Información Financiera conforme a lo establecido en el Reglamento (CE) nº 1606/2002 del Parlamento Europeo y el Consejo del 19 de julio de 2002 (en virtud de los cuales todas las sociedades que se rigen por un estado miembro de la Unión Europea, y cuyos títulos valores coticen en un mercado regulado de alguno de los Estados que la conformen, deberán presentar sus cuentas consolidadas de los ejercicios que se inicien a partir del 1 de enero de 2005 de acuerdo con las NIIF que hayan sido convalidadas por la Unión Europea). En España, la obligación de presentar cuentas anuales consolidadas bajo NIIF aprobadas en Europa ha sido, asimismo, regulada en la disposición final undécima de la Ley 62/2003, de 30 de diciembre de 2003, de medidas fiscales, administrativas y de orden social.	The consolidated financial statements of XXX, S.A., for the year ending 31 December 2005 have been prepared in accordance with the International Financial Reporting Standards in accordance with the terms of Regulation (EC) nº 1606/2002 of the European Parliament and the Council on 19 July 2002 (under which all companies governed by the Law of a Member State of the European Union with securities listed on an official market of any Member State must file their consolidated returns for the years beginning as from 1 January 2005 in accordance with the IFRSs, as approved by the European Union). In Spain, the obligation to file consolidated financial statements in accordance with the IFRSs as approved in Europe has also been regulated in Final Provision Eleven of the Tax, Administrative and Social Measures Law 62/2003, dated 30 December 2003.	5 10 15 20 25

As these two examples suggest, there is often more freedom for sentential reorganization in this kind of text than in a text having the force of law, although there are existing International Financial Reporting Standards or United States Generally Accepted Accounting Principles translations of such texts. Using this freedom, have a go at translating this paragraph from a Report supporting a consolidated financial statement:

ST 2

> El Consejo de Administración de la Compañía de fecha de 27 de mayo
> de 2005, haciendo uso de la delegación que, conforme al artículo 153.1b)
> de la Ley de Sociedades Anónimas (LSA), acordó la Junta General
> Extraordinaria de 4 de febrero de 2005, aprobó la realización de una
> ampliación de capital con aportación dineraria en la cuantía de 19.367.118   5
> euros, mediante la emisión y puesta en circulación de 9.683.559 acciones,
> todas de la misma serie y clase, en la proporción de 1 acción nueva por
> cada 4 que estaban ya previamente emitidas. La prima total de la emisión
> ascendió a 13.556.982,60 euros, siendo el desembolso efectivo de la
> ampliación de 32.924.100,60 euros. La operación se elevó a público,   10
> mediante escritura número 1.286 del Notario de Alcobendas (Madrid), D.
> Jesús Alejandre Alberruche. Se solicitó la admisión a cotización de la
> nueva emisión en las Bolsas de Madrid y Barcelona, pasando los nuevos
> títulos a cotizar en el Mercado continuo.
>
> (Europac 2005b: 67)

Finally, in terms of genre, big companies typically produce a hybrid text, combining the statutory financial statements with a lavishly illustrated narrative report of the firm's activities, which amounts to an advertising pitch. A further element here is that the glossy description inevitably contains a lot of technical information, depending on what the company manufactures. So the translator may well need to be familiar not just with the language of accountancy, but also with, for example, the latest in paper and cardboard manufacture and products or the telecommunications industry or computer software. Some translation firms will give the financial statements to one translator and the glossy material to another – but even then, the person doing the advertising material will not be able to escape the language of finance entirely. There is an example of this in Practical 2.2. If you did this assignment, we recommend looking at it again as an illustration of some of the points made in the present chapter. If you did not, it is worth doing as part of Practical 13.

Here is a more purely financial ST than the one in Practical 2.2, for comment on salient features and draft translation. Make notes on the elements that raise translation problems, and how they can best be tackled. If necessary, consult friends studying economics, management and accountancy. The text is from the section on 'Gestión de riesgos' in the *Informe Anual 2006*, of Telefónica, S.A., a leading telecommunications company with subsidiaries worldwide:

ST 3

Riesgo de tipo de interés

> Los costes financieros de Telefónica están expuestos a las oscilaciones de
> los tipos de interés. En 2006, los tipos de corto plazo con mayor volumen
> de deuda expuesta a ellos fueron fundamentalmente el Euribor, el Libor

de la libra (con motivo de la adquisición de O_2), la tasa SELIC brasileña, 5
el Libor del dólar y la UF chilena. A 31 de diciembre de 2006, el 45,4%
de la deuda total (o el 46,3% de la deuda a largo plazo), tenía su tipo fijado
por un periodo superior a un año. Del 54,6% restante (deuda a flotante o
a tipo fijo con vencimiento menor a un año) 41,1 puntos porcentuales
tenían el tipo de interés a acotado por un plazo superior a un año (o el 10
23% de la deuda a largo plazo), mientras que a 31 de diciembre de 2005
estaba fijado el 66% de la deuda a largo plazo. La nueva deuda tomada a
lo largo del año, en especial ligada a la adquisición de O_2, también ha
supuesto una exposición a los tipos (tanto a corto como a largo plazo)
vigentes en el momento de la contratación o la cobertura. Asimismo, 15
la actualización financiera de los pasivos de prejubilaciones se ha ido
realizando a lo largo del año con la curva de tipos de interés implícita en
los mercados de swaps. El aumento de los tipos ha supuesto una
disminución del valor de dichos pasivos.

(Telefónica 2007b: 51)

To sum up, in translating Spanish legal and financial texts, the accent will
be on accuracy, clarity and avoidance of ambiguity. In TTs that do not have
the force of law, some referring expressions ('el Código civil', 'la disposición
final undécima de la Ley 62/2003, de 30 de diciembre de 2003') may need
a touch of exegesis and/or gist translation to show that they refer to the SL
culture and not the TT culture: 'the Spanish Civil Code', 'Spanish corporate
legislation'. If the TT does have the force of law (e.g. a contract), there is no
such latitude: there will still need to be reference to the Spanish Civil Code,
but details of specific laws and articles must also be spelt out as in the ST. With
some texts, it may be necessary to include footnotes or translators' notes. But
it is essential to remember that it is never the translator's job to add anything
that constitutes comment on, or interpretation of, substantive points of law
(Hickey 1998: 224–6). The prerequisite is to know what the purpose of the TT
is. Is it being used in a legal action? Is it the subject of controversy or dispute?
No text of any kind is produced in a vacuum, and the more that is known about
the subject matter of the ST, the more fit for its purpose the TT will be.

As with any area, the debutant translator should build up for reference
purposes a portfolio of 'parallel texts' in both languages, such as contracts and
tenders, balance sheets, certificates and official documents. This makes it
possible to get a feel for the specialist language used, the different types of
document and register, to understand how they work and what they are for.
The conventions used in both languages will gradually become apparent, and
can be automatically applied to translation. The Internet is an increasingly
useful source of such information, for example www.findlaw.com, www.
freshfields.com, www.tradulex.org, and the LIFT network of the Institute of
Translation and Interpretation (see www.iti.org.uk for details). A lot of the
translation work being done in the fields covered by this chapter is handled
by specialist agencies, which build up their own computerized resources –

previous translations, translation memories, glossaries and terminology banks. And for this and many other areas of professional translating activity, there is an excellent information and advice service called 'The Bottom Line', by Fire Ant & Worker Bee at www.accurapid.com/journal.

Practical 13

13.1 Legal translation

Assignment

After class discussion of problems encountered in translating the excerpt from the tenancy agreement (p. 230), compare your TT with a specimen given to you by your tutor.

13.2 Legal translation

Assignment

After class discussion of the problems encountered in translating STs 1 (i) and (ii) on pp. 233–4, compare your TT with a specimen given to you by your tutor.

13.3 Legal translation

Assignment

(i)   You are translating a contract, from which the following ST is taken. The contract is for the sale of a property, under Spanish law, by a Spanish person to a Briton. The Spanish and English texts will be printed alongside one another throughout the contract; articles and paragraphs should therefore be numbered identically in ST and TT. Discuss the strategic decisions that you have to take before starting detailed translation of this ST, and outline and justify the strategy you adopt.

(ii)   Translate the ST into English (or each half of the class translates half of the ST).

(iii) Explain the main decisions of detail you took.

Contextual information

The contract is headed 'Contrato de compraventa de vivienda'. It has twenty pages, and opens by designating the parties and property involved. It concerns the transfer of property from a building contractor to a client, who has the option of taking on a mortgage directly from the builder or financing the purchase by other means. The price and details of the payment of the deposit are laid out in 'Estipulaciones', which also covers the protection of both parties should the sale fall through. An 'Anexo de las Condiciones Generales' lists the documentation with which the buyer should be supplied, and is followed by a transcription of the relevant parts of the Spanish civil code. The 'Condiciones generales de contrato de compraventa' detail the information laid out in the opening part of the 'Contrato' and the 'Estipulaciones'. The ST consists of extracts from the 'Condiciones generales'.

Source text

CUARTA – SUBROGACIÓN EN EL PRÉSTAMO HIPOTECARIO SUSCRITO POR LA PARTE VENDEDORA.

4.1 Contenido y alcance de la subrogación

Si la parte compradora ha optado por subrogarse en el contrato de préstamo con garantía hipotecaria sobre la vivienda, asumiendo tal   5 compromiso por cláusula contractual específica, el comprador retendrá en su poder y descontará, la cantidad que se ha obtenido como prinicipal del préstamo hipotecario, por cuyo motivo la parte compradora faculta a la parte vendedora para percibir de la entidad de crédito dicha cantidad, comprometiéndose a asumir en el momento de la firma de la escritura 10 pública de compraventa y de subrogación en el préstamo la condición jurídica de deudor y, consecuentemente, a hacer efectivo su pago, así como el de los intereses, comisiones y amortizaciones que correspondan, en los plazos y condiciones que sean fijados, subrogándose no sólo en la garantía hipotecaria, sino también en la obligación personal y demás responsabi- 15 lidades derivadas del préstamo hipotecario con aquélla garantizada; siempre que la entidad de crédito preste su conformidad expresa o tácita, según lo dispuesto en el artículo 118 de la Ley Hipotecaria.
[. . .]

4.3 Repercusión de gastos por no subrogación o demora   20

4.3.2 En lo que concierne a los intereses del préstamo la parte vendedora vendrá obligada a pagar los que se devenguen con anterioridad al otorgamiento de la escritura o subrogación en el préstamo. No obstante, serán de cuenta de la parte compradora los intereses devengados desde la puesta a disposición de la vivienda si el otorgamiento de la escritura y 25 subrogación se demoran por causa que le sea imputable. Asimismo, y dado que el precio se estipula como pago al contado, en tanto no sea abonada por la entidad de crédito la última de las entregas correspondientes al préstamo, la parte compradora se compromete a abonar a la parte vendedora el importe de los intereses que devengue la parte no recibida 30 del mismo al tipo aplicable a dicho préstamo. El importe total de estos intereses deberá ser satisfecho por la parte compradora a la parte vendedora dentro del plazo de los treinta días siguientes al que esta última le notifique el correspondiente cargo.

13.4 Financial translation

Assignment

After class discussion of problems encountered in translating ST 2 on p. 238 ('El Consejo . . .'), compare your TT with the published one, which will be given to you by your tutor.

13.5 Financial translation

Assignment

After class discussion of problems encountered in translating ST 3 on pp. 238–9 ('Riesgo de tipo de interés . . .'), compare your TT with the published one, which will be given to you by your tutor.

14 Translation of consumer-oriented texts

A real translation, as distinct from a translation done as a training exercise, is always produced in response to the specific demands of the person or organization that commissions it: a government department, an international organization, an advertising agency, a publisher, a manufacturing company (see the discussion of skopos in Chapter 4). This puts a particular kind of pressure on the translator. We have tried to simulate such demands and pressures in some of the practicals in this course. These exercises are necessarily artificial, but they should make it clear that TTs are purpose-made texts, their manner of formulation heavily influenced, both strategically and in detail, by who and what they are intended for. It is to emphasize this vital point that we are giving an entire chapter to consumer-oriented texts, for the decisive influence of 'translation-for-a-purpose' is nowhere more strongly felt than in translating such texts. Of course, all texts are in a certain sense consumer-oriented (or user-oriented). One may assume that every type of text responds to the tastes or demands of a particular audience. In that sense, short stories are consumer-oriented to satisfy readers who enjoy short stories, television soap operas are consumer-oriented to satisfy viewers who like watching soaps, and so forth. The first thing a publisher asks when offered a manuscript is what potential readership there is for the text. The whole question of marketability turns primarily on this kind of consumer orientation.

However, consumer orientation takes a much more acute form in texts that do not merely promote themselves, but have other things to promote. These are texts that fall into the persuasive/prescriptive genre, texts whose main purpose is to recommend commodities, attitudes or courses of action. The most transparently consumer-oriented subcategory of this genre is advertising. Indeed, one may initially think of this genre as epitomized by advertising copy. The self-evident consumer-oriented purpose of advertising is to boost sales of particular commodities. However, many advertising campaigns show that sales promotion techniques shade into the promotion of opinions, beliefs, attitudes and courses of action. Examples are government health warnings about driving under the influence of alcohol, drug abuse and AIDS. Along with party-political election campaigns, these examples point to a flourishing genre of texts directly aimed at instructing and persuading audiences to do or not to do (as well as to think or not to think) a wide gamut of things. Consumer-oriented texts consequently share common imperatives: they must capture attention and hold it, they must in some sense speak directly to their public, and they must convey their message with neatly calculated effect. That much is clear. What is perhaps less immediately clear is that the range of texts suitably grouped under the heading of 'publicity' is wider than one would think at first sight. It includes, for instance, things like tourist brochures and information leaflets, public notices, posters and even instructions for the use of appliances, recipe books and so on.

It is therefore necessary to bear in mind that the title or explicit description of a text (for example, 'Instructions for Use') does not always clearly indicate that the text belongs to the same persuasive genre as those that are explicitly labelled as advertisements. It could be argued, in fact, that some of the most successful advertisements are those that appear to belong to some other genre, masking their consumer-oriented purposes under the guise of being informative or educational, or even literary. The upshot of this is that translators may sometimes have to look carefully at STs in order to recognize and identify their covert consumer-oriented persuasive/prescriptive features. Take the average recipe book, for instance. On the face of things, it may seem to belong to the category of empirical/descriptive genres, for it appears to classify different cooking techniques in a descriptively systematic manner, to offer factual and objective accounts of the contents and appearance of dishes, as well as of their preparation. In itself, this almost makes recipe books sound like scientific texts. But it does not account for a number of manifest textual features of recipe books: even the most apparently factual recipe books are rarely written in a technical and scientifically neutral style; their use of tonal register is often calculated to draw the reader into a comfortable, possibly flattering relationship; they have a transparently helpful organization, beyond what could be expected of the most indulgent scientific textbook; and they are often lavishly furnished with glossy pictures. (Some of these features are illustrated in the three extracts from recipe books on pp. 249–50.) Such features indicate a consumer-oriented purpose in these recipe books, and are well worth looking out for when translating certain kinds of 'commercial' ST. Even if not directly consumer-oriented to the sale of particular foodstuffs or the promotion of fashionable cuisine, most recipe books are, at the very least, specimens of a hybrid genre characterized by the dual purpose of description and persuasion.

One must, then, be alert to covertly persuasive STs, in order to be able to translate them into appropriately persuasive TTs. But this is only the tip of the iceberg. The more methodologically interesting aspects of consumer orientation in STs and TTs are revealed when it is realized that literal translation of persuasive STs is likely to produce TTs that are far from persuasive for TL audiences. This point, too, shows up most transparently of all in the case of advertising copy. To find examples hinging on cultural difference one need only observe differences of style and impact in different English-speaking cultures. For instance, hectoring and hard-sell styles appear in general to be more acceptable in American than in British advertising, where earnestly overpraising a product may provoke scepticism and thus become counter-productive. Much of British television advertising is based on comic or ironic effects of some kind or another, whereas American-style advertisements may strike British customers as bombastic and unsubtle. For the rest, the tendency in British advertising is to stereotype the customer as a discerning equal, not someone to be browbeaten or patronized; consequently, the tonal register of some American advertisements might be considered offensive by some British customers. In cultures where they are in favour, hard-sell techniques may spread over the entire range of persuasive genres – not just commercial, but also ethical and political publicity, as well as many of the less obviously consumer-oriented textual types. To the extent that this is so, importing, for example, an American-style consumer-oriented text without modification from an American to a British context runs the risk of producing adverse effects on British consumers.

This intercultural comparison holds a lesson for translators. The fact that different cultures (even those nominally speaking the same language) have different expectations with regard to style in consumer-oriented genres explains why literal translations of persuasive STs are likely to prove less than persuasive in the TL. In other words, persuasiveness in consumer-oriented texts is culture-specific. The advice to the translator of persuasive/prescriptive texts is therefore the same as for translating any other genre of text. Look not only at the style of the ST, but also at the style(s) of other SL texts in the same or similar genres. Look not only at the surface literal meaning of the ST, but also at the details of the stylistic choices made in the ST. From detailed observation of stylistic choices in a number of texts in a given genre it is possible to build up a general picture of the stylistic tendencies or expectations associated with particular types of text in a given culture. Naturally, only a specialist will have the requisite time and experience to develop a clear and detailed sense of stylistic appropriateness in a given genre. (Practicals 14.2 and 14.3 may be seen as a first step towards becoming a specialist translator of recipe books, by considering some general tendencies in the style of Spanish recipes as compared with English ones.)

Further recommendations to the translator of consumer-oriented texts concern the nature of TTs. Here again, the same principles apply as to any other text: do not be afraid to break away from literal translation where the needs of persuasive effect indicate such a break; do not produce TTs without having first built up a knowledge of the style of specimen TL texts in the appropriate genre. First-hand analysis of such TL specimens means build-ing up, through careful observation, a kind of 'genre grammar' consisting of generalizations concerning the stylistic norms, tendencies and expectations typical of the genre of the eventual TT. This does not mean that the TL speci-mens are models for slavish copying; but comparing the stylistic tendencies of the ST genre with those of the TT genre is the best starting-point for tackling decisions about departures from literal translation. Conducting the kind of investigation we are talking about may typically involve contrasting texts relating to the same product in the SL and TL. An example is given here from the English and Spanish versions of instructions for the use of a German-made gardening tool. This should be prepared for discussion in Practical 14.1.

Spanish text	*English text*
Motoazada eléctrica GARDENA (EH 600/20, EH 600/36)	*GARDENA Electric Hoe (EH 600/20, EH 600/36)*
Bienvenido al jardín GARDENA . . .	Welcome to the Garden of GARDENA . . .

Por favor, lea atentamente estas instrucciones y observe las indicaciones contenidas en las mismas. Familiarícese mediante estas instrucciones con las características de la motoazada eléctrica, con su uso correcto y con las indicaciones de seguridad. Por motivos de seguridad no está permitido el uso de esta motoazada eléctrica a niños menores de 16 años y a las personas que no estén familiarizadas con estas instrucciones. Por favor, guarde estas instrucciones para consultas posteriores.	Please read these operating instructions carefully and observe the notes given. Use these instructions to familiarise yourself with the Electric Hoe, its correct use and the notes on safety. For safety reasons, children under the age of 16 as well as persons not familiar with these operating instructions should not use this Electric Hoe. Please keep these operating instructions in a safe place.	5 10 15

1 Aplicaciones de su motoazada eléctrica GARDENA	*1 Where to Use Your GARDENA Electric Hoe*	
Aplicación La motoazada eléctrica GARDENA está prevista para trabajos en suelos gruesos o endurecidos en superficies pequeñas hasta medianas en el jardín doméstico o de aficionados a la jardinería. Se consideran aparatos para jardines domésticos o de aficionados los que no son utilizados en jardines públicos, parques, calles, instalaciones deportivas, así como en explotaciones agrícolas y forestales. El cumplimiento de las instrucciones adjuntas de GARDENA es condición previa para el uso correcto de la motoazada eléctrica.	*Intended use* The GARDENA Electric Hoe is designed for loosening large lumps and hardened soil in small to medium-sized cultivation areas in domestic gardens and allotments. It is not designed for use for public grounds, parks, sports centres, roads, agriculture or forestry. Compliance with these instructions provided by GARDENA is a prerequisite for using the Electric Hoe correctly.	20 25 30

Spanish text . . . continued	English text . . . continued
A observar Debido al peligro de lesiones no está permitido usar la motoazada eléctrica GARDENA para desmenuzar piedras o para cavar superficies de hierba o césped.	*Please note* Attention! The Electric Hoe must not be used for breaking up stone or for turning over areas of lawn because of 35 the danger of physical injuries.

2 Para su seguridad	*2 For Your Safety*
Observe las indicaciones de seguridad en la motoazada eléctrica.	Please observe the notes on safety on the Electric Hoe.

¡Atención!	*Warning!* 40
• Leer las instrucciones de servicio antes de la puesta en marcha. • ¡Proteja el aparato de la lluvia y de la humedad! • ¡Mantenga a terceros fuera del área de trabajo! • ¡Herramientas rotatorias! ¡Herramienta gira por inercia! (Gardena 2006: 52–3)	• Read instruction handbook! • Do not use in rain or wet conditions! • Keep bystanders away! • Rotating tools! The hoe blades take a while to stop after turning off the 45 engine. (Gardena 2006: 11–12)

Strictly speaking, the texts above are not a ST and a TT; rather, they are two slightly different presentations of the same subject matter (presumably both translated from German). The contrasts between them are informative in that they may suggest possible culture-specific differences between British and Spanish instructions for use. We have recommended departures from literal translation in translating consumer-oriented STs where it is considered necessary; however, this does not mean the kind of freedom that might be exercised for stylistic reasons in the translation of literary texts. The translator of instructions for the use of a product, for example, owes a prime responsibility to the manufacturer (and its customers) to give a correct, unambiguous and comprehensible account of how the product is to be used, and therefore gives a higher priority to the accurate transmission of this functional information than to reproducing linguistic features of the ST. The successful comprehension of the information by TL users may demand adjustments to style and shifts of emphasis, since patterns of textual cogency and conventions for providing information and giving instructions are to some extent culture-specific. Consequently, readers from one culture might find the logic of presentation of a given text patronizingly overexplicit, whereas readers from another culture might find it over-economical and unclear. The faithfulness of such corresponding texts is more a matter of avoiding the falsification of the technical details described than of a TT faithfully matching the form of the ST. In the example above, the fact that the play on words with which the English text greets its readers ('the Garden of Gardena') is completely absent from the Spanish text may have some effect on the consumer's attitude towards the product but has no functional importance whatsoever.

Furthermore, it is not unusual to find that, in certain fields, different pieces of background knowledge will be expected from SL consumers and TL consumers. Thus the text in one of the languages may take for granted details which it is considered necessary to include in the text in the other language. For example, in the Gardena instance, the point of keeping the instructions in a safe place is not made explicit to English-speaking consumers, whereas Spanish-speaking consumers are advised to do this 'para consultas posteriores'. Conversely, the warning about the blades continuing to turn after the motor has been switched off is made in more technical terms in the Spanish version ('Herramienta gira por inercia') than in the English. If, for cultural reasons, a higher degree of sophistication is to be expected from either SL or TL consumers, that difference in sophistication may need to be reflected by formulating TTs in either more technical or less technical ways than the corresponding STs.

Closely related to these considerations is the question of register. The social and tonal registers of ST and TT often need to differ in ways reflecting different consumer expectations. Features of register in consumer-oriented texts are indicators of three key factors: how the purveyors of the commodity present themselves and their product; how the targeted consumers are seen by the purveyors; and the proposed relationship between the two parties. It may be that in the ST the relationship between purveyor and consumer is stereotyped as being, for example, one of the expert addressing poorly informed non-experts, while, for cultural reasons, the relationship in the TT is more aptly stereotyped as one of expert to other experts, or of non-expert to non-experts. Recipe books are a case in point: it is probably a fair assumption that a British reader of a recipe book is less likely to feel insulted by being 'talked down to', but more likely to react adversely to curt directives, than most Spanish readers. (There will be a chance to test this assumption in Practicals 14.2 and 14.3.)

The choice of ways of expressing commands plays a major role in configuring these perceptions and relationships. A simple imperative is an obvious option in both Spanish and English, but this may be modulated in different ways: texts in English may be more likely to soften the imperative with 'please', while Spanish offers a choice between familiar and formal forms of address (although most advertisements in Spanish now favour the familiarity of 'tú', operating instructions tend to be presented as a serious matter requiring the formality of 'usted'). Spanish also offers the option of using the infinitive form of a verb as an imperative, the effect of which is often to make the command more impersonal. Instructions in English may make more use of passive constructions, including phrases with 'must' or 'should'; those in Spanish are likely to favour constructions with 'se' instead (including 'se debe'). The ways in which commands are formulated in the Gardena texts would repay discussion in Practical 14.1.

Various other linguistic elements may be involved in a strategy aiming to make transpositions on functional or cultural grounds: vocabulary; grammatical/syntactical structure (for example, active and personal constructions may be preferable to passive and impersonal ones); sentential structure (for example, the presence or absence of parenthetical clauses, or colloquial or formal use of sentential markers, illocutionary particles and connectors); discourse structure (for example, marked or less marked use of devices signalling textual cohesion, more or less transparent textual layout); and so on. In principle, every level of textual variable may be drawn on to signal register. In particular, features of tonal register may need to be altered between ST and TT in order to establish and maintain a certain desired relationship between TT and consumer which is different from that between ST and consumer. The genre-specific tendencies of the ST may, for instance, lead one to expect a text that addresses the SL consumer in a formal tonal register, whereas the chosen genre of the TT may lead one to expect a text that addresses the TL consumer in an informal tonal register. In a situation like this, the knock-on effects of a change of register, may imply quite drastic departures from the framework of the ST, on any or all levels of textual variables discussed in Chapters 6 and 7.

All other considerations apart, choosing a register for a consumer-oriented TT can in some cases be problematic for the simple reason that there may be little in common between the groups of consumers targeted by the ST and the TT. In any case, any TL genre selected as a prototype for the TT will probably provide specimens in widely divergent styles and registers, leaving the translator with a number of possible models. We end this chapter with extracts from three different recipe books in English that amply illustrate these potential problems of choice. Thanks to their manifest consumer orientation, the extracts are also clear concluding reminders that every text – and therefore also every TT – is made for a specific purpose and a specific audience.

BOUILLABAISSE

NOTE: This, the most famous of all fish soups, is made chiefly in the South of France, different districts having particular recipes. It is a kind of thick stew of fish which should include a very wide mixture of different kinds of fish. The original French recipes use many fish not available in Great   5
Britain. The following recipe is adapted to use the available fish. In order to get a wide enough variety a large quantity must be made.

[Ingredients listed]

Clean the fish, cut them into thick slices and sort them into 2 groups, the firm-fleshed kind and the soft kind. Chop the onion; slice the leek, crush   10
the garlic; scald, skin and slice the tomatoes. In a deep pan make a bed of the sliced vegetables and the herbs, season this layer. Arrange on top the pieces of firm-fleshed fish; season them and pour over them the oil.
[. . .]

                                                              (Beeton 1962: 119)

ZUPPA DA PESCE

It doesn't matter whether you call it bouillabaisse, cippolini, zuppa da pesce, or just fish stew; whether it has lots of liquid, or, like this, is simmered in its own richly aromatic juices. It's not just good, it's wonderful. To put it in the oven is somewhat illegitimate, but you are less 5
apt to overcook it. Serve with Spanish rice (for the hearty ones), tossed green salad, French bread to sop up the juices.

[Ingredients listed]

Put the olive oil and garlic in a warm, deep casserole and heat. Place the 10
large fish on the bottom, then the mussels and shrimp. Season, and sprinkle the parsley over all. [. . .] Baste from time to time with the juices, using an oversized eyedropper called a baster. Serve in deep hot plates. Serves 6 generously. Time: 45 minutes.

(Tracy 1965: n. p.)

FISH CAKES

[Ingredients listed]

1   Chop the parsley with both hands, one on the knife handle and one on the top of the knife blade. This chops the parsley smaller and keeps 5
    your fingers safely out of the way of the knife.
2   Put the potatoes on one plate and mash them up with the fork. Add the fish and mash it up too. Add the butter, parsley, salt and pepper. Mix them all together.
3   Turn the mixture out on to the board and make it into a roll with your 10
    hands like a big sausage. Cut off rounds with the knife. [. . .]

(Anderson 1972: 26)

Practical 14

14.1 Consumer-oriented translation: instructions

Assignment

(i)   Compare and contrast the texts from the English and Spanish versions of the Gardena electric hoe operating instructions, given on pp. 246–7.
(ii) Determine what general conclusions can be drawn from the comparison.

14.2 Consumer-oriented translation: recipes

Assignment

(i)   Compare and contrast the texts from different English recipe books given on pp. 249–50.

(ii)   Compare and contrast the Spanish and English recipes given below.
(iii) Discuss what general conclusions can be drawn from these contrasts.

Contextual information

The texts below are taken, respectively, from a Spanish and an English recipe book chosen at random. The Spanish text is from Simone Ortega's *Mil ochenta recetas de cocina* (1972).

Text 1

RODAJAS DE MERLUZA EN SALSA VERDE

(6 personas)

6 rodajas gruesas de merluza
   cerrada (unos 200 gr.
   cada una),
4 cucharadas soperas de aceite,
1 cucharada sopera de harina,
1 cebolla mediana (80 gr.),
1 diente de ajo,
unas ramitas de perejil,

1 cucharada sopera de perejil
   picado muy menudo,
1½ vasos (de los de agua) de   5
   agua fría,
1 lata pequeña (125 gr.) de
   guisantes (facultativo),
1 ó 2 huevos duros
   (facultativo),   10
sal y pimienta.

En una sartén se pone el aceite a calentar; cuando está, se echa la cebolla a freír. Mientras tanto, en el mortero se machaca el diente de ajo y las ramitas de perejil con un poco de sal. Cuando la cebolla se va poniendo transparente (unos 5 minutes más o menos), se añade la harina, se dan 15 unas vueltas con una cuchara de madera y se agrega poco a poco el agua fría, se cuece un poco esta salsa y se coge un par de cucharadas, que se añaden a lo machacado en el mortero, revolviendo muy bien. Se incorpora el contenido del mortero a la salsa de la sartén y se revuelve todo junto.

En una cacerola de barro o porcelana (resistente al fuego) se cuela la 20 salsa por un chino o un colador de agujeros grandes. Se colocan las rodajas de merluza ligeramente saladas y holgadas de sitio. La salsa las debe cubrir justo; si es necesario, se puede añadir algo más de agua (teniendo en cuenta que la merluza soltará agua también al cocerse). Se espolvorea un poco de pimienta molida, el perejil picado y los guisantes (si se quiere). Se 25 agarra la cacerola por un costado y se sacude suavemente durante unos 15 minutos. Esto es fundamental para que se trabe bien la salsa. Se prueba entonces la salsa y se rectifica si fuese necesario. Se pican los huevos duros y se espolvorean por encima del pescado (esto es facultativo).

Se sirve en seguida en su misma cacerola de barro.   30

(Ortega 1972: 359–60)

Text 2

POLLOCK IN GREEN SAUCE

To serve 6

3 lb. pollock steaks, each cut ½ inch thick, or substitute halibut, fresh cod or other firm white fish steaks cut ½ inch thick	¾ pint water
	4 tablespoons dry white wine
	1 scant teaspoon finely chopped parsley 5
2¾ oz. flour	1½ teaspoons salt
4 tablespoons olive oil	1½ tablespoons cooked fresh green peas or thoroughly
1½ oz. finely chopped onions	defrosted frozen peas (optional) 10

Remove the skin from each steak with a small, sharp knife, and pat the steaks dry with kitchen paper. Sprinkle them with salt, then dip the steaks in 2 oz. of the flour, and shake them vigorously to remove any excess.

Heat the olive oil over a moderate heat in a large, heavy frying pan until a light haze forms above it. Add the fish and cook for about 4 minutes on 15 each side, turning the steaks and regulating the heat so that they brown evenly without burning. Remove the pan from the heat and with a bulb baster transfer the oil remaining in the pan to a heavy, medium-sized frying pan. Cover the fish steaks in the larger pan to keep them warm while you prepare the sauce. 20

Heat the oil again until a light haze forms above it. Add the onions and, stirring constantly, cook for about 5 minutes, until they are soft and transparent but not brown. Stir in the rest of the flour, mix thoroughly and pour in the water and wine. Cook over a high heat, stirring constantly with a whisk until the sauce comes to the boil and thickens slightly. Reduce 25 the heat to low and simmer for about 3 minutes.

Meanwhile, mash the garlic, parsley and salt to a smooth paste, using a pestle and mortar or the back of a wooden spoon. Thin it with about 3 tablespoons of the simmering sauce, then whisk it into the rest of the sauce. Cook, stirring constantly, for a minute or so. Taste for seasoning. Scatter 30 the peas, if you are using them, on top of the fish steaks, pour the sauce over them and cook uncovered over a low heat for about 3 minutes, basting occasionally until the fish and peas are just heated through. Serve at once on a large heated dish.

14.3 Consumer-oriented texts: recipes

Assignment

(i)   Discuss the strategic decisions confronting the translator of the following text, and define your own strategy for translating it.

(ii)   Translate the text into English to appear in a book of Spanish recipes published in an English-speaking country.

(iii)   Explain the main decisions of detail you made in producing your TT.

Contextual information

The text is from Simone Ortega's *Mil ochenta recetas de cocina* (1972).

Text

BRAZO DE GITANO

(8 personas)

2 cucharadas soperas de fécula de patata,	1 cucharada (de las de café) de levadura Royal,
4 cucharadas soperas de harina,	un pellizco de sal, 5
5 cucharadas soperas de azúcar,	1 paño limpio,
3 huevos,	mantequilla para untar la chapa,
1 clara,	azúcar glass.
un pellizco de vainilla en polvo,	

Se montan a punto de nieve muy firmes las cuatro claras, con un pellizquito 10 de sal. Se les añaden las yemas, después el azúcar y por último, cucharada a cucharada, la mezcla de la harina, la fécula y la levadura (estos tres elementos se mezclarán en un plato sopero antes de usarlos).

Se unta muy bien con mantequilla una chapa de horno bastante grande (37 × 26 cm. más o menos) y poco alta; en el fondo se coloca un papel 15 blanco también untado con mantequilla. Se mete a horno más bien suave unos 35 minutes. Tiene que estar la masa cocida (al pincharla con un alambre, éste tiene que salir limpio), pero no muy dorada.

Se moja el paño de cocina en agua templada y se retuerce muy bien para que esté húmedo pero sin agua. Se extiende en una mesa y en seguida 20 se vuelca el bizcocho. Se quita el papel pegado, se extiende el relleno con mucha rapidez y se enrolla el brazo de gitano ayudándose con el paño. Una vez bien formado, se pone en una fuente cubierto con un papel, hasta que se enfríe, y al ir a servir se cortan las extremidades y se espolvorea con azúcar glass. 25

Rellenos:

1°.) Crema pastelera

½ litro de leche,	1½ cucharadas soperas de maizena,
3 yemas de huevo,	½ cucharada sopera de harina,
5 cucharadas soperas de azúcar,	un pellizco de vainilla.

2º.) Mermelada de frambuesa o grosella y nata montada   30
Una vez el bizcocho en el paño de cocina, se extiende una capa muy fina
de mermelada con un cuchillo. Encima de ésta se extiende nata montada
dulce y se enrolla rápidamente. Hará falta más o menos ½ kg. de nata.

(Ortega 1972: 589–90)

14.4 Consumer-oriented texts: promotional leaflet

Assignment

(i)   Discuss the strategic decisions confronting the translator of the following
       text, and define your own strategy for translating it.
(ii)   Translate the text into English, assuming that it will be distributed to
       English-speaking tourists.
(iii) Explain the main decisions of detail you made in producing your TT.

Contextual information

The text is an extract from a tourist brochure entitled *Santo Domingo Tours*
produced by the Santo Domingo Sheraton Hotel.

Source text

  Tour en la ciudad

  Salida: 9:00 a.m.
  Duración: 3 horas

  Esta excursión, de aproximadamente 3 horas, visita la más vieja ciudad
  de América, saliendo de su hotel en la mañana.   5
  La primera parada se efectuará en la Primera Catedral del Nuevo
  Mundo (1540), Santa María La Menor. Este imponente monumento tiene
  el honor de albergar los restos de Cristóbal Colón, el descubridor de nuestra
  isla. Durante el recorrido por la zona colonial, usted podrá admirar
  impresionantes edificaciones, como son: la Torre del Homenaje, Casa de 10
  Tostado, Museo de las Casas Reales, Casa del Cordón y la primera calle
  del Nuevo Mundo, Calle las Damas.
  Nuestra segunda parada, será en el Alcázar de Colón, casa de Diego
  Colón, hijo del descubridor. Aquí se podrá observar el modo suntuoso de
  vida de la época de la colonia. Caminando unos pasos hacia La Atarazana, 15
  con sus bellas casas al estilo colonial, usted encontrará una gran variedad
  de tiendas de joyas y 'souvenirs'.
  Luego de finalizar el recorrido por la Zona Colonial, usted será llevado
  a la ciudad moderna, pasando por el Palacio Nacional y la Plaza de la
  Cultura, donde podrá ver el Museo del Hombre Dominicano, el Teatro   20
  Nacional, el Museo de Arte Moderno, y la Biblioteca Nacional, toda esta

área rodeada por hermosos jardines, en el centro de los cuales está la fuente 'Rosa de los Vientos', un trabajo de arte hecho por Crismar. También, usted podrá dar un vistazo a los centros de diversión nocturnos, los sectores residenciales de Santo Domingo, cuyas avenidas están plantadas 25 con árboles como la Palma Real, Caoba y Laurel; y finalmente, usted será llevado de vuelta a su hotel.

(from a leaflet distributed by the Santo
Domingo Sheraton Hotel)

15 Stylistic editing

Throughout the course, we have considered translation sometimes as a process, and sometimes as a product (a TT). The assessment of existing TTs has been an important feature in practicals. In this chapter, we turn our attention to the final stage of translation as a process, where the proposed TT is actually examined as a product. This stage is known as **editing**. A TT is only really complete after careful stylistic editing.

Any form of textual editing is intrinsically an operation carried out in writing on a pre-existent written text. (Even editing spoken dialogue is normally performed on a written transcript.) That is, the editor already has at least a tentative draft form of a text. Basic editing, of course, is concerned with eliminating outright errors – anything from incorrect spelling or punctuation, through ungrammatical constructions to obscure, ambiguous or misleading sentential configurations; all the linguistic levels of textual variables require checking for mistakes. When the object of editing is a TT, this process has to include checking back to the ST to make sure that its basic literal meaning has not been misrepresented in the TT. Nevertheless, much of this stage of textual editing is done on the TT as a TL text in its own right, without reference to the ST. In a sense, therefore, the transitional process of editing is a post-translational operation used for tidying up an almost complete TT, and is done with as little reference as possible to the ST.

In principle, no TT is ever finished and polished to the point where it could not be edited further. It is a practical question whether further editing will actually improve it. In practice there must, sooner or later (and for busy professional translators it is likely to be sooner), come a point where one has to stop tinkering with a TT. However, there is plenty of work to be done before that point is reached.

Just as basic editing presupposes at least a draft written text, so stylistic editing presupposes a text that is reasonably finished in such respects as literal meaning, grammar and spelling. This may turn out in practice to have been an unwarranted assumption, but it has to be the methodological starting-point. (A text might be rejected as unsuitable for stylistic editing if it were clearly not substantially correct.)

In the stylistic editing of a TT the translator considers only the alternative ways of expressing the literal meanings of parts of the text, rather than the possibility of altering the substance of what is expressed. This is admittedly a thin dividing line (as will be seen in Practical 15), because the way something is expressed is, to a great extent, part of what is expressed. Nevertheless, methodologically speaking, stylistic editing is purely a process of tinkering with stylistic effects in a TT. Thus it is not, in essence, a bilingual operation. It is perfectly possible for someone with no knowledge of, for example, Arabic to be called in to help with the stylistic editing of a TT translated from Arabic. As this observation suggests, the primary concern in editing is to enhance the quality of the TT, less as a translation than as a text produced in the TL for the use of a monolingual audience. Indeed, it is not uncommon for translations to be done by collaboration between one translator whose contribution is knowledge of the SL and another translator whose contribution is knowledge of the TL. With any luck, such collaboration would help in avoiding blunders like these classic captions:

Our milk comes from brucellosis accredited herds.

Why kill your wife with housework? Let electricity do it for you!

Stylistic editing is most effective if the editor lays the ST aside and concentrates on assessing the probable effects of the TT on a putative TL audience. One of the biggest problems in translating is that it is hard to put oneself in the shoes of a TL reader looking at the TT with a fresh eye. This is why translations from Spanish often have a Hispanic flavour which immediately signals that the text is a translation. Even the translator who manages to avoid outright translationese is not best placed to judge how well the TT would convey particular meanings or nuances for a reader who did not know the ST. There is therefore a lot to be said for asking an independent TL-speaking observer, who does not know the ST, to help with the editing.

Perhaps the most central features for stylistic editing are connotative meanings, because they require to be triggered by the context of the TT alone. The translator, who is inevitably immersed in the ST context, is unlikely to be able to assess confidently whether a connotation that is crystal clear in the context of the ST and the SL is equally clear to someone who only looks at the TT from the viewpoint of the TL culture. It is vital that this be checked. It is just as vital to check the converse – that there are no obtrusive unwanted connotations evoked by the TT. At best, such unwanted connotations show that the translator has failed to anticipate the stylistic effects the TT is liable to produce on its TL audience, and is not fully in control of its style. At worst, they may distort and subvert the overall content and impact of the TT, or they may create textual anomalies, contradictory connotations clashing either with one another or with the literal meaning.

Of course, it is easier for the independent editor to help with the second of these constraints than with the first. For instance, whatever the ST expression may be, the phrase 'a world authority in French letters' risks unfortunate innuendo and the editor may suggest that the translator think again. (Going back to the ST, the translator may then decide that the TT is an unfortunate rendering of 'una autoridad mundial en letras francesas', and opt for 'a world authority in French literary studies' instead.) But, without knowing the ST, how can editors tell when connotations are *missing* from a TT? The best thing is to give them the ST and hope that they do not get so deeply immersed in it that they, too, cannot see the TT objectively. Otherwise, if there is time, the translator can put the TT away for a month and then look at it with fresh eyes; even so, there is no guarantee that missing connotations will be spotted.

The twin constraint of spotting both missing connotations and unwanted ones is best illustrated in cases of connotative clash. The elimination of connotative clashes is one of the principal aims of stylistic editing. Thus, for instance, only an unbiased reading of the TT may reveal that juxtaposed literally exact expressions in the TT convey conflicting attitudinal meanings which make the text anomalous by virtue of the clash between contradictory attitudes ascribed to the author or speaker. Such textual anomalies leave the TT audience in doubt as to how to take the attitudes connoted in the text. Attitudinal anomalies are exemplified in the first of the Sastre TTs discussed in Chapter 4 (pp. 62–3):

> Éste es mi verdadero traje. Y vuestro 'verdadero traje' ya para siempre.
> This is my true garb. And your 'true garb' henceforth.

The connotations of this TT extract are likely to convey an attitude of lofty idealism, the sentences reading as an expression of praise and appreciation, even flattery, for the men addressed, not a thinly veiled threat. This clashes with the attitudes of the speaker conveyed elsewhere in the TT, from which it is clear that the Cabo's attitude to soldiering is one of pride mixed with a hard-nosed determination, while his attitude to the recruits is contemptuous and threatening. Stylistic editing might produce a better suggestion: 'This is my proper suit. And that goes for you lot too from now on.'

> Lo demás son ropas afeminadas . . ., la vergüenza de la especie.
> Anything else is effeminate clothing . . ., a disgrace to mankind.

The phrase 'a disgrace to mankind' has inappropriate attitudinal connotations suggesting a situation of solidarity and equality between the speaker and the addressees, whereas the context demands a blustering expression of contempt in which any of the recruits who do not qualify as 'real men' are automatically included: 'Anything else is for pansies . . ., the scum of the earth' conveys exactly the right nuances, given the bullying machismo implicit in the situation.

Clashes like these tend to reduce the connotative content of the TT to absurdity and paradox. Where the ST is not itself deliberately enigmatic and paradoxical, this constitutes a distortion of its overall meaning. However, even where no outright clashes occur, translators should be careful not to let gratuitous attitudinal meanings insinuate themselves into the TT. These should be picked up and eliminated, as far as possible, at the stylistic editing stage.

Similar considerations apply for all other types of connotation. Thus, for instance, the loss of an allusive meaning with a subtle but thematically important role in the ST is a significant translation loss. Gustavo Adolfo Bécquer's poem 'Es un sueño la vida' (Bécquer 1961: 52) provides an example, as discussed in Chapter 9 (pp. 177–8). The title alludes to Calderón's famous play *La vida es sueño* and creates irony by means of the contrasting moods of the poem and the play. A translation from which an appropriate allusion is missing would, therefore, be unsatisfying.

Reflected meanings in a ST are also notoriously difficult to render adequately in a TT; and, conversely, unforeseen and potentially embarrassing reflected meanings can create translation loss by jeopardizing the seriousness of a TT through unwanted comic effects or innuendo, as in the example of the French letters given above.

As regards collocative meanings, the most obvious flaws to look out for are miscollocations. These are a likely result of the translator's immersion in the ST and the SL at the earlier stages of translating. (Even where, strictly speaking, they do not trigger problems of collocative meaning as such, they are a common source of translation loss on the grammatical level. Our discussion here embraces miscollocations in general, as well as collocative meaning.) Some miscollocations may actually amount to outright grammatical errors, not merely stylistic ones. For example, the collocation of superlative 'más' and any adjective is grammatical and idiomatic in Spanish, but is ungrammatical with many adjectives in English; compare 'la más vieja ciudad' with 'the most old city'. This kind of grammatical mistake will presumably be eliminated at an early editing stage. However, there may be collocations that are not categorically ungrammatical in the TL, yet introduce a jarring note into the TT. It is sometimes hard to pin down just what makes a certain collocation seem ungainly. At best, one can suggest that speakers of a language have a sense of 'euphonic order' by which they judge certain collocations to be more acceptable than others. For example, Spanish 'ir y venir' is felicitous where 'venir y ir' is not; whereas, in English, 'come and go' is felicitous but 'go and come' is not. Similarly, Spanish 'de pies a cabeza' may, according to context, need to be rendered as 'from top to toe', 'from head to toe' or 'from top to bottom', but never as 'from toe to top' or 'from toe to head', and rarely as 'from bottom to top'.

When differences between felicitous collocations in one language and those in another are overlooked, a TT will often signal, by its clumsiness, the fact that it is a translation and not an indigenous text. Here are some examples of such translationese:

De acá para allá	from here to there
	(*Edit to*: back and forth/up and down)
niños de 2 a 5 años	children from 2 to 5 years
	(*Edit to*: children between 2 and 5)

un film en blanco y negro	a film in white and black
	(*Edit to*: black and white film)
Ya lo sabía yo	I knew it already
	(*Edit to*: I thought as much)
Se pasa todo el tiempo	He spends all the time studying
estudiando	(*Edit to*: He spends all his time studying)

As seen in the last example, deictic and anaphoric elements often create collocational problems of a stylistic rather than a grammatical nature. Deictic elements like 'this', 'that', 'the' and 'a' are often involved in subtle and complex collocational euphonics. So, for example, 'my hand hurts' and 'this hand hurts' convey different messages and seem both to be felicitous; 'that hand hurts' is (depending on context) less so, while 'the hand hurts' and 'a hand hurts' are in most contexts unacceptable. (Note that Spanish avoids the use of a possessive adjective where the verbal form makes possession unambiguous; for example, 'me duele la mano izquierda', 'my left hand hurts' or 'Jaime llevó la chaqueta verde', 'Jaime wore his green jacket'.) 'When I aim, I close an eye' is somewhat ungainly, while 'when I aim, I close one eye' is felicitous. Anaphorics, too, show clearly that there are collocational choices to be made on the basis of felicity or infelicity in a given language. For example, 'aquel libro lo leí en dos días' is usually better rendered as 'I read the book in two days' than as 'that book, I read it in two days'. The translation of deictics and anaphora is far from being a straightforward matter of literal translation. Here are some examples:

El agua es enfriada por transferencia de calor desde hielo con *el* que se halla *ésta* en contacto.	Water is chilled by heat transfer from ice with which *it* is in contact.
y además ...	and for another *thing* ...
... me pareció que estaba más contenta	... *she* seemed happier to me
La segunda parte de *la* excursión es *la* visita *al* Jardín Botánico.	The second part of *the* tour is *a* visit to *the* Botanical Gardens.
[In directions for the use of a product] Aplicar *el* PREPARADOR mediante fibra tipo Scotch Brite.	Apply PREPARER with *a* ScotchBrite-type abrasive pad.
Más grave que *el* materialismo conceptual tan típico del siglo XIX es *este* materialismo activo que ...	More serious than *the* conceptual materialism of the 19th century is *the* active materialism that ...

Infelicity in the use of anaphora and deictics may in some cases originate from a factor of tedious repetition. That is, collocational possibilities may be stylistically affected by some kind of textual 'boredom factor'. If this is the case, however, it must be said that different textual genres in different languages have very different tolerances to repetition. In an English novel, for example, there may be countless repetitions of 'he said', without this repetition being thought obtrusive or tedious. If the dialogue is translated into Hungarian, however, the translator soon begins to feel the need to vary the formula through translating 'he said' by various verbs descriptive of the manner of utterance (the Hungarian counterparts of 'he replied', 'he queried', 'he whispered', 'he affirmed', and so on). Thus it would seem that, in certain genres at least, the English-speaking reader's tolerance to the 'boredom factor' caused by continual use of 'he said' is higher than the Hungarian reader's tolerance of repetitions of the corresponding formula in Hungarian.

In a similar vein, it is clear that Spanish has in general a lower tolerance than English for the repetition of adverbial suffixes when they are joined by a conjunction, as exemplified by the clear preference for 'ni rápida ni eficazmente' (as opposed to 'ni rápidamente ni eficazmente'), 'lenta y decididamente' (as opposed to 'lentamente y decididamente'), 'política y económicamente' (as opposed to 'políticamente y económicamente'), and so on. These differential tolerances and preferences have obvious implications for translating and for stylistic editing.

It is clear from these examples that stylistic editing is in part an exercise in taste. Even if it means taking liberties with the literal faithfulness of TT to ST, rooting out unidiomatic collocations is a recommended editing process, except, of course, where the ST deliberately exploits them. This last proviso, however, highlights a vital point concerning all stylistic editing: while it is highly desirable to test the TT on SL speakers who do not know the ST, and to take careful account of their suggestions, *the ultimate editing decisions must always be taken by the translator, with reference to the ST.*

Rooting out unidiomatic collocations is one thing, but there is, of course, also the converse case to consider, where the TT collocation is idiomatic to the point of being clichéd. Clichés can be obtrusive in their own way, and are therefore capable of creating their own unwanted stylistic effects. In particular, if the ST produces unusual twists by means of unexpected collocations, the use of clichés in the corresponding TT amounts to significant translation loss, trivializing the text or even falsifying it. This effect is illustrated in an example from the Lorca text in Practical 9.1:

Por el cuerpo le subían	Soft around her body
los caracoles del agua.	curled the water like a snail.

As we have suggested, it should not be forgotten that collocative clashes may be used deliberately. In such cases it will usually be appropriate for the TT to coin equally deliberate miscollocations. The main thing then is to make sure that the contrived miscollocations in the TT are stylistically plausible in the light of the TL, and are clearly recognizable as deliberate ploys, not stylistic hitches. Here is a good example from the Rubén Darío text in Practical 9.2:

El sol como un vidrio redondo y opaco
The sun like a sheet of glass opaque and round
(*Edit to*: The sun like an opaque globe of glass.)

In this example, the ST presents an unusual simile of the sun likened to a globe made of glass. Since glass is normally thought of as two-dimensional (as in 'a sheet of glass'), it is the function of the contrived collocation of 'vidrio' with 'redondo' (rounded) to provide the image with its necessary three-dimensional quality. The innovative 'vidrio redondo' contrasts with such standard collocations as 'vidrio cilindrado' (plate glass), 'vidrio plano' (sheet glass), which convey two-dimensional images, or, for that matter, 'vidrio pintado', which evokes colour.

For affective meanings, and stylistic uses of language varieties of all sorts, the same considerations hold as for the types of connotative meaning we have been discussing. These considerations can be summed up by calling attention to four problems: the problem of losing from the TT important connotations contextually triggered in the ST; the problem of accidentally creating unwanted connotative effects in the TT; the problem of bringing about connotative clashes in the TT; and the problem of deliberately introducing gratuitous connotations into the TT. These are the main points to look for in stylistic editing.

One other thing that should be reviewed at the stylistic editing stage is the textual effects of language variety – alternatives associated with different social registers, dialects, sociolects and tonal registers. Even though conscious choices have been made about these things at the drafting stage, stylistic editing offers one more chance to weigh up how successful the outcome of these choices is over the TT as a whole. The four problems outlined above are all likely to arise here as well, *mutatis mutandis*. It is also particularly important, when using a marked language variety in a TT, to avoid the two extremes of 'too little' and 'too much'. Editing offers the chance to make sure that the TT contains enough features of language variety to prevent its coming across as a neutral, standard sample of the TL, but not so many that it seems caricatural. The 'boredom factor' we referred to earlier can also be invoked here, and so can an 'irritation factor': over-using stylistic features all signalling the same language variety can very easily lead to tedium, embarrassment or exasperation (as witness some of the dialectal features of D.H. Lawrence's writing).

There is always a threat of connotative clash in the stylistic use of language variety. There is only one genuine excuse for mixing features from different registers, dialects and sociolects in a TT, and this is when the ST itself deliberately uses code-switching for specific thematic purposes, as for instance in the text from *Flor de Otoño* used for Practical 11.2 (p. 208). (If the mixture is accidental, then the ST will probably not be worth translating anyway, unless it is a potboiler that has sold a million copies and been turned into a television series with an all-star cast – in which case, the last thing the likely readership is going to be interested in is accuracy of language variety.)

Finally, here are two passages manifestly in need of stylistic editing, and which are well worth discussion in class:

(i)   The Ministry of Education and Science has granted, on its fifth edition, the Scientific Research National Awards 'Santiago Ramón y Cajal', Technical Research 'Leonardo Torres Quevedo', Humanistic and Social Research 'Ramón Menéndez Pidal' and for young scientists 'Rey Juan Carlos I'. The Jury for these awards was composed by specialized professors in each area. These awards will be handed over by Their Majesties the King and Queen at an act to be held at the Royal Palace.

(ii)   The Offices for the Transfer of Research Results (OTRIs) came into being in 1988 for promoting the transfer of scientific and technical offerings to productive sectors, thereby enabling universities and public research centres (CPI) to interrelate with companies in a coherent, planned and activated way.

Practical 15

15.1 Stylistic editing

Assignment

Discuss the two passages given immediately above and edit them to read better where you think they are stylistically or idiomatically defective. Earmark points where you think editing may be necessary but cannot be done without reference to the ST.

15.2 Stylistic editing

Assignment

(i)   Working in groups, each taking roughly equal amounts of the text, edit the following English TT to read better where you think it is stylistically or idiomatically defective.

(ii)   Earmark points where you think further editing may be necessary but can only be done with reference to the ST.

(iii) After discussion of your provisional edited version, you will be given the ST and asked (a) to assess the accuracy of the TT and (b) to complete the editing of the TT.

Contextual information

The text is taken verbatim from a travel brochure entitled *Colombia: país de Eldorado; the Country of Eldorado* distributed by Avianca airlines in the late 1980s.

Target text

Colombia

The country of Eldorado

When the Spanish Conquer started in the actual colombian territory during
the XVI century a legend was born: Eldorado . . . a fabulous treasure
supousedly hidden beneath every water, buried in every cave, hit an in   5
every mine . . .

Nonethe less the conquerors could not find that immense richness
which if only described exalted the spirits and gave courage to the
cowards . . .

The conquerors did not know that every shining thing is not always gold   10
and that all treasures can not be minted: the treasure was evident, It was
just on the surface . . . the treasure was the weather, the generous fruits,
the open skies, the plains and mountains: Colombia was the Eldorado!!!

Thus, this country located at the extreme northern tip of South America
was undescribable in the usual language of tourist booklets. In order to   15
talk about it you have to be possesed by passion, use the language habitual
to legends weavers . . .

Very sure you have read One Hundred Years of Solitude, that famous
novel by the colombian author Garcia Márquez, where girls fly and the
deads keep on tied up to the trees or stroll throgh the old mansions . . .   20

Well then, you already have an aproximate idea about this misterious
country . . . full of unatainable dreams. Believe every thing they tell you
about Colombia . . . This is an excessive country . . . Our territory is already
a surprising amount of fullness, coastal borders on two oceans, inviolable
jungles (some of them with airports), three outstanding mountain systems   25
and big rivers giving surviving to inaccountable towns . . .

Colombia has been called a country of cities . . . We have to many . . .
small . . . quiet . . . and traditional, full of historic relics . . . Some are
modern . . . up to the XXth Century, thrown into progress . . . But all of
them connected by a net of good roads, railroads and airways . . .   30

16 Summary and conclusion

The idea of translators as active and responsible agents of the translation process has played a constant and central part throughout this course. Indeed, the personal responsibilities of translators are, in our view, of paramount importance. Although loyalties may genuinely be divided between responsibilities to the author of the ST, to the manifest properties and features of the ST (in particular, with a view to what is there in black and white in a written ST, as opposed to what its author may have intended), to the 'paymaster' by whom a TT has been commissioned, and to a putative public for whom the TT is meant, it is, in the end, the translator who is responsible for submitting a particular TT. Responsibility entails decisions, and it is with this in mind that we have insisted at every juncture on the key notions of strategy and decisions of detail, stressing the idea that decisions of detail should be rationally linked to the prior formulation of an overall strategy for translating a particular text in a particular set of circumstances.

The adoption of an appropriate translation strategy means ranking the cultural, formal, semantic, stylistic and generic properties of the ST according to their relative textual and functional relevance and the amount of attention these properties should receive in the process of translation. The aim is to deal with translation loss (see especially Chapter 2), and the attendant necessities of compromise and compensation (see the discussion in Chapter 3), in a rational and systematic way based on clear priorities: in short, by sanctioning the loss of features that have a low degree of textual relevance, sacrificing less relevant textual details to more relevant ones, and using techniques of compensation to convey features of high textual relevance that cannot be more directly rendered.

Textual relevance is a qualitative measure of the degree to which, in the translator's judgement, particular properties of a text are held responsible for the overall impact carried in and by that text. In a sense, textually relevant features are those which stand out as making the text what it is – marking it as belonging to a particular genre and determining how it is received by listeners or readers. This is not as trivial and circular as it might sound. On the contrary, it is the basis for the only reasonably reliable test of textual relevance. No such test can, of course, escape a degree of subjectivity, but the most objective test of textual relevance is to imagine that a particular textual property is omitted from the text and to assess what difference this omission would make to the overall impact of the text as a whole. If the answer is 'little or none', we may take it that the property in question has a very low degree of textual relevance. If, on the other hand, omission of a textual property would mean a palpable loss in either the genre-typical or the individual (perhaps even deliberately idiosyncratic) character of the text, we may attribute a high degree of relevance to the textual property in question.

We have referred above to 'textual *and functional* relevance', and our discussion of genre in Chapter 4 emphasizes the crucial connection between the analysis of formal textual properties and the identification of two kinds of purpose: that of the ST within the SL culture and that of the TT with respect to the requirements of a particular translation task (the skopos). While functional considerations have to some extent become implicit in the chapters dealing primarily with textual features and kinds of language (5 to 11), they have regained prominence and explicitness in the chapters dealing with specialized fields of translation (12 to 14), in which real-world constraints and requirements are of decisive importance. These three chapters are not intended to provide a comprehensive or self-contained training in technical, institutional and consumer-oriented translation, and they should not be used in isolation from the rest of the book. Their main purpose is to provide more concrete contexts for the application of the methods developed in the preceding chapters, grounding the principles of the formulation of translation strategies in realistic practical examples.

The most concise synopsis of factors to be taken into account in the assessment of textual relevance is contained in the 'Schema of textual filters' presented in the Introduction (pp. 6–7). The issues discussed and the methods proposed in Chapters 4 to 11 are all summarized in the schema, dividing the process of planning a translation into a series of levels of analysis so as to encourage a systematic, self-critical approach and facilitate the assignment of priorities. Having studied and discussed all sixteen chapters and having put methods and principles to the test in practical exercises, users of this book should now have a good grasp of the meaning, implications and functional value of each of the components of the schema, and should be able to make effective use of it as a checklist for ensuring that their translation strategies are rigorously formulated, coherent and productive, as well as for the analysis of completed TTs (their own and those of other translators). Each of the 'filters' corresponds to a series of questions that need to be posed about the ST and the translation skopos, generating awareness of a range of options and an understanding of the implications of each option.

We have emphasized at every stage that nothing should be taken for granted, nothing automatically ruled in or ruled out. Translators need to be equipped to consider the full range of options available to them and to articulate precisely why one decision is preferable to another. We have offered no hard-and-fast rules for how to deal with generic and cultural specificity, phonic and graphic effects, syntactical and semantic gaps, or particularities of register and dialectal or sociolectal variation. What we have attempted to provide is clear, coherent guidance reinforced by constructive, well-targeted practice in order to develop the kinds of linguistic and cultural awareness, analytical acumen and decision-making capabilities required for the translation of any kind of text. In short, the message is that thinking translation means better translation.

Glossary

affective meaning   the emotive effect worked on the addressee by the choice of a particular **linguistic expression**, in contrast with others that might have been used to express the same literal message; affective meaning is a type of **connotative meaning**.

alliteration   the recurrence of the same sound/letter or sound/letter cluster at the beginning of two or more words occurring near or next to one another in a text.

allusive meaning   the **connotative meaning** of a **linguistic expression**, which takes the form of evoking the meaning of an entire saying or quotation of which that expression is a part. (NB: If a saying or quotation appears in full within a text, that is a case of citation; we speak of **allusive meaning** where only a recognizable segment of the saying or quotation occurs in the text, but that segment implicitly carries the meaning of the entire 'reconstructed' saying or quotation.)

anaphora   in grammar, the replacement of previously used **linguistic expressions** in a **text** by simpler and less specific expressions (such as pronouns) having the same contextual referent; in rhetoric, the repetition of a word or phrase at the beginning of successive clauses.

associative meaning   the **connotative meaning** of a **linguistic expression** which takes the form of attributing to the referent certain stereotypically expected properties culturally associated with that referent.

assonance   the recurrence of a sound/letter or sound/letter cluster in the middle of words occurring near or next to one another in a **text**.

asyndeton   the omission of conjunctions.

attitudinal meaning   the **connotative meaning** of a **linguistic expression** which takes the form of implicitly conveying a commonly held attitude or value judgement towards the referent of the expression.

audiovisual translation   the translation of dialogue in films, video, television programmes and opera or theatre performances, either by means of dubbing and voiceover, or by means of subtitles or surtitles.

calque   an instance of **literal translation** in which a TT expression is modelled on the grammatical structure and/or lexical collocation of a ST expression; it represents a minimal degree of **cultural transposition** –

translating the components of a culture-specific item in the ST without giving it idiomatic viability in the TL.

code-switching   the alternating use of two or more recognizably different language variants (varieties of the same language, or different languages) within the same **text**.

cogency   the 'thread' of intellectual interrelatedness of ideas running through a **text** (a combination of **coherence** and **cohesion**).

coherence   the tacit, yet intellectually discernible, thematic development that characterizes a cogent **text**, as distinct from a random sequence of unrelated sentences.

cohesion   the explicit and transparent linking of sentences and larger sections of **text** by the use of overt linguistic devices that act as 'signposts' for the **cogency** of a text.

collocative meaning   the **connotative meaning** lent to a **linguistic expression** by the meaning of some other expression with which it frequently or typically collocates in a grammatical context; that is, collocative meaning is an echo of the meanings of expressions that partner a given expression in commonly used phrases.

communicative translation   a style of **free translation** involving the rendering of ST expressions by contextually/situationally appropriate counterparts in the TL; that is, the TT uses an expression that a TL speaker would be likely to use in that situation (in preference to **literal translation**).

compensation   the technique of making up for unacceptable **translation loss** by deliberately introducing a more acceptable one; important **ST** features being approximated in the **TT** through means other than those used in the ST. (NB: Unlike, for example, an unavoidable, conventional **grammatical transposition** or **communicative translation**, compensation is not forced on the translator by the constraints of **TL** structures – it is a conscious, careful, free, one-off choice.)

conative function   using language (verbal or non-verbal) to prompt the listener to do something, rather than to convey information (an aspect of **pragmatics**).

connotative meaning   the implicit overtones and nuances that **linguistic expressions** tend to carry over and above their **literal meanings**. (NB: The overall meaning of an expression in context is compounded of the literal meaning of the expression plus its contextually relevant connotative overtones.)

cultural borrowing   the process of taking over a SL expression verbatim from the ST into the TT (and, more broadly, into the TL as a whole). The borrowed term may remain unaltered in form or may undergo minor alteration or transliteration.

cultural transplantation   the highest degree of **cultural transposition**, involving the replacement of source-cultural details mentioned in the ST with cultural details drawn from the target culture in the TT – that is, cultural transplantation deletes from the TT items specific to the source culture, replacing them with items specific to the target culture.

cultural transposition   any degree of replacement of ST features specific to the SL culture with features designed to be more familiar to TL readers; cultural transposition entails a certain degree of TL orientation.

dative of interest   see **ethic(al) dative**

decisions of detail   in translating a given **text**, the decisions taken in respect of specific problems of grammar, lexis, and so on; decisions of detail are ideally taken in the light of previously taken **strategic decisions**.

deixis (adjective **deictic**)   a **linguistic expression** (for instance, a demonstrative, a personal pronoun, a temporal or spatial expression) referring to or determined by the circumstances in which an utterance is made – who is speaking, who is being addressed, where, when.

dialect   a language variety with features of accent, vocabulary, syntax and sentence formation (for example, **illocutionary particles**, intonation) characteristic, and therefore indicative, of the regional provenance of its users.

discourse level   the textual level on which whole utterances or texts (or sections of whole texts) are considered as self-contained, coherent and cohesive entities; the ultimate discourse structure of texts consists of a number of interrelated sentences, these being the lowest analytic units on the discourse level.

domesticating (or **naturalizing**) **translation**   a TL-biased translation strategy aiming to make the TT seem as accessible and familiar as possible to TL readers, especially on the cultural level (in contrast with **exoticizing translation**).

editing   the last stage of the translation process, consisting of checking over the draft of a written TT with a view to correcting errors and polishing up stylistic details.

ethic(al) dative or **dative of interest**   the use of an indirect object pronoun ('se, le, me', etc.) to indicate that the person referred to is associated with the direct object ('his hands, my shoes') or the action being carried out.

exegetic translation   a style of translation in which the TT expresses and explains additional details that are not explicitly conveyed in the ST; that is, the TT is, at the same time, an expansion and explanation of the contents of the ST.

exoticism   an instance of zero **cultural transposition**, whereby a ST feature (having its roots exclusively in the SL and source culture) is taken over verbatim into the TT; that is, the transposed term is an ostensibly 'foreign' element in the TT.

exoticizing (or **foreignizing**) **translation**   a SL-biased translation strategy aiming to retain features of the ST and the SL culture in the TT (in contrast with **domesticating translation**).

expressive function   using language (verbal or non-verbal) to communicate the feelings of the speaker, rather than to convey information (an aspect of **pragmatics**).

foot   a prosodic/metric unit in versification, consisting of a rhythmic pattern of stressed and/or unstressed syllables; in certain languages (for example, English or Latin, but not Spanish), feet are the basic units of poetic rhythm.

foreignizing translation   see **exoticizing translation**.

free translation   a style of translation in which there is only a global correspondence between units of the ST and units of the TT – for example, a rough sentence-to-sentence correspondence, or a still looser correspondence in terms of even larger sections of text.

generalizing translation, generalization   rendering a ST expression by a TL **hypernym** – that is, the literal meaning of the TT expression is wider and less specific than that of the corresponding ST expression; a generalizing translation omits details that are explicitly present in the literal meaning of the ST.

generic or **androcentric masculine**   the use of the masculine gender to refer to male and female referents, or to describe a mixed-sex group.

genre (or **text-type**)   a category to which, in a given culture, a given **text** is seen to belong and within which it is seen to share a type of communicative purpose with other texts; that is, the text is seen to be more or less typical of the genre.

gist translation   a style of translation in which the TT purposely expresses a condensed version of the contents of the ST; that is, the TT is, at the same time, a synopsis of the ST.

grammatical (or syntactical) level   the level of linguistic structure concerned with words, morphology (the decomposition of inflected, derived or compound words into their meaningful constituent parts), and syntax (the patterned syntactic arrangement of words into phrases, and phrases into yet more complex phrases).

grammatical (or syntactical) transposition   the technique of translating a ST expression having a given grammatical structure by a TT expression with a different grammatical structure containing different parts of speech in a different arrangement.

hypernym   a **linguistic expression** whose literal meaning is inclusive of, but wider and less specific than, the range of literal meaning of another expression: for instance, 'parent' is a hypernym of 'mother'.

hyponym   a **linguistic expression** whose literal meaning is included in, but is narrower and more specific than, the range of literal meaning of another expression; for example, 'younger sister' is a hyponym of 'sibling'.

hypotaxis (in syntax)   the use of compound sentences containing subordinate clauses with a hierarchical relationship; the main clause is modified or added to by one or more subordinate clauses, each of which plays a syntactical role within the structure of the main clause (that is, they are embedded within it).

idiom   a fixed figurative expression whose meaning cannot be deduced from the literal meaning of the words that make it up.

idiomatic   what sounds 'natural' and 'normal' to native speakers – a **linguistic expression** that is unexceptional and acceptable in a given context.

idiomizing translation   a translation that respects the ST message content, but typically uses TL idioms or familiar phonic and rhythmic patterns to give an easy read, even if this means sacrificing nuances of meaning or tone.

illocutionary particle   a discrete element not integrated into the syntactical structure of a sentence which reinforces the illocutionary force or function of the utterance – that is, its main pragmatic purpose, what the speaker is trying to achieve by uttering those words (primarily in spoken language but also reflected in written texts). For example, 'please', 'for God's sake!', 'surely', 'qué va', '¿no?', 'coño'.

interlineal translation   a style of translation in which the TT provides a literal rendering for each successive meaningful unit of the ST (including affixes) and arranges these units in their order of occurrence in the ST, regardless of the conventional grammatical order of units in the TL.

interpreting   translation of an **oral** ST into an oral TT (usually a **gist translation**); either consecutive (producing an oral TT based on notes after the ST has been delivered), simultaneous (an oral TT is delivered at the same time as the ST) or bilateral/liaison (mediating an exchange between speakers of the SL and TL).

intersemiotic translation   translating from one semiotic system (that is, system for communication) into another. For a translation to be inter-semiotic, either the ST, or the TT, but not both, may be a human natural language.

intertextuality/intertextual level   the level of shared culture on which texts are viewed as bearing significant external relationships to other texts (for example, by allusion, by imitation, by virtue of genre membership).

intralingual translation   the re-expression of a message conveyed in a particular form of words in a given language by means of another form of words in the same language.

lexis (adj. **lexical**)   the totality of words in any given language.

linguistic expression   a self-contained and meaningful item in a given language, such as a word, a phrase, a sentence.

literal meaning   the conventional range of referential meaning attributed to a **linguistic expression** (as abstracted from its **connotative** overtones and contextual nuances).

literal translation   a word-for-word translation, giving maximally accurate literal rendering to all the words in the ST as far as the grammatical conventions of the TL will allow; that is, literal translation is SL-oriented, and departs from ST sequence of words only where the TL grammar makes this inevitable.

metalingual function   using language in a self-referential way to discuss language itself or how something has been expressed (an aspect of **pragmatics**).

naturalizing translation   see **domesticating translation**.

nominalization   the use of a noun which, in the same language or in a TT, could be replaced by an expression not containing a noun; it is a typical feature of technical texts.

onomatopoeia   a word whose phonic form imitates a sound, which is the referent of the word or which is associated with the referent.

oral language/genre/discourse/text   spoken or sung as opposed to written; includes both live and recorded speech/performance. Can be broadly categorized as: conversation, oral narrative, oral address, oral reading, dramatization, sung performance.

parataxis   phrases, clauses and sentences which are placed next to one another without subordinating relationships or explicit connecting elements.

partially overlapping translation   rendering a ST expression by a TL expression whose range of **literal meaning** partially overlaps with that of the ST expression – that is, the literal meaning of the TT expression both adds some detail not explicit in the literal meaning of the corresponding ST expression, and omits some other detail that is explicit in the literal meaning of the ST expression; in this sense, partially overlapping translation simultaneously combines elements of **particularizing** and **generalizing**.

particularizing translation, particularization   rendering a ST expression by a TL **hyponym**; that is, making the **literal meaning** of the TT narrower and more specific than that of the corresponding ST; a particularizing translation adds details to the TT that are not explicitly expressed in the ST.

phatic function   using language (verbal or non-verbal) to communicate shared feelings, maintain social interaction and fill gaps in conversation, rather than to convey information (an aspect of **pragmatics**).

phonemic translation   a technique of translation that consists of an attempt to replicate in the TT the sound sequence of the ST, while allowing the sense to remain, at best, a vague and suggested impression.

phonic/graphic level   the level of linguistic structure concerned with the patterned organization of sound-segments (phonemes) in speech, or of letters (graphemes) in writing.

phrasal verb   in English, a verb formed with an adverb, preposition or both.

poetic function   using language in a way that focuses on formal qualities (sound, rhythm, patterning, graphic presentation) rather than on sense or cohesion (an aspect of **pragmatics**).

pragmatics   the study of language as used for particular purposes in particular situations, focusing on communicative acts rather than grammatical structures (what users are doing or intending to achieve by expressing themselves in particular ways).

prosodic level   the level of linguistic structure concerned with metrically patterned stretches of speech within which syllables have varying degrees of prominence (in terms of such properties as stress and vowel-differentiation), varying degrees of *pace* (in terms of such properties as length and tempo) and varying qualities of *pitch.*

reflected meaning   the **connotative meaning** lent to a **linguistic expression** by the fact that its *form* (phonic, graphic, or both) is reminiscent of a homonymic or near-homonymic expression with a different **literal meaning**; that is, reflected meaning is an echo of the literal meaning of some other expression that sounds or is spelt the same, or nearly the same, as a given expression.

register   see **social register** and **tonal register**

rephrasing   the exact rendering of the message content of a given ST in a TT that is radically different in form, but neither adds nor omits details explicitly conveyed in the ST.

sentential level   the level of linguistic structure concerned with the formation of sentences as complete, self-contained linguistic units ready-made to act as vehicles of oral or written communication. (NB: Over and above the basic grammatical units – which may be elliptical – that it contains, a sentence must be endowed with sense-conferring properties of intonation or punctuation, and may in addition contain features of word order, and/or **illocutionary particles**, all of which contribute to the overall meaning, or 'force', of the sentence.)

skopos   the specific purpose of a translation seen as an assignment fulfilling the requirements of the person or organization that commissions it.

social register   a style of speaking/writing appropriate to a given social situation, which may give grounds for inferring relatively detailed stereotypical information about the social identity of the speaker/writer. (NB: 'Social identity' refers to the stereotypical labelling that is a constant feature of social intercourse.)

sociolect   a language variety with features of accent, vocabulary, syntax and sentence formation (for example, intonation, **illocutionary particles**) characteristic of a particular social group, and therefore indicative, for example, of the class affiliations of its users.

source language (SL)   the language in which the **text** requiring translation is expressed.

source text (ST)   the text requiring translation.

strategic decisions   the general decisions taken, in the light of the nature of the ST and the requirements of the TT (the skopos), as to what ST properties should have priority in translation and the overall style and register of the TT; **decisions of detail** are ideally taken on the basis of these strategic decisions (though, conversely, decisions of detail may have an effect on altering initial strategic decisions).

synonymy   the highest degree of semantic equivalence between two or more different **linguistic expressions** having exactly identical ranges of **literal meaning**. (NB: Synonymous expressions usually differ in **connotative**, and therefore in 'overall', meaning; that is, they are unlikely to have perfectly identical meanings in textual contexts – compare 'automobile' and 'jalopy', for instance.)

syntactical (or grammatical) level   the level of linguistic structure concerned with words, morphology (the decomposition of inflected, derived or compound words into their meaningful constituent parts), and syntax (the patterned syntactic arrangement of words into phrases, and phrases into yet more complex phrases).

target language (TL)   the language into which a given **text** is to be translated.

target text (TT)   the text proffered as a translation (that is, a proposed TL rendering) of the ST. (NB: 'Publishing' a target text is a decisive act that overrides the necessarily relative and tentative success of the target text.)

text   any given stretch of speech or writing produced in a given language (or 'mixture of languages' – see code-switching) and assumed to make a self-contained, coherent whole on the discourse level; a text may contain elements (images or sounds) that are not verbal.

text-type   see **genre**

textual variables   all the ostensible features in a **text**, and which *could* (in another text) have been different; that is, each textual variable constitutes a genuine *option* in the text.

tonal register   a style of speaking/writing adopted as a means of conveying the affective attitudes of speakers/writers to their addressees. (NB The **connotative meaning** of features of tonal register is an **affective meaning**. This connotative meaning is, strictly speaking, conveyed by the *choice* of one out of a range of expressions capable of conveying a particular literal message; for example, 'Give me the money, please' versus 'Chuck us the dosh, will you?')

translation loss   any feature of inexact correspondence between ST and TT. (NB: Where a TT has properties, effects or meanings that are *not* present in the ST, the addition of these counts as a translation loss. That is to say, translation loss is not limited to the omission from a TT of properties, effects or meanings present in the corresponding ST.)

transposition   see **grammatical transposition** and **cultural transposition**.

word system   a pattern of words (distributed over a text) formed by an associative common denominator and having a demonstrable function of enhancing the theme and message of the text (for example, an alliterative pattern emphasizing a particular mood).

written language/genre/discourse/text   recorded in the form of graphic symbols, either hand-written or printed onto a physical medium such as paper, or in a digital medium. Can be broadly categorized as: literary/ fictional/imaginative; religious/devotional/ritual; theoretical/philosophical/ speculative; empirical/descriptive/analytical; and persuasive/prescriptive/ normative.

References

ABC Cultural (1996) 'El caso Aldo Moro', *ABC Cultural,* Madrid, 6 December 1996.

Alarcón, P.A. de (1993) *El sombrero de tres picos*, Barcelona: Crítica.

Alas, L. (1984) *La Regenta*, trans. J. Rutherford, Harmondsworth: Penguin.

—— (1991) *La Regenta*, Madrid: Cátedra.

Allende, I. (1984) *De amor y de sombra*, Barcelona: Plaza & Janés.

Alonso, D. (1980) *Letras*, La Habana: Letras Cubanas.

Álvarez Gil, A. (2002) *Naufragios*, Sevilla: Algaida.

Álvarez Pellitero, A.M. (ed.) (1990) *Teatro medieval*, Madrid: Espasa-Calpe.

Amestoy, I. (2001) 'Valle-Inclán, García Lorca y Buero Vallejo: crónica, impresión y memoria; tres legados del teatro español al teatro universal del siglo xx' in M. de Paco and F.J. Díez de Revenga (eds), *Antonio Buero Vallejo dramaturgo universal*, Murcia: Cajamurcia, pp. 9–22.

Andalú (2008) *Andalú: L'enziklopedia libre'n andalú*. Online. Available: http://andalu.wikia.com (accessed 31 March 2008).

Anderson, V. (1972) *The Brownie Cookbook*, London: Hodder & Stoughton.

Aphek, E. and Tobin, Y. (1988) *Word Systems: Implications and Applications*, Leiden: E.J. Brill.

Araujo, E. (1997) 'Los Roques: una puerta de sol abierta al mundo', *El Nacional*, Caracas, 7 January 1997. Example in Real Academia Española, *Corpus de referencia del español actual*. Online. Available: www.rae.es (accessed 25 March 2008).

Arias, F. (2004) 'Navidad 2004', *El Universal*, Caracas, 27 December 2004. Online. Available: www.eluniversal.com/2004/12/27/opi_art_27491A.shtml (accessed 25 March 2008).

Ayala Castro, M.C. *et al.* (2002) *Manual de lenguaje administrativo no sexista*, Málaga: Ayuntamiento de Málaga/Universidad de Málaga. Online. Available: www.ayto-malaga.es/pls/portal30/docs/folder/mujer/manual_no_sexista.pdf (accessed 31 March 2008).

Aymerich, J. (2001) 'Generation of Noun–Noun Compounds in the Spanish–English Machine Translation System SPANAM(r)', in *MT Summit VIII: Machine Translation in the Information Age, Proceedings, Santiago de Compostela, Spain, 18–22 September 2001,* Santiago de Compostela: EAMT, Xunta of Galicia, Instituto Cervantes, European Commission, pp. 33–7. Online. Available: www.eamt.org/summitVIII/papers/aymerich.pdf (accessed 1 April 2008).

Barcelona Turismo (2006) *Guía de Barcelona*. Online. Available: www.barcelona-turismo.es (accessed 25 March 2008).

Bassnett, S. (2002) *Translation Studies*, 3rd edn, London: Routledge.

Batchelor, R.E. and Pountain, C.J. (2005) *Using Spanish: A Guide to Contemporary Usage*, 2nd edn, Cambridge: Cambridge University Press.

Bécquer, G.A. (1961) *Rimas, leyendas y narraciones*, New York: Doubleday & Company.

—— (1985) *The 'Rimas' of Gustavo Adolfo Bécquer*, trans. B. Phenix, Braunton: Merlin.

Beeby Lonsdale, A. (1996) *Teaching Translation from Spanish to English: Worlds Beyond Words*, Ottawa: University of Ottawa Press.

Beeton, M. (1962) *Mrs Beeton's Family Cookery*, London: Ward, Lock & Company.

BOE (2007) 'LEY 52/2007, de 26 de diciembre, por la que se reconocen y amplían derechos y se establecen medidas en favor de quienes padecieron persecución o violencia durante la guerra civil y la dictadura', *Boletín Oficial del Estado*, 310 (27 December 2007), Madrid: Ministerio de la Presidencia/Iberlex. Online. Available: www.boe.es/g/es/bases_datos/doc.php?coleccion=iberlex&id=2007/22296 (accessed 25 March 2008).

Bonavia, D. (1984) 'La importancia de los restos de papas y camotes de época precerámica hallados en el valle de Casma', *Journal de la Société des Américanistes*, 70: 7–20.

Buero Vallejo, A. (1964) *Hoy es fiesta*, London: Harrap.

Butt, J. and Benjamin, C. (2004) *A New Reference Grammar of Modern Spanish*, 4th edn, London: Arnold.

Cabrera, J. (1999) *Cine: 100 años de filosofía, Una introducción a la filosofía a través del análisis de películas*, Barcelona: Gedisa.

Cabrera Infante, G. (1993) *La Habana para un infante difunto*, Barcelona: Plaza y Janés.

Cantera Palacios, F. (1971) 'Tecnología de los principales procesos de potabilización de las aguas de mar: congelación', *Dyna*: 267–8; repr. in L. Hickey (1977) *Usos y estilos del español moderno*, London: Harrap, pp. 127–8.

Carrión, I. (1989) 'Himno', *El País*, Madrid, 15 November 1989. Online. Available: www.elpais.com/articulo/ultima/Himno/elpepiult/19891115elpepiult_6/Tes (accessed 31 March 2008).

Carroll, L. (1954) *Alice's Adventures in Wonderland and Through the Looking-Glass*, London: J.M. Dent.

—— (1973) *A través del espejo y lo que Alicia encontró al otro lado*, trans. J. de Ojeda, Alianza: Madrid.

Castellanos, R. (1961) *Balún Canán*, México DF: Fondo de Cultura Económica.

Castro, F. (1979a) 'Discurso pronunciado por el comandante en jefe Fidel Castro Ruz, primer secretario del Comité Central del Partido Comunista de Cuba, presidente de los consejos de estado y de ministros y presidente del Movimiento de Países no Alineados, ante el XXXIV periodo de sesiones de la asamblea general de las Naciones Unidas', United Nations, New York, 12 October. Online. Available: www.cuba.cu/gobierno/discursos/1979/esp/f121079e.html (accessed 25 March 2008).

—— (1979b) '19791012', Castro Speech Database, The Latin American Network Information Center: Cuba. Online. Available: http://lanic.utexas.edu/la/cb/cuba/castro/1979/19791012 (accessed 25 March 2008).

Catullus, G.V. (1969) *Catullus (Gai Valeri Catulli Veronensis Liber)*, trans. C. and L. Zukofsky, London: Cape Goliard.

Colombia.com (2008) 'Foro: Política y gobierno', January 2008. Online. Available: www.colombia.com/foros/forum.asp?FORUM_ID=38 (accessed 5 March 2008).

Corbett, G.G. (1991) *Gender*, Cambridge: Cambridge University Press.

Cortázar, J. (1976) *Los relatos: juegos*, Madrid: Alianza.

—— (1984) *Rayuela*, Madrid: Cátedra.

Darío, R. (1987) *Prosas profanas y otros poemas,* ed. I.M. Zuleta, Madrid: Castalia.

Delibes, M. (2002) *Cinco horas con Mario*, Barcelona: Destino.

Delibes de Castro, M. (2001) *Vida: la naturaleza en peligro*, Madrid: Temas de Hoy.

Demonte Barreto, V. and Bosque, I. (1999) *Gramática descriptiva de la lengua española*, Madrid: Real Academia Española/Espasa-Calpe.

Díaz, L. (1993) *La radio en España (1923–1993)*, Madrid: Alianza.

Díaz Cintas, J. and Remael, A. (2006) *Audiovisual Translation: Subtitling*, Manchester: St Jerome.

Díez de Revenga, F.J. (2001) 'Escenarios poéticos en Buero Vallejo' in M. de Paco and F.J. Díez de Revenga (eds), *Antonio Buero Vallejo dramaturgo universal*, Murcia: Cajamurcia, pp. 23–38.

Doggart, S. and Thompson, M. (eds) (1999) *Fire, Blood and the Alphabet: One Hundred Years of Lorca*, Durham: Durham Modern Languages Series.

EFE (2007) 'Rienda esquió de nuevo tras su lesión', *Diario As*, Madrid, 12 May 2007. Online. Available: www.as.com/mas-deporte/articulo/rienda-esquio-nuevo-lesion/daimas/20070512dasdaimas_11/Tes (accessed 20 March 2008).

Ejército Zapatista de Liberación Nacional (2005a) 'Sexta Declaración de la Selva Lacandona'. Online. Available: http://palabra.ezln.org.mx/comunicados/2005/2005_06_SEXTA.htm (accessed 31 March 2008).

—— (2005b) 'Sixth Declaration of the Selva Lacandona', trans. 'Irlandesa'. Online. Available: www.anarkismo.net/newswire.php?story_id=805 (accessed 31 March 2008).

Electoral Commission (2007) 'Postal Vote: Frequently Asked Questions', The Electoral Commission. Online. Available: www.aboutmyvote.co.uk/FAQ/ByPost.cfm?PCode=CB12PR&CFID=13724223&CFTOKEN=81748979 (accessed 31 March 2008).

Enciclopedia Universal Ilustrada Europeo-Americana (1993) Suplemento Anual, 1991–1992, Madrid: Espasa-Calpe.

Espinosa, E. (1995) *Jesús el bisabuelo y otros relatos*, México DF: Siglo XXI.

Europac (2005a) *2005 Annual Report*, Madrid: Europac.

—— (2005b) *Informe anual 2005*, Madrid: Europac.

Franco, F. (2003–2008). 'Pensamiento político de un general: Franco; democracia orgánica'. Online. Available: www.generalisimofranco.com/Discursos/pensamiento/00002.htm (accessed 31 March 2008).

Franco Aixelá, J. (1996) 'Culture-Specific Items in Translation' in R. Álvarez and M.C. África Vidal (eds), *Translation, Power, Subversion*, Clevedon: Multilingual Matters, pp. 52–78.

Gallardo, A. (2007) 'Unicaja cumple el trámite pendiente de la enfermería', *Diario As*, Madrid, 12 September 2007, p. 48.

Gallego, C. (1990) *Adelaida*, Madrid: Marsó-Velasco.

García Lorca, F. (1987) *Yerma*, ed. and trans. I. Macpherson, J. Minett and J. Lyon, Warminster: Aris & Phillips.

—— (1995) *Sonetos del amor oscuro; Poemas de amor y erotismo; Inéditos de madurez*, ed. J. Ruiz-Portella, Barcelona: Áltera.

García Márquez, G. (1996) *Noticia de un secuestro*, Buenos Aires: Sudamericana.

Garcilaso de la Vega (1996) *Poesías castellanas completas*, 3rd ed., Madrid: Castalia.

Gardena (2006) 'Manual de instrucciones: Motoazada eléctrica/Operating Instructions: Electric Hoe. Gardena EH 600/20 (Art. 2414), EH 600/36 (Art. 2415)', Gardena Manufacturing GmbH. Online. Available: www.gardena.com/servlet/INT/resources/ES/es/manuals/02414-20_man_ESes.pdf (Spanish) and www.gardena.com/servlet/INT/resources/CA/en/manuals/02414-20_man_CAen.pdf (English) (accessed 31 March 2008).

Gentzler, E. (2001) *Contemporary Translation Theories*, 2nd edn, Clevedon: Multilingual Matters.

González Muela, J. and Rozas, J.M. (eds) (1986) *La generación poética de 1927*, Madrid: Istmo.

Goscinny, R. and Uderzo, A. (1965) *Astérix et Cléopâtre*, Neuilly-sur-Seine: Dargaud.

—— (1966) *Astérix chez les Bretons*, Neuilly-sur-Seine: Dargaud.

—— (1967) *Asterix en Bretaña,* (trans.) J. Perich, Barcelona: Grijalbo-Dargaud.

Goytisolo, J. (1976) *Señas de identidad*, Barcelona: Seix Barral.

—— (1988a) *Marks of Identity,* trans. G. Rabassa, London: Serpent's Tail.

—— (1988b) *Reivindicación del conde don Julián*, Barcelona: Seix Barral.

—— (1989) *Count Julian*, trans. H.R. Lane, London: Serpent's Tail.

Grandes, A. (2002) *Los aires difíciles*, Barcelona: Tusquets.

Guambia (2003) 'Guambia: suplemento de Humor', *Últimas Noticias*, Montevideo, 2ª Época, 409, 24 May 2003.

Guillén, J. (1950) *Cántico*, Buenos Aires: Sudamericana.

—— (1968) *Aire nuestro: Cántico, Clamor, Homenaje*, Milan: All'Insegna del Pesce d'Oro.

Guillén, N. (1976) *Motivos de son,* in *Sóngoro Cosongo; Motivos de son; West Indies Ltd.; España: poema en cuatro angustias y una esperanza*, Buenos Aires: Losada.

Hatim, B. and Munday, J. (2004) *Translation: An Advanced Resource Book*, London: Routledge.

Hermans, T. (1999) *Translation in Systems: Descriptive and Systemic Approaches Explained*, Manchester: St Jerome.

Hickey, L. (1998) 'Perlocutionary Equivalence: Marking, Exegesis and Recontextualization', in L. Hickey (ed.) *The Pragmatics of Translation*, Clevedon: Multilingual Matters, pp. 217–32.

Holmes, J.S. (1988) *Translated!* Amsterdam: Rodopi.

Hulme, J. (1981) *Mörder Guss Reims*, London: Angus & Robertson.

Jakobson, R. (1960) 'Linguistics and Poetics', in T. Sebeok (ed.), *Style in Language*, Cambridge, MA: MIT Press, pp. 350–77.

—— (1971) *Selected Writings, vol. 2: Word and Language*, The Hague: Mouton.

Johnston, D. (1993) *Lights of Bohemia, Plays International*, 9.2: 32–48.

—— (1998) 'Valle-Inclán: The Mirroring of Esperpento', *Modern Drama*, 41.1: 30–48.

—— (2000) 'Valle-Inclán: The Meaning of Form', in C.-A. Upton (ed.) *The Moving Target: Theatre Translation and Cultural Relocation*. Manchester: St Jerome, pp. 85–99.

Jones, R.R., Sevilla, C.M. and Uelman, G.F. (1988) *Disorderly Conduct: Real Life Comedy from the Courtroom*, London: Angus & Robertson.

Jovellanos, G.M. de (1840) 'Humanidades', in *Obras,* vol. 5, Barcelona: Oliva, pp. 94–159.

Junta de Andalucía (2007) 'Símbolos de Andalucía: Estatuto de Autonomía'. Online. Available: www.juntadeandalucia.es/SP/JDA/CDA/Secciones/Simbolos_de_Andalucia/ JDA-Indice_Simbolos/0,20314,,00 (accessed 28 March 2008).

Koller, W. (1995) 'The Concept of Equivalence and the Object of Translation Studies', *Target*, 7: 191–222.

Lázaro Carreter, F. (2003) 'Fernando Lázaro Carreter: "La Academia necesita más filólogos y menos creadores" (entrevista)', *El Cultural*, Madrid, 3 April 2003. Online. Available: www.elcultural.es/Historico_articulo.asp?c=6749 (accessed 31 March 2008).

Lea, R. (2007) 'Lost: Translation', *The Guardian*, 16 November 2007. Online. Available: http://books.guardian.co.uk/departments/generalfiction/story/0,,2212304,00. html (accessed 31 March 2008).

Leech, G. (1974) *Semantics*, Harmondsworth: Pelican.

Lemebel, P. (2001) 'La música y las luces nunca se apagaron', in *La esquina es mi corazón*, Santiago de Chile: Seix Barral, pp. 119–23.

López-Grondona, F. *et al.* (2003) 'Monosomia 1p36: un síndrome clínicamente reconocible', *Boletín del ECEMC: Revista de Dismorfología y Epidemiología*, V.2: 11–14. Online. Available: http://lis.isciii.es/mono/pdf/CIAC_02.pdf (accessed 31 March 2008).

López Guix, J.G. and Minett Wilkinson, J. (1997) *Manual de traducción: inglés-castellano; teoría y práctica*, Barcelona: Gedisa.

McCluskey, B. (1987) 'The Chinks in the Armour: Problems Encountered by Language Graduates Entering a Large Translation Department', in H. Keith and I. Mason (eds), *Translation in the Modern Languages Degree*, London: Centre for Information on Language Teaching and Research.

Mackenzie, I. (2001) *A Linguistic Introduction to Spanish*, Muenchen: LINCOM.

Machado, A. (1982a) *Poesías completas,* ed. M. Alvar, Madrid: Espasa-Calpe.

—— (1982b) *Selected poems,* trans. A.S. Trueblood, Cambridge, MA: Harvard University Press.

—— (1987) *Solitudes, Galleries and Other Poems*, trans. M. Predmore, Durham: Duke University Press.

Malof, J. (1970) *A Manual of English Meters*, Bloomington, IN: Indiana University Press.

Mañas, J.Á. (1998) *Historias del Kronen*, Barcelona: Destino.

Maradona, D.A. (2000) *Yo soy el Diego*, Barcelona: Planeta.

Marías, J. (1994) *Mañana en la batalla piensa en mí*, Barcelona: Anagrama.

—— (1999) *Corazón tan blanco*, Madrid Alfaguara.

—— (2000) *A Heart So White*, trans. M. Jull Costa, New York: New Directions.

Martín Gaite, C. (1994) *La Reina de las Nieves*, Barcelona: Anagrama.

Martín-Santos, L. (1973) *Tiempo de silencio*, Barcelona: Seix Barral.

Mercado, M.L. *et al.* (2006) 'Proyección del estudiante de Patología y Clínica Estomatológica desde el ámbito del claustro de la Facultad al Hospital Público: registro retrospectivo de las patologías observadas', *Avances en Odontoestomatología*, 22: 279–85. Online. Available: http://scielo.isciii.es/scielo.php?script=sci_art text&pid=S0213-12852006000500004&lng=es&nrm=iso (accessed 1 April 2008).

Merino, R. and Rabadán, R. (2002) 'Censored Translations in Franco's Spain: The TRACE Project – Theatre and Fiction (English-Spanish)', *TTR (Traduction, Terminologie, Rédaction)*, 15.2: 125–52. Online. Available: www.erudit.org/revue/ttr/ 2002/v15/n2/007481ar.html (accessed 1 April 2008).

Merriam-Webster (2007–2008) *Merriam-Webster OnLine [Abridged] Dictionary*. Online. Available: www.merriam-webster.com (accessed 1 April 2008).

Ministerio de Cultura (Spain) (2007) 'Panorámica de la edición en España.' Online. Available: www.mcu.es/libro/MC/PEE (accessed 31 March 2008).

Ministerio del Interior (Spain) (2007) 'Voto por correo, 2007. Preguntas y respuestas', Elecciones Locales 2007. Online. Available: www.elecciones.mir.es/locales2007/faq04.html (accessed 31 March 2008).

Montero, R. (1981) *La función delta*, Madrid: Debate.

—— (1983) *Te trataré como a una reina*, Barcelona: Seix Barral.

—— (2000) *Temblor*, Barcelona: Seix Barral.

Morón, G. (1986) *El gallo de las espuelas de oro*, Caracas: Monte Ávila.

Munday, J. (2001) *Introducing Translation Studies: Theories and Applications*, London: Routledge.

Navarro Tomás, T. (1991) *Métrica española*, Barcelona: Labor.

Newmark, P. (1981) *Approaches to Translation*, Oxford: Pergamon.

Nida, E. (1964) *Towards a Science of Translation*, Leiden: Brill.

Niranjana, T. (1992) *Siting Translation: History, Post-Structuralism and the Colonial Context*, Berkeley: University of California Press.

Nissen, U.K. (2002) 'Aspects of Translating Gender', *Linguistik Online*, 11: 25–37. Online. Available: www.linguistik-online.de/11_02/nissen.html (accessed 25 March 2008).

Nord, C. (1997) *Translating as a Purposeful Activity: Functionalist Approaches Explained*, Manchester: St Jerome.

OED (1989–2008) *Oxford English Dictionary*, 2nd edn, Oxford: Oxford University Press. Online. Available: http://dictionary.oed.com (accessed 25 March 2008).

Ortega, S. (1972) *Mil ochenta recetas de cocina*, Madrid: Alianza.

Palavecino, N. (2004) *Nutrición para el alto rendimiento*. Libros en Red. Online. Available: www.librosenred.com (accessed 25 March 2008).

Pedrero, P. (1999) *Juego de noches: nueve obras en un acto*, Madrid: Cátedra.

Penella, M. (1995) *Tu hijo: genio en potencia; las claves fundamentales para su educación*, Madrid: Espasa-Calpe.

Pérez Galdós, B. (1971a) *Lo prohibido*, Madrid: Castalia.

—— (1971b) *Miau*, Puerto Rico: Universitaria.

—— (1991) *La de Bringas*, Madrid: Cátedra.

—— (1996) *That Bringas Woman*, trans. C. Jagoe, London: J.M. Dent.

Pinchuk, I. (1977) *Scientific and Technical Translation*, London: Andre Deutsch.

Pöchhacker, F. (2004) *Introducing Interpreting Studies*, London: Routledge.

Pratchett, T. (2003) *El segador*, trans. C. Macía, Barcelona: Random House-Mondadori.

Pring-Mill, R. (1990) *'Gracias a la vida': The Power and Poetry of Song*, London: Department of Hispanic Studies, Queen Mary and Westfield College, University of London.

Publishers Association (UK) (2007) 'Market Information and Statistics.' Online. Available: www.publishers.org.uk/en/home/market_reports_and_statistics (accessed 4 December 2007).

Querci, M. (2007a) 'Sesión nº 2: Presentación del manual, métodos de trabajo e introducción del curso', in M. Querci, M. Jermini and G. van den Eede, *Curso de formación sobre análisis de la presencia de organismos genéticamente modificados en muestras de alimentos; manual de participante*. Online. Available: http://

bookshop.europa.eu/eubookshop/FileCache/PUBPDF/LBX107033ESC/LBX
107033ESC_002.pdf (accessed 4 December 2007).

—— (2007b) 'Session 2: Manual Presentation, Working Methods and Course Introduction', in M. Querci, M. Jermini and G. van den Eede, *The Analysis of Food
Samples for Genetically Modified Organisms: A Training Manual*. Online. Available: http://bgmo.jrc.ec.europa.eu/home/documents/Manual%20EN%202006/Session
02.pdf (accessed 4 December 2007).

Real Academia Española (1975–2008) *Corpus de referencia del español actual
(CREA)*. Online. Available: www.rae.es (accessed 31 March 2008).

—— (2001–2008) *Diccionario de la lengua española*, 22nd edn. Madrid: Real
Academia Española. Online. Available: www.rae.es (accessed 31 March 2008).

—— (2007) 'La política lingüística panhispánica'. Online. Available: www.rae.es/
rae%5CNoticias.nsf/Portada4?ReadForm&menu=4 (accessed 31 March 2008).

Rodríguez González, F. (ed.) (1996) *Spanish Loanwords in the English Language*,
Berlin: Mouton de Gruyter.

Rodríguez Méndez, J.M. (1979) *Bodas que fueron famosas del Pingajo y la Fandanga;
Flor de Otoño*, Madrid: Cátedra.

—— (2001) *Autumn Flower*, trans. M. P. Holt, New Brunswick, NJ: Estreno.

Romaine, S. (1999) *Communicating Gender*, Mahwah, NJ: Lawrence Erlbaum
Association.

Rommel, B. (1987) 'Market-Orientated Translation Training', in H. Keith and I. Mason
(eds) *Translation in the Modern Languages Degree*, London: Centre for Information
on Language Teaching and Research, pp. 11–16.

Ruiz, G., Pellón, R. and García, A. (2006a) 'Resumen: análisis experimental de la
conducta en España', *Avances en Psicología Latinoamericana*, 24: 71–103. Online.
Available: www.rlpsi.org/apl/resumenes/volumen24/6.htm (accessed 31 March
2008).

—— (2006b) 'Análisis experimental de la conducta en España', *Avances en Psicología
Latinoamericana*, 24: 71–103. Online. Available: www.rlpsi.org/articulos_2006/apl_
vol_24_2006_analisis_en_espana.pdf (accessed 31 March 2008).

Sacerio-Garí, E. (2006) 'Bemboguaba' in *Poetic Solutions*. Online. Available: www.
poeticsolutions.com/Jabberwockyps.html (accessed 31 March 2008).

Sastre, A. (1969) *Escuadra hacia la muerte*, Madrid: Escelicer.

Serrano Cueto, J.M. (2002) 'Jorge Rivera, director del s. XXI' (interview), *La
Ratonera: Revista asturiana de teatro*, 5 (May 2002). Online. Available: www.
la-ratonera.net/numero5/n5_rivera.html (accessed 31 March 2008).

Simon, S. (1996) *Gender in Translation: Cultural Identity and the Politics of
Transmission*, London: Routledge.

Snell-Hornby, M. (1988) *Translation Studies: An Integrated Approach*, Amsterdam:
John Benjamins.

Sopeña Monsalve, A. (1994) *El florido pensil: memoria de la escuela nacionalcatólica*,
Barcelona: Crítica.

Steel, B. (2006) *Spanish Translation Exercises and Tests With a Contrastive Analysis
of Key Aspects of Spanish Syntax*. E-book available from www.briansteel.net
(accessed 31 March 2008).

—— (2007) *A Textbook of Colloquial Spanish*. Electronic re-issue available online
from www.briansteel.net. Originally published Madrid: SGEL, 1985.

Stewart, M. (1999) *The Spanish Language Today*, London: Routledge.

Suárez, I. (2001) 'Desde El Mangrullo', *Noticiero De Norte a Sur*, 242 (Octubre). Online. Available: www.denorteasur.com/asp/articulo.asp?numero=242&id=834 (accessed March 25 2008).

Telefónica (2007a) *Annual Report 2006*, Madrid: Telefónica.

—— (2007b) *Informe anual 2006*, Madrid: Telefónica.

Teresa de Jesús (1957) *The Life of Saint Teresa of Avila by Herself*, trans. J.M. Cohen, Harmondsworth: Penguin.

—— (1978) *Su vida*, 8th edn, Madrid: Espasa-Calpe.

Toury, G. (1980) *In Search of a Theory of Translation*, Tel Aviv: The Porter Institute for Poetics and Semiotics.

—— (1995) *Descriptive Translation Studies and Beyond*, Amsterdam: John Benjamins.

Tracy, M. (1965) *Modern Casserole Cookery*, London: Studio Vista.

Tymoczko, M. (2007) *Enlarging Translation, Empowering Translators*, Manchester: St Jerome.

US Department of Education (2003) 'Disclaimers in Spanish and English for IDEA'97 Translation'. Online. Available: www.ed.gov/espanol/policy/speced/reg/disclaimer.html (accessed 31 March 2008).

'Uño que escribe con eñe' (2007) *Zoziedá pal Ehtudio 'el Andalú: Foro zobre la lengua andaluza*, 9 November 2007. Online. Available: www.my-forum.org/foros.php?id=96785 (accessed 4 December 2007).

Unión General de Trabajadores (2007) 'La integración de trabajadores y trabajadoras en la gestión preventiva de la empresa', *Salud Laboral*. Online. Available: www.saludlaboralcanarias.org (accessed 20 February 2008).

Valenzuela, L. (1982) *Cambio de armas*, Hanover, NH: Ediciones del Norte.

—— (1983) *Cola de lagartija*, Buenos Aires: Bruguera.

—— (1992) *The Lizard's Tail*, trans. G. Rabassa, London: Serpent's Tail.

Valle-Inclán, R.M. del (1993) *Lights of Bohemia/Luces de Bohemia*, trans. and ed. J. Lyon, Warminster: Aris & Phillips.

Van Rooten, L.D'A. (1968) *Mots d'heures: gousses, rames*, London: Angus & Robertson.

Vandaele, J. (2007) 'Take Three: The National-Catholic Versions of Billy Wilder's Broadway Adaptations', in F. Billiani (ed.), *Modes of Censorship and Translation: National Contexts and Diverse Media*, Manchester: St Jerome, pp. 279–310.

Venuti, L. (1992) 'Introduction' in L. Venuti (ed.), *Rethinking Translation: Discourse, Subjectivity, Ideology*, London: Routledge.

—— (1995) *The Translator's Invisibility: A History of Translation*, London: Routledge.

Walters, D.G. (2002) *The Cambridge Introduction to Spanish Poetry*, Cambridge: Cambridge University Press.

Wolosky, S. (2001) *The Art of Poetry: How to Read a Poem*, Oxford/New York: Oxford University Press.

Yablon, S. (2003) 'Un capítulo de *La dimensión desconocida*', *Film Online*, Buenos Aires, 6 July 2003.

Index